A Different Day

Greta de Jong

A Different Day

African American Struggles

for Justice in Rural

Louisiana, 1900–1970

THE UNIVERSITY OF NORTH CAROLINA PRESS

Chapel Hill and London

Designed by Nancy Ovedovitz and set in Century Expanded type by
Keystone Typesetting, Inc.

The paper in this book meets the guidelines for permanence and
durability of the Committee on Production Guidelines for Book
Longevity of the Council on Library Resources.

Library of Congress Cataloging-in-Publication Data
De Jong, Greta.
A different day : African American struggles for justice in rural Louisiana,
1900–1970 / Greta de Jong.
    p. cm.
Includes bibliographical references and index.
ISBN 0-8078-2711-8 (alk. paper) — ISBN 0-8078-5379-8 (pbk. : alk. paper)
1. African Americans—Civil rights—Louisiana—History—20th century. 2. Civil
rights movements—Louisiana—History—20th century. 3. African American
civil rights workers—Louisiana—History—20th century. 4. African Americans—
Louisiana—Politics and government—20th century. 5. African Americans—
Louisiana—Social conditions—20th century. 6. Rural population—Louisiana—
History—20th century. 7. Louisiana—Race relations. 8. Louisiana—Rural
conditions. 9. Louisiana—Politics and government. I. Title.
E185.93.L6 D38 2002
323.1′1960730763′0904—dc21   2001057824

cloth   06 05 04 03 02   5 4 3 2 1
paper   06 05 04 03 02   5 4 3 2 1

For mum and dad

Contents

Illustrations,
Tables, and Maps

Illustrations

Tables

Maps

Acknowledgments

I am profoundly indebted to all of the freedom fighters who allowed me to interview them for this project: Ronnie Sigal Bouma, Harrison and Earnestine Brown, Wilbert Guillory, Clifton Hall, Eual Hall, John Henry Hall, Lawrence Hall, Lorin Hall, Eunice Hall Harris, Robert and Essie Mae Lewis, Eunice Paddio-Johnson, Meg Redden, Clarence Reed, Lola Stallworth, Martin Williams, Moses Williams, and John Zippert. Their courage, intelligence, and insights contributed enormously to black people's struggles for justice in Louisiana and to this book.

As with the freedom movement itself, economic factors played a significant part in shaping the possibilities and final results of my work. The Department of History and the Research and Graduate Studies Office at the Pennsylvania State University provided funding that helped me to complete much of the research for this project. Writing the first few drafts was greatly facilitated by a two-year predoctoral fellowship awarded by the Carter G. Woodson Institute for Afro-American and African Studies at the University of Virginia. The J. N. G. Finley postdoctoral fellowship at George Mason University enabled me to work on revising the manuscript for publication, and some additional funds provided by the Department of History assisted in further research. At the turn of the millennium, a visiting assistant professorship at the University of Nevada, Reno, saved me from deportation just as my visa was due to expire and I thought my world was going to end. I am very grateful for the financial support I received from all of these institutions.

I will never be able to repay my debt to the commissary of my dissertation adviser and friend, Professor Nan Elizabeth Woodruff. I thank her with all my heart for her strong encouragement, rigorous criticisms, outrageous jokes and stories, and home-cooked meals. Thanks also to the other members of my doctoral committee, Professors Gary Cross, Thavolia Glymph, Daniel Letwin, and Clyde Woods, who carefully read the initial versions of this book and offered many thoughtful suggestions for improvement. Professor Charles Payne of Duke University made time in his busy schedule to serve as a special member on my committee, and his comments and assistance were greatly appreciated.

It is hard to imagine a more supportive environment than the one I enjoyed in the Department of History at the Pennsylvania State University during my graduate years. Faculty and fellow graduate students alike warmly welcomed me into their community, making the 6,700 mile separation from my Pacific island homeland much easier to endure than it might have been. When I left Pennsylvania, I never thought I would be so fortunate again—yet, incredibly, I was. Since 1997 I have relocated to a different university and a different part of the country almost every year, and every time I have found myself once more among extremely likable, generous, humorous, and inspiring colleagues. Through both formal seminars and informal conversations over coffee or lunch, their ideas and suggestions have helped to shape my thinking and contributed to the analysis presented in this book. Thank you Bill and Mary Ann Blair, Clarissa and John Confer, Gary and Eileen Gallagher, Charles (Middleton) Holden, Isabel Knight, Lynn Vacca, and Melissa Westrate at the Pennsylvania State University; Eve Agee, Reginald Butler, Lisa Lindquist Dorr, Scott French, John Gennari, Natasha Gray, Andrew Lewis, Rolland Murray, Vânia Penha-Lopes, Ian Strachan, Lisa Severson Swales, Phillip Troutman, and Robert Vinson at the Woodson Institute; Jack and Jane Censer, John Cheng, Robert DeCaroli, Matthew Karush, Alison Landsberg, Lawrence Levine, Roy Rosenzweig, Suzanne Smith, and Jeffrey Stewart at George Mason University; Scott Casper, Linda Curcio, Richard Davies, Andy Donson, Dennis Dworkin, Jerome Edwards, Frank Hartigan, Martha Hildreth, Carolyn Knapp, Bruce Moran, Elizabeth Raymond, Bill Rowley, Hugh Shapiro, Kevin Stevens, and Barbara Walker at the University of Nevada, Reno; and John Buenker, Frank Egerton, Laura Gellott, Jerry Greenfield, Oliver Hayward, and Steve Meyer at the University of Wisconsin-Parkside. Very special thanks to Mary Hebert at Louisiana State University, who assisted greatly with logistical matters during my research trips to Louisiana and who generously shared with me ideas and sources that grew out of her project on the civil rights movement in Baton Rouge.

I could not have asked for better administrative support than I received from the staffs of the universities where I worked, especially those whose jobs involved dealing with the U.S. Immigration and Naturalization Service on my behalf. In addition to answering my many questions and processing paperwork, some of them had to help me out of bureaucratic tangles more than once. If I could, I would give them all huge raises. My profound thanks to Maureen Costello, Karen Ebeling, Darla Franks, Lynn Moyer, Linda Nihart, Judy Shawley, and Karin Weaver at the Pennsylvania State University; Mary Farrer and Gail Shirley-Warren at the Woodson Institute; Julia Friedheim and Elizabeth Spencer at George Mason University; Debbie Hammersmith and Margaret Hellwarth at the University of Nevada, Reno; and Cheryl Gundersen and Luella Vines at the University of Wisconsin-Parkside.

Librarians and archivists at the State Historical Society of Wisconsin, the Amistad Research Center and the Howard Tilton Library at Tulane University, the Historic New Orleans Collection, the Hill Memorial Library at Louisiana State University, the New Orleans Public Library, the Earl K. Long Library at the University of New Orleans, the Center for Regional Studies at Southeastern Louisiana University, the Louisiana State Archives, the National Archives, the Library of Congress, the Federal Bureau of Investigation National Headquarters, the National Agricultural Library, the Southern Labor Archives at Georgia State University, and the Fisk University Library Special Collections Department were universally helpful, often offering valuable advice and assistance as I searched for materials related to my work. In addition to allowing me access to their collections of taped interviews, archivists at the T. Harry Williams Center for Oral History at Louisiana State University provided the recording equipment and guidance that enabled me to conduct my own. Staff members of the interlibrary loan services of Pattee Library at the Pennsylvania State University and Alderman Library at the University of Virginia displayed considerable tolerance in processing my requests for endless reels of microfilm and in helping me to track down obscure references.

I am deeply grateful to Pete Daniel of the National Museum of American

History in Washington, D.C., as well as the anonymous reviewers for the University of North Carolina Press, for reading and commenting on various versions of the manuscript as it made its way to publication. Thanks also to the editors and production staff who helped to guide me in this process; David Perry, Mark Simpson-Vos, and Paula Wald made this experience less intimidating than I thought it would be, and their patience and understanding were much appreciated as I tried to meet deadlines in between job hunting, preparing courses, and moving from Virginia to Nevada to Wisconsin in the space of two years. Stevie Champion did an excellent job as copyeditor, eliminating many ill-phrased sentences in addition to ensuring consistency in the citations and slashing the number of endnotes in half.

Throughout my long exile in the United States, family and friends back home in New Zealand have helped me through periods of culture shock and homesickness, keeping me in touch with my kiwi roots through their letters, e-mail messages, and phone calls. My parents, Daphne and Keith de Jong, have supported and encouraged everything I have chosen to do, despite the years of separation this has meant. Lisette, Kris, Martin, and Kimmy de Jong remind me every time I speak to them that "car" is pronounced "cah," not "carr"; the round things with the chocolate chips are called "biscuits," not "cookies"; and VEGEMITE RULES. My two best buddies, Megan Claridge and Greg Locke, might have been geographically distant, but they were always present in some way when I needed them.

To everyone back home: Although I could have done without the phone calls at 2:00 A.M., my time, I thank you all. I love you, and I miss you.

Abbreviations

AAA	Agricultural Adjustment Administration
AFBF	American Farm Bureau Federation
AFL	American Federation of Labor
ASCS	Agricultural Soil Conservation Service
CAP	Community Action Program
CCC	Civilian Conservation Corps
CIO	Congress of Industrial Organizations
CORE	Congress of Racial Equality
FaHA	Farmers' Home Administration
FBI	Federal Bureau of Investigation
FEPC	Fair Employment Practice Committee (President's Committee on Fair Employment Practice)
FERA	Federal Emergency Relief Administration
FFM	Ferriday Freedom Movement
FSA	Farm Security Administration
GMVPC	Grand Marie Vegetable Producers' Cooperative
IWA	International Woodworkers of America
LCTA	Louisiana Colored Teachers' Association
LFU	Louisiana Farmers' Union
MOWM	March on Washington Movement
NAACP	National Association for the Advancement of Colored People

NAWU	National Agricultural Workers' Union
NFU	National Farmers' Union (Farmers' Educational and Cooperative Union of America)
NRA	National Recovery Administration
OEO	Office of Economic Opportunity
OWI	Office of War Information
PVL	Progressive Voters' League
SAFE	Students' Association for Freedom and Equality
SCC	Southern Consumers' Cooperative
SCLC	Southern Christian Leadership Conference
SCU	Share Croppers' Union
SEDFRE	Scholarship, Education, and Defense Fund for Racial Equality
SNCC	Student Nonviolent Coordinating Committee
STFU	Southern Tenant Farmers' Union
UCAPAWA	United Cannery, Agricultural, Packing and Allied Workers of America
VEP	Voter Education Project
WAAC	Women's Auxiliary Army Corps
WAC	Women's Army Corps
WPA	Works Progress Administration

A Different Day

Introduction

One of the archival sources used in the research for this project was a collection of taped interviews with local black people who became involved in the civil rights movement in rural Louisiana. The interviews were conducted in 1966 by Miriam Feingold, a member of the Congress of Racial Equality (CORE) who had worked with local activists on voter registration projects in the region for several years. Taking what would seem to be a logical approach, Feingold began several of the sessions by asking questions like "When did the civil rights movement begin in your community?" or "When did you first become involved in the movement?" Often, the interviewees seemed taken aback or perplexed by these inquiries—as if, to them, the questions did not make sense. Bogalusa Voters' League leader A. Z. Young paused for a moment, then stated, "I've been involved in the movement all my life." Zelma Wyche, a veteran of the movement in Madison Parish, referred to "a constant struggle for human rights." Joseph Carter of West Feliciana Parish told Feingold that his cousin had been killed by some white men when he was a boy, and he had vowed then that one day he would do something "to break up this mess of the white folk shooting the colored people down like they do rabbits."[1]

Like many black people, these activists viewed the civil rights movement as part of an older, broader struggle for freedom and justice, one that they had lived in and participated in for as long as they could remember. Recent scholarship on the black freedom movement has begun to mirror this perspective, shifting our attention away from the events of the 1960s to earlier time periods and to the wide variety of strategies that African Americans used to fight their oppression.[2] Zelma Wyche might well have been summarizing an emerging theme in the historiography as much as his own experiences when he told Miriam Feingold, "There were lean years when we didn't do anything, but we were constantly trying to do something."[3]

This book examines black political activism in a rural southern community over seven decades, attempting to show how earlier struggles for citizenship were related to the civil rights movement and how they were shaped by changing social conditions that, at certain times, encouraged a shift from informal resistance to organized protest. The study focuses on the northern and southeastern regions of Louisiana where CORE conducted its voter registration and community organizing efforts in the 1960s. These parishes were chosen for several reasons. Most accounts of African American strategies of resistance in the Jim Crow era have focused on urban areas, whereas black activism in the rural South before the arrival of civil rights workers has largely gone unnoticed. Black farmers in several of the parishes had been involved in union organizing activity in the 1930s, yet little was known about the Louisiana Farmers' Union (LFU) and its role in the fight for equality. Finally, although CORE workers encountered conditions similar to those endured by the Student Nonviolent Coordinating Committee (SNCC) in Mississippi, their activities in Louisiana have not received nearly the same amount of attention from scholars. This study therefore adds to our knowledge in several areas. In addition, by taking a longitudinal approach and by viewing events as much as possible through the eyes of local black people who lived in the region during the Jim Crow and civil rights eras, I aim to provide a new perspective on the twentieth-century freedom struggle.

CORE focused on seventeen parishes in rural Louisiana: Caddo, Claiborne, Concordia, East Feliciana, Iberville, Jackson, Madison, Ouachita, Pointe Coupee, St. Helena, St. Landry, St. Tammany, Tangipahoa, Tensas, Washington, Webster, and West Feliciana.[4] Historically, these had mostly been majority-black cotton and sugar plantation parishes but included some areas of hill country characterized by smaller diversified farms. By the 1960s plantation agriculture was no longer as dominant as it had once been in rural Louisiana, though its legacy of exploitation and violent oppression pervaded many of the communities that CORE workers sought to organize. Black migration away from the region meant that African Americans were no

Map I.1. Parishes, Principal Cities, and Rivers of Louisiana

longer the majority in eleven of the parishes. However, black residents in all the parishes made up a substantial proportion of the population, ranging from 27 percent in St. Tammany Parish to 65 percent in Tensas Parish.[5]

I have concentrated primarily on nine parishes that were representative of the larger area covered by CORE (Concordia, East Feliciana, Iberville, Madison, Pointe Coupee, St. Helena, St. Landry, Washington, and West Feliciana), occasionally drawing evidence from the other CORE parishes and from parishes throughout Louisiana that resembled those in the main sample, particularly those along the Red River and the southern stem of the

Mississippi River where the LFU was active in the 1930s. Neither CORE nor the LFU reached into the predominantly white, rice-growing parishes in the southwestern corner of the state, and they are not part of this study. Although New Orleans and other major cities are also largely neglected, it sometimes seemed appropriate to extend my scope to urban areas—as, for example, in the chapters on the two world wars, when migrants from the rural parishes swelled the black populations of the cities and contributed to an increase in protest activity. This book is not meant to be a comprehensive account of the freedom struggle in the entire state.[6] The parishes studied do not represent all of Louisiana's diverse regions, but they are a suitable basis for examining the links between black resistance and protest in the Jim Crow era and the civil rights movement, and that is my main purpose.

The book begins with a brief chapter outlining the historical background and development of the state in the first few decades after the Civil War. Chapters 2 and 3 cover the first half of the twentieth century, describing the limits that were placed on political activism and the ways that African Americans attempted to subtly challenge white supremacy. These chapters also establish four main themes that represent key aspirations of black people in the rural parishes: economic independence, education, political participation, and safety from violence. The themes recur throughout the study, with each successive chapter showing how changing social contexts enabled African Americans to pursue these goals in different ways. Chapters 4 and 5 demonstrate how activity that was usually clandestine and ineffective became more open and organized during World War I and the Great Depression, without becoming strong enough to significantly alter the social order. Chapters 6 and 7 link the emergence of the modern civil rights movement to shifts in the political economy of the rural South after World War II and the rise of a new class of relatively prosperous, economically independent African Americans who were better placed than earlier generations to press their demands for citizenship. Chapter 8 examines the interaction between CORE workers and local activists in the 1960s, highlighting local people's adherence to an indigenous political tradition that had its roots in the informal and organized struggles of earlier decades.

This work draws on and contributes to three sets of historiography: the literature on the civil rights movement, studies of working-class and peasant resistance, and analyses of the transformation of the South wrought by the New Deal and World War II. Bringing all of these together, it demonstrates that rural black southerners were important participants in the freedom struggle throughout the twentieth century, and it highlights the connections between social protest and broader economic and political conditions.

Traditional narratives of the civil rights movement have closely associated its origins and outcomes with the rise to prominence of Martin Luther King Jr., whose powerful articulation of African American demands for equality touched millions of people and helped move the nation toward abolishing legalized discrimination. Studies of King and of national organizations like the Southern Christian Leadership Conference (SCLC), the National Association for the Advancement of Colored People (NAACP), SNCC, and CORE often seem to imply that before the 1960s, working-class and rural poor black people in the South represented an inactive, apathetic mass, only realizing their collective power after middle-class civil rights activists arrived from outside the region to encourage voter registration and protests against racism.[7]

More recent scholarship has begun to present a different picture. Two excellent books on the movement in Mississippi, John Dittmer's *Local People: The Struggle for Civil Rights in Mississippi* (1994) and Charles Payne's *I've Got the Light of Freedom: The Organizing Tradition and the Mississippi Freedom Struggle* (1995), reveal the central importance of local leaders and participants, challenging the notion that rural black southerners played only supporting roles. Adam Fairclough's *Race and Democracy: The Civil Rights Struggle in Louisiana, 1915–1972* (1995) also makes a significant contribution, tracing the development of local movements since World War I. However, his study focuses largely on urban areas that had strong NAACP branches, giving little attention to either informal or organized political activity in the rural parishes before the 1960s.

Certainly, as Fairclough and others have pointed out, the repressive plantation regime placed limits on black people's ability to contest the social order. Most African Americans in the rural South lived and worked as tenant farmers, day laborers, or domestics, closely supervised by their white employers. Poverty, inadequate education, disfranchisement, and the threat of violence discouraged organizing efforts, while plantation owners' control over economic resources, political offices, and the law enabled them to stifle most challenges to the system. Black people who dared to protest these conditions risked being evicted, jailed, beaten, or murdered. The conditions that African Americans endured are well documented in studies such as Neil McMillen's *Dark Journey: Black Mississippians in the Age of Jim Crow* (1989) and Leon Litwack's *Trouble in Mind: Black Southerners in the Age of*

Jim Crow (1998). The oppressiveness of the Jim Crow era and its crippling impact on black activism cannot be ignored. However, as other scholars have noted, it is difficult to see how the freedom movement of the 1960s could have emerged from among the fearful, apolitical black southerners depicted in some studies of the period.[8]

My research suggests that African Americans in rural Louisiana were not waiting passively for CORE activists to inspire them to action. Within the confines of the southern social order, local black people developed their own ways of fighting injustice in the early twentieth century. The analysis presented here reflects the influence of a growing body of literature that suggests scholars must look beyond traditional conceptions of politics to fully appreciate the extent that African Americans and other oppressed peoples have participated in their liberation movements. This field has a long lineage reaching back to innovative works on slavery by Herbert Aptheker and Eugene Genovese, E. P. Thompson's pioneering studies of the English working class, and Lawrence Levine's perceptive analysis of black culture as a site of resistance.[9] These and more recent books by James Scott, Robin Kelley, and others indicate that even in contexts of extreme oppression, people find ways to express opposition to the social order. Proletarians in England, slaves and workers in the United States, and peasants in Africa, Latin America, and Southeast Asia have all engaged in what James Scott termed "infrapolitics"—subtle or unorganized forms of resistance such as creating their own cultural worlds and value systems, working slowly or poorly, stealing from their employers, destroying property, running away or quitting work, and occasionally engaging in violent attacks against their oppressors.[10]

Scholars have argued over the significance of such activities and the extent that they reflected the political consciousness of those who engaged in them. It is often impossible to determine exactly what motivated actions like theft or malingering, and these tactics did little, if anything, to alter the power relationships between subordinate and dominant groups.[11] Trying to decide which elements to include in a study of black political activism presents something of a dilemma. Focusing narrowly on organized movements excludes the majority of black southerners from the history of the freedom struggle and creates the perception that they were apathetic and uninterested in politics. But there are also problems in viewing nearly all aspects of black society and culture as forms of protest. Placing blues singers (or gangsta rappers) who complain of injustice on the same level as African

Americans who faced down tear gas, fire hoses, and police dogs to try to *end* injustice seems a little unfair.

We need not commit such an offense to appreciate the importance of black people's informal strategies of resistance. Infrapolitics and politics exist on a continuum, and it is difficult to define when one stops and the other begins. Rather than trying to decide whether some acts are more political than others, it makes more sense to see both subtle and overt expressions of dissent as different parts of the same process. Music, art, and folklore represented one layer of the struggle, presenting an analysis and a critique of the social system that were reflected in small acts of resistance as well as organized political action. Black freedom fighters might engage in some or all of these activities simultaneously or at different times, intensifying the struggle for justice whenever possible, and reverting to less obvious forms of resistance in response to repression.

In this study the terms "resistance" and "infrapolitics" refer to those actions short of organized, open protest that suggest an awareness of the sources of oppression and were aimed at circumventing white supremacists' attempts to keep African Americans powerless and poor. This includes both informal, individual acts such as violent attacks on white people that, although open, were unplanned, as well as more structured activities like institution building that, although they were collective, did not directly confront the system in the same way that forming unions or NAACP branches did. By showing how similar objectives drove both informal and organized political activities, I aim to clarify the relationship between various forms of black resistance and protest.

Central to understanding the twentieth-century freedom struggle is that racial oppression was also class oppression, and African Americans fought both of these on many different fronts. Analyzing just those actions directed at overcoming segregation or disfranchisement reveals only part of the story. As Nan Elizabeth Woodruff has argued, rural black people's notions of citizenship encompassed economic rights as well as political and social rights.[12] In addition, as this study shows, economic advancement facilitated the elimination of legalized discrimination. Attempts to break the bonds of class were therefore vital elements in the concurrent struggle against racism, even though many of the strategies employed were not unique to African Americans.

During the Jim Crow era black people in rural Louisiana rarely tried to register to vote or to openly criticize the white supremacist social order. Yet in a multitude of other ways, they attempted to improve their living and working conditions and to assert their citizenship rights. Many of the issues that motivated rural black people's participation in the civil rights movement were prefigured in activities such as leaving or stealing from employers, developing strategies for educating black children, creating strong community institutions, and fighting back against white violence. Incorporating everyday forms of resistance as well as organized politics into our definition of black activism reveals some continuity in the goals of rural black people, even though the methods of achieving them did not remain static. This study lends support to the idea that infrapolitics is "real politics," and that more powerful social movements can emerge from the base it provides when social conditions encourage such transitions.[13]

The political and economic changes that swept the South in the 1930s and 1940s have been the focus of rich scholarly inquiry in recent years. Historians such as Pete Daniel and Jack Temple Kirby have described the ways New Deal agricultural policies enhanced the power of plantation owners and exacerbated the problems of sharecroppers, tenants, and small farmers in the region.[14] Donald Grubbs and Robin Kelley have examined rural poor people's responses to these developments in their studies of the Southern Tenant Farmers' Union (STFU) and the Alabama Share Croppers' Union (SCU).[15] Recent scholarship has suggested links between the struggles of farmers and workers in the 1930s and those of black Americans in the 1960s, although the exact nature of the relationship has yet to be delineated.[16]

Placing the social movements of these two decades in a broader historical context reveals how they are intertwined. Black activists in rural Louisiana took advantage of political and economic developments between 1933 and 1945 to take the freedom struggle to the level of organized protest. With the help of the communist organizers of the SCU, poor white and black farmers formed the LFU to fight planter abuses of the New Deal and demand a fair share of federal aid. African Americans, in particular, embraced the union as an ally in their ongoing fight to gain fair compensation for their labor, adequate education for their children, a chance to participate politically, and protection from violence. Black people's involvement in the LFU showed an awareness of the power of collective action and an appreciation of the causes of their problems that resurfaced when similar opportunities presented themselves during and after World War II.

The nation's mobilization for war in the 1940s accelerated changes in the social order initiated by the New Deal. Thousands of farmworkers left the plantations to take new jobs in defense industries, and the resulting labor scarcity encouraged cotton and sugar growers to mechanize as many tasks as possible. Agricultural historians have described these developments at the macro level, but we do not have many detailed studies of their effect at the local level.[17] Examining the impact of economic transformations on black individuals and communities provides some insight into the reasons why the civil rights movement emerged when it did, and not before.

Black farm owners, businesspeople, factory laborers, students, homemakers, and unemployed workers who had escaped agricultural labor and were no longer tied to the plantation economy provided the backbone of the postwar freedom movement. In the 1950s these former sharecroppers and their children established voters' leagues, formed NAACP branches, joined unions, and openly demanded equal economic, educational, political, and legal rights. In the 1960s they welcomed CORE workers into their homes and communities. Local black people's courage and persistence, combined with the financial and other resources provided by national organizations, were crucial to the success of the civil rights movement.

Change did not come easily to rural Louisiana or anywhere else in the South. Though participants in the struggle were no longer as subject to white reprisals as in previous decades, no one was ever completely immune from retaliation. Black people who became involved in the movement still faced the threat of physical violence and of having their businesses, churches, and homes bombed or burned. But terrorist acts like these involved more planning and greater risks on the part of white supremacists than the methods they had most often used to combat challenges to their power, namely firings and evictions. White southerners' increasing resort to violence and arson was in itself a sign that the political and economic balance in the region had changed. And it was those kinds of actions that captured national attention and finally forced the federal government to intervene. The Civil Rights and Voting Rights Acts were a culmination of many decades of struggle by black people, who were newly empowered in the 1960s to press their demands for citizenship. For African Americans, the post–World War II era truly was what local activist Earnestine Brown called "a different day."[18]

1

And Did Not Pay Them a Cent: Reconstruction and the Roots of the Twentieth-Century Freedom Struggle

Louisiana's geographic diversity and its unique history of colonization by the Spanish and French before the arrival of Anglo-Americans in some ways set it apart from the other Deep South states. Scholars have typically distinguished between French Catholic parishes and Anglo-Protestant parishes, between New Orleans and the rural areas, and between the different agricultural regions that developed along the rivers, on the southwestern prairies, and in the hill country of the north central and southeastern parts of the state. Attempts to classify parishes according to environmental, economic, and cultural characteristics have resulted in estimates ranging from two to thirteen distinct regions of Louisiana.[1]

For the purposes of this study, the rural parishes (which for much of the period covered meant the entire area outside New Orleans) can be divided into four main types. Along the southern stem of the Mississippi, the parishes from Pointe Coupee in the north to Terrebonne and Plaquemines in the south made up the Sugar Bowl area, characterized by large sugar plantations. This region retained many aspects of the language and culture of early French settlers. In contrast to other parts of the South, most residents of the sugar parishes were Catholic rather than Protestant. Relationships between white and black people also varied slightly from the rigid color lines that were drawn elsewhere. French colonists had accepted interracial marriages and partnerships to a greater extent than the Americans who arrived later on, giving rise to a significant population of native Louisianans with mixed ancestry. Lighter-skinned African Americans were not treated equally with white people yet enjoyed privileges that set them apart from most other black people in the South. Even after their incorporation into the United States, the French-speaking, Catholic parishes of southern Louisiana retained reputations for being more racially tolerant than those farther north.[2]

Stretching along the V-shape formed by the Red River and the northern Mississippi lay the cotton plantation parishes. Northern Louisiana was settled largely by Anglo-Americans who migrated to the region in the early nineteenth century. Many came from other southern states, seeking new territory in which to make their fortunes as landowners and slaveholders. These parishes closely resembled the rest of the Anglo-Saxon, Protestant South. More specifically, they were very much like the plantation regions of neighboring Mississippi and Arkansas. As in the sugar parishes, black people comprised the majority of the population, sometimes outnumbering white people by more than ten to one. White supremacy was strictly, often violently enforced. Researchers in the early twentieth century noticed an undercurrent of fear among the black population of the northern parishes that contrasted with the relatively relaxed atmosphere that prevailed in southern Louisiana.[3]

East of the Mississippi and on either side of the Red River, alluvial plains gradually merged into rolling hills that were unsuitable for plantation agriculture. In the parishes of this area white and black small farmers eked a living from less fertile plots of land, growing a mixture of subsistence and cash crops. As in the northern plantation regions, Anglo-Saxon, Protestant influences dominated here. Though most white people in the region had little need for black labor, competition for land, jobs, and resources often created strong racial tensions. Less likely than plantation workers to suffer violence at the hands of their employers, African Americans in these parishes still had to fear the random acts of aggression that endangered black lives throughout the South in the Jim Crow era.[4]

Below the Red River in the southwest were sparsely populated prairies and marshes, first settled by Cajun people who subsisted by growing rice, hunting, and raising cattle. After the Civil War, migrants from the Midwest introduced large-scale rice production and mechanized farming methods.

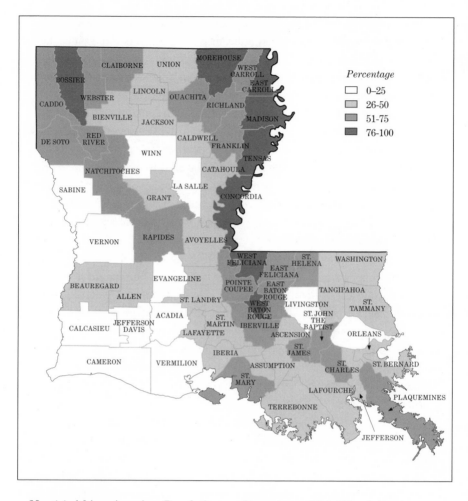

Map 1.1. African American Population as a Percentage of Total Population in
Louisiana Parishes, 1900
Source: Bureau of the Census, *Twelfth Census of the United States Taken in the
Year 1900, Population, Part 2* (Washington, D.C.: GPO, 1902), 187.

Like the sugar parishes, the region retained much of its French Catholic
heritage. There were some differences, however. Rice farmers preferred to
hire white workers over black people because of the skill required to operate machinery, so African Americans usually represented only a small percentage of the population in these parishes. Less dependent than sugar
growers on black labor and having no need to fear a large black majority,

white people in the southwest could afford to be more racially tolerant than those in either of the plantation regions.[5]

Despite these regional variations, Louisiana was dominated politically and economically by a plantation- and business-owning elite whose behavior seemed influenced by its financial interests more than by its religious beliefs or cultural backgrounds. Whether French or Anglo, Louisiana's plantation parishes were among the most repressive areas in the nation, with reputations for the savage handling of black people dating back to the antebellum period.[6] Even after slavery was abolished, neither the state's former slaveowners nor the northern investors who helped rebuild the plantation economy were willing to accord freed people the same rights to life, liberty, or property that they claimed for themselves. Successful cultivation of the state's staple crops depended on the availability of a reliable, cheap labor force that planters assumed would be provided by former slaves. When African Americans resisted that role, white Louisianans responded with intimidation, violence, and legislative measures designed to limit political participation and economic opportunities for black people.[7]

Planter priorities became apparent immediately after the Civil War, when state and local governments attempted to coerce freed people back onto the plantations by passing laws that restricted their mobility. In Opelousas, for example, ordinances prevented African Americans from buying property, limited the types of jobs they could hold, and prohibited black people who were not employed by white people from living in the town. In 1865 the state legislature discussed a series of measures to deny freed people any alternatives to plantation labor. At the end of the session, a new vagrancy law made unemployed or "idle" African Americans subject to arrest and hiring out to private employers if they were unable to pay the required bond, and legislation governing agricultural employment locked workers into year-long contracts with plantation owners. In addition, lawmakers set rules for laborers' behavior that allowed employers to impose fines or deduct wages for infractions such as "feigning" sickness, disobeying orders, leaving without permission, impudence, and swearing.[8]

Planters also used physical violence to force black people to work for them. African Americans who deserted their employers, argued over working conditions, or attempted to rent or buy land of their own were harassed, beaten, and murdered. According to freedman Henry Adams, when two

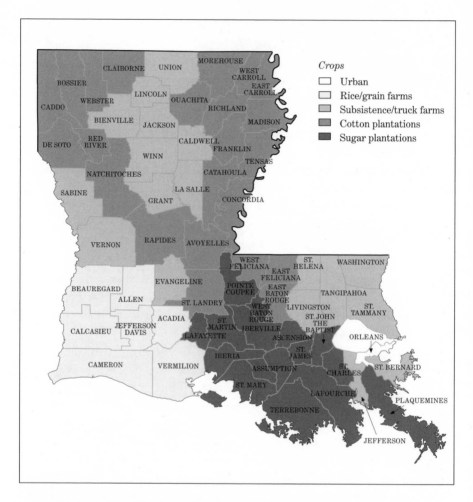

Map 1.2. Agricultural Regions of Louisiana, 1900–1930

Sources: Charles Robert Goins and John Michael Caldwell, *Historical Atlas of Louisiana* (Norman: University of Oklahoma Press, 1995), 4; Bureau of the Census, *Thirteenth Census of the United States Taken in the Year 1910, Volume 6: Agriculture* (Washington, D.C.: GPO, 1913), 690–95, and *Fifteenth Census of the United States: 1930, Agriculture, Volume 2: Reports by States, Part 2: The Southern States* (Washington, D.C.: GPO, 1932), 1265–71.

black men who had worked without pay for three months on a plantation near New Orleans complained to their employer, the white man "took his gun and shot at them, and did not pay them a cent." Adams and other witnesses reported that landowners in Louisiana continued to whip black workers as they had done under slavery, and that hundreds of freed people who attempted to leave the plantations in 1865 had been killed.[9]

Congress responded to reports of violence against freed people by introducing harsher policies toward the South and weakening the plantation elite's political power. During Radical Reconstruction, many former Confederates were disfranchised while African Americans were allowed to vote and hold office. The result was massive and enthusiastic participation by black people in politics. Approximately 90 percent of black males of voting age were registered in Louisiana in 1867. Although not officially allowed to vote, black women influenced the political agenda by expressing their views at mass meetings and by encouraging men to vote for the candidates whom they believed would best protect their interests. African Americans' voting strength and their active involvement in the Republican Party helped to elect a new state legislature in 1868 that was evenly divided between white and black representatives. African Americans also held the offices of lieutenant governor, state superintendent of education, and state treasurer. At the parish level, scores of black people served as sheriff, mayor, police juror, justice of the peace, tax collector, and in other administrative positions.[10]

Reconstruction legislators enacted laws to protect African Americans' civil rights as well as social welfare provisions to help poor people.[11] In response to demands from freed people, the Republican government introduced a system of universal education in Louisiana that was open to white and black children equally. African Americans expressed their desire for education in other ways as well. Black people of all ages flocked to classes organized by the Freedmen's Bureau and northern white missionaries to teach them to read and write. Many freed people also made access to education a condition of signing labor contracts with plantation owners.[12]

Most black families would have preferred to acquire land and work for themselves rather than continuing to labor for white people on the plantations. But the failure of the federal government to redistribute economic power as well as political power in the South after the Civil War left freed people dependent on their former masters for employment. Lacking the financial resources to strike out on their own, the majority of black people had few options apart from agricultural labor. Yet they resisted efforts by

white employers to impose conditions resembling slavery. Freed people refused to work in gangs under the supervision of white overseers, forcing
plantation owners to allow them to work as families on small plots of land
in return for a portion of the crops that were raised. The sharecropping
system thus initially emerged as a compromise between planters' desire
for a tightly controlled labor force and freed people's demands for land
and autonomy. Though it caused much misery for African Americans in the
twentieth century, sharecropping represented a small victory for freed people in their struggle for independence in the Reconstruction era.[13]

From the beginning, Radical Reconstruction faced strong opposition from
many white Louisianans. Members of the planter aristocracy and newly
arrived northern entrepreneurs resented the heavy taxes levied to pay for
public services like schools, hospitals, and aid for unemployed people. They
argued that prosperity could be regained only by keeping taxes and wages
low to revive production of the state's staple crops and encourage investment. Although many poor white people benefited from and supported Republican economic policies, numerous others felt only the humiliation and
bitterness of military defeat and occupation. In addition, for most white
Louisianans, the loss of social superiority over black people was difficult
to accept.[14]

Opponents of Reconstruction gravitated toward the state's reactionary
Democratic Party, using violence, intimidation, and fraud to gain control of
the state. Plantation owners and merchants denied land, credit, and supplies
to people who supported the Republican Party, coercing many into voting
for the Democrats instead. White supremacist groups like the Ku Klux Klan
and the Knights of the White Camellia terrorized black communities to
discourage African Americans from participating politically. Between 1866
and 1876 more than thirteen hundred black people were killed by white
people in rural Louisiana, with political motivations underlying the vast
majority of these murders.[15]

African Americans frequently fought back against these attacks, establishing a tradition of armed self-defense that continued into the twentieth
century. During Reconstruction they commonly carried guns with them to
political meetings, and some even armed themselves at work in the fields.
Several "race riots" occurred in the spring of 1868 after black people shot
back at white vigilantes in Bossier, St. Landry, St. Bernard, and Orleans
Parishes. Black communities sometimes responded to threats of white violence by organizing into armed bands to protect themselves. Often, however,

African Americans were outnumbered and faced opponents who had superior weaponry. In a shootout in the town of Colfax in 1873, black Republicans' shotguns proved no match for a small cannon deployed by their Democratic adversaries. More than one hundred black people were killed, the worst massacre in the history of Reconstruction.[16]

By 1876 politics in many parts of the state had deteriorated into a virtual civil war. Political turmoil in Louisiana and elsewhere in the South disgusted northerners and convinced them to end the Reconstruction experiment. The federal government withdrew its forces from the region in 1877, leaving African Americans without the military and legal protections they needed to preserve the gains they had made. Fearing unrestrained violence and repression by white supremacists, thousands of black Louisianans left the state in 1879, joining similar numbers of "Exodusters" from other parts of the South who migrated to the Midwest after the end of Reconstruction.[17] Those who remained behind experienced a steady deterioration in living and working conditions, along with the negation of their political rights.

With their opponents removed from office, conservative legislators passed measures that favored the state's wealthiest citizens. Funding for schools and other public services dropped off dramatically, while planters and businesspeople received hefty tax breaks. These actions plus successive economic crises in the late nineteenth century sparked a series of revolts by poorer people who demanded a government more responsive to their needs. In the 1880s and 1890s labor unions, farmers' alliances, and the Populist movement gained widespread support from hard-pressed farmers and workers, both white and black. Plantation and business owners responded by employing the same violent methods they had used to overthrow Reconstruction. A strike by black sugar workers organized by the Knights of Labor in 1887 led to evictions and then to a massacre at Thibodaux that left over thirty people dead and hundreds more injured.[18] Democrats punished supporters of the Populists with economic reprisals, social ostracism, beatings, and sometimes death. Conservatives did not even attempt to deny the deliberate miscounting of votes and other forms of corruption that became regular features of state and local elections. One northern Louisiana newspaper editorialized: "It is the religious duty of Democrats to rob Populists and Republicans of their votes whenever and wherever the opportunity presents itself and any failure to do so will be a violation of true Louisiana Democratic teaching. The Populists and Republicans are our legitimate political prey. Rob them! You bet! What are we here for?"[19]

By the late 1890s the state's progressive forces had largely been defeated, leaving legislators free to create the basic structures of an oppressive, white supremacist social order that remained intact for the next half century. Restrictive labor laws once again limited the mobility of plantation workers by imposing penalties if they left employers before their contracts had expired and prohibiting them from leaving at all if they owed their landlords money. The Louisiana Constitution of 1898 disfranchised the majority of African Americans (along with thousands of poor white people) by imposing literacy tests, residency requirements, and poll taxes as qualifications for voting. The same document mandated segregation in the state's public schools, supplementing both earlier and later statutes that solidified racial discrimination into law. African Americans were purged from political offices, leaving government and legal processes to be administered by white people who set policy and enforced the law in ways that protected their own interests at the expense of the state's black inhabitants.[20]

For African Americans at the turn of the century, the future looked bleak. Yet for a brief period in the late 1860s and early 1870s, black Louisianans had enjoyed many of the same rights as their white counterparts. African Americans had participated in politics, sent their children to free public schools, negotiated with employers for better wages and working conditions, and gained access to the law. As Eric Foner has noted, Radical Reconstruction "allowed scope for a remarkable political and social mobilization of the black community, opening doors of opportunity that could never again be completely closed."[21] Though it lasted only a short time, individual and collective memories of Reconstruction influenced the twentieth-century freedom struggle in Louisiana, providing an example of what could be achieved and inspiring black activists in their fight to regain what had been lost.

2

Our Plight Here Is Bad: The Limits of Protest in a New South Plantation Economy

In 1939 Louisiana planter Tom Alexander offered nine African American men free transportation and one dollar per hundred pounds of cotton they picked to work on a plantation he owned in Mississippi. The men agreed. After they had worked for one week, Alexander paid each man just two dollars and told them that they must buy their rations for the following week out of that amount.[1] According to Bernice Wims, who reported the incident to the U.S. Department of Justice, "One man, Frank Hanes . . . made a protest. Tom Alexander told Hanes to come to the commissary, which he did. Then Tom Alexander and another white man, set upon the Negro and beat him to death with ax handles." Five of the other black men tried to escape but were captured and beaten by Alexander and some of his neighbors. "Tom Alexander's plantation Negroes are under rigid control," Wims wrote. "They must report an escape. If an escape is made without their having reported it, then, they themselves receive a beating."[2]

Wims contacted the attorney general on behalf of Tom Elliot, the only one of the nine laborers who got away. She told him that Elliot was willing to cooperate with investigators and stated, "He is appealing to your Department to immediately protect his unfortunate companions from the imminent danger of enslavement and perhaps death." In response, she received only a brief note from Assistant Attorney General O. John Rogge explaining that the brutal treatment of African Americans on Tom Alexander's plantation did not violate any federal statute, so there was nothing the Justice Department could do. Rogge suggested that Wims bring these matters to the attention of state law enforcement agencies. Wims replied that it was futile to notify authorities in either Louisiana or Mississippi because "Negroes are not American citizens in the states of the far south." Like most white southerners who committed such acts, Tom Alexander went unpunished for the murder of Frank Hanes.[3]

Students of southern black history soon become familiar with horrifying stories like this one. Accounts of peonage, beatings, and lynchings could be considered another of the region's primary crops, and those of us with the stomach to labor in these fields eventually come to appreciate V. O. Key's observation concerning the high incidence of despair and tendencies toward "self-destruction" that seem to exist among people who write about the South.[4] The fate of Frank Hanes encapsulates many of the themes that permeate the historical record: the exploitation of black people as workers, the threat of violence or other reprisals if they protested maltreatment, their status as noncitizens unprotected by the law, and the failure of federal authorities to intervene on their behalf even in cases of extreme injustice. It demonstrates, powerfully, both the execrable workings of the Jim Crow social order and the complicity of national leaders in allowing it to persist into the mid-twentieth century.

The political and economic systems that allowed wealthy white Louisianans like Tom Alexander to control, cheat, and abuse black people took shape in the decades after the end of Reconstruction, guided by a coalition of former slaveholders and new entrepreneurs who migrated to the region from the North and West. This chapter outlines the development of those systems and the obstacles they placed in the way of black political activity. Although it was neither static nor uncontested, the New South political economy proved highly resilient for the first half of the twentieth century. Chapters 2 and 3 cover the decades up to World War II, because it was only after the 1940s that rapid economic change, the emerging civil rights movement, and federal intervention enabled the construction of a more equitable society.

Historians have debated whether the laws that segregated, disfranchised, and limited economic opportunities for black southerners in the late nineteenth century represented an attempt by white reactionaries to reestablish traditional racial hierarchies or whether they were part of the process of modernization itself.[5] Louisiana's plantation parishes provide examples of the way old and new people, money, and ideologies blended together in the New South to create a hybrid political economy based on neither slavery nor completely free labor. White Louisianans rejected northern political domination but they were desperate for northern capital. The Civil War had left most landowners without cash or the basis for obtaining credit that had previously been provided by slave ownership. Local merchants and professionals whose fortunes survived the war, along with entrepreneurs from outside the region, saw that they could provide financial assistance to impoverished planters and in doing so profit themselves. Some of them bought or leased plantations from their owners, hoping to grow rich from cultivating cotton and sugarcane. Others established general stores in rural areas and allowed farmers to purchase supplies on credit in return for liens on the crops they expected to produce. Simultaneously, northern-financed extractive industries, particularly lumber companies, began to exploit the state's natural resources. Agricultural and commercial interests gradually overlapped as merchants and other businesspeople accumulated enough wealth to purchase landholdings of their own. Recent migrants sometimes formed alliances with older residents through economic partnerships or marriage. Their sons attended college and entered medical, financial, or legal professions in addition to helping to operate the family estates. Out of this mix emerged a new elite comprised of planters, business owners, bankers, lawyers, doctors, and industrialists who dominated economic and political life in the rural parishes for much of the twentieth century.[6]

Former Confederates and Yankee fortune seekers merged into a single, conservative ruling class.[7] According to an account of the development of Madison Parish in the late nineteenth century, families that had lived for generations in the area welcomed immigrants in a "wonderful spirit of harmony."[8] Some local governments and community leaders actively encouraged northern investment and industry, emphasizing low taxes, abundant natural resources, and the availability of cheap labor as the region's main attractions.[9] State legislators generously exempted the owners of railroads, factories, sawmills, and mines from paying taxes for the first ten years of the twentieth century and empowered the State Board of Agriculture and Immigration to adopt "needful measures" to bring about the "peopling with a desirable population the vast unoccupied areas" of Louisiana.[10]

At the same time, the idea that farming was best approached as a business enterprise gained influence among planters. Corporate owners bought some of the old plantations in both the sugar and cotton parishes, reorganizing them to maximize efficiency and profits. Native Louisianans who had managed to hold onto their land readily adapted to new management and operating systems that promised greater productivity and higher incomes. In 1887 the region's most prominent sugar planters formed the Louisiana Sugar Planters' Association, urging members to adopt modern business practices and scientific farming methods. Five years later plantation owners in the northern parishes organized the North Louisiana Cotton Association to disseminate information, lobby for better freight rates and prices, and encourage the development of cotton production along scientific lines.[11] In the next few decades many Louisiana plantations came to resemble the rationalized, efficiency-driven enterprises associated with northern capitalism and industry. Corporate owners and absentee landlords gave little thought to the welfare of their workers, with whom they rarely had any direct contact. Agricultural laborers increasingly came to be viewed as statistics in plantation record books, important only to the extent that they counted as profits or losses.[12]

Despite the devastation caused by the Civil War, a rejuvenated Louisiana experienced remarkable economic growth in the late nineteenth and early twentieth centuries. In 1880 the state had only 652 miles of railroad, mostly traveling from east to west. By 1915 railroads totaling 5,728 miles crisscrossed its entire area, creating new markets and opening previously undeveloped forests and farmland to exploitation. In roughly the same period Louisiana's population almost doubled, increasing from 939,946 to 1,798,509. Although the state remained overwhelmingly rural until the 1940s, there was some industrial expansion in the early part of the century. Between 1899 and 1914 the number of manufacturing establishments in Louisiana increased from 1,826 to 2,206, raising the number of wage earners employed in industry from 40,878 in 1880 to 77,648 in 1920.[13]

Although this seemed like progress to some people, the black residents who made up nearly half of the population did not fare well in the new economic order. Lack of resources, inadequate education, and discrimination confined the majority of them to unskilled, low-paid jobs. In 1910, 76 percent of the state's black workers labored in agriculture or domestic service, usually for white employers. Another 7 percent worked in logging camps and sawmills, where wages and conditions were similar to those that prevailed on the plantations. Cotton, sugar, and lumber production were all labor-intensive enterprises subject to changing weather, market, and credit conditions. Plantation and lumber company owners operated with a chronic shortage of capital and often incurred heavy debts. Periods of prosperity alternated with times of economic hardship, buffeting these entrepreneurs about and frequently making life miserable both for them and their employees.[14]

In all three industries, ready access to a large, cheap labor force at crucial times in the production process was necessary for success. Sugar growers, for example, had only a small window of time each year to harvest their crops before exposure to cold weather reduced the sucrose levels in the cane, causing it to decrease in value or destroying it altogether. Lumber contractors and sawmill operators could (and did) incur thousands of dollars in losses when labor shortages prevented them from fulfilling their obligations to their customers. The end of the crop year was a dreaded experience for both cotton and sugar planters who could never be sure of retaining enough laborers to work their lands in the coming seasons. Plantation manager Henry Stewart of West Feliciana Parish gave expression to the exasperation that annually afflicted many agricultural employers when, in December 1906, he wrote: "The labor conditions here are frightful. My negroes have all cleared moving and were the first negroes to want to start moving, two families have left me and I have moved several but still I am short of last or this year. . . . How can any one accomplish anything with the whole country upset in any such way, every year?"[15]

The financial uncertainty and other problems associated with rural Louisiana's three main commercial enterprises encouraged attempts by employers to squeeze the most out of their employees for the least possible cost. Since the majority of laborers were African American, ruthless exploitation and brutal methods of controlling them were easy to justify. Henry Stewart advised a neighbor not to consider paying her workers more because "it is simply money thrown away (money given a negro is always thrown away) and setting a premium of worthlessness." Comparing management practices on the Bowman family's plantations in West Feliciana, Iberville, and Pointe Coupee Parishes, Sarah Bowman found those under the charge of a strict overseer to be more profitable; she concluded that when it came to dealing with black workers, "fear is far better than love." According to an article that appeared in the *Madison Journal* in 1928, African Americans had less need for food or clothing than white people. Its author claimed: "The negro . . . can weather the fiercest winter gale, clad in only a pair of cotton overalls and a blue jumper. . . . He can live a week on three soda crackers, a box of sardines, and five cents worth of cheese. . . . His surplus money he spends on entertainment. . . . and it very often happens that when the birds begin to sing, Mr. Negro is seized with wanderlust and suddenly disappears."[16] The prevailing view among white Louisianans could be summarized as follows: black people would not work unless they were coerced, they could survive on less money than other people, and offering them higher wages only caused them to become shiftless and unreliable.

Most African Americans in the cotton parishes worked as tenants and sharecroppers, closely supervised by plantation owners or managers. Although tenancy had traditionally been a rental arrangement that allowed landless farmers to lease land in return for paying either cash or a portion of the crops they raised as rent to their landlords, on large "business plantations" like those that emerged in Louisiana's delta regions it evolved into something more resembling wage labor. State courts recognized clear differences between two sets of relations that could exist on plantations: that of lessor and lessee, and that of employer and employee. The status of lessee applied only to tenants whose agreements with their landlords allowed them some autonomy, giving them control over management decisions and the sale of their portion of the crops. Where landowners or their managers supervised the work on plantations, tenants were merely employees, with no right to the products of their labor until after these had been sold and the proceeds divided by their landlords, who had legal ownership of the crops.[17] Common usage and the U.S. census after 1920 defined those workers who provided their own farm animals and equipment as tenants, distinguishing them from sharecroppers, who had only their labor to contribute to the production process. In reality, as Harold Woodman has observed, the differences were not so obvious. When landowners or overseers assigned workers tasks, decided when to harvest and sell the crops, and controlled the division of earnings, tenants became simply sharecroppers with mules, the only difference being that they received a larger share (usually two-thirds) as payment for their labor than sharecroppers, who received one-half.[18]

Census statistics do not reveal the exact status of individual farm families, but they do provide a general indication of the prevalence of farm ownership and the different types of tenancy. In 1910, 80 percent of Louisiana's 54,879 black farmers were tenants. Of those, 20 percent were cash tenants, 76 percent were share tenants, and 4 percent were listed as share-cash or unspecified tenure. By 1930 the percentage of nonwhite farmers who were tenants had increased to 86 percent, and the proportion who were cash tenants had

Table 2.1 African American Farm Operators in Louisiana, 1910 and 1930

Tenure	1910		1930	
	Number	Percentage	Number	Percentage
Owners[a]	10,725	20	10,503	14
Managers	77	(-)[b]	54	(-)
Tenants	44,077	80	63,213	86
Total	54,879	100	73,770	100
Tenants	44,077	100	63,213	100
Cash	8,723	20	6,692	11
Share[c]	33,596	76	32,214	51
Other	1,758	4	24,307	38

SOURCES: Bureau of the Census, *Thirteenth Census of the United States Taken in the Year 1910, Volume 6: Agriculture* (Washington, D.C.: GPO, 1913), 12, 684, and *Fifteenth Census of the United States: 1930, Agriculture, Volume 2: Reports by States, Part 2: The Southern States* (Washington, D.C.: GPO, 1932), 2–3, 1219.

[a]Farm operators listed as part owners in the census (i.e., those who owned part of the land they worked and rented other parts) are included in the category of farm owners.
[b](-) indicates less than 0.5 percent.
[c]Farm operators listed as share tenants in the 1910 census included all those who labored in return for a portion of the crop. In the 1930 census, this figure included only sharecroppers (i.e., share tenants who owned no farm animals or equipment). A large number of farmers classed as share tenants in 1910 were therefore listed as "other tenants" in 1930.

decreased to 11 percent.[19] (See Table 2.1.) A 1941 study of farm tenancy in Louisiana that divided tenants into "independent," "semi-independent," and "supervised" categories according to the extent of their managerial responsibilities found that African Americans were most likely to be supervised, especially if they resided on plantations in the Mississippi or Red River delta parishes.[20]

Usually, all members of tenant families who were old enough worked. The crop year began with plowing in the spring, a task that was performed by

Children picking cotton, location unknown, n.d. In the early twentieth century, sending children to the fields instead of to school for much of the year was both an economic necessity and a condition of employment for many tenant families. RG 83-ML-4-90, National Archives, Washington, D.C.

men and older boys. Women and younger children joined male workers in the fields to plant the cotton seeds, and they helped with the weeding and thinning that were needed periodically between late spring and midsummer. When the plants grew tall enough to survive on their own, the crops were "laid by" for a few weeks and work was temporarily suspended. All hands returned to the fields again during the cotton-picking season, beginning late in the summer and lasting until the fall or winter.[21]

Tenants were not paid until after the harvest, when they received a share of the income from the crops they had raised. Lacking cash for most of the year, plantation workers relied on their employers for housing, food, clothing, and other necessities. These were purchased on credit and the costs, plus interest, deducted from their wages at "settlement time." Planters often charged usurious interest rates on credit extended to their employees, arguing that these were necessary because of the high risks involved. Landlords had sole responsibility for keeping accounts and selling the crops, so that workers had to take their employer's word for how much they had earned and how much they owed. At the end of the year, most tenants either just broke even or landed in debt. Civil rights leader Harrison Brown, who grew up in a sharecropping family in Tensas Parish in the 1920s, recalled that he never saw any money. "Negroes didn't even sell crops in those days," he stated. "All he did was raise them, and pick them, and after that he'd see nothing."[22]

In the sugar plantation regions farther south, tenant farming was less common. African Americans in these parishes were mostly wage laborers who worked in gangs watched over by white supervisors. Like cotton growers, sugar planters had experimented with tenants in the decades following the Civil War but found these arrangements unsatisfactory. Sugar production required a highly disciplined, tightly supervised labor force, and the considerable financial investments that planters had in sugarhouses and other specialized equipment made them unwilling to rely on tenants for their maintenance. In addition, there was no way to accurately measure the amount of sugar that each tenant's cane produced, making a fair division of the proceeds difficult and discouraging more widespread use of tenancy in the sugar parishes. By the 1930s almost 80 percent of the Louisiana sugar crop was produced using wage labor, with African Americans making up 75 percent of the resident workforce.[23]

Sugar production divided into three main phases: plowing and planting (in the spring and fall), cultivating (from late March until early July), and harvesting (from October to January). Plowmen and their families provided the core labor supply and were hired on year-long contracts. Men prepared the fields at the beginning of the season, and women planted the seed cane. The rows then had to be weeded every ten days until June or July, when the cane was left to mature. During the sugar harvest planters employed extra workers from the surrounding areas, including many cotton farmers from northern Louisiana and Mississippi who came south to cut cane after their crops had been laid by.[24]

Payment arrangements varied. To ensure that year-round employees fulfilled their contract obligations, some planters paid them half of their earnings every two weeks and withheld the other half until after the harvest. Others paid both permanent and temporary employees weekly or daily wages. Whatever the method, wages were universally low, averaging about eighty-five cents to one dollar a day during the planting and cultivating seasons and slightly more at harvest time.[25] Though employers customarily

Women cutting sugarcane on a plantation near Baton Rouge, April 1939. Poverty forced many black women into the workforce in the early twentieth century, either as agricultural workers or as domestics. RG 69-GU-2-886, National Archives, Washington, D.C.

provided houses, garden plots, firewood, and medical care, there was a growing tendency in the early twentieth century to eliminate these benefits. Plantation owners knew that there was money to be made in furnishing employees with food and other necessities. Like their counterparts in the cotton parishes, some sugar workers never saw any cash. Employers either paid them in scrip redeemable only at plantation stores or simply kept a record of their purchases and labor.[26]

In the late nineteenth and early twentieth centuries, lumber companies joined cotton and sugar planters as major employers of African Americans in Louisiana. Northern speculators and corporations purchased large tracts of forest, built sawmills and railroads, and began exporting lumber to other parts of the United States and to Europe. Farmers whose landholdings included wooded areas sometimes built small, portable mills that they used to clear stands of trees, moving on when the task had been completed.

Operators employed mostly black male workers to cut and trim the timber, then transport it by river or rail to the sawmills, where the logs were sawed into planks and dried. The work was difficult, dangerous, and poorly compensated. The fifty to seventy-five cents per day that most sawmill workers earned in 1910 were the lowest wages paid by any nonagricultural southern industry. Weather conditions could sometimes put men out of work for days or weeks, and they depended on credit extended by their employers or local merchants to carry them over periods of unemployment. In some places there emerged company towns that resembled plantations in the organization and treatment of labor. Payment in scrip and employer-operated stores were common throughout the lumber camps of Louisiana.[27]

Though there were some differences in the experiences of cotton, sugar, and lumber workers, there were also important similarities. Low incomes, the centrality of credit, and the "furnish system" held many black families in perpetual poverty or indebtedness. Some employers deliberately cheated workers out of their earnings, either by overcharging them at commissaries or manipulating accounts. One family of sugar workers in Pointe Coupee Parish that kept records of its purchases from a plantation store discovered, when the time came to settle the account, that its employer had debited twice the correct amount. Although it is difficult to quantify the extent of these practices, an article that appeared in the *Madison Journal* in 1926 suggests that they were common and that white people made no attempt to deny them. Under the heading "Madison Parish; Its Customs—Yesterday and Today," an old-time resident reminisced about the day one of the most prominent planters in the area hired a woman to tutor his son, instructing her to "Teach him how to figger. Teach him how to beat the nigger out of his half, take the other half and leave him satisfied."[28]

Many plantation owners and lumber companies used such methods to hold their workers in peonage, assisted by an 1892 law that made it illegal for workers to leave employers without paying their debts.[29] White people were never able to completely restrict laborers' movements, and the extent of coercive practices varied according to the needs of employers. Black mobility was also assisted by competition among planters for labor and by the practice of allowing workers to leave if another employer agreed to pay off what they owed.[30] When planters wanted workers, however, holding employees in debt was a useful means of labor control. One resident of Claiborne Parish estimated in 1903 that there were an "average five or six peon slave holders and workers in every parish and county throughout the cotton

"The home of a negro plantation worker," New Roads, Louisiana, October 1938. Many rural black families lived in dilapidated shacks like this one well into the later twentieth century. LC-USF34-31792-D, Library of Congress, Washington, D.C.

belt" and reported that approximately twenty black people were working under such conditions in Claiborne itself. In 1905 Henry Stewart of West Feliciana Parish commented on the difficulty of finding black tenants who were not too indebted to their previous employers to move, saying, "I fear that the planters make as much money selling negroes as they do selling cotton."[31]

In the early 1900s the U.S. Department of Justice attempted to stamp out involuntary servitude and enforce the Thirteenth Amendment in the South, leading to investigations and trials of several plantation owners in Louisiana and the modification of some state laws.[32] However, control over local police and the courts remained with the planters. Even after the legislation that prohibited indebted laborers from moving was declared unconstitutional in 1918, those who attempted to leave without settling their accounts remained subject to arrest, harassment, and violence well into the later twentieth century. In 1937 a white resident of Caddo Parish reported:

These large planters and ranchers here in Louisiana, Arkansas and Texas, have men (White and Black) working and farming for shares. . . . When the cotton is picked and ginned and sold. . . . The rancher figures up their bills and says they owe him $200.00 to $300.00 after the sale of the cotton is take off of the bills that they owe, and he makes them stay on his place for the next year. . . . Some times the man slips his family out and goes to some other rancher. The rancher finds out where he is goes after him whips him (usually) and makes him return to work his debts out. Which he can never do. They are really held in bondage or slavery.[33]

As late as the 1950s, an investigation into working conditions in the sugar parishes found that if a field worker attempted to move off a plantation without the landowner's consent, "he may find a deputy sheriff's car parked in front of his house with a notice that he is to pay an accumulation of debts and obligations—some legitimate, some doubtful, before he can reach the highroad with his belongings."[34]

Limiting black people's access to education was another way to restrict their economic opportunities. According to one newspaper editor, it was well known that "the negroes, as soon as they can read and write with facility, seem to feel that they have entered a new era of existence and that they are raised above the necessity of having to till the soil." Educational policy in the rural parishes reflected the belief shared by many landowners that "an educated Negro is a ruined field hand."[35] School terms accommodated planters' need for labor during the crop seasons, with most black children attending classes for only three or four months a year.[36] Teachers often lacked proper qualifications and were poorly paid. Even those who were competent instructors faced difficulties such as overcrowding, lack of equipment, and dilapidated buildings. In many parishes African Americans received only an elementary education, as no high school existed. In 1910 only 1,199 of the state's 76,868 black youths aged between fifteen and nineteen were enrolled in high school, and 1,101 of these students were attending private institutions. White and black reformers were able to gain some improvements in the first few decades of the twentieth century, but as late as 1940 only twenty-six of the state's sixty-four parishes had more than one high school for African Americans, and fourteen parishes still had no facilities for providing secondary education to black children.[37]

White attitudes toward education for African Americans were not monolithic. In parishes where small farms predominated, black people sometimes fared a little better than their counterparts in the plantation regions. Washington Parish schools, for example, were relatively well equipped and housed, and black principals reported having little trouble with local officials. Some white administrators actively supported efforts to improve conditions in the black schools. One superintendent persisted for twenty years in his attempts to build a new school in his parish and finally succeeded. Another recalled the support he had received from a school board member who made the construction of a black high school in his parish his life's work, then retired from the board after his goal had been achieved. State Department of Education officials also expressed concern about inequities in the educational system, although they seemed powerless to alter practices at the local level.[38]

Proponents of black education faced strong opposition from those who believed that teaching African Americans to read and write was a waste of resources and a threat to the social order. State Agent for Negro Education Leo Favrot reported that he had met with the school superintendent of Terrebonne Parish in 1920 and found the man supportive of a program to improve black schools. Visiting the parish three years later, however, Favrot found that the superintendent had given up his efforts. Favrot concluded, "It must be, since the school board seemed so willing to go forward with Negro education, that the superintendent was deterred either by prominent sugar planters in his parish whose influence he feared, or by the influence of a neighboring superintendent who is distinctly hostile to Negro education and who seems to dominate school affairs to some extent in that section of the state."[39]

Workers who could not read, write, or count were unlikely to move out of agricultural and other unskilled jobs; they also made easy targets for the dishonest practices some employers used to cheat them out of their earnings. One analyst in the 1930s noted, "All educational improvements are vigorously fought by the rich sugar growers, who find it more profitable to engage poor and ignorant labor."[40] In the plantation parishes, officials who were too supportive of black education risked losing their jobs. The school superintendent of Concordia Parish explained to researchers, "You know we've got to live here with these people and we have to get along with them even if we can't convince them about the right thing to do. . . . We can't get the things done we need to get done because whenever we start with anything some big fellow will object and if he wants to . . . he'll make it very difficult for you."[41]

Louisiana's decentralized political structure left reformers with few options apart from trying to persuade individual school boards to do a better
job. State authorities supervised the superintendents and provided some
funding for education, but most control over the schools lay at the local level.
Parish officials decided how many and what kinds of schools to build, how
many teachers to hire, how long the school terms should be, and how to
distribute funds. Inequality and corruption permeated the educational system, with parish boards commonly misappropriating money that the state
provided for training black children. In the 1936–37 school year, only six
parishes directed the entire amount of their grants to facilities for African
Americans, and of those parishes four had negligible black populations. The
overall spending rate was 70 percent, but in many parishes the proportion
was much less—St. Landry Parish, for instance, received $153,262 but allo-
cated only $39,033 (25 percent) to its black schools, diverting the remainder
to white children. These statistics prompted the state superintendent of
education to conclude that there was "no serious intention in most of the
parishes to provide school facilities for Negro children."[42]

African Americans who acquired or aspired to higher levels of education
were wise to keep this to themselves, for few threats seemed more dangerous to white Louisianans than black people who appeared to be smart.
Black lawyer Johnnie Jones, who grew up in West Feliciana Parish in the
1930s, recalled that another young man he knew was killed by the supervisor
of the railroad yard where he worked after displaying a little too much
mathematical ability in counting planks of wood. Sharecropper Sonny Smith
of Pointe Coupee Parish received similar treatment from his landlord after
defying an order not to attend school. The plantation owner beat Smith so
severely that he never went to another class.[43]

For most African Americans in the South, wherever they worked or lived,
violence was a pervasive fact of life. Recent studies of lynching have shown
that black plantation workers were the most likely victims of this and other
forms of brutality. Some planters in Louisiana routinely used violence to
discourage laborers from protesting their working conditions or attempting
to leave. Civil rights activist Moses Williams noted that on the plantation
where he lived as a child, people were beaten if they were late for work
or questioned an order given by the landlord. Several decades after witness-
ing one such incident, he could still describe in detail the hooked stick the
planter had used to beat a man "half to death." Testimony at the trial of Joel
F. Johnson, the owner of a plantation in Madison Parish accused of practicing

peonage in 1909, revealed that "Negroes on his plantation were worked without pay and many of them were horribly beaten." According to witnesses, several workers who had tried to escape from the plantation were captured and "severely whipped by a colored man . . . acting under directions of Joel F. Johnson." Similar abuses occurred on the plantation of Tommy Walker in Webster Parish. A federal investigator found that the Walker family was well known for its tyrannical treatment of black laborers, and that Tommy Walker's brother, Lee Walker, had reportedly "killed several negroes in cold blood, and forced others to work for him against their will."[44]

Not all plantation owners were as vicious as these men. Other planters in Webster Parish condemned the actions of the Walkers, and the files of federal government departments contain enough letters from concerned white Louisianans to suggest that at least some of them were troubled by the injustices that African Americans in their communities suffered. Many of the black people who were interviewed for this study remembered white people who had shown kindness, or helped them, or supported their struggles for equality in some way.[45] But white sympathizers often found it difficult to intervene on black people's behalf. For instance, when Armas Sylvester attempted to stop a mob from whipping one of his tenants, he was told that "if he interfered, they would give him the same dose." As black leader Martin Williams explained, not all white people were bad, but "good white people was scared of his neighbor."[46]

White liberals' powerlessness cannot compare with that of African Americans themselves. Without a voice in local or state government, black people lacked access to legal processes that might have protected them from abuse. An informant in the Walker peonage case stated, "the plain fact is that there isn't any law around Shongaloo, Louisiana, and . . . the negroes are very badly treated."[47] There were federal and state laws against peonage, assault, and murder, of course, but local political and judicial systems made it almost impossible to enforce them. Sheriffs and deputies often were relatives or friends of wealthy planters and business owners, so employers could mistreat their workers without much risk of arrest.[48] In the rare instances when lawbreakers were prosecuted, all-white juries generally acquitted the perpetrators of even the most horrifying crimes. Late in 1914 a spate of lynchings occurred in Caddo Parish, including one where an elderly black man was tortured and then burned to death. The levels of cruelty involved in these incidents so shocked state officials that they ordered an investigation of the killings. After much difficulty (witnesses were reluctant to name members of the mob), Attorney General Ruffin G. Pleasant finally identified five men believed to be the ringleaders and recommended charging them with murder. In April 1915 a grand jury declined to act on the recommendation and instead issued a report criticizing the sheriff's office for "failing to make any attempt to prevent the examples of mob law."[49]

The "better classes" of white Louisianans often attributed beatings, lynchings, and other violence to the actions of poor white people, whose virulent racism supposedly contrasted with their own benevolent attitudes toward African Americans. In reality, all classes of white people participated in such acts, and plantation owners, merchants, lawyers, police, and parish officials were themselves among the worst offenders. "Public sentiment among the leading white people in this section of the state approve[s] lynching," wrote J. Leo Hardy of Shreveport in 1918, after the president of a local bank had attempted to reassure the "good niggers" of the town that only "guilty" African Americans need fear for their lives.[50] Ample evidence supports Hardy's contention. In 1935, for instance, a black man who was arrested and jailed in Iberville Parish after fighting with a white neighbor was found the next day hanging from a tree. There being no signs that anyone had broken into the jail, the most obvious suspects in the murder were the police who had him in custody. But as was common with lynchings, the coroner's report stated that the man "came to his death at the hands of unknown parties."[51] When black driver James Smith was involved in a car accident in West Feliciana Parish on his way to New Orleans in 1940, he filed a lawsuit against Ewan Ritchie, the white man whose vehicle had collided with his. At the trial in St. Francisville the court returned a verdict in favor of Ritchie, and afterward a group of white men ambushed Smith, took him to some woods, and beat him. Smith identified four of his attackers as follows: Sheriff T. H. Martin, "who appeared to be the ring-leader"; A. P. LeBlanc, a prominent businessman who had appeared as a witness for Ritchie; Sam J. D'Amico, Ritchie's attorney; and Ritchie himself.[52]

Even when they did not participate in such activities themselves, middle- and upper-class white Louisianans were complicit in the violence that pervaded black people's lives. Whippings and lynchings could not have occurred without the acquiescence of the planters, business owners, and professionals who dominated economic and political life in these communities. Local police could prevent vigilante action when they wanted to, as in the case of one sheriff in Rapides Parish who told a mob that it would have to kill him and his deputies first if it wanted to take a black prisoner from his jail. A story told by Johnnie Jones reveals where the real responsibility for life or death decisions lay. When Jones was blamed for a car accident that killed a white woman in West Feliciana Parish in the 1930s, there were rumors that he might be killed himself until powerful white friends of his father put a stop to such talk. As Jones stated, "when the white power structure speak . . . other white just shut their mouths up."[53]

The plantation elite's control over people and resources in rural Louisiana was never absolute, but it often seemed close to being so. Some parishes resembled personal fiefdoms, governed by a few individuals or families whose influence extended over everyone in the community, white or black. In the first few decades of the twentieth century, St. Landry Parish planter, merchant, and postmaster J. P. Savant monopolized power in the town of Whiteville and its surrounding areas. Savant kept his workers in peonage, threatened them with death if they tried to leave, and beat them if they displeased him. "All the negros [for] several miles are afraid of him and do any thing he says," one resident reported. "The white as well as the negros are afraid to say a word for if they offend Mr Johnie they know that they will have to move or be carried out of the neighborhood."[54] A similar situation existed in Madison Parish, where the sheriff and other officials in Tallulah took their orders from Andrew Yerger, a cotton grower and president of the police jury. According to black activist Martin Williams, "the Yergers was running this town back then, a bunch of rich plantation owners, and everybody had to dance by their music."[55]

The enormous power of people like J. P. Savant and Andrew Yerger was most evident within the boundaries of their own properties. Unlike wage laborers in the North who could normally escape the influence of their employers once the work day ended, agricultural workers in the South were constantly under surveillance. Planters or their business allies or relatives owned the houses they lived in, the stores they shopped in, the land their churches and schools were built on. Landlords controlled the mail and telephones, enabling them to limit the amount of contact tenants had with the world outside the plantation. Planters also bestowed money, gifts, and favors on black people who kept them informed of developments within the African American community. In these ways plantation owners monitored not only black people's working lives, but their social lives as well. The knowledge that planters were likely to find out about any expression of dissatisfaction or any attempt to organize workers made challenging the system extremely difficult. Harrison Brown explained: "You couldn't be known

Plantation store and post office, Melrose, Louisiana, June 1940. In the rural parishes, large landowners often combined agricultural and business interests, as well as holding public offices such as postmaster. These overlapping interests afforded some planters an extraordinary amount of power within and over their communities in the first half of the twentieth century. LC-USF34-54608-D, Library of Congress, Washington, D.C.

resisting against the powers.... They always had a way to reach you and get you, you know. So . . . you'd have to take it slow."[56]

Conditions in the lumber camps were no more conducive to black political activity. Loggers and mill operators often had even worse reputations than plantation owners for using peonage, violence, and spying to control their workers.[57] Company-owned towns provided all of the employees' needs from housing, food, and clothing to schools and recreation. Many of these settlements were temporary and were dismantled when the timber ran out. Others, like Bogalusa in Washington Parish, lasted into the late twentieth century. The owners of the Great Southern Lumber Company founded Bogalusa in 1906, building houses, banks, hotels, schools, a hospital, and a store in addition to a sawmill. The company employed its own police force, and its manager, William Henry Sullivan, served as mayor until he died in 1929. According to one source, Sullivan's control over Bogalusa was "as complete as any ante-bellum master over his plantation."[58] Black (and white) laborers who challenged his power were as likely to be fired, evicted, beaten, or shot as those who worked for "real" planters.[59]

The few African Americans who were not directly employed by white people nonetheless remained subject to their authority. Black teachers depended on local school boards for their salaries, and they generally avoided actions that might jeopardize their livelihoods. Religious leaders in Louisiana's rural parishes also seemed reluctant to become involved in such activities. Few could survive solely on the contributions of the poverty-stricken tenants, domestic workers, and unskilled laborers who made up their congregations. Some ministers supplemented their incomes by farming or doing odd jobs, but others chose to improve their economic and social positions by accepting the patronage of prominent white people in return for discouraging challenges to the social order.[60] Even ostensibly independent landowners or businesspeople might not be immune from manipulation, since prosperous black southerners often owed their success to white benefactors who loaned them money, secured business permits or political offices for them, and protected them from violence.[61]

Johnnie Jones's father was one of those who earned such privileges. At one time, he and another black man were appointed to the West Feliciana Parish school board by a white man who wanted to increase his own influence over educational policy. Later Jones often teased his father about his years on the board, asking him, "Daddy, when you was on the school board what did you do?" His father always replied, "Whatever Mr. Argus told us."[62] In 1940 the control that white people had over nearly all aspects of African American life drove an NAACP member in East Carroll Parish to despair. "Our plight here is bad," he wrote in a letter to the national office. "A bunch of hopeless and helpless people with most preacher and school teachers being used by their white Lords to keep the people humble."[63]

Perhaps the only entity capable of altering the southern social order in any meaningful way was the federal government. But except in times of crisis or war, national political leaders rarely showed any interest in ensuring equality or justice for African Americans. When they did decide to take action, sensitivity to local elites' desire for control over their own affairs usually undermined these efforts, as was the case with the Justice Department's attempts to combat peonage at the turn of the century. Although lawyers for the United States managed to persuade the Supreme Court to declare some state laws unconstitutional, gaining convictions for individuals who used coercion or violence to control workers was more difficult. White southerners were apt to become upset over violations of "state rights" when federal officials interfered with their local law enforcement procedures. For this reason, the department usually tried to encourage punishment of offenders by local authorities before intervening itself. Convictions in these instances were rare, and even when cases were tried in federal courts, lawyers still had to contend with local juries' sympathy for (or fear of) the defendants.[64]

Southern plantation owners exerted a considerable amount of influence in shaping national as well as local policy. Political corruption and the one-party system resulted in the election of the same senators and representatives from the region year after year, enabling these politicians to achieve a disproportionate amount of seniority and power within the national government. Southern Democrats often controlled the most important policy-making committees and positions. As a result, attempts to enforce the U.S. Constitution in the South were usually stymied. In the first half of the twentieth century, every proposed antilynching bill and most other measures aimed at increasing federal protection of black people's civil rights were killed by filibusters in the Senate or by the threatened withdrawal of southern Democrats' support for other legislation deemed more important by national political leaders.[65]

Louisiana's Senator Allen J. Ellender, a member of a prominent sugar planting family, served his state for thirty-six years between 1937 and 1972. During one filibuster in 1938, he held the Senate floor for twenty-seven hours, arguing that the federal government should repeal the Fifteenth Amendment and outlaw interracial marriage instead of wasting its time debating legislation to prevent lynching. Throughout his term, the senator acted to protect the interests of Louisiana plantation owners and defeat measures aimed at increasing wages or improving conditions for sugar workers. In the 1950s farm union organizer H. L. Mitchell blamed Ellender for "perpetuating the labor conditions which have changed but little in the past 80 years when the Negro plantation workers in Louisiana were chattel slaves, openly bought and sold in the market like animals."[66]

As Mitchell and scores of other white activists and officials discovered, the plantation system presented formidable obstacles to anyone desiring to bring law, democracy, equality, or justice to rural Louisiana. To black people living in the region, the difficulties often seemed insurmountable. Not surprisingly, local civil rights leaders who came of age in the decades before

World War II remembered those years as times of much poverty, hardship, and violence, and little political activity. Harrison Brown recalled, "You'd do what you could, but—I don't know how to explain it, but you couldn't have the freedom to do or to be exposed to what was there to be exposed to. You couldn't take a part with it, you know." Moses Williams stated, "You didn't have no kind of organization, no kind of resistance, nobody jumping on the boss man . . . if you raised up and hit one of them then, you'd be killed before sundown, or you'd have to run for the rest of your life."[67] As the next chapter will show, however, the absence of organized protest against white supremacy did not necessarily mean that African Americans in the region passively accepted their fate.

3

They Will Not Fight in the Open:
Strategies of Resistance in
the Jim Crow Era

"Got one mind for white folks to see / 'Nother for what I know is me," went a song that was well known among black southerners in the Jim Crow era.[1] Behind the mask of subservience and acceptance of the social order that many black people presented to the world lay a clandestine culture of resistance. In their music, folklore, religion, and value systems, African Americans in the rural South analyzed their world and critiqued the economic and political systems that kept most of them in poverty. At the same time, black individuals and communities adopted a variety of methods to undermine white people's efforts to keep them powerless and poor. That these forms of resistance were usually subtle or ineffective does not mean that they were unimportant. Many of the concerns that motivated organized political activity were also reflected in less obvious, "infrapolitical" strategies that black people employed to challenge their oppression during this period.

This chapter outlines the ways rural black Louisianans quietly struggled to gain economic opportunity, education, political power, and safety from violence in the Jim Crow era. Although these activities did not directly confront white supremacy and affected the social order only slightly, they reflected participants' awareness of the sources of their oppression and provided the foundations of the twentieth-century freedom struggle. The goals and themes established by informal resistance carried over into the attempts at collective action discussed in later chapters of this book.

No movement to overthrow white supremacy could have emerged in the twentieth century if large numbers of black people had not believed that the system was unjust. Criticisms of the social order usually were not expressed openly for fear of reprisals, but they permeate the songs, stories, and jokes collected by students of black culture and folklore in the twentieth century. Had Louisiana sugar planters listened carefully to the verses sung by their black field hands, they might have detected a reproachful assessment of the economic arrangements that transferred most of the profits from black people's labor to white people who had done little to deserve them. Cane cutters frequently swung their knives to a work song containing these lyrics:

> White folks want de niggers to work and sweat
> Wants dem to cut de cane till dey is wringin' wet
> We poor niggers gits nothin' atall
> White boss cusses and gits it all.[2]

Visiting the state in the 1930s, black writer Zora Neale Hurston heard a similar complaint from a friend who told her a folk tale ending with the rhyme, "ought's a ought, figger's a figger; all for de white man, none for the nigger." As Lawrence Levine has noted, music and storytelling provided forums for protest and social criticism when the usual avenues for political expression had been closed to black southerners.[3]

African American blues musicians drew on these cultural traditions to create one of the most important forms of creative expression to emerge within the United States in modern times. Historians of the blues have traced its origins to the plantation regions of the Deep South in the late nineteenth and early twentieth centuries, just when the gains of Reconstruction were being negated by segregation, disfranchisement, and narrowing economic opportunities for African Americans. The distinctive, melancholy sounds of blues harmonicas, guitars, and voices, along with lyrical themes expressing sadness, anger, loss, and betrayal provided the soundtrack to the period commonly referred to as the "nadir" of African American history. J. D. Miller, a record company owner who worked with local musicians in the Baton Rouge area in the 1940s, described some of the influences that shaped the songs of many artists that he recorded when he spoke to an interviewer about Lightnin' Slim (Otis Hicks). "His father was a tenant farmer," Miller explained, "and they lived out there in the country and after the men would get through work they used to sit out and they'd start playin' and singin' you know. And they'd sing these ole blues and the blues was generally bad luck and the troubles they have had." Other Louisiana musicians grew up listening and playing at juke joints that catered to workers in the state's lumber and turpentine camps, traveling the "barrelhouse circuit" from tiny town to tiny town along a well-worn route from Alabama to Texas.[4]

Bluesmen and women took their experiences of oppression and turned them into art. Though some listeners found these tunes depressing and fatalistic, for others the blues offered comfort, inspiration, and hope. In rundown shacks and makeshift bars, black workers gathered on Friday and Saturday nights to drink, socialize, play music, sing, and dance, enjoying brief moments of relief from the hard, physical labor that filled most of their days. Such activities were central elements in the lives of many rural black people, despite the disapproval that was occasionally expressed by more upright, churchgoing African Americans in their communities. For some black people, religion and the blues were not so far apart. Of church services, blues player Willie Thomas noted, "They sing: Lord—have mercy . . . / Lord—have mercy . . . ooooh, / Lord—have mercy . . . save poor me. He's in the church singin' that! He got the blues in church!"[5]

In many ways, churches and juke joints served similar functions. Both offered respite from the harsh realities of daily life, provided sustenance for the soul, and fostered a sense of community among people who shared the same problems and experiences. Both were spaces where black people asserted that they were more than just bodies forced to labor for others, and where they created distinct cultural and value systems away from the influence of white people.[6] For Willie Thomas, the music was something that African Americans could own, in a world where most forms of opportunity and property were denied them. He explained: "The white man could get education and he could learn to read a note, and the Negro couldn't. All he had to get for his music what God give him in his heart. And that's the only thing he got. And he didn't get that from the white man; God give it to him."[7]

The blues were an important form of self-expression that helped black people endure oppression and hardship. For those musicians who were fortunate enough to make a living from their art, playing the blues also offered more material benefits. Traveling entertainers enjoyed a greater degree of mobility, autonomy, and creativity than most African Americans in the early

Bar and juke joint, Melrose, Louisiana, June 1940. Many rural black people gathered in establishments like this one on Friday and Saturday nights to drink, socialize, listen to music, and dance. These pursuits offered a brief respite each week from the hard labor that filled their days. LC-USF34-54355-D, Library of Congress, Washington, D.C.

twentieth century. Some chose this profession precisely because it offered an alternative to economic exploitation and tight control by white employers. In the 1930s wandering minstrel Carolina Slim justified his rootless existence to a group of Louisiana folklorists by singing them a song that ended:

> The boys in Noo 'Leans they oughta be dead
> They go to work for fish and bread.
> . . . And I ain't bluffin',
> I ain't gonna work for nothin'.[8]

Similarly, blues musician Black Ace (B. K. Turner) remembered the lucrative career he made out of playing at house parties in Shreveport during the depression. "I couldn't get a li'l job nowhere," he explained. "So I would go aroun' play at house parties with this boy—make a dollar-an'-a-half whilst other folks was gettin' that for one day's work on relief. . . . I get three or four parties, man—I made a *lot* of money. . . . Dollar-an'-a-half for fun!"[9]

African Americans who managed to evade plantation labor and other low-paid jobs were in the minority. Yet many others sought to improve their economic positions in whatever ways they could. Thousands of agricultural workers left their employers at the end of each year in search of higher wages and better treatment.[10] To the chagrin of plantation owners, some of them did not even wait that long, preferring to abandon their crops before harvest time rather than endure beatings or face the probability of coming out in debt. Planters complained that black sharecroppers and laborers were "always dissatisfied and moving from one place to another," often attributing this to their supposedly inherent shiftlessness and unreliability.[11] Contrary to white people's assumptions, black workers' peripatetic tendencies were not random or unpurposeful. The statement given by sharecropper John Pickering to a notary public in Texas after he moved there from Louisiana in 1926 shows that his decision resulted from a carefully considered, accurate analysis of the plantation system and his chances of making a living if he had stayed with his previous employer. "I moved off of the place of the said William Wilson because he would not give me a fair settlement on what I had made and what I earned and would not account to me for my share of the cotton crop," Pickering said. "I being an ignorant negro he would not furnish me with a statement showing what the cotton sold for and what goods I had procured from him, but insisted that, notwithstanding his getting all the cotton, I still owed him three hundred dollars. When I found out he would not give me a fair settlement and was getting all of my earnings, I decided to move into the State of Texas because I knew that in the State of Louisiana the big planters buy and sell negroes and never let one get out of debt."[12]

Many other black people shared Pickering's views. Harrison Brown believed that white people aimed to maintain the supply of "free" (meaning unpaid) labor that they had enjoyed before the Civil War. Outlining the difficulties sharecroppers faced in finding good landlords or saving enough money to buy land of their own, he stated, "We mostly had to do their work, you know. . . . They didn't intend for you to get out." Describing conditions in Bossier Parish in the 1920s, cotton farmer W. C. Brown wrote, "We as a rule gets everything but a square deal both in business and in law. . . . We are all through picking and ginning our cotton and the white people as a whole have it all in their hands and many have lived hard and will clear good money but the white people will wait until a few days to Christmas and then try to put the good and the bad in the same class and give them just what they want us to have and not mention justice to them." James Willis related to an interviewer in 1939 how hard his parents worked on a sugar plantation in Iberville Parish and how little they received for their labor. He said, "Ma and pa couldn't figure, so they took whatever the man on the farm gave 'em. The folks said that pa worked himself a house. Yeah, in other words Pa made enough money to git him a house, but he never did git it. . . . And there is a lot of things I don't know about but I do know that pa was gipped."[13]

Moving from plantation to plantation or from state to state was one of the few means available to agricultural workers to protest their working conditions. Though employers generally denied any connection between black migration and unfair labor practices, they sometimes admitted that it existed. Early in the twentieth century, newspapers in northern Louisiana reported that attempts by planters to "restore a form of forced labor" in the state had resulted in a mass exodus of African Americans to Arkansas, where they hoped to gain better treatment.[14] In 1907 cotton planter Henry Stewart complained to a friend: "There is not enough labor here to go around and what is here is too unreliable and *I think* thoroughly organised. If one has labor one year it is a good sign that they will be short the next year, so in reality you make a little money one year and the next the place lies idle for the negro is punishing you for some small misdemenor which you have committed."[15]

Black workers who stayed with their employers often took every opportunity they could to supplement their earnings. After inspecting his cousin Sarah's plantation in West Feliciana Parish in August 1910, Robert Stirling found one tenant "pasturing of horses" as well as making the expected crops, and told her, "He trades in horses at your expense." Of another employee, Stirling advised his cousin not to charge any less than fifty dollars a month for rent because "Vattore is getting $50.00 per month from Ry Co. and yet he is trying to get house rent free from you[;] he and his boy also have quite a lot of cattle in your pasture." Other planters in the parish found it necessary to post weekly notices in the local newspaper asking members of the public not to purchase wood, posts, livestock, or other farm products from tenants on their plantations without first gaining permission from the owners.[16]

For Louisiana planters in the late nineteenth and early twentieth centuries, theft was a serious problem. "The negroes around here have reduced cattle stealing to a fine art," bemoaned Henry Stewart in 1906. "Some years

African American family moving, Opelousas, Louisiana, October 1938. For many plantation workers, abandoning their employers at the end of each crop year was one of the few means through which they could express their dissatisfaction with working conditions without risking eviction or physical violence. LC-USF33-011863-M3, Library of Congress, Washington, D.C.

ago we had 160 head and now I can count but 76 head of branded cattle and none sold in these years. I wonder if cows evaporate." A year later, the owner of Hazelwood Plantation in West Feliciana Parish reported that several black tenant families had stolen cotton from the place, in spite of her manager's "seeming watchfulness." Other items likely to disappear included harnesses, small pieces of machinery, hogs, corn, and seeds that workers either used themselves or sold to unscrupulous merchants in the dead of night.[17]

Black domestic workers as well as field hands commonly appropriated property from the homes of the white families they worked for. Taking away leftovers, or "pan toting," was a widely accepted custom throughout the South. But as Jacqueline Jones has noted, "the service pan expanded in proportion to a black woman's needs and resourcefulness," often without the knowledge or consent of employers. One white Louisianan who complained of being without domestic help in the 1940s stated that despite having to cook meals herself, "It is rather nice not to have a *nigger* eating up all your food and carrying off what they can't eat!" White people resented their servants' tendency to take more than what was willingly given them, but domestic workers usually saw nothing wrong in these actions. One black cook chided an employer who initially refused to allow her to take home leftover food, saying, "The only thing we cullud people can do is get home and eat a little sumpin' you white folks can't eat. Has that ever crossed yo' mind, Missus Jakes? Is you humanity?" Smuggling food and other necessities out of the house to take home to their own families helped compensate for the low wages these women earned. Given the conditions of poverty that most were forced to endure, the justification was plain: white people had more than they could eat, and black people did not have enough, therefore they had a right to take what they needed. African Americans used theft to partially redress inequalities in the social order that white Americans had created.[18] One white southerner observed that black people were "like the Isr[ae]lites when they left the land of Egypt, think they have a right to borrow and take all they could beat the Egyptians out off. The negro still think they have this right and exercise it when opportunity affords."[19]

Though attempts by African Americans to improve their material status might be seen as simply matters of survival, they were more than that. As many black people realized, economic independence was a prerequisite to achieving real freedom and equality. They knew that during Reconstruction, their ancestors had voted and held political offices, and that those gains had been lost through violence, intimidation, and economic reprisals.[20] As long as they too were forced to rely on white people for food, shelter, and other necessities, they could not hope to launch a powerful movement for change. In 1918 the president of a struggling NAACP branch in Shreveport suggested to the national office that the organization make some effort to provide "relief for the farmer that is swindled and cheated out of his money.... Loan these men and women (farmers) money assist them in securing credit and in a great many other ways help them." Two decades later, another local leader noted the restraints that economic dependence placed on some African Americans' ability to take part in organizing efforts, saying, "The man who has your job has you."[21]

Activists Eual and Lorin Hall, who came from a family of black landowners in St. Helena Parish, remembered how this idea was passed down (and continues to be passed down) through the generations. "If you have no land, and no money, you're worthless," Eual Hall stated. "There's nothing you can do, there's no fear you can put into nobody." The Halls' parents, grandparents, and great-grandparents were "independent and free" and determined to keep themselves that way. Some were farmers, some were self-employed entrepreneurs, "and they were very, very strong in unity. . . . They believed in keeping things together . . . they would help one another maintain their property, whatever had to be done." Older members of the Hall family still emphasized to younger people the importance of economic and political independence, both for themselves and for African Americans as a group. Identical values were impressed upon Willa Suddeth during her childhood. Raised on a farm near Shreveport, she recalled that her father told her repeatedly to "own your own," and to strive for autonomy. "Grandfather and his brother went to great lengths to buy their own land," she told an interviewer, "and it's still in the family."[22]

Equally important to the freedom struggle was education. Since the passage of the first laws prohibiting enslaved people from learning to read and write, African Americans have recognized the empowering potential of literacy. In the twentieth-century South, the lessons were no less clear than they had been in the antebellum period. David Bibens, who grew up on a plantation in Pointe Coupee Parish, remembered that his grandfather's reading abilities and mathematical skills prevented the manager from cheating him at settlement time. After other sharecroppers began asking him to calculate their accounts as well, the manager arranged for some local thugs to administer a beating, causing him to stop this practice. Civil rights leader Robert Lewis of Concordia Parish recalled a similar incident that occurred on the plantation where he had lived as a boy. A sharecropper who had kept his own records confronted the landlord with his account book after being told that he had come out in debt, making the white man so angry that he refused to settle any more accounts that day. In the end the sharecropper received his money but was ordered to leave the plantation. Bibens, Lewis, and other rural African Americans were keenly aware of the value of education and the possibilities it offered for creating a better life for themselves and their children. Harrison Brown succinctly expressed the feelings of many black people when he stated, "Education—I ain't got it but I know the benefit of it."[23]

Rural black people devised a variety of strategies to circumvent plantation owners' efforts to deny them knowledge and power. By following their teachers as they moved from one regional classroom to the next, some students extended the length of time they attended school beyond the limits set by their parish school boards. Families living in communities that lacked high schools commonly sent older children to stay with friends or relatives in neighboring parishes to complete their secondary education. When state and local governments refused to build schools for black communities, African Americans constructed their own or held classes in churches and fraternal society halls. In a typical case, a study of schools in St. Helena Parish conducted in the 1940s found that the school board owned only two of the buildings used for educating African Americans. The remaining twenty-eight, attended by over 80 percent of the black children, were "housed in churches and in buildings erected mainly at the expense and efforts of the Negroes themselves."[24]

Such feats were the result of a long history of school-building efforts by black communities dating back to Reconstruction. After conservatives ousted the Republicans from office in the 1870s, northern white philanthropists helped to fill the financial void left by state and local governments that refused to support black education. In the early twentieth century, donations from the Slater Fund, Anna T. Jeanes Fund, General Education Board, and Julius Rosenwald Fund supplemented the money raised by black communities to construct buildings, hire and train teachers, and buy equipment for classrooms. Small one- and two-teacher schools sprang up in parishes across the state, standing as tiny wooden monuments to African Americans' commitment to education. After a decade of these efforts Leo Favrot reported to Julius Rosenwald, "No single effort in Negro education in Louisiana has created as much enthusiasm for better schools among these people as your benefaction. It will not be possible to supply the demand for new schoolhouses this year." Between 1917 and 1932 the Rosenwald Fund helped to finance 435 school buildings that catered to more than 51,000 black students in Louisiana.[25]

Accepting help from white sympathizers was not without its problems. In return for their generous contributions, northern philanthropists expected teachers and administrators of the schools they funded to produce model black citizens who knew their "place."[26] Grambling College, the primary training ground of teachers for the rural schools, sought to make every graduate "an able teacher, a community leader, a farmer, a handyman, and an ambassador of good will between the races," according to its president. The State Department of Education's *Course of Study for Negro High Schools and Training Schools* (1931) required teachers to "develop in the pupils an

Rosenwald school under construction, Millikens Bend, Louisiana, n.d. Efforts to ensure access to education for black children were among the most important elements of the long-term freedom struggle. L1167, Papers of Jackson Davis, Special Collections Department, University of Virginia Library, Charlottesville.

appreciation of the dignity and importance of manual labor," and to impress upon students that *"professional and 'white collar' jobs cannot absorb all."* Robert Lewis recalled that in the black schools of Concordia Parish, students never learned about African American rebels like Nat Turner or Harriet Tubman but were taught to admire "Booker Uncle Tom Washington" and other accommodationist leaders instead.[27]

Yet a willingness to outwardly conform to social expectations often benefited black individuals and communities. Robert Lewis learned this when he watched an older man persuade white people to allow him to fish on their property by talking to them in a subservient manner. Martin Williams of Tallulah consciously "worked the system" using accommodationist tactics. "That was my strategy," he said, and usually it was effective. In his hometown of Jackson, Alabama, Williams had a job driving a grocery delivery truck and became a favorite of several white families on his route by giving their children rides home from school whenever it rained. As a result, they always treated him well. Williams could not see any point in upsetting white people because, as he put it, "we ain't got no money." Leaders like Williams reasoned that it was necessary to work through white people to get anything done because they were the ones who controlled the finances in Louisiana's rural communities. Willie Crain, a schoolteacher in Washington Parish, phrased it this way: "My race is alright, but they can't do anything for you." Crain then related the story of how an extra room came to be added to the black schoolhouse. When the need for the addition first arose, some of the other teachers offered to donate money. But they were so poor that there was no way they could raise the necessary funds themselves. Crain said, "Then they had a meeting one Sunday afternoon, and I had Mr. Bateman [the superintendent] out to it, and he give us this extra room, just like that." Both Williams and Crain were adept at persuading white people to provide needed resources for black communities. In their own way, these men and others like them were participants in the freedom struggle.[28]

Despite the assistance of white benefactors, most of the burden of improving educational conditions fell on African Americans. To construct a high school in the 1930s, residents of East Feliciana Parish had to first overcome the opposition of some white members of the community who argued that "the time is not ripe for one here because the colored children were needed on the farm or could work in the sawmill." Next, they set about raising money and soliciting contributions. "We had to disrupt the school program and have teachers be responsible for a certain amount of money and the giving of entertainment made it impossible to conduct classes normally," said the woman who spearheaded the effort. "But that was the only way we were able to get the training school." In this and countless other cases, local black people initiated school-building programs, donated money and materials, and did most of the work themselves. As James Anderson has noted, African Americans incorporated financial aid from other sources into an existing tradition of self-help and fund-raising to provide for their own education.[29]

The struggle for education reflected and reinforced strong community ties that African Americans developed in their families, churches, benevolent societies, and fraternal orders. These institutions offered valuable support networks that black Louisianans relied on for survival. Sugar workers in Pointe Coupee Parish recalled that when people became ill and unable to work, friends and relatives "took up orders" for them at plantation stores, charging food and other necessities to their own accounts so that families who had fallen on difficult times did not starve.[30] In a study of black workers

on two plantations in West Baton Rouge and St. Mary Parishes, white investigator J. Bradford Laws noted derisively that his subjects had "an unfortunate notion of generosity, which enables the more worthless to borrow fuel,
food, and what not on all hands from the more thrifty." Laws and other white
people criticized black people's failure to adopt entirely the individualistic,
profit-seeking values of capitalist society, citing it as a major reason for their
general poverty. But it was partly in response to poverty and insecurity that
African Americans developed such mutualistic practices. The idea that no
one should have to starve because of a bad crop, bad landlord, or bad luck
held immense appeal to people who were acutely aware of their own vul-
nerability to economic disaster. Ruth Cherry explained the dominant philosophy among black people in her parish this way: "What you have, I have.
What would hurt one, would hurt the other. Hospitality they call it, but it
was the only way we made it through." By emphasizing people's interdepen-
dence and their obligation to look after one another, black communities offered what James Scott calls "an alternative moral universe" in opposition to
the dominant culture's self-centeredness and materialism.[31]

In addition to relatives and neighbors, African Americans could rely on
their churches for spiritual, emotional, and material assistance. A study of
twenty parishes conducted in the 1940s found that almost every black person belonged to a church and attended services and other meetings regularly. "To the church they contributed seemingly enormous amounts of
money in proportion to their meager and inconceivably low incomes," the researchers wrote. "Even those persons unemployed with no apparent source
of income frequently stated that they made regular contributions to the
support of the church. They have placed their utmost faith in this institution
and willingly support it in all programs which it undertakes." For many, the
church was a haven, a place that offered some respite from work and suffering. One youth's account of a conversion experience reveals how religion
brought joy to people whose lives offered few opportunities to savor such
emotions: "Look like everything was new and I felt happy . . . and I told the
Lord if He freed my soul, I'd serve Him all my days. . . . That was the
happiest time my family had—when my brother and I got religion."[32]

Some analysts have viewed the black church as a conservative force that
deflected people's concerns away from the problems of this world and encouraged them to think only of what awaited them in the next. There is some
truth in this assessment. In Louisiana, many African Americans belonged to
the Roman Catholic Church, and their spiritual guides were usually white

Inside a plantation worker's home, Melrose, Louisiana, June 1940. As the pictures decorating this bedroom suggest, religion was a central part of many black people's lives. LC-USF34-54651-D, Library of Congress, Washington, D.C.

priests and nuns who had been assigned to, not chosen by, their communities. White religious leaders taught acceptance of white supremacy as a reflection of God's will and discouraged attempts by black people to rise above their prescribed station in life.[33] In the black-controlled Protestant churches, limited training and a tendency to avoid challenging the social order made most rural preachers ineffective community leaders; even members of their own congregations sometimes viewed them with suspicion and scorn. Several Louisiana folk songs alluded to lazy, thieving, or philandering ministers, traits that seemed common among those who claimed that God had called them to preach. "I wouldn't trust a preacher out o' my sight," went one tune, "'Cause dey believes in doin' too many things far in de night."[34]

Despite these problems, black churches could and did act as agents of social change. Religion was an empowering force in many black people's lives, providing hope and a sense of being valued that counteracted messages of black inferiority and worthlessness projected by the white supremacist social system. Churches were places where African Americans met not only to pray, but also to socialize, disseminate information, make plans, and raise money to carry them out. In the early twentieth century religious institutions were central elements in school-building programs and other community projects. Moreover, they provided important social services such as health care, sickness and disability insurance, and assistance for those who were unemployed or too old to work.[35]

For a small fee, black Louisianans could join any number of other organizations that offered similar safeguards. In West Feliciana Parish, members of the Morning Star Society received medical and burial benefits for fifty cents per month. The Progressive Funeral Home owned by Dora B. Davis of Bunkie operated a hearse and ambulance service over a radius of two hundred miles, catering to over seven thousand people in six parishes. Black churches in Iberville, Pointe Coupee, East Feliciana, and West Feliciana Parishes contributed one dollar a month to the Home Mission Baptist Association in Baton Rouge in return for the care of elderly and infirm church members. The Knights and Ladies of Peter Claver, an organization of black Catholics founded in 1909, drew a large proportion of its membership from Louisiana. Aware that African Americans were "ruthlessly exploited economically" and that Catholics were persecuted in many parts of the United States, the order aimed to provide financial help, comfort for sick or disabled members, and opportunities for socializing.[36]

African Americans created a complex, overlapping system of benevolent societies, fraternal orders, insurance agencies, parent-teacher associations, and youth groups that reached into isolated rural areas as well as towns and cities in Louisiana. With the exception of a few exclusively male fraternal orders, membership and meetings were open to all. By enhancing economic security and assisting those in need, these organizations contributed greatly to the well-being of individuals and communities. In addition, they encouraged participation in efforts to improve conditions for black people. Activities sponsored by these institutions included attempts to increase employment opportunities for African Americans, alleviate racial tension, and improve health, sanitation, and educational facilities. According to one report, such concerns were less likely to be rejected by white people when they were raised by general community groups instead of more overtly political organizations like the NAACP. The author observed that although they seemed innocuous, many societies did "tend to show a civic interest that can only be made manifest through them yet they have no claim to the name of a so-called civic organization. These civic interests are accepted by many of the opposite race because their attitude towards the sponsoring group is not warped by preconceived ideas of their functions that may have been called out by a civic named club."[37]

Black community institutions were subversive in other ways as well. Churches and society halls provided some of the few spaces where rural black people were relatively free from white supervision, and within their walls African Americans engaged in decision-making and other political processes that were denied them in the wider society. The St. Mary Parish Benevolent Society, for instance, established guidelines for acceptable behavior among its members and set fines for those who engaged in gambling or fighting. Many African Americans viewed these transgressions as harmful to their communities, but they were often ignored by local law enforcement officers as long as no white people were hurt. The society also provided short-term, interest-free loans, offering members an alternative to falling further into debt to white creditors in cases of emergency. At monthly meetings of the Bethel Baptist Church in Natchitoches Parish, representatives of the church's various districts followed standard parliamentary procedures as they discussed and voted on issues such as the disbursement of funds to needy members, censure and fining of those who were guilty of misbehavior, and long-term policies and programs.[38]

The social networks that rural black people established in their churches and societies went some way toward combating plantation owners' efforts to keep them isolated and unaware of developments in the outside world. In 1928 one observer wrote: "Every negro mouth is a transmitter and ear a receiver. If anything of importance happens on a plantation to-night, every negro for forty miles around will know it by morning."[39] Throughout the twentieth century, this kind of "wireless telegraphy" was instrumental in enabling African Americans to seize opportunities to press their demands for equality when political or social developments encouraged them to do so. In 1934, for instance, black Louisianans who belonged to the Improved Benevolent and Protective Order of Elks of the World managed to collect ten thousand signatures for a petition endorsing a federal antilynching bill then being considered by Congress. Black community institutions assisted in the organization of the LFU in the 1930s, and they were vital to the success of voter registration efforts and other forms of black protest after World War II.[40]

Despite the important sustaining roles they played and their potential political uses, churches and societies were not strong enough to overcome black Louisianans' general poverty and powerlessness in the Jim Crow era. Disfranchisement and lack of access to the law forced black people to find other ways to fight injustice. Given white Louisianans' frequent use of beatings, whippings, and lynchings, it should not be surprising that African Americans also sometimes resorted to aggressive tactics. In 1921 the NAACP's New York headquarters received the following report of an incident that occurred in Iberville Parish: "We heard a sugar cane farmer horsewhipped one of his Negro laborers—the Negro took the thrashing then shot the owner—four times. The white man went to his house for his gun—the Negro met him coming out of the door—and shot him again—this time in the mouth—then rear! . . . He was put in to jail and lynched that same night. The white man meanwhile lies in Baton Rouge hospital."[41]

Individual reactions like these occurred with some frequency, with white antagonists often receiving more grievous wounds than those suffered by the Iberville Parish sugar planter. In 1926 black sharecropper Joe Hardy raised what he thought was a good crop on the plantation of John S. Glover in Caddo Parish. Expecting to clear several hundred dollars, he was surprised when Glover claimed that he owed sixty dollars instead. Hardy did not want to risk any trouble so he said nothing at the time. Later, he approached a neighboring planter who agreed to hire him for the next year and to pay his debt to Glover. When Hardy took his new employer's check to Glover, the planter attacked him and in the fight that followed, Hardy shot and killed his former landlord.[42]

A similar incident occurred near Franklinton, Washington Parish, a decade later. One morning in July 1934, white stock inspector Joe Magee stopped at the home of John Wilson, a prosperous black farmer, and became involved in an argument with Wilson's son Jerome about whether or not a mule he saw standing in the corral had been dipped. After the altercation Magee telephoned the sheriff, saying that he had been mobbed and threatened by the Wilson family. A short while later Magee returned to the Wilsons' farm with Deputy Sheriff Delos C. Woods and two other white men. Jerome told them to take the mule for dipping if they wanted to. When Woods told him that they had come not just for the mule but for him also, Jerome asked to see an arrest warrant. Woods responded by grabbing Jerome, and when the black man resisted, the deputy shot and wounded both Jerome and one of his brothers. Jerome staggered into the house and returned with his gun. He fired one shot, the white men shot back, and either Jerome's or someone else's bullet killed Deputy Woods.[43]

Although African Americans generally tried to avoid dangerous situations, when they did encounter circumstances like those faced by Joe Hardy and Jerome Wilson it was not unusual for them to fight back.[44] In the decades before national leaders and organizations began advocating nonviolent protest as a strategy to overcome racism, most rural black people placed more faith in their shotguns than in appeals to the consciences of white people when harm threatened. Johnnie Jones's father did not rely solely on his white friends to protect his son from violence after the car accident mentioned in Chapter 2. With the whole family expecting a mob to arrive at their house, Jones recalled, "My daddy didn't, didn't back up, he just loaded up his shot gun and loaded up his .44, that's the kind of pistol he had, and just waited for whatever would come, but nothing ever came." Black lawyer Lolis Elie remembered being told about a similar incident when he was a young boy. In the 1930s Elie's mother was visiting her foster parents in Pointe Coupee Parish when the sheriff drove by and called out "Hey gal" as she walked along the road toward their house. She ignored him, and when he pulled the car over in front of her and asked why she had not answered him, she replied, "My name ain't 'Hey gal,' my daddy ain't no white man, and I don't have to answer you if I don't want to." Her foster mother witnessed this exchange with horror. After Elie's mother entered the house, the older woman scolded her and locked all the doors and windows, expecting the sheriff and his deputies to come back and kill them. But when Elie's grandfather came home and heard what had happened, he told them to unlock everything and stationed himself outside with his shotgun. "They may come through that gate," he said, "but ain't none of them gonna be alive to get to my porch."[45]

African Americans who chose to defend themselves against harassment or violence took enormous risks, especially if a white person was killed or injured in the process. Jerome Wilson was eventually lynched for his role in the shooting of Delos Woods. Joe Hardy narrowly escaped this fate, but most were not so lucky. A black man in Tallulah and another from Caddo Parish both paid with their lives after shooting their white employers. In a tragic incident that occurred near Alexandria in 1928, an angry mob retaliated against William Blackman's entire family after he shot a deputy in self-defense and was shot and killed himself. The mob lynched Blackman's two brothers, burned seven homes, and drove all his remaining relatives out of the parish.[46]

"Homicide" was the reason given for nearly 2,000 recorded lynchings that occurred in the South between 1882 and 1946. "Felonious assault" accounted for another 202 of these murders, "robbery and theft" for 231, and "insult to white person" for 84.[47] Perhaps nothing more effectively captures the ambiguous meaning of infrapolitical activity than these statistics. On one hand, they show that African Americans were far from acquiescent in the first half of the twentieth century. On the other, they reveal the limits of protest in a setting where white people's political, economic, and firepower always overwhelmed any resources that black people had access to.

The effect that individual, informal acts of resistance had on the southern social system is much more difficult to gauge than the achievements of organized political movements. But evidence suggests that they had at least some impact. Beneath the surface of newspaper articles proclaiming that harmonious "race relations" existed in the region, white Louisianans lived in a constant state of tension with their African American neighbors. In letters to his fiancée, Henry Stewart complained incessantly of problems with black workers on the two plantations he managed in West Feliciana Parish in the early 1900s. Their faults included taking unexpected holidays, disregarding his advice about when to pick their cotton, and leaving at the slightest provocation.[48] In 1908, after the arrival of the destructive cotton boll weevil provided an incentive to cut back his cotton crop and rely less heavily on African American labor, Stewart wrote with some relief, "I would not return to the negro and cotton for anything."[49]

Other planters had similar problems. In 1933 a social worker who visited a plantation owner and his wife in Tensas Parish noted that they were having trouble with one family of tenants, writing in her report: "They are very anxious to get rid of this family, for the reason that they keep the plantation in an uproar nearly all the time. This type of people nearly always instill an instin[c]t of fear into their employers, due to their treacherous and revengeful natures. They will not fight in the open, but will burn your house down when your back is turned."[50]

The knowledge that black people were not completely docile had a more significant effect than keeping the white community perpetually on edge. One of the reasons why the Wilson family of Washington Parish had been so successful before the shootout in 1934 was that they knew *both* how to get along with white people *and* when to stand up for their rights. Jerome Wilson was the grandson of Isom Wilson, a former slave who achieved land ownership with the help of the family he had served before the Civil War. One day in the early 1900s Isom's daughter Ophelia was plowing a field near a road when a white man rode by and asked, "Say, gal, you want to do a little business?" Ophelia screamed, bringing Isom running across the field with his shotgun. The white man had to flee for his life. According to Horace Mann Bond, "News of that got around, too, and didn't anybody try to joree with any of Isom's girls after that."[51]

As this story suggests, incidents of armed self-defense sometimes had a lasting impact on white behavior. After Jerome Wilson was killed in January 1935, African Americans in Washington Parish were afraid that there might be more lynchings and white people were just as afraid that the black community might retaliate. For several weeks, it seemed, white inhabitants were extremely careful not to offend anyone. "They ain't bother you," a local black woman reported. "Mr. Barker says they can't be too nice in the stores. They jump around trying to wait on you." In the early 1940s a school principal claimed that relationships between white and black people in Washington Parish were "very good." He explained: "It seems that some shooting which occurred about five years ago made things better. We had a series of murders during that time, starting off with the shooting of a white sheriff by an unknown Negro. When a Negro was killed by a white man, then the Negroes would turn around and kill a white man. The white people developed the saying—'You know, these niggers around here will kill you.'" The shootings prompted a group of prominent white residents to meet with black community leaders to discuss the situation, and after that the violence subsided.[52]

Although they courted disaster, the actions of people like Isom and Jerome Wilson drove home to white people the danger of pushing African Americans too far. Just as black people knew that retaliating against white violence risked death, white people were aware that instigating violence also invited death, even if to a much lesser extent. African Americans only had to shoot back occasionally to influence white people's actions. Sporadic use of armed self-defense meant that white supremacists never knew when they might exceed black people's limits of tolerance, with potentially lethal consequences for themselves. That African Americans' behavior was not always predictable might have been why Johnnie Jones's father and Lolis

Elie's grandfather did not have to use their guns in the incidents mentioned earlier, although they were fully prepared to do so.

Both national and local civil rights leaders in the first half of the twentieth century recognized the role that armed self-defense played in the freedom struggle and encouraged its use. Antilynching campaigner Ida B. Wells-Barnett noted in 1892 that of the many black people who had been the victims of mob violence during the year, the only ones who managed to escape death were those who had guns and used them to fend off their attackers. "The lesson this teaches and which every Afro-American should ponder well," Wells-Barnett wrote, "is that a Winchester rifle should have a place of honor in every black home, and it should be used for that protection that the law refuses to give. When the white man who is always the aggressor knows he runs as great risk of biting the dust every time his Afro-American victim does, he will have greater respect for Afro-American life." In a 1916 issue of the NAACP's *Crisis* magazine, W. E. B. Du Bois strongly criticized the black people of Gainesville, Florida, for their inaction during a recent lynching. He argued, "The men and women who had nothing to do with the alleged crime should have fought in self-defense to the last ditch if they had killed every white man in the county and themselves been killed. . . . In the last analysis lynching of Negroes is going to stop in the South when the cowardly mob is faced by effective guns in the hands of people determined to sell their souls dearly." Five years later, in the wake of a riot in Tulsa, Oklahoma, that followed the attempted lynching of a black youth charged with rape, the *Baltimore Afro-American* praised the courage of African Americans in the city who had shown that they would "rather die than submit to mob law."[53]

Black newspapers in Louisiana also commented favorably when the victims of attack fought back. After a black man shot and killed a white student during a fight in New Orleans in 1930, the *Louisiana Weekly* editorialized, "We do not condone the killing of this white student, but we will state that every Negro will not pass lightly by the insults and vituperations heaped upon their heads by roving bands intent on having fun at the expense of their darker brothers." They also observed that several riots had been averted in the city because African Americans showed their willingness to defend themselves.[54] The following year the *Weekly* praised the actions of a black man who took his son back to a store where a white boy, encouraged by the clerks, had hit him. The man demanded that his son be allowed to fight the white boy on equal terms, and after the white men agreed, the black boy beat his opponent. The report urged African Americans not to accept abuse, saying, "This boy's courage will increase, and as he grows older he will develop the true spirit which our race is so badly in need of.[55]

Although the accuracy of the newspaper's prediction in this particular case cannot be ascertained, the lives of many people who became involved in the civil rights movement seem to support the general thesis. In her study of the young black people who formed CORE's New Orleans chapter in the 1960s, Kim Lacy Rogers found that they were often the children of militant parents who had encouraged them to engage in informal acts of resistance against white supremacy. Rudy Lombard, who later became the project director for CORE's voter registration efforts in rural Louisiana, once defied the state's segregation laws by throwing a ball into a white-only park and inviting his friends to join him in playing there. For this action, his father rewarded him with a case of root beer. Lolis Elie described his parents as people with little money or education who nonetheless had "a great deal of pride." His father once stood up to a foreman who harassed him at work and "told the story over and over how he took that white man on." Jerome Smith remembered watching his father remove segregation signs on streetcars and said that his mother always insisted that white merchants address her as "Mrs." Asked when he first became active in the freedom movement, Smith found it difficult to answer, explaining, "When I entered the civil rights struggle in a formal sense I had been involved in things in a personal and private sense for so long."[56]

Local activist Robert Lewis's experience also reflected the connection between infrapolitics and organized politics. Lewis frequently expressed his dissatisfaction with the social order in small ways before CORE arrived in Concordia Parish and provided a structure for more open protest. When the white high school in Ferriday invited children from the black school to watch their football team play, Lewis and his classmates arrived to find that they would not be allowed into the stadium. They were expected to go to one end of the field where there was a gap in the fence and peer through that. Lewis refused to be insulted in this way and left. Another time Lewis took revenge on a fast-food vendor who always made African Americans wait at a side window while he served white people at the front of his van. "I ordered about five hot dogs, chili dogs with the works, and five chocolate malts, and while he was fixing them, when he got on the last one I got on my bicycle and . . . left him there," he said. "I learned how to protest, I guess, in my way."[57]

Despite the enormous obstacles to black political activity in the first half of the twentieth century, African Americans in rural Louisiana were not apathetic or inactive during this period. By leaving plantations where they were mistreated, ensuring access to education for their children, creating strong social institutions, and fighting back against violence, black people showed that they did not accept their assigned place in the social order and laid the foundations for protest that organized movements built on. As the following chapters will demonstrate, when changes in the political and economic landscape of the region opened space for action, black activists were quick to take advantage of opportunities to openly demand their citizenship rights.

4

We Feel You All Aut to Help Us:
Struggles for Citizenship,
1914–1929

The outbreak of war in Europe in 1914 presented African Americans in rural Louisiana with an opportunity to challenge the repressive social system that had emerged in the South after Reconstruction. Northern industrialists' supply of cheap immigrant labor halted abruptly, causing employers to look to the southern states for replacement workers. The result was a mass departure of black people from the region that had profound consequences for the freedom struggle. The Great Migration swelled the African American population of the North, contributing to the emergence of newspapers, civil rights organizations, and political leaders dedicated to the eradication of discrimination and the recognition of black people's citizenship rights. Historians have long acknowledged World War I as a signal event in African American history, and northern migrants have been the focus of some excellent scholarship in the last decade.[1]

Less well known are the stories of those who remained behind. Wartime rhetoric and encouragement from the NAACP inspired a small number of black southerners to form their own organizations and to openly demand justice. Meanwhile, white people responded to the threatened loss of their labor supply with a mixture of coercive legislation and improvement measures aimed at persuading African Americans to remain on the plantations. Rural black Louisianans made some gains during this period, but they did not last long. The end of the fighting in Europe brought a new wave of violence and repression in the United States as white supremacists acted to prevent African Americans from converting the fight to "make the world safe for democracy" into a battle for equal rights at home.

Contemporary observers viewed the movement of thousands of rural black southerners to the North during World War I as the natural result of economic "push" and "pull" factors. Demand for labor in the North was increasing at the same time that crop failures caused by flooding and the boll weevil drove many southern farmworkers from the land. According to some analysts, African Americans were responding to changes caused by forces beyond their control as a matter of survival.[2] Others, especially white southerners, argued that labor agents and northern black newspaper editors were responsible. Black people in the South were well treated and content, they claimed, and would not think of moving unless irresponsible outsiders encouraged them to do so. Neither of these interpretations accorded migrants much capacity for analyzing their situation on their own, or of acting independently to improve the conditions of their lives.[3]

In a report on black migration prepared in the 1930s, African American scholar Charles S. Johnson presented a different view. Johnson referred to the exodus of 1916–18 as "a leaderless mass-movement" and stated, "Such mass-movements can result only after a long period of gestation." Connecting migration out of the South to the constant movement between plantations and states within the region that had long been a feature of the rural black experience, Johnson suggested that dissatisfaction with the southern social order was the main reason why African Americans had left. As he noted, black people "had been churning about in the south, seeking newer fields for many years before hope dawned for them in the industries of the north." Symbolically, the major routes northward during the Great Migration were roughly the same as those of the Underground Railroad that some African Americans had used to escape enslavement in the decades preceding the Civil War.[4]

Letters written by migrants themselves also placed their actions squarely within the tradition of black resistance and protest, revealing that something more than impersonal economic forces was at work. The motives of many were summarized by one black Louisianan who was "desirous of leaving the South for the beterment of my condition generaly." Another stated that he and many others he knew wanted to go north, writing: "please notifie me at once bee cors I am tired of bene dog as I was a beast and wee will come at wonce. So I will bee oblige to you if you will help us out of the south." A black man from Ouachita Parish explained that he and his brother wanted to leave Louisiana "to get where we would be able to have a chanse in the world and get out from among all of the prejudice of the southern white man."[5]

When they were more specific, black Louisianans cited multiple reasons for leaving their state that reflected their ongoing struggles against the plantation regime. Prominent among the factors that attracted them to the North was the promise of higher wages. "I am working hard in the south and can hardly earn a living," was one variation on a common complaint. A young woman from Alexandria stated, "There isnt a thing here for me to do, the wages here is from a dollar and a half a week. What could I earn Nothing." Another writer emphasized this point, saying, "Compared with other things to which we have almost become resigned, the high cost of living coupled with unreasonably low wages is of greatest concern."[6] Later in the war, a government study of labor shortages in the South concluded that one of the chief determinants of whether black tenants and sharecroppers left the region or stayed was the fairness of working arrangements. The author wrote, "With a proper agreement, the labor will remain, but with a poor one it will leave."[7]

The desire for better educational opportunities also motivated numerous migrants. One parent wrote, "I has been here all my life but would be glad to go wher I can educate my children where they can be of service to themselves, and this will never be here." For some people, the urge to move north represented a continuation of earlier efforts to achieve similar goals. A man who had recently moved his family to New Orleans explained, "I have been living here . . . only seven years I formerly live in the country but owing to bad conditions of schools for my children I sold my property and moved here I didnt think there was any justice in my paying school taxes and had no fit school to send [m]y children to."[8]

Many black people wrote of their hopes of escaping mistreatment and violence when they requested information about migrating north. One man declared that he was willing to move anywhere "away from the Lynchman's noose and torchman's fire." Another wanted only to live out his life peacefully and "without fear of molestation." Acts of violence against African Americans during the war sometimes precipitated the evacuation of entire black communities. Even some white people admitted that brutal lynchings and beatings, more than the persuasive tactics of labor agents, contributed to the movement of black workers from the South.[9]

Finally, the chance to participate politically attracted many black people to the North. Migrants often registered to vote as soon as they arrived in their new home states. In the second ward of Chicago, the section of the city with the highest proportion of African American inhabitants, 72 percent of eligible voters were registered in 1920 compared with 66 percent for the city as a whole. By the next decade, more than one-fifth of the nation's black population had settled in the North, forming a constituency that national political parties could no longer afford to ignore. The entry of large numbers of black people into politics made possible the election of black Republican congressman Oscar DePriest in 1928 and enabled African Americans to gain some significant concessions at the national level in the decades that followed.[10]

Approximately half a million black people left the South between 1916 and 1919, followed by another million in the 1920s.[11] Although migrants often experienced poverty and racism in the North that was as bad as anything they had experienced in their home states, they enjoyed a greater degree of freedom. Membership in civil rights organizations and the circulation of black newspapers like the *Chicago Defender* shot up exponentially, reflecting migrants' liberation from supervision and control by white employers. On a smaller scale, hundreds of mini-migrations that occurred within the South as rural people moved from plantations to towns and cities encouraged some protest activity there as well. In 1918–19 alone, the NAACP grew from 80 branches with 9,200 members to more than 229 branches with 62,000 members. Almost half of the branches and 23,500 members were in the southern states.[12]

Louisiana's first NAACP branch was born in Shreveport in 1914. Located in Caddo Parish in the northwestern corner of the state, the city originated as a trade center for cotton planters in the Red River delta region, and its growth was further boosted by the discovery of oil deposits in the parish in 1906. By 1910 Shreveport's population had grown to 28,015 and included 13,896 African Americans. In the next decade, the number of black residents increased to 17,485. The twenty people who founded the NAACP branch worked as real estate agents, insurance agents, porters, laborers, small business owners, waiters, and cooks—a diverse range of occupations that embraced the entire class spectrum of the African American community. Black people in New Orleans (1917), Alexandria (1918), Baton Rouge (1919), and Monroe (1925) also established NAACP branches, with memberships that were similar to the branch in Shreveport. Businesspeople represented the largest proportion of members in most branches, followed by laborers and semiskilled workers like mechanics and railroad brakemen. A small number of physicians and dentists also participated, along with a few ministers and teachers.[13]

Black people in some smaller communities also organized during this period. Truck farmers and laborers made up the majority of African Americans who chartered an NAACP branch in St. Rose, a tiny settlement of about five hundred people located in St. Charles Parish. Members of the Clarence branch in Natchitoches Parish were all farmers except for one minister and one man who gave his occupation as "public work."[14]

One of the appeals of the NAACP to black Louisianans was its investigative and publicity campaigns against lynching. Caddo Parish had one of the worst records for mob violence of any region in Louisiana in the early twentieth century, and members of the Shreveport branch made this issue their first priority. In August 1914, following the lynching of seven black people in the state in seven days, they asked Governor Luther E. Hall to lend his authority by speaking out against the sadistic practice. In making this request, they stated, "We ask no favors, no privileges, no special advantages . . . but instead we pray for a living chance; an opportunity for defense before the Courts and justice at the hands of the law."[15] Several years later, branch president George Lewis suggested that NAACP headquarters send someone to the parish to investigate another lynching, saying, "If the members of the branch can get your assistance in this matter it will greatly stimulate them." Similarly, black people in Clarence looked to the national organization for the protection they believed it could provide. Local leader Forest Trottie wrote to branch director Robert Bagnall in January 1922 asking him to quickly mail back the members' charter so that their activities might appear to have more legitimacy. "Send it at wonse or just as soon as you can Because the white people here are Talking about against this move of ours so please get the charter out to us soon as possible," he urged.[16]

Both national and local civil rights leaders hoped that black Americans' participation in the war to defend freedom and democracy might result in the extension of those ideals to African Americans. Most black newspapers and magazine editors encouraged their readers to lend all possible support to the war effort, arguing that if they did so, white Americans could not continue to deny them equality.[17] Writing in the *Crisis*, W. E. B. Du Bois predicted, "Out of this war will rise, too, an American Negro with the right to vote and the right to work and the right to live without insult"; he urged

African Americans to put aside their grievances and stand "shoulder to shoulder with our own white fellow citizens and the allied nations that are fighting for democracy." Echoing these sentiments, the New Orleans NAACP's newsletter reassured African Americans: "If we keep the Huns on the run, we will get everything that we have been desiring for the past sixty years. Men let's fight for our rights."[18]

Not everyone agreed with this strategy. Writing to the national office in 1917, Shreveport NAACP member T. G. Garrett expressed his disgust with black community leaders who had spoken at a recent patriotic meeting held in the city. Enclosing some newspaper reports on the event, he stated: "Thes is some of the things that is so much harm to the negro in the southland. This is one of the ways that the negros is being rushed into the war. What has the Southern white man ever done for us. Thes kind of negros is the ones that making it so hard for us today. Thay want some money that all thay want."[19]

Continued discrimination and mistreatment of African Americans during World War I proved skeptics like Garrett right. Black men who served in the U.S. armed forces remained subject to Jim Crow laws, harassment, and physical violence from their commanding officers, local law enforcement agents, and private citizens. Moreover, most black soldiers served as laborers in supply regiments. Their housing and recreational facilities were inferior to those provided for white soldiers and their movements more restricted. Often they suffered harsh treatment from white officers who believed this was the only way to train black people. In addition, local residents resented the presence of African Americans in military training camps in the South, sometimes expressing their opposition violently.[20]

White southerners feared that the training of black men as soldiers and their service overseas might encourage them to think of themselves as equals. Following a trip to France in 1918, Louisiana congressman James B. Aswell predicted, "The war will [raise] serious questions to us, one of which is the race question." Aswell had noticed the French people's comparatively tolerant attitude toward interracial couples and worried that "Negro soldiers who walk the streets with white women and white girls for several years will give trouble at home."[21] The actions of African Americans who remained in the United States were also cause for concern. Racial tensions evolving out of consistent disregard for segregation laws by black soldiers stationed near Houston, Texas, exploded into riots in the summer of 1917 after a white police officer used excessive violence in arresting one offender. Fifteen white people were killed and twelve others injured, pointing to the emergence of what some wartime analysts called the "New Negro"—black people who were determined to demand equal rights and who were unafraid to fight back against abuse.[22]

Black Americans' aspirations for "social equality" and violent altercations like the incident in Texas were relatively minor concerns compared with a much larger problem that confronted southern plantation owners during the war. Touring Louisiana early in 1919 to assess the farm labor situation, one War Department official saw "hundreds of acres of untouched land formerly cultivated, and what land was planted proved to be in bad shape because of the lack of hands. . . . Scores of mules in pasture because there was no help to hitch them to the plow. . . . Tons and tons of cane soured on the ground, left from last year for lack of men."[23] The draft and migration created severe difficulties for planters, whose workers left rural areas by the thousands to take advantage of new economic opportunities. Between 1910 and 1920 Louisiana's black population dropped by 13,617. Although this was only about a 2 percent decrease for the state, the decline in the number of African Americans living in the sugar- and cotton-growing regions was much greater. Most of the plantation parishes lost between 15 and 30 percent of their black inhabitants during this period. (See Table 4.1.) Without their customary access to abundant and cheap labor, plantation owners faced the prospect of decreased production and declining profits.

An incident that occurred even before the beginning of the war in Europe foreshadowed some of the later responses of Louisiana landowners. In March 1914 a group of armed sugar planters from Assumption Parish appeared at the Texas and Pacific Railroad passenger depot and dispersed about sixty African Americans who were awaiting the arrival of a northbound train. Witnesses reported that the white men were "among the most prominent and influential citizens of the lower Assumption neighborhood," and that their action was designed to "put a stop to the work of the labor agents who have been enticing large numbers of negro fields hands away from this section during the last several weeks." A newspaper article about the incident explained that initially the agents had not been a problem because there had been a large surplus of workers in the parish, but that "this surplus has long since been exhausted, and if the supply of labor is still further depleted the planters will face a serious situation in the cultivation of their crops."[24]

The following month the *Houma Courier* reported that a "new messiah" had recently appeared in Terrebonne Parish to lure black sugar workers away to the cotton parishes of northern Louisiana with promises of higher wages. The writer noted that the loss of labor from the parish was a serious problem and urged planters to take action to stop it. The article pointed out, "Other parishes warn these messiahs to keep out, and they find it healthier to heed the warning." In December, Madison Parish plantation owners held a meeting to discuss the problems they too were experiencing with people who were attempting to "entice away" their labor. The result was a notice to labor agents, printed in the *Madison Journal*, that stated: "The planters of Madison Parish . . . will not tolerate any one in the parish enticing or in any way interfering with our labor. All white or colored strangers will be called upon to explain their business in Madison Parish and if they are not Labor Agents they will be welcome."[25]

After 1916, when the problems caused by migration reached acute proportions, labor agents faced more serious obstacles to their recruiting efforts. Local and state authorities passed legislation to restrict their activities, imposing expensive licensing fees and taxes along with hefty fines for violating the regulations governing their work. Those who still managed to continue their recruiting efforts risked physical violence when they ventured into rural towns and parishes. Plantation owners became so suspicious of outsiders that any strange face they encountered in their communities might be subject to attack. For instance, when Hizzie Pringle went to pay his sister's debt to her landlord, Benjamin Kinchen, the planter assaulted him with no provocation. According to an investigator, Kinchen justified his action "on the grounds that he thought Pringle was a labor agent."[26]

At the same time that they attempted to halt the flow of migrants to the North, white Louisianans sought to force all black people who remained in the state into "useful" employment, a term that often seemed to describe only those low-wage occupations that African Americans had traditionally held. Wartime necessity and the federal government's efforts to direct all the nation's resources into achieving victory offered employers and legislators a powerful tool for this purpose. In May 1918 Selective Service director Enoch Crowder issued a "work or fight" order mandating that all able-bodied men in the United States either serve in the armed forces or be engaged in a necessary civilian occupation. Local authorities eagerly enforced the order. The Louisiana state legislature applied the ruling to all men between the ages of seventeen and fifty-five (compared with the Selective Service age limit of forty-five) and empowered sheriffs to seek out and punish those not in compliance. Some parishes passed resolutions requiring

Table 4.1 African American Migration in Louisiana during World War I

| Parish | Number of African Americans in Parish | | Percentage Change |
	1910	1920	
Cotton Parishes			
Avoyelles	12,039	10,353	−14
Bossier	16,735	15,730	−6
Catahoula	5,195	5,122	−1
Claiborne	14,938	14,798	−1
Concordia	11,941	9,823	−18
De Soto	17,932	17,914	−(-)[a]
East Carroll	10,390	9,701	−7
East Feliciana	14,536	12,004	−17
Franklin	5,264	10,720	+104
Madison	9,455	9,060	−4
Morehouse	13,971	13,140	−6
Natchitoches	20,334	20,697	+2
Red River	6,212	7,589	+22
Richland	10,463	11,996	+15
St. Landry[b]	31,234	26,507	−15
Tensas	15,613	10,314	−34
Webster	9,900	11,387	+15
West Carroll	2,724	2,370	−13
West Feliciana	11,012	10,187	−7
Sugar Parishes			
Ascension	11,255	9,490	−16
Assumption	10,105	7,487	−26
Iberia	14,474	10,898	−25
Iberville	19,145	15,372	−20
Lafayette	10,734	10,811	+1
Lafourche	7,973	5,888	−26
Plaquemines	6,847	5,393	−21
Pointe Coupee	17,147	14,981	−13
St. Charles	6,720	4,347	−35
St. James	13,164	11,602	−12
St. John the Baptist	8,126	6,415	−21
St. Martin	9,836	7,902	−19

Table 4.1 Continued

| | Number of African Americans in Parish | | Percentage |
Parish	1910	1920	Change
St. Mary	21,266	15,174	−29
Terrebonne	11,194	8,742	−22
West Baton Rouge	9,223	7,485	−19
Rice/Grain Parishes			
Acadia	6,546	7,526	+15
Allen	NA[c]	6,352	NA
Beauregard	NA	6,105	NA
Cameron	538	585	+9
Jefferson Davis	NA	4,837	NA
Vermilion	4,500	4,560	+1
Subsistence/Truck Parishes			
Bienville	9,464	8,619	−9
Caldwell	3,465	2,983	−14
Evangeline	NA	5,681	NA
Grant	4,869	4,045	−17
Jackson	3,996	4,006	+(-)
Jefferson	6,785	5,880	−13
La Salle	1,953	1,525	−22
Lincoln	7,289	6,310	−13
Livingston	1,377	1,667	+21
Sabine	4,164	4,364	+5
St. Bernard	1,933	1,597	−17
St. Helena	4,573	4,229	−8
St. Tammany	6,731	7,648	+14
Tangipahoa	9,135	8,892	−3
Union	7,448	6,114	−18
Vernon	3,716	5,103	+37
Washington	5,458	7,391	+35
Winn	3,931	3,385	−14
Parishes with Cities of 10,000 People or More			
Caddo	36,142	37,801	+5
Calcasieu[b]	16,562	8,736	−47

Table 4.1 Continued

Parish	Number of African Americans in Parish		Percentage Change
	1910	1920	
East Baton Rouge	21,342	23,098	+8
Orleans	89,262	100,930	+13
Ouachita	14,153	13,897	−2
Rapides	21,445	24,992	+17
Total for Louisiana	713,874	700,257	−2

SOURCES: Bureau of the Census, *Thirteenth Census of the United States Taken in the Year 1910, Volume 2: Population* (Washington, D.C.: GPO, 1913), 790–91, and *Fourteenth Census of the United States Taken in the Year 1920, Volume 3: Population* (Washington, D.C.: GPO, 1922), 393–99.

[a](-) indicates less than 0.5 percent.
[b]The decreases in African American population in St. Landry and Calcasieu Parishes between 1910 and 1920 resulted in part from boundary changes.
[c]NA indicates data not available (parishes created after 1910).

women as well as men to work; others tightened the enforcement of vagrancy laws to ensure that no "slackers" escaped performing their patriotic duty.[27]

Often these efforts seemed directed particularly at African Americans. Perhaps (but probably not) by coincidence, a list of nonessential occupations prepared by the Louisiana State Council of Defense in September 1918 ruled out many jobs traditionally held by self-employed black people. Those who worked in barber shops, poolrooms, gambling establishments, shoe shine stands, fruit stands, and as porters were not recognized as contributing anything to the war effort and faced the threat of arrest unless they found some other employment. Rumors circulated among African Americans that the new work or fight laws would allow people to be forced to labor under conditions resembling peonage. The chairman of the federal government's War Labor Policy Board dismissed these concerns, saying that the orders simply reflected "the national spirit and the national will,—that everyone

should contribute to the service for freedom upon which the nation is engaged either in useful industry or in useful military service."[28]

Whatever the intentions of lawmakers, black people's fears were well
founded. When the NAACP's Walter White visited several southern states
in 1918 to investigate complaints of abuse, he found that employers were
indeed using compulsory work laws to force African Americans to labor for
low wages. In St. Mary Parish, the sheriff walked into a black restaurant one
morning and told its owner that two young men he employed must go and
work at a nearby mill. When the restaurateur protested and pointed out that
the youths were younger than drafting age, the sheriff swore at him, then
told him to close his business down because he too would have to work at the
mill or go to jail. Black people in Caddo, Rapides, and Ouachita Parishes told
White of similar incidents. Civil rights leaders reported these abuses to
federal agencies, but the authorities did nothing to prevent such practices.
Director of Negro Economics George E. Haynes explained that the federal
government had no power to interfere with local or state laws, regardless of
how unjust they might be.[29]

Coercive labor legislation seems only to have encouraged more African
Americans to leave the South, as did the increasing levels of violence that
accompanied frustrated planters' efforts to prevent black people from going.
Attempts to enlist the aid of prominent African Americans in encouraging
workers to remain in the region were not successful either. A government
researcher sent to investigate the causes of migration from Mississippi and
Louisiana in 1917 found that black community leaders in those states did
little to stop the exodus, for they knew that the resulting labor shortages
could be used to force concessions from white people and improve conditions
for those who remained behind. According to his account, African Americans were "silently hoping that the migration may continue in such increasing proportions as to bring about a successful bloodless revolution, assur-
ing equal treatment in business, in the schools, on the trains, and under
the law."[30] A letter written by New Orleans NAACP secretary H. George
Davenport to the national office in May 1917 suggests that the investigator
was right. Davenport planned to move to Chicago in June and stay there
permanently. "[I] am tired of the South," he wrote, "protest has failed here
so far, the exodus will solve the problem quicker than protest I am sure,
because the crackers here are all worked up over it, the planters held a
meeting here to try and discourage migration north."[31]

Having failed to coerce black people into staying in the South, white people eventually realized that a more effective strategy might be to make the region a better place to live in. Heeding the advice that many black and some white observers had long been giving them, planters and local authorities began advocating higher wage rates, better treatment of tenants and sharecroppers, improvement of housing and schools, and efforts to protect black people from mob violence.[32] In a speech delivered at an NAACP conference in 1919, Louisiana's state agent of rural schools explained that plantation owners and other employers of black labor usually showed scant interest in providing education for African Americans, but "the World War helped to broaden our vision. The Negro migration opened our eyes. Many of our large employers are ready now to provide school facilities for the colored youth." He then outlined the improvements that many parishes were making in the quality of instruction provided to black children. St. Mary Parish had recently set aside six thousand dollars for African American schools, and Terrebonne Parish, "which never owned one dollar's worth of colored school property," was completing one of nine schoolhouses that would eventually cost twenty thousand dollars. Natchitoches, Tangipahoa, Caddo, Bienville, Lincoln, Morehouse, Bossier, East Caroll, Beauregard, and Winn Parishes all had similar building plans.[33]

One of the most effective measures taken to stem the migration, and one that benefited many rural black people, was the expansion of the federal government's Agricultural Extension Service. The Extension Service had its origins in government efforts to combat the boll weevil in the late 1890s. Agents from the U.S. Department of Agriculture visited farmers to educate them about the disease and to teach them methods of controlling it. By the early twentieth century, Extension Service functions had broadened to include training in a variety of techniques to produce better crop yields and higher incomes for farmers. However, its efforts mostly aided prosperous landowners who could afford to take advantage of new technologies and ignored poorer people—especially African Americans—at the bottom of the agricultural ladder.[34]

In 1906 black educator Booker T. Washington initiated the first agricultural extension project among African Americans through the "Movable School," a program that sent teachers from Tuskegee Institute into rural Alabama to demonstrate new farming equipment and techniques. Washington's attempts to persuade the Department of Agriculture to establish a more wide-ranging program of black extension work met with only limited success until the beginning of World War I and the Great Migration. Fears that food shortages might result from the scarcity of labor and the need to supply European allies with agricultural products encouraged the Extension Service to pay more attention to black farmers. Administrators instructed white agents to assist African Americans in their districts and hired more black agents in the hope that they might persuade tenants and sharecroppers to remain on the plantations. Black extension agents thereafter became a permanent, though underfunded, part of the federal Extension Service.[35]

Extension work among African Americans in Louisiana began in 1913, when Tuskegee Institute graduate Thomas J. Jordan was assigned to two northern parishes. He operated in his first year without a salary, surviving on funds raised for him at church meetings and gifts of farm produce from the black people he worked with. In 1914 the Smith-Lever Act provided for the cooperative funding of extension agents through federal, state, and local authorities, and over the next four years sixteen more black extension agents were employed in Louisiana. The scope of their activities depended to a large extent on money provided by parish police juries and school boards, whose motivations were conservative. A report on the work of black agents written in 1920 emphasized the role they had played in decelerating the migration of African Americans out of the region. A white agent who worked with African Americans in a parish not served by any black agent revealed where planter priorities lay when he proudly noted, "I have practically accomplished to keep cheap labor here for all." As soon as the war ended, six of the state's seventeen black agents were dropped because of "lack of funds."[36]

Black extension workers' dependence on local elites' willingness to finance their services and close supervision of their activities by white agents meant that they were unlikely to become outspoken proponents of racial justice. An agent in Caddo Parish lost his position because, according to a report, he "failed to distinguish between his duties as an agent and his rights as a citizen."[37] Most others avoided doing anything that could be construed as interfering with "race relations" or encouraging political activism. In many ways extension agents fulfilled a similar role to the middle-class black reformers discussed in recent studies by Evelyn Brooks Higginbotham and Kevin Gaines.[38] Their work helped to reinforce white supremacy by serving the interests of plantation owners, but agents also challenged dominant racial ideologies by attempting to "uplift" African Americans, individually and collectively. Despite the limits placed on them, extension agents' efforts to improve the lives of black agricultural workers and the enthusiasm they brought to this task achieved some significant gains.

A measure of the extension agents' contribution is that rural black people welcomed and appreciated their aid. Parish reports regularly praised the efforts of African American farmers and the dedication they showed in carrying out the new techniques they learned. In 1919 a white agent in Pointe Coupee Parish stated that he had "found many negro farmers very much alert and ambitious to learn more about better methods of farming." Another agent reported that he had "many Negro friends of Demonstration work. They would utilize all my time if I would permit it." T. J. Watson found black farmers in Madison Parish to be "responsive and apparently anxious for advice on better methods of farming, stock raising, poultry, gardening, orchard and general improvement of the home and its surroundings." Some agents even concluded that African Americans were more interested in extension work than white farmers. According to the state administrative report for 1922, it was "a fact well recognized by County Agents and Specialists that the negro farmer responds to suggestions much more readily than does the white farmer."[39]

Black participants in the programs viewed extension agents as potential allies in their struggle for economic independence. Harrison Brown recalled that agents offered sharecropping families valuable training in how to make their small plots of land more productive, saying, "That's what we mostly suffered for in every area—training, you know."[40] When the use of fertilizer or new seed varieties resulted in a better crop, tenants as well as plantation owners stood to benefit. Perhaps more importantly, extension agents encouraged "live at home" programs designed to free farmworkers from their dependence on planters and merchants for food that they could produce themselves. As a boy, Thomas Jordan had known many families who ended every crop year in debt to their landlords; he had heard his father say that these people would have been able to do better if they had not owed so much to the plantation commissary for food. Much of his and other extension agents' work in Louisiana focused on increasing African Americans' self-sufficiency.[41]

Following the advice of agents, some black farm families prospered as they never had before. In 1915 S. W. Vance reported that sharecroppers on a plantation where he conducted one demonstration "made a good crop and owed very little the 1st year and only one came out behind. The second year . . . every negro has paid out of debt and has a lot of corn." Two years later Vance stated that four of the African American families he had worked with in the past few years had recently bought land of their own, five had saved enough money to make the first payments on their farms, and "every cooperator was able to pay his account and have money left and they are buying good mule buggies and household furnitu[r]e and in fact have improved their condition wonderfully."[42]

Greater demand for agricultural products and high prices made the war years prosperous times for most American farmers, and this more than the activities of extension agents might have contributed to the increased prosperity of tenant families.[43] But even during the postwar recession of the 1920s, farmers who had access to extension services generally did better than those who did not, suggesting that the agents did have an impact. Like many others who faced losing their land after a sudden drop in farm prices, black farmer Mose Matthews of West Feliciana Parish was heavily in debt and about to give up when agent J. E. Ringgold first met him in 1921. After four years of farming under Ringgold's direction, Matthews was debt-free and his crops were thriving. Ringgold stated in his 1925 report that he "could mention a score of men that have been able to finish paying for their homes and who are living happy by becoming demonstrators and following the advice and instructions as laid down in Farm Demonstration work."[44] Black farm ownership in West Feliciana almost doubled between 1925 and 1930, and increases occurred in other parishes as well.[45] In 1931 the state agent for Louisiana noted that, at a time when farm ownership in general was on the decline and tenancy increasing, all of the nine parishes that had African American extension agents gained in farm ownership during the year.[46]

The impact of the Extension Service went beyond the individual farmers who cooperated on projects. Agents were required to formulate ways to maximize the number of people who could be reached with the department's limited staff. One of the questions that had to be answered in their annual reports was, "Have you so thoroughly organized your county that you have someone in every community or school district assisting you in extension work and through whom you can reach EVERY farm family in your county?" Churches and other meeting places provided convenient forums for this purpose, with agents enlisting the aid of ministers and schoolteachers to disseminate information to large numbers of people at a time.[47] The role of those chosen as demonstrators was not only to improve their own farming methods, but also to teach others what they knew. Black agent Myrtis

Magee explained: "Information and help is given this group and they pass it along to their cooperators and others interested. . . . Economic and Civic conditions have been greatly improved through the tireless efforts of leaders and other agencies cooperating."[48]

Extension agents often sponsored projects designed to enhance the lives of all black people in their parishes. In 1918 O. G. Price reported that he arrived in St. Helena Parish to find African Americans eager to do demonstration work but hampered by their lack of education and suitable farm equipment. "I visited the negro schools of this parish with the Superintendent of Education and saw the teachers teaching two months terms at twenty dollars per month in church houses, old boxed houses, and in log cribs," he wrote. "I decided the first thing the negroes needed was better schools." After years of fund-raising by the local black people and lobbying for donations from white philanthropists, construction of a new industrial high school in the parish began in December 1921. J. E. Ringgold in West Feliciana Parish also assisted in raising money "to build schools, extend school terms and help the community generally." In a tribute to black extension agent Myrtis Magee on his death in 1940, the *Louisiana Weekly* asserted, "Everywhere he was known as a hard cooperative worker and a real friend of the poor. He has built in Louisiana a monument, which will represent service, and which can be looked upon by generations to come."[49]

In some ways extension agents were the first "outside agitators" to arrive in rural Louisiana. They did not encourage people to try to vote, or challenge segregated facilities, or organize mass marches against discrimination, or engage in any of the other activities associated with the civil rights movement. They operated at another level of the freedom struggle, working to reduce poverty and subtly undermining plantation owners' attempts to keep African Americans uneducated and immobile. Many black Louisianans took full advantage of the knowledge and resources extension agents brought to the region, recognizing them as valuable weapons in the fight against inequality and exploitation.

The reactions of white landowners and officials to extension work among black people suggest that they too perceived the potential threat to the social order posed by the agents. Some people openly opposed the service, arguing that it encouraged African Americans to aspire to property ownership or professional careers instead of being content to work for white employers. Black agents were unable to assist many tenants and sharecroppers whose landlords refused to allow them to participate in demonstration programs. During debates over passage of the Smith-Lever Act, southern congressmen defeated amendments designed to ensure an equitable distribution of federal funds between the white and black agricultural colleges that administered extension work in each state. The money was instead channeled through the white colleges, ensuring separate and unequal services to black farmers.[50] Planter-dominated local governments provided little funding for black agents, forcing them to perform their duties with minimal budgets and few resources. In 1930 Louisiana's state director of extension work noted the difficulties that afflicted African American agents, saying: "We have never been able to get any local support in the negro work. On this account, we have necessarily had to keep the salaries of the negro agents on a low basis and they scarcely have enough to get by with."[51]

At the same time, extension work among white farmers resulted in the formation of a powerful new organization to advance the interests of wealthy landowners. Created in 1920, the American Farm Bureau Federation (AFBF) grew out of county farmers' bureaus that extension agents had established to facilitate their educational efforts. The AFBF and the Extension Service developed close cooperative relationships, often working together to formulate policy and lobby for legislation to benefit the nation's farmers. In many communities, the AFBF paid part or all of the county agent's salary. Planters dominated the AFBF in the South, and through their influence over extension agents they exerted a considerable amount of control over who received assistance and the types of programs that were available. Farmers who did not belong to the AFBF often complained of being neglected by their county agents. Despite efforts by the Department of Agriculture to ensure that extension services were available to all farm families, in the decades after World War I most poor white and black people were once again excluded from participation.[52]

Wary of the subtle challenge to the racial order presented by black extension agents, white supremacists were even less tolerant of more open civil rights activity. Instead of extending democratic rights to African Americans as leaders like Du Bois had hoped, at the end of the war they quickly acted to negate the gains black people had made and force them back into their customary roles. African Americans suffered disproportionately from the postwar economic recession, many of them losing their jobs to returning white servicemen. Federal offices that had been created and staffed with black appointees in an attempt to reassure African Americans that the government was concerned about their problems were abolished soon after the fighting ended. Worst of all was the increasing friction between white and black Americans that often exploded into violence. In the summer of 1919 race riots occurred in twenty-six cities across the nation, resulting in dozens of deaths and injuries. Black analyst Emmett J. Scott observed, "Instead of a tendency to extend the right of franchise there has been something like a recrudescence . . . of the Ku Klux Klan so as to intimidate the Negroes of the South that they may not seek to reach this end."[53]

Disturbed by these developments, the NAACP sent Herbert Seligmann to southern troublespots to investigate the sources of racial tension. Seligmann discovered that white southerners deeply resented the defection of their black workers during the war and believed that military service had encouraged African Americans to think of themselves as equals. One Louisiana politician told him that black people should never be allowed to vote or acquire education and argued that lynching and other forms of violence were necessary to maintain white supremacy.[54]

Nine African Americans were lynched in Louisiana in 1918, and three more were killed by mobs in the first six weeks of the following year. Many of the victims were former soldiers like Lucius McCarty, who was executed in Bogalusa by a crowd of over one thousand people after a white woman accused him of attacking her. Black novelist Ernest Gaines, a native of Pointe Coupee Parish, later depicted in fictional form a shocking yet common experience that African American servicemen encountered after the war. In *A Gathering of Old Men* (1983), one character recalls his return home to Louisiana after serving on the front lines in France and earning decorations for his bravery. "I was proud as I could be," he says, "till I got back home. The first white man I met, the very first one . . . told me I better not ever wear that uniform or that medal again no matter how long I lived. He told me I was back home now, and they didn't cotton to no nigger wearing medals for killing white folks."[55]

Such behavior toward those who had risked their lives for the nation and for world democracy was depressing enough. Even more frustrating was the federal government's failure to do anything to stop the wave of violence that threatened black Americans' lives and property. In a letter informing President Woodrow Wilson of a series of atrocities that occurred in Morehouse Parish in 1919, one black Louisianan wrote: "Mr Officer of USA we feel you all aut to help us in some way as you all got the power & as we Have put up our Lives for this U.S.A. We have ben in France on Front lines we have Lost our sons on acct of USA . . . & still we treated like we wasnt men."

In 1921 an anonymous letter from Shreveport referred to a lynching that had recently occurred there and asked that U.S. soldiers be sent to the region to prevent more violence against black people. "We needs help here in La," the author stated, "Because this is a Slave Country Down here."[56]

No troops materialized, and the post–World War I period turned out to be one of violent repression aimed not only at African Americans, but also against all potential threats to the social order. Extreme anticommunism in the wake of the Russian Revolution led to the systematic destruction of progressive social movements by business leaders, vigilante groups, and the federal government. Civil rights activists, immigrants, socialists, feminists, and labor unionists all came to be seen as dangerous radicals and enemies of the state. During the postwar "Red Scare" and continuing through the 1920s, many Americans were harassed, jailed, beaten, or killed for their political beliefs.[57]

In this climate, the owners of the Great Southern Lumber Company responded to union organizing efforts by white and black workers in Bogalusa with intimidation, evictions, and murder. Early in 1919 two unions affiliated with the American Federation of Labor (AFL) began a campaign to organize lumber workers in eastern Louisiana and southern Mississippi. The United Brotherhood of Carpenters and Joiners focused on white skilled workers, while the International Union of Timber Workers attempted to encourage unskilled laborers, mostly African Americans, to join the effort. Organizers found both white and black workers in Bogalusa receptive to the call, especially after company managers diminished their incomes by raising house rents. Great Southern's owners attempted to obstruct unionizing by offering bribes to leaders and threatening members. Bogalusa's Self-Preservation and Loyalty League, an organization of white business owners formed during the war to enforce the state's work-or-fight legislation, then began terrorizing workers to force them to withdraw from the union. Mob violence wreaked havoc in the town on the night of 21 November 1919, and the following day members of the Loyalty League shot and killed four white union men who obstructed their attempt to arrest black organizer Sol Dacus. Dacus fled the area, state and federal authorities refused to investigate the incident, and the union campaign disintegrated.[58]

Similarly, economic depression, the revival of the Ku Klux Klan, and intimidation by local officials exacted a devastating toll on black southerners' fledgling civil rights organizations. More than half of the NAACP's 342 branches were "completely delinquent" in July 1920, having reported no new members or renewals and made no contributions to the national office in the past seven months. Nationwide, membership in the organization dropped from a wartime high of around 91,000 to a mere 23,500 in 1928.[59]

The seven NAACP branches that black Louisianans managed to form between 1914 and 1925 struggled to survive, but their activities were hindered by poverty and the threat of reprisals against members. The Baton Rouge branch's charter was revoked after three years of inactivity, and civil rights work in most other areas outside New Orleans also faded. In 1923 H. C. Hudson of Shreveport reported to the national office: "The N.A.A.C.P. is deeply hated in this section. . . . As to the conditions elsewhere I cannot state with any degree of certainty, but you can rest assure that any man that is actively engaged in this work is liabl[e] to the same treatment. . . . That accounts for the large number of good towns with no branches in them." Both the Shreveport and Alexandria branches lapsed and then revived several times over the next ten years, reflecting cycles of organized protest followed by repression.[60]

Postwar reaction crushed any hope that the ideological implications of World War I and black Americans' participation in it would force the nation to abolish racial discrimination. The freedom struggle in rural Louisiana was once again pushed underground, awaiting the next opportunity to emerge from its subterranean existence. In 1929 the beginning of the Great Depression set in motion the events that made possible a resurgence of open political activism.

5

With the Aid of God and the F.S.A.:
The Louisiana Farmers' Union
and the Freedom Struggle in the
New Deal Era

Beginning with a sharp drop in agricultural prices soon after the end of World War I, rural Americans were the first to experience the effects of the economic crisis that eventually afflicted the entire nation. Severe flooding in 1927 followed by the worst drought on record compounded the situation in Louisiana's plantation parishes. Landowners lost their farms, tenants' debts increased, and competition for jobs drove down wages. National economic growth began to slow in 1929, and the financial panic of October that year precipitated a wave of bank failures, forced businesses into bankruptcy, and threw millions of people out of work. The effects of the Great Depression were particularly harsh for African Americans. Already among the poorest and most vulnerable segments of the population, black people's incomes now dropped even further below subsistence level. In the parish where Moses Williams grew up in the 1930s, farmers who could no longer afford to buy shells for their shotguns were reduced to chasing rabbits and other wildlife with sticks to obtain food for their families.[1]

Similar scenes of desperation were repeated all over the nation. The United States had experienced economic slumps before but never on such a wide scale. The extent and duration of the depression provided the rationale for a decade of experimentation by the federal government in an attempt to find solutions to social problems. Although President Franklin Roosevelt's New Deal policies brought some benefits for African Americans, the limits of these reforms were soon exposed in the South, where local elites used their control over the administration of government programs to further enhance their power. Meanwhile, left-wing groups organized farmers and working-class people across the nation to push for more far-reaching changes.

Encouraged by the communist organizers of the SCU, poor white and black farmers in rural Louisiana formed the LFU to challenge federal agricultural policies that mostly benefited large, corporate landowners. African Americans provided the union's strongest leadership and support and used their locals to demand economic justice, better schools, political rights, and the safeguarding of their lives and property. Plantation owners responded with threats, evictions, violence, and attacks on government farm programs that assisted poor people. By the end of the decade the forces of reaction had succeeded in turning back reform efforts and minimizing threats to the social order. Nonetheless, the New Deal era brought important changes to the region and to the lives of African Americans, portending even greater transformations that encouraged more protest activity in later decades.

The small group of elite white people who monopolized power in Louisiana had not been without opposition in the early twentieth century. Poor white farmers and workers whose interests clashed with those of planters, merchants, and corporation owners nurtured deep resentment toward the state's conservative rulers, and middle-class progressives hated the rampant corruption that characterized electoral processes. Pressure from these groups resulted in some educational and political reforms during the governorships of Newton Blanchard (1904–8) and John Parker (1920–24), but real change came only with the election of Huey Long in 1928. A native of Winn Parish, an area that was mostly populated by white small farmers who had a long history of antiplanter sentiment, Long garnered mass support by pledging to pass legislation to curb the power of the wealthy minority and enhance the fortunes of people who were less well off. In a paradox that has invited both condemnation and praise from his biographers, Long combined corrupt and brutal political practices that placed Louisiana under a virtual dictatorship with measures designed to help the state's poor. During his term he abolished the poll tax, introduced a graduated income tax, regulated utility rates, and increased spending on public schools and transportation networks.[2]

Although Long was no less racist than the conservatives he replaced, for African Americans his governorship was an improvement over previous administrations. The *Louisiana Weekly* acknowledged that "Huey Long was for the common man, definitely throwing all his legislation in their favor, and as Negroes are certainly classed with the commoners, they benefited by Long's work." Another source noted that despite Long's tendency to "mispronounce" the word "Negro," African Americans shared in the better roads, free school textbooks, lower taxes, and reductions in phone, gas, and electricity rates that were among the achievements of Long's regime.[3] An assassin killed Huey Long in 1935, but his legislative program for the most part remained intact even after his political opponents regained power. In addition, the growing economic crisis and demands for action from across the United States encouraged the federal government to implement similar social welfare measures on a national scale.

The 1930s were promising years for Americans who believed that some regulation of capitalism was necessary to alleviate the effects of economic insecurity inherent in the system. The depth of the depression exposed the inaccuracy of the belief that prosperity was guaranteed to anyone who worked hard and obeyed the law. Poverty or the fear of poverty affected people of all classes, making them more willing to accept change. Nowhere was this truer than in the South. Some of Roosevelt's strongest supporters were rural southerners whose livelihoods were endangered by falling crop prices and crippling debts. In the early part of the decade, even the region's conservative plantation owners joined in demanding government intervention to protect farmers from the ravages of the free-market economy.[4]

Roosevelt and a newly elected Democratic majority in Congress took power in 1933. Over the next decade the administration enacted a string of measures aimed at mitigating poverty and restoring economic stability. The Federal Emergency Relief Administration (FERA) and later the Works Progress Administration (WPA) allocated approximately $14 billion to the states to be used either as direct payments to unemployed people or wages for work on public projects. The National Recovery Administration (NRA) attempted to standardize business operations and improve workers' lives by establishing industrywide codes for maximum hours and minimum wages. The Civilian Conservation Corps (CCC) provided jobs and training for young Americans on reforestation, swamp drainage, and flood control schemes. To rescue the nation's farmers, the Agricultural Adjustment Administration (AAA) paid subsidies to those who voluntarily reduced their crop acreages in an effort to eliminate overproduction, increase prices, and raise rural people's living standards. The Resettlement Administration and its successor agency, the Farm Security Administration (FSA), provided low-interest loans and other assistance to marginal farmers to help them achieve self-sufficiency.[5]

The New Deal raised black people's expectations, encouraging them to believe that they might finally be recognized as citizens. Federal policy stipulated that the newly established relief agencies must treat everyone equally, and First Lady Eleanor Roosevelt achieved notoriety among white southerners for speaking out against racism. Franklin Roosevelt's record in this respect was more ambiguous, but most black people nevertheless viewed his presidency as a positive development. In the 1930s those who were able to vote defected in large numbers from the Republican Party to the Democratic Party. For the first time since the Civil War and Reconstruction, African Americans believed that the government was on their side. A black sharecropper whose crops had been stolen by his landlord in Red River Parish expressed this new mood when he appealed to the Department of Justice for help. "I am told that President Roosevelt is a true friend to the negro people," he wrote. "I want you and him to aid me, please."[6]

The New Deal did improve the lives of many African Americans. Between 1933 and 1939 approximately 8,600 young black people in Louisiana took part in the CCC program, with significant benefits for themselves and their families. Enrollees received thirty dollars per month and were required to send twenty-five dollars home to their parents or dependents. In addition, the training and opportunities offered enabled many of them to pursue careers other than unskilled farm labor. Madison Parish civil rights leader Martin Williams, who spent several years working at CCC camps near his hometown in Jackson, Alabama, remembered well the effect that the project had on participants. "We had some boys come there, had never seen a tractor or piece of heavy equipment," he said. "Give them two weeks, they'd do anything you wanted done. They learned so quick—all they need is a chance." As well as providing the basic education that many rural black people lacked, the CCC gave instruction in vocations such as carpentry, mechanics, landscaping, and clerical work. One project for African Americans in Pointe Coupee Parish offered a journalism course as well as classes in reading, writing, history, government, and debating. Such curricula were unlike anything most black people had been exposed to in the state's regular school system, and they were quick to recognize the value of these programs. Attendance at classes was voluntary but averaged around 90 percent. As one government study noted, African Americans used the camps "as a means of escaping the

Civilian Conservation Corps camp, location unknown, n.d. Thousands of African Americans in Louisiana took part in the CCC program between 1933 and 1939. The camps provided education and training for jobs—such as clerical work—that most rural black people had not had access to before the 1930s. RG 35-G-41-2124, National Archives, Washington, D.C.

hardships of farm life and for [the] purpose of securing better pay and learning a trade." This was exactly the path followed by Martin Williams, who came from a sharecropping family, trained as a drycleaner as part of the CCC program, and later established his own business in Tallulah.[7]

Other relief programs offered similar chances to escape from plantation labor or brought improvements to rural communities that benefited both white and black inhabitants. Access to government aid made African Americans less dependent on white employers and more likely to assert themselves when they thought they were being mistreated. Unemployment benefits and wages earned on public works projects provided recipients with stable incomes and pumped money into local economies, helping communities to recover from the depression. Louisiana reported a 4.3 percent increase in industrial employment between July and October 1936, with some regions experiencing economic growth for the first time since 1929. In Tallulah, the Chicago Mill and Lumber Company added a power plant, veneer mill, and box factory to the sawmill it had built there in 1928, creating more than four hundred new jobs.[8] Operating under the NRA codes after 1933, the company paid sawmill workers a minimum wage of twenty-four cents per hour for a forty-hour week, significantly more than most farmworkers could expect to earn at that time.[9] Both Martin Williams and Harrison Brown moved to Tallulah in the 1930s to take advantage of the new opportunities, forming part of a migration that increased the town's black population by a little over two thousand.[10]

Another promising development for African Americans came in the area of education. Efforts to eliminate illiteracy in Louisiana initiated by state officials in the 1920s received added impetus when the federal government provided more funding for adult education programs. State WPA officials reported in 1937 that nearly ten thousand African Americans had enrolled in literacy classes and were learning "for the first time to read, write their names, figure the amount of their crops." By 1939 more than twenty-five thousand black people were receiving instruction. Black people's dedicated participation in the program defied white stereotypes that had portrayed them as uninterested in education or incapable of learning. One account stated that students were "rearranging their entire lives in order to take advantage of the opportunity for knowledge," noting that a group in De Soto Parish attended lessons during its noon break in the cotton fields each day. An issue of the Louisiana WPA's newsletter *Work* printed a photograph of some rural black people clustered around a table in a plantation schoolroom with the caption: "Both men and women have put in a hard day in the fields— but they never miss a class."[11]

Having been deprived of education for so long, black students were not about to pass up the chance of achieving literacy when it presented itself. In a letter to President Roosevelt, J. H. Chapmon stated, "I truly do thank God for the blessing that he extended to the colored race here through you and those who took part in this great program. . . . I am thinking of when I was a school boy. They only let the colored people have four months in which to go to school. . . . Now you are helping me to get that that I was debarred of then." Leola Dishman of Ferriday expressed similar sentiments. "We are trying and doing our best to learn the things heretofore we haven't had a chance to get," she told the president. "We thank you for the privilege." Annette Nelson from Ouachita Parish wrote to WPA administrator Harold

Adult literacy class being held in a "plantation shack," Louisiana, 1938. This photograph appeared in a publication of the Louisiana Works Progress Administration with the caption "Both men and women have put in a hard day in the fields—but they never miss a class," indicating participants' determination to take advantage of this educational opportunity. Work, *April 1938, 4, Hill Memorial Library, Louisiana State University, Baton Rouge.*

Hopkins, "I am doing all in my power to grasp this wonderful opportunity.... Thanks for the opportunity."[12]

The WPA's efforts to reduce illiteracy among black Louisianans were among the most significant contributions of the New Deal. In many other areas, the effects of government programs were disappointing. One of the chief limitations of federal relief measures was that the amount of money allocated was inadequate to provide for all those who needed assistance. The federal government's rural rehabilitation programs, for instance, reached only a fraction of the nation's low-income farmers.[13] Similarly, public works projects could not provide employment for every person seeking a job. As was the case throughout the nation, many more people applied for aid in Louisiana than officials were able to handle. In July 1936 the WPA posted notices in local newspapers asking residents not to attempt to enroll in the program, since the relief quota for the state had been filled and no more applicants could be accepted.[14]

Governor Richard Leche received hundreds of letters from impoverished Louisianans who had been rejected at their local welfare offices and did not know where else to turn. Charlie Young, a seventy-one-year-old black man from St. Mary Parish who was half blind and unable to work, was refused assistance because he had three children who supposedly were able to support him. He told Leche, "They Said for my children to help me But my children aint got nothing Them self." Lillie Pearl Jackson begged the governor to help her find employment. She wrote, "I am hungry my two children are hungry we are without clothes, and shoes my husband needs medicine will you please help me? I do not mind working but I cannot get a job. . . . Please, please, please help me if you please or I will starve." In 1938 twenty-four unemployed residents of Concordia Parish sent a petition to Leche demanding that he do something about their plight. "We have exhausted every known means at our disposal without avail in an effort to obtain work—or even information about work," they stated. "Our credit has been exhausted through inability to pay; our rent is long overdue because of lack of funds. We are without *food*! We are *hungry*! We are *desperate*! . . . *We look to your* OFFICE *as a last desperate appeal*!"[15]

The inadequacy of relief affected both white and black Louisianans. African Americans faced the added problem of racism. Establishing a general commitment to equality at the national level was easier than ensuring the impartial administration of programs at the local level, particularly in the South. In 1933 the higher wages and shorter hours demanded by NRA codes resulted in mass layoffs of black workers, whose jobs were given to white people. The *Louisiana Weekly* reported that although the official policy of the government was to "thunder against discrimination," employers were "disregarding it right and left, where Negro labor is concerned." Louis Israel informed black lawyer A. P. Tureaud that African Americans in Iberville Parish received lower wages than the white laborers employed on public works and were being treated unfairly in other relief programs. In 1935 federal WPA director Aubrey Williams told a congressional committee that racism was a serious problem in New Deal agencies, attributing it to "'local traditions' invoked in many sections of the country."[16]

Rather than discouraging or undermining the South's "local traditions," in many respects the New Deal reinforced existing power relationships. Throughout the region, administrators were selected by the same planters and business owners who dominated everything else. In West Feliciana Parish, some of the men appointed to oversee federal programs included merchant, farmer, and sheriff T. H. Martin, plantation owner Howard Spillman, and storekeeper Thomas Woods. Wealthy landowners like Dr. J. H.

Hobgood served on the parish board of public welfare in Pointe Coupee Parish. A survey of the landholdings of AAA committee members in the Louisiana sugar belt found that the majority were large growers and corporation owners unsympathetic to the problems of small farmers, tenants, and sharecroppers. Control over crop acreage allotments enabled planters to ensure that they received the biggest share, while the amount of land other farmers could cultivate was drastically reduced. As had always been the case, the authority to decide who would or would not receive aid lay with the most powerful people in towns and parishes. Access to federal dollars in addition to their own wealth only increased their influence.[17]

The policy of placing New Deal programs in the hands of local elites proved disastrous for black people. One man who informed the WPA's national office about the terrible working conditions and low wage rates African Americans endured on a project in Louisiana stated, "We are now worser off on the WPA . . . than our foreparents was in slavery. If we open our mouths to say anything we loses our job, which the Federal government have provided for us." In 1936 C. L. Kennon of Webster Parish complained, "just because I would not leave my home and go work on half [as a share-cropper] for another man they cut me of[f] the relief—and won't let me back on. I have ben begin this relief office hear for 6 month to put me to work so I can buy my little children some clothe and shoes to send them to school." In Iberville Parish, merchants subverted relief programs by having food and other supplies intended for needy people sent to their stores, where they sold the goods instead of distributing them to the poor.[18]

White employers believed that government handouts made black people "lazy" and discouraged them from accepting work when jobs were available. Welfare payments and the wages paid by the WPA were meager, but they were still more than African Americans could earn as agricultural laborers and domestics. Many people showed an understandable preference for government over private employment. According to one official, a household workers' training project that operated in Louisiana for about a year "spoiled Negro women" by offering wages of up to seven dollars a week compared to the three or four dollars a week most had previously been paid. Now, he said, they thought they were "superior maids who could command big wages." Some of them refused to do any domestic work at all, preferring "sewing or some other WPA project." The white extension agent in West Feliciana Parish reported that "farm laborers and tenants have received so much assistance from relief agencies . . . that a great many of them have concluded that the Government will take care of them whether they work or not, and, therefore, they take things easy and get by with [as] little work as possible." In a similar vein, Guy Campbell of Monroe complained to Senator Allen Ellender that New Deal programs were having the "worst possible evil effect" on African Americans in the region. He claimed that black laborers who drew ten dollars a week on relief refused to go to work picking cotton despite plantation owners' desperate need for their services.[19]

Faced with such threats to the social order, white community leaders sought to prevent black people from taking advantage of the alternatives to plantation labor offered by federal agencies. Public works projects could be established only in response to requests by local officials, and police juries seemed reluctant to take the initiative. A WPA administrator who had been trying to encourage statewide plans for building farm-to-market roads reported, "many of the parishes are unable to pay engineering costs and in other cases, the Police Jurors who are the governing bodies of the parish, have been very slow in getting up data for projects. I am inclined to believe that they have been told to do nothing and not to cooperate with us." Similarly, district supervisor Mildred Taylor found that a black women's sewing unit in Concordia Parish was poorly operated, observing, "The Sponsors have contributed nothing and apparently have showed very little interest." Complaints that African Americans made too much money on WPA projects resulted in new regulations that cut the amount of time they were allowed to work in half, so that black people could earn only $19.25 for two weeks of labor a month instead of $38.50 for the full thirty days.[20]

As in the past, some white people used violence to try to force African Americans back into their traditional roles. In 1933 and 1934 a number of beatings and murders occurred in Union Parish to discourage black men from signing up for relief. A letter reporting the incidents to the Department of Justice listed two men who had been killed and four others who had been whipped (along with the names of twenty-one white men who were responsible for the terror) and added, "9 men run away from home all had to leave their homes wives and children to keep white people from killing them." Two near-riots occurred in St. Landry Parish when a black CCC camp was established there in June 1933. An investigator attributed the trouble to "intense racial feeling" in the community. A more specific motive was implied in a similar case reported to the U.S. attorney general by the secretary of the National Negro Congress in 1940. The Ku Klux Klan harassed and intimidated residents of a job-training camp for African Americans, posting signs that read, "Niggers your place is in the cotton patch."[21]

Plantation owners complained incessantly that federal programs encouraged black people to refuse to work and created intolerable labor shortages in rural areas. N. Watts Maddux of St. Bernard Parish claimed that he knew of hundreds of former farmworkers whose talents were being wasted on useless WPA projects that seemed "purposely long-drawn-out and needlessly so." In October 1942 a sugar grower in Avoyelles Parish who was unable to match the wages paid by relief agencies politely requested the closing of WPA camps in the region until the cane-cutting season was over. The same year, the Caddo Parish police jury passed a resolution calling for the suspension of welfare programs, stating that an "extreme shortage of labor" had been caused by "giving public funds to undeserving persons, who wish to be supported by the government in idleness."[22]

Most complaints about labor shortages were exaggerated if not completely fabricated. In one case, an investigator found that employers were able to provide the names of only two workers believed to be on WPA projects instead of laboring in the fields. His report concluded that "complaints made about pickers not being available were generally made without facts to substantiate the claims and were of such a general nature that they were of no help to the W.P.A. in relieving the situation; that W.P.A. did release all workers with the proper background and that the needs of the growers were satisfied."[23] Referring to the Caddo Parish resolution, a state department of labor official informed Governor Sam Jones that "it was not a question of lack of labor but the low wage scale which controlled that situation." Plantation owners in the region had offered workers only $1.25 per hundred pounds of cotton picked when their competitors on the state's eastern borders were paying from $1.50 to $2.00. As the harvest season progressed and more labor became available, the Caddo Parish planters reduced their rates to $1.00, indicating that no real crisis existed.[24]

In fact, as these investigators' comments suggest, administrators worked hard to ensure that New Deal programs did not interfere with rural labor markets. State WPA director J. H. Crutcher warned his staff in 1936 that the agency would "under no circumstances be a party to creating a labor shortage, and District Directors will be held personally responsible for seeing that no such condition exists in localities where persons are employed on W.P.A. projects and undertakings." He told them not to wait for private employers to complain, but to ensure that labor was available by releasing workers from projects whenever necessary. The WPA's newsletters and public announcements stated repeatedly that its aim was to provide employment for farmworkers only during the off-season. Relief programs were routinely shut down during agricultural harvest times so that welfare recipients could work in the fields, thus protecting the interests of employers who were unwilling to compete with the wage scales offered by public works projects.[25]

At the same time that they demanded a ready supply of cheap labor at certain times of the year, plantation owners were becoming less willing to support surplus workers when they were no longer needed. One of the most significant consequences of the New Deal for rural black people was the displacement of thousands of sharecroppers and tenants as a result of the federal government's farm policies. With the reduction in crop acreages brought about by the AAA, plantation owners' need for labor decreased. In addition, many growers invested their subsidy payments in machinery that further reduced their need for workers. Farm implement companies had been experimenting with labor-saving agricultural technologies since the nineteenth century, and by the late 1920s mass-produced all-purpose tractors like International Harvester's McCormick-Deering Farmall were widely available. Tractors could be used instead of mules for plowing and planting cotton, and with special attachments they could also perform a range of functions in sugar cultivation. Large landowners in the Mississippi River delta regions were the first to begin using the new machines in the South, and sales to southern planters increased rapidly after 1935. Between 1930 and 1940 the number of tractors in Louisiana almost doubled, increasing from 5,016 to 9,476. The state's plantation parishes showed the highest increase (386 percent) in the number of tractors per thousand acres of crops harvested of any southern region in the same period.[26]

With fewer acres in cultivation and the use of tractors spreading, the number of black tenant families in Louisiana dropped by nearly fifteen thousand in the 1930s. The Department of Agriculture attempted to ensure that employers retained tenants on their plantations and shared AAA payments with them, but loopholes in the agency's regulations allowed unscrupulous planters to avoid these obligations. Welfare officials in Louisiana noticed the prevalence of "old plantation negroes who are no longer able to work for a living" on their rolls and concluded that many landlords were taking advantage of the New Deal to rid themselves of unproductive laborers.[27]

Workers who remained on the plantations were easily cheated out of their AAA payments. Government officials decided that federal policy should not interfere with traditional labor contract arrangements in the South, allowing planters to continue manipulating accounts and limiting their employees' incomes. In its first two years of operation, the AAA distributed subsidy checks to landlords and entrusted them with the task of disbursing the appropriate portions of these funds to sharecroppers and tenants. Many agricultural workers failed to receive their share, so in 1936 the administration began mailing plantation owners multiple checks made out in the names of individual employees. It remained an easy matter for landlords to coerce workers into signing the checks over to themselves. Illiterate sharecroppers were forced to mark these mysterious slips of paper with an X without fully understanding what that meant. Another ploy was to make sure that the money could only be spent at plantation stores. Harrison Brown remembered "when the government had ordered you'd get a check or something after you settled . . . they took that check. . . . And the way they took it you couldn't cash it in town nowhere, you had to go by your merchant and let him sign it to cash it in—that was so he could get his hands on it, but you'd have to go by them."[28]

Planter abuses of New Deal programs did not go unchallenged. The massive social upheaval caused by the depression gave rise to radical workers' and farmers' movements that struggled to influence national policy and enhance equality, opportunity, and security for all Americans. In 1931 members of the Communist Party began working among rural black people in Alabama, encouraging them to form the SCU in an effort to increase the bargaining power of agricultural workers and help them gain fair treatment from landlords. Socialists in Arkansas organized the interracial STFU in 1934 to fight the mass eviction of tenant families caused by the AAA. The STFU spread into Missouri, Oklahoma, Texas, and parts of Mississippi, attracting thousands of members. At the same time, liberals in the Farmers' Educational and Cooperative Union of America (more commonly called the National Farmers' Union or NFU) began to increase their influence over that union's leadership, advocating federal legislation that was more responsive to the needs of small farmers. The activities of these rural unions and the publicity generated by plantation owners' violent opposition were instrumental in drawing nationwide attention to the plight of southern tenants and sharecroppers. The modification of some AAA policies in the later half of the 1930s and the expansion of programs to help displaced and low-income farmers buy land of their own resulted in part from union pressure.[29]

The LFU was formed in the mid-1930s, originating as an offshoot of the SCU. In Alabama, lynchings, beatings, and evictions had driven the SCU underground, forcing its members to meet secretly and limiting its effectiveness. After a strike by cotton pickers in Lowndes County was violently crushed in 1935, union leaders began searching for ways to strengthen the organization. Strong interest shown by black farmers in Louisiana encouraged the SCU to focus some of its attention on that state, and initially it seemed that the union would meet less resistance there than in Alabama. In January 1936 SCU secretary Clyde Johnson reported from Louisiana, "We have locals of 20 to 175 members that meet in churches and school houses and when some little terror did start against one member one of our leaders went to see the Sheriff in the name of the Union and the Sheriff didn't say a word about him being a Union member." Communist organizers worked with local people to make contact with black farmers and encourage them to attend meetings to discuss the union. Those who were interested in forming a local then elected officers and recruited more members by approaching family, friends, and neighbors. The social networks that existed within churches and other community institutions provided useful structures for disseminating information about the union. By May 1936 the SCU had approximately one thousand members in Louisiana, and the union had moved its headquarters to New Orleans.[30]

The SCU's New Orleans office was staffed by a small group of activists that included (at various times) Clyde Johnson, Gordon McIntire, Clinton Clark, Peggy Dallet, and Reuben Cole. Most were white southerners in their early twenties who shared a commitment to progressive causes and viewed their work as part of the fight for social justice. Clyde Johnson was the only northerner in the group and Clinton Clark the only African American. Originally from Minnesota, Johnson had attended City College in New York and worked as an organizer for the National Student League before joining the Communist Party and being assigned to Alabama in 1934. Though he eventually left the party, he remained committed to workers' struggles throughout his life.[31] Texan Gordon McIntire had attended Commonwealth College in Arkansas (a school that was closed down by the state in 1941 for "teaching anarchy") before arriving in Alabama to work with Johnson and the SCU in 1935. Clinton Clark was a native of Louisiana who helped establish union locals in St. Landry, Avoyelles, and Pointe Coupee Parishes in 1936. Peggy Dallet had been involved in organizing local chapters of various left-wing organizations in New Orleans, including the American League for Peace and Democracy, the League for Young Southerners, and the North American Committee to Aid Spanish Democracy. She became the union's office secretary in 1937 and later married Gordon McIntire. Reuben Cole came from a

sharecropping family in Georgia. Like McIntire, he had attended Commonwealth College and joined the other activists in Louisiana in May 1937.[32]

Members of the New Orleans staff acted as effective grassroots organizers, offering advice and aid to union members but encouraging local people to make key decisions about issues affecting them. The first issue of the
union newspaper, the *Southern Farm Leader*, invited members to send in
letters expressing their concerns and ideas for action, describing conditions
in their communities, and reporting on the activities of their locals. Clyde
Johnson recalled that whenever a new policy or position needed to be formulated, "everyone available met to talk it over. If it involved a basic union
position we discussed it all over the union and tried to have a state meeting
approve a position. . . . We believed the members had to understand and
approve an action to have it be successful. Rubber stamps can't cooperate."[33]

Relationships between organizers and local activists were characterized
by mutual respect. At their first convention in 1936, union members passed a
resolution thanking Clyde Johnson for his efforts on their behalf, calling
him "one of the outstanding champions of the Southern day laborers, sharecroppers, tenants and small farmers." Three years later Gordon McIntire
noted the rapid growth of the union in Louisiana, saying, "Much of the credit
must go to the Local leaders of the Union, whose courageous desire to improve the economic conditions and protect the democratic rights of brother
farmers throughout the agricultural fields has been repaid by the success of
the Union."[34]

After establishing itself in Louisiana, the SCU attempted to further
strengthen its position by joining forces with other farmers' and laborers'
unions. In May 1936 Johnson wrote an editorial in the *Southern Farm
Leader* suggesting that all of the 60,000 southern sharecroppers, tenants,
and small farm owners who currently belonged to the SCU, the STFU, or
the NFU unite in the largest of the three organizations, the NFU. Johnson
had maintained friendly relations with STFU leader H. L. Mitchell since
1934, and the two unions sometimes cooperated on issues affecting them
both. However, Mitchell and others in the STFU were wary of the SCU's
communist affiliations, and they rejected the idea of a merger.[35] The SCU's
overtures toward the NFU were more successful. Hard-pressed small farmers and tenants among the NFU's all-white membership were beginning to
see the value of uniting with black farmers to fight government agricultural
policies that mostly benefited large growers. The union's more progressive
elements saw an opportunity to strengthen their position by encouraging

the transfer of SCU members to their organization.[36] In return, NFU charters offered the former SCU locals the protection they so badly needed.[37] Clyde Johnson hoped that the charters would enable union members to "meet openly without interference," and that uniting with an established organization that had more than 100,000 members in thirty-eight states would "give the Black Belt farmers a much greater backing" in their struggles against plantation owners.[38]

In 1937 the SCU's locals in Alabama and Louisiana began transferring into the NFU, and the LFU was chartered as a state division of the national union.[39] At the annual convention of the NFU in November, delegates from the southern states played an important part in electing new executive officers and replacing the union's traditional emphasis on banking and money reform with a program more in line with the needs of poor farmers. Resolutions called for legislation to help tenants achieve farm ownership, mortgage relief, crop loans, and price control, as well as cooperation between farmers' organizations and industrial workers' unions.[40]

Since the problems confronting agricultural day laborers were different from those of farm operators, SCU leaders urged that they be organized into a separate union affiliated with the AFL.[41] In 1937 farm wageworkers in Alabama gained an AFL charter to form a union, but shortly afterward they joined the United Cannery, Agricultural, Packing and Allied Workers of America (UCAPAWA), a new organization of farm and food processing workers sponsored by the Congress of Industrial Organizations (CIO). Clyde Johnson then left the South to work with UCAPAWA lobbyists in Washington, leaving Gordon McIntire to head organizing efforts in Louisiana. McIntire encouraged wage laborers to join UCAPAWA and small farmers, tenants, and sharecroppers to join the LFU. The LFU maintained a stronger presence in the state than the CIO union, however, especially when financial difficulties forced UCAPAWA to abandon most of its rural labor organizing activities after 1938.[42] To complicate matters, many LFU members worked as seasonal wage laborers at sugarcane-cutting time in addition to raising cotton or other crops during the year. For these reasons the LFU did not limit its activities to issues affecting tenants and sharecroppers, and its locals consisted of all types of agricultural workers.[43]

The union's "family membership" structure mirrored the tradition of earlier black community institutions in encouraging participation by women and young people as well as men. Dues were $1.50 per year for adult males; women and young men between the ages of sixteen and twenty-one could join for free. Non-dues-paying members were called honorary members but they had the same rights and privileges in local, county, and state unions as dues-paying members. Women took an active part in the union at both the local and state levels. Often more literate than men, they performed valuable services like writing letters, passing on information from printed sources, keeping records, and teaching other members how to read and write.[44] Women delegates at the union's 1936 convention confidently expressed their opinions and ideas for action. Among the resolutions passed were several calls for measures to improve conditions for farm women, including equal pay for equal work, higher wages for domestic workers, free medical attention for pregnant women, and a maternity insurance system.[45]

The LFU welcomed white as well as black people, and strong local leadership was provided by members of both groups. As with all interracial unions in the South, the LFU's mixed membership presented problems.[46] In keeping with the Communist Party's antiracism, organizers at first did not allow segregated locals, though they avoided challenging southern racial practices too openly. According to Johnson, "To be for equal rights, for freedom and for self-defense was enough. It covered all our problems. We never advocated 'social equality' in those words because in the white mind it was synonymous with demanding that a black marry his daughter. The racist propaganda hung so heavy on this that it was futile to argue."[47] In later years the policy on interracialism was not rigidly enforced, especially after opponents charged that the LFU was a "nigger union" in an attempt to discourage white people from joining. Gordon McIntire refuted the claim in the December 1936 issue of the *Southern Farm Leader*, explaining that the perception arose after a mass meeting in Opelousas where the black farmers appeared to overwhelm the white members in attendance. "They later realized that their enthusiasm had worked against them," he wrote. "Both white and colored generally prefer to have their own locals and meet separately."[48]

No precise statistics showing the ratio of white to black members are available, but the majority of LFU locals seem to have consisted of African Americans. The union did make some headway among poor white people in rural Louisiana. White farmer John Moore of Simmesport, for example, led efforts to organize a local in Avoyelles Parish before being attacked and driven from his home by a mob in July 1936. Most of the other local leaders were black, including John B. Richard (who served as vice-president of the state union), Abraham Phillips, and Willie and Irene Scott. The black men and women who joined the union were cotton farmers and sugar workers who welcomed the legal assistance, skills, and resources that organizers brought to the freedom struggle. The grievances that LFU members expressed in letters to the union newspaper and in convention resolutions reflected many long-standing concerns of rural black people, such as unfair crop settlements, inadequate schools, exclusion from decision-making on government policies that affected them, and lack of protection from violence. Joining the LFU signaled their intention to intensify the fight against inequality and injustice.[49]

The LFU's first real battle occurred in St. Landry Parish in 1936. For several months the union had been involved in a range of activities there, including forming a farmer-labor cooperative with maritime workers in New Orleans and pressuring state and federal authorities to provide relief to farmers after the region was struck by drought.[50] In November, plantation owners in the parish made their first attempt to destroy the union, precipitating a fight that set LFU members against planters and their associates in local office. With the help of federal officials, the LFU gained a partial victory, but the incident showed that the union was far from welcome in Louisiana and that some white people were determined to do everything in their power to prevent it from interfering with the plantation system.

The struggle began when twenty families on St. Landry Farm learned that they were to be evicted because the bankers who owned the land wanted to sell it to the Resettlement Administration. Local administrators responsible for choosing farmers to participate in the planned resettlement project decided that LFU members would be excluded. Most of those who were told that they would have to leave were African American sharecroppers and belonged to the union. According to former manager Albert de Jean, all of them were good farmers. The families were served eviction notices in late November and ordered to move off the plantation by the end of the next month. As a statement prepared by the LFU pointed out, most rural workers made employment arrangements for the following crop season in July and August. The only landowners likely to have farms available this late in the year were "'ornery' landlords" who abused their workers. The St. Landry Farm families did not want to move.[51]

Eight union locals joined together to protest the action, demanding that the sharecroppers either be allowed to stay and participate in the resettlement program or be placed on good farms elsewhere with loans to buy their own equipment and supplies. Planters and parish officials responded by intimidating organizers and members. A group of white men that included Sheriff D. J. Doucet harassed Gordon McIntire when he went to collect affidavits from plantation residents in December. At a meeting held in Opelousas, vigilantes threatened McIntire and other union leaders while local resettlement supervisor Louis Fontenot "stood among the hoodlums grinning." Toward the end of December, the Resettlement Administration sent Mercer G. Evans to investigate the LFU's charges of discrimination. After speaking to local officials, Evans said that he found no evidence of policy violations but suggested that the displaced sharecroppers might receive loans if they found new farms and applied for aid. Under continued pressure from the union, federal administrators finally agreed to loan the evicted families between four and five hundred dollars each to help them establish farms of their own.[52]

The LFU achieved similar success in a confrontation with landlords in Pointe Coupee Parish in 1939. Plantation owners had responded to stricter regulations forcing them to share AAA checks with workers by evicting sharecroppers and altering tenancy agreements so that they could keep a bigger proportion of the government subsidies for themselves. Tenant families were told that they must accept the new arrangements or leave. Union officials advised the farmers to stand firm while they lobbied the federal government to intervene. According to local leader Abraham Phillips, "One bad week followed another, for we never knew when the boss would stop bluffing and really put us out in the cold. But we kept building our membership during those anxious days, we appealed to the federal government, and finally won the support of the Farm Security Administration, so that we got better rent contracts for 1939 than we'd ever had before." The FSA agreed to lease the plantations from the owners and arranged for tenants to pay cash rents of six dollars an acre. The settlement allowed the families to receive their full AAA payments, sell their own cotton, and follow a live-at-home program, offering them a chance to save some money and get out of debt that most had not previously had.[53]

The LFU also became involved in efforts to improve conditions for sugar workers. Under the Sugar Act of 1937, growers who wished to take advantage of the AAA subsidy program had to adhere to certain regulations, including the payment of "fair and reasonable" wages. These were to be determined each year by the Department of Agriculture after hearings were held to give planters, processors, and laborers the opportunity to present testimony to government officials.[54] In October 1937 hearings to set wages for the coming harvest season were held at Louisiana State University, a segregated venue that prevented African Americans (who made up the majority of sugar workers) from attending. The morning session was taken up with growers who spoke of the poor prices they received for their product, implying that they could not afford to pay cane cutters any more than the current rates (on average, $1.10 per day or 65¢ per ton).[55] In the afternoon, Gordon McIntire spoke on behalf of approximately one thousand LFU members whose complaints included inadequate wages, inaccurate weighing of cane, payment in scrip, excessively high prices charged at company stores, and inability to grow their own food. Some of the planters responded by praising the "beautiful paternalism of the old plantation system," arguing that because workers received free housing, medical care, and other benefits, they did not need higher wages. Others claimed that black people were lazy and wasted all their money on gambling, so it was pointless to pay them more. However, since wage increases seemed inevitable, the growers indicated that they might accept rates of $1.25 per day or 75¢ per ton. After the hearings the LFU urged members to write to Joshua Bernhardt, chief of the AAA's Sugar Section, telling him why they needed higher wages.[56] The final wage determination set minimum rates at $1.20 per day for women and $1.50 per day for men, or 75¢ per ton. The regulations prohibited growers from reducing wages "through any subterfuge or device whatsoever" and stated, "the producer shall provide laborers, free of charge, with the perquisites customarily furnished by him, e.g., a habitable house, a suitable garden plot with facilities for its cultivation, pasture for livestock, medical attention, and similar incidentals."[57]

The Department of Agriculture held additional hearings in February 1938 to establish wages and working conditions for the planting and cultivation seasons. Peggy Dallet presented a statement by the LFU describing the miserable poverty that year-round employees on the sugar plantations suffered and calling for minimum wages of $1.20 per day for women workers and $1.50 for men. She refuted planters' contentions that the provision of free housing and medical care compensated for low pay, saying that in most cases accommodations were not fit for human habitation and sick people paid their own doctors' bills. Dallet requested that all payments be in cash and that workers be allowed to grow gardens and raise livestock for food. In July the AAA announced its regulations for the coming season, requiring growers to pay women at least $1.00 and men $1.20 per day and to provide the customary perquisites free of charge. Though the new wage determination was not as high as the LFU had hoped, it still represented a 20 percent increase over previous rates.[58]

These wage rates held steady for the next four years.[59] Once the rules were established, workers fought to ensure that planters abided by them. The LFU taught its members how to keep records of what they were owed for the labor they performed each day and encouraged them to file complaints against employers who violated the law. Louisiana sugar workers submitted nearly four hundred wage claims to local and federal authorities in August and September 1939. At the request of the LFU, the Department of Agriculture withheld AAA subsidies from plantation owners until the claims were settled, and government agents investigated reports that employers in several parishes had threatened and intimidated their workers. The same year, union members in Pointe Coupee Parish refused to accept wages of one dollar per day from a planter who had evicted some families the previous year for filing complaints. As a result, they reported, he was "forced to live up to the law."[60]

Support for the LFU grew steadily in the late 1930s. Between 1936 and 1938 the number of dues-paying members more than doubled, increasing from 400 to 891. Although this represented only a tiny fraction of the LFU's potential constituency, it was an encouraging start.[61] Organizers found the response from African Americans especially gratifying. In November 1939 more than three hundred delegates from locals in twenty-five parishes attended the third annual convention of black members held in Baton Rouge, where they presented reports of their activities and listened to guest speakers from the AAA and FSA informing them of their rights under the federal government's agricultural programs. Gordon McIntire declared that it was "probably the largest meeting of sharecroppers and tenants ever held, but if not I will guarantee that it was the most unified meeting, and surely accomplished more than any that I have ever attended." The delegates voted to work toward establishing parishwide organizations to coordinate the efforts of their union locals. Moreover, to make it easier for cash-deprived tenant farmers to join the union, they agreed to allow the collection of dues for 1940 after the current year's harvest.[62]

Some white observers in Louisiana ridiculed black people's participation in the LFU, arguing that the communists wanted only to manipulate the state's poor, ignorant sharecroppers for their own purposes. One report on the union stated that it was "a trouble making organization in that it puts ideas in the minds of the negro tenant farmers in Louisiana which could not possibly have originated there." But African Americans were not as easily misled as these analysts believed. Black members saw the union as a powerful ally in their fight against exploitation and discrimination. They did not need to read Karl Marx or be "duped" by communist propaganda to sense the logic in the LFU's initiatives. Union organizers could not have been so successful if their analysis had not accurately described many aspects of rural black people's lives. As the Urban League's monthly newspaper *Opportunity* pointed out, black tenant farmers in Alabama and Louisiana knew nothing about theories of economic determinism or Marxist philosophy, "But these things they do know. They know of grinding toil at miserably inadequate wages. They know of endless years of debt. They know of two and three months school. They know of forced labor and peonage."[63]

African Americans in rural Louisiana had been battling these evils in their own way before the arrival of union organizers. Membership in the LFU offered the chance to fight their oppressors on more even terms. Writing to the *Southern Farm Leader* "about the dirty landlords, and how they rob us poor tenants," one Pointe Coupee activist stated, "When I heard about this union and what it was for, I joined it and I am proud to be a member of the Farmers' Union and I am willing to help every good effort for our justice and rights." Another member wrote, "When our Creator brought us into this world, He gave each and every man a right to inherit some of land that He created. I'm looking to the Union to open the door for me."[64] With the power of organization behind them and with the help of sympathetic federal officials, union members gained some limited concessions from plantation owners in the 1930s.

A key issue that had always concerned rural African Americans was gaining fair settlements at the end of the crop seasons. According to Clyde Johnson, one of the first things sharecroppers and tenants wanted was "a way of having a voice. They wanted their account with the landlord to be on paper." The LFU taught its members how to keep records of purchases from plantation stores so that they would know if planters tried to cheat them. At the same time, the union lobbied to make the provision of written contracts with employers a standard practice under federal farm programs. Although administrators had always encouraged the use of contracts, they were not compulsory. In 1938 the FSA announced that it would insist on having written leases drawn up between its clients and their landlords, attempting to pacify planters by saying that this was for the protection of both parties.

"We know from experience that both profit from having their agreement in written form," an FSA official stated. Another supervisor explained, "The landlord must be protected against abuse of the land and improvements, abandonment of crops and the like, while the tenant must have assurance of occupancy, a fair division of crop proceeds and renumeration for improvements made." These statements aside, most of the provisions on the FSA's standard lease form seemed designed to improve conditions for tenants, including minimum requirements for the quality of housing and a guarantee that renters be allowed to follow a live-at-home program.[65]

Complementing the campaign for written leases, black people used their union locals to continue the struggle for decent schools. Shortly after his arrival in Louisiana, Clyde Johnson reported: "The Negro people, contrary to the teaching of the landlords, are very hungry for education and culture. Union members are already writing to the state depart[ment] of education explaining that they get only 3 or 4 months schools with very poor fa[cil]ities and insisting that they be given longer and better school terms." In a resolution calling for resettlement loans for the evicted sharecroppers of St. Landry Farm, LFU Local 2 also demanded "better equipped school houses and free text books, longer school terms, higher salaries for Negro teachers, and free transportation for Negro children." A few months later the *Southern Farm Leader* reported that a group of union women in the parish had successfully lobbied for improvements at their children's school. The women raised $15.50 for the purpose themselves, then sent a delegation to request more aid from parish officials, who agreed to match the amount. The money was used to install new toilets, new steps, and a fence to enclose the school grounds.[66]

Union members in other communities carried out similar activities, often making education a top priority. In 1937 the secretary of a newly established local reported, "Our first demand is for a school bus, some of the children have as much as 5 miles to walk." The following year, when the LFU endorsed the Harrison-Fletcher Bill providing for federal aid to education, one member told Gordon McIntire, "I saw in the Bulletin where you said you had been to Washington to get aid for rural schools. To my judgement that is one of the most important things you could have done for us especially in West Feliciana Parish. . . . I can see and understand that you are on the job and I pray that you and all others keep working for improvement."[67]

The LFU also attempted to give members a voice in the administration of federal farm policies. In 1937 Gordon McIntire represented the union at hearings held by the President's Committee on Farm Tenancy in Dallas, Texas. He joined three representatives of the STFU in urging the federal government to allocate more money to its rural rehabilitation programs so that assistance could be given to the thousands of farm families who needed it. A common complaint among rural poor people was that agents of the federal government's Agricultural Extension Service often failed to address the needs of small farmers, tenants, and sharecroppers. "County agents are chosen by the landlords to be of service to the landlords," an article in the *Southern Farm Leader* explained. "Its hard for a square dealing County Agent who wants to be of service to share cropers and tenants and small farmers, to keep his job. He is soon fired by the landlords." The newspaper encouraged readers to demand that county agents be elected by white and black farmers and farmworkers so that they might be more responsive to the needs of the majority of rural people instead of serving the narrow interests of plantation owners. Administrators of federal loan programs also came under attack for discriminating against African Americans and LFU members. Union leaders urged members to write to the heads of government agencies and their representatives in Congress to ask that administration of the programs be placed in the hands of committees elected by all the farmers in the areas they served.[68]

These efforts to democratize federal agricultural policy and increase black people's political influence were largely unsuccessful.[69] At the local level, however, union agitation gained access to New Deal programs for black farmers who otherwise would have been excluded. A measure of the LFU's achievement in this area is that in Pointe Coupee Parish, where the union had many strong locals, more than 80 percent of FSA clients in 1937 were black.[70] Union leaders disseminated information about federal loans that were available and helped members to complete the application process. Black farmers who encountered discrimination from local officials could call on the LFU to assist them in gaining fair treatment. Abraham Phillips, for instance, was repeatedly turned down for an FSA loan by his parish committee because of his "general reputation as a trouble maker and a busy body" (a reference to his union organizing activity). The LFU's persistent appeals on his behalf caused the committee members to relent in January 1942. They finally approved Phillips's application in an attempt to "harmonize the labor situation" in Pointe Coupee.[71]

African Americans were intensely interested in obtaining credit from sources other than white landowners and merchants. In letters and statements to government authorities, black farmers often expressed the belief that all they needed was a chance to prove their ability free from the constraints of exorbitant interest rates and the dubious accounting practices of landlords.[72] This theme permeated the affidavits collected by Gordon McIntire during the struggle to gain resettlement loans for the sharecroppers of St. Landry Farm. Almost all of those threatened with eviction wanted to buy the land they worked and believed that they would be able to support themselves if they could borrow money at reasonable interest rates. Harry Jack Rose summarized the prevailing view when he stated, "If I can just have the chance I sure would like to buy this farm. . . . I know how to work and I have eight children and four good hands. I can work 40 acres or more. If I can get a little piece with the government I know I can defend myself."[73]

African Americans' faith in their own abilities was borne out by the experiences of many of those who did receive federal assistance. The first black farmer to pay back an FSA loan did so thirty-six years ahead of schedule. Over all, in the six years following the creation of the first rural rehabilitation agencies, the number of farmers who defaulted on federal loans amounted to only 2.6 percent of borrowers. As one study pointed out, a major achievement of the government's lending programs was the "liberation of the negro and white tenants from bondage to the 'furnish' system under which tenants paid an average of 20% to 50% for production credit and were consequently kept in perpetual debt—or perpetually in flight from unpaid obligations."[74]

Breaking the strangleholds of expensive credit and permanent debt allowed for great improvements in the lives of some African Americans. Between 1935 and 1937 FSA farmers in Pointe Coupee Parish increased their average net worth from $108 to $567.[75] Rehabilitation loans enabled people to achieve a higher standard of living, with many black clients building "houses of the most modern design and with all the conveniences of a city home." Some tenants became landowners, helping to reverse the trend from farm ownership to tenancy that had been the pattern in the previous three decades. Between 1935 and 1940 the proportion of black farm operators in Louisiana who owned part or all of the land they worked rose from 15 to 19 percent. Noting a similar increase in Tensas Parish, black extension agent J. A. M. Lloyd predicted, "With the present programs of the Federal Government continuing to exist . . . within the next ten or fifteen years every colored farmer in Tensas Parish will be well established on his own farm."[76] Such pronouncements were not very realistic, but the federal government's tenant loan programs nonetheless gave recipients cause for optimism. In 1938 an LFU member expressed these feelings in a letter to the union newspaper, saying, "My crop is coming along fine. With the aid of God and the F.S.A. I hope to establish a better home for myself and family and to help my fellow brothers."[77]

The same developments that held such promise for rural poor people elicited negative and sometimes violent responses from their employers. Union organizers' initial hopes of operating free from harassment in Louisiana were not realized. After its early successes in the mid-1930s, the LFU encountered increasingly strong opposition from white landowners, politicians, and business people in the rural parishes. Opelousas newspapers accused the union of stirring up "class hatred" and turning "the negro against the white man, the sharecropper against the land owner." Planters tried to discourage farmworkers from joining, claiming that the LFU only wanted to exploit them. One member reported: "Ed B. went to his boss' office to get $2. that Mr. H. owed him. Mr. H. told Ed., 'Now don't take this money and give it to that Union because you are only making some fellow rich in New Orleans.'"[78] Another landlord called all his workers together one morning and told them not to join the union or there would be trouble: "You fellows going around writing to the government, it will be too bad. And anyone of you who joins that thing, you will have to move." Gordon McIntire encountered intense hostility from planters, merchants, and local officials whenever he ventured into the rural parishes. One man told him, "We don't want a Union here. . . . We'll keep it out . . . with our lives if we have to."[79]

As always, plantation owners could rely on law enforcement officers and other public servants to protect their interests. One night Sheriff D. J. Doucet of St. Landry Parish visited the secretary of the LFU's Woodside local, threatened him, and gave him five days to leave the parish. In 1940 union members in Natchitoches Parish reported that "the landlords are telling the sheriff and deputies to visit all the meetings of the farmers and beat the people until they break up the unions." Police in the parish held and interrogated one black sharecropper for two hours, telling him that it was illegal for people to pay any dues to the union. Local administrators of federal programs also discouraged farmers from joining the LFU by withholding aid from members. Resettlement Administration officials in Pointe Coupee Parish relocated those who had joined the union to poorer land, took their equipment away so that the farmers had nothing to work with, and held up their AAA checks. The secretary of one local in the parish complained, "The landlords are bitterly against the union in this section," and added, "Resettlement and county agents are carrying on the same crooked work against us."[80] The danger posed to organizing efforts by the frequent overlap of planter and public authority was most clearly revealed in Rapides Parish during the struggle over sugar workers' wages in 1939. According to Gordon McIntire, immediately after wage claims were submitted to the local agricultural committee, "terror broke out in Rapides Parish, where one of the big landlords against whom we had entered several claims, was Chairman of the Parish Committee."[81]

Union members lived with constant threats of evictions, beatings, imprisonment, and death. One man who dared to ask his landlord if his AAA payment had arrived reported that his employer "seemed to get offended because I asked about my check, and he told me I had been with him too long for him to hurt me, so I had better move before he killed me. And he gave me 24 hours to be gone off the farm." In June 1937 a group of white men broke into the home of Willie Scott in West Feliciana Parish, seeking to lynch him. Finding only his wife Irene, they beat her severely in an attempt to gain information. Irene Scott survived by pretending to be knocked unconscious and fleeing to some woods while the men waited outside the house for her husband to return. With the help of other union members, the Scotts escaped to New Orleans. Frightening attacks like this were common. By the late 1930s most LFU members probably felt a lot like Joe Beraud, who feared that he would soon be murdered by his landlord. "MR. WARREN is going all around telling both whites and blacks that he is going to kill me," he wrote in a letter to Gordon McIntire. "He is carrying his gun for me. . . . My life has come to be like a rabbit's."[82]

Black Louisianans who had joined the LFU in the hope of achieving better living and working conditions struggled determinedly against plantation owners' attempts to repress their efforts. African Americans in Woodside responded to the threats made against their union secretary by forming an armed guard to watch over his home and family. Communist organizers supported the right of black people to protect themselves against violence and encouraged the use of armed self-defense. In a letter to LFU members during the St. Landry Farm fight, for instance, Gordon McIntire wrote, "If any members house is threatened by crazy hoodlums they have a right to protect their home with guns. We are not going to make trouble but must protect our rights."[83] A 1937 report on the situation in West Feliciana Parish noted that "some of the negro union officers were quite capable of deter-

mined, courageous and effective leadership and quite competent to take care
of themselves in a test of strength with the whites." Despite planters' attempts to kill them, Willie and Irene Scott returned to the parish and continued their union activities. The LFU newsletter reported in February
1938 that members in West Feliciana had "bandaged up the victims and dug
deep into their pockets for food and other aid," and that the parish locals remained strong even though they could not meet as openly as before. "Maybe
poor folks just don't have good sense," the report stated, "but when other
people are getting shot at, poor folks want to know why. And so more people
join up and the Union rocks on, for Union men are hard to scare."[84]

The LFU's ability to call on federal assistance in the 1930s might have contributed to its members' tenacity. After Gordon McIntire had complained
repeatedly to government officials, both the Department of Agriculture and
the Federal Bureau of Investigation (FBI) finally sent investigators to the
sugar parishes in 1939.[85] In its September newsletter, the LFU assured
members that government officials were "determined to investigate every
case of intimidation or any other violations of civil liberties." Although this
statement greatly exaggerated the Roosevelt administration's commitment
to ensuring justice in the sugar parishes, the mere presence of the federal
agents had a positive effect. The interest that events in rural Louisiana
attracted from people outside the region threatened to undermine the tight
control that planters had over their communities. Consequently, they sought
to avoid actions that might provide material for sensational headlines in
northern newspapers or draw national attention. Fear of federal intervention prevented officials in Natchitoches Parish from lynching Clinton Clark
after he was arrested and jailed there in 1940. According to one account,
there was every likelihood that Clark would be killed until the state attorney general made a telephone call to the parish district attorney. "No—no
lynching!" he reportedly stated. "We've got to be careful. The State is on the
spot. Can't afford that kind of thing with the federal government like it is."[86]
Violence continued in Natchitoches and other parishes where the union was
active, but the situation almost certainly would have been worse had it
not been for the contacts that the LFU had established with officials in
Washington.

Southern political and economic leaders deeply resented the encroachment of national authority into local affairs. Although they welcomed efforts
to stabilize agricultural prices and benefited greatly from the AAA, planters
viewed any attempt by the federal government to address more fundamen-

tal issues of poverty and inequality with suspicion. Plantation owners had been wary of the New Deal from the time of its inception, and they grew increasingly uneasy as the decade progressed. The new federal presence in the South and the encouragement that liberal officials in Washington provided to organizations like the LFU threatened the existing social order. In the early 1940s southern lobbyists joined forces with conservative northern business leaders to demand an end to the government's "socialistic" experiment.

Much of this opposition focused on the FSA. Critics charged that the FSA's efforts on behalf of poor farmers interfered with natural economic forces that dictated the failure of inefficient or incompetent enterprises, that its encouragement of cooperative farms was "communistic," and that attempts to combat the high incidence of disease among its poverty-stricken clients risked introducing "socialized medicine" into the United States. The agency was vilified in country newspapers and at mass meetings of plantation owners throughout the South, and enemies of the FSA in Congress succeeded in passing budget amendments in 1940 that restricted appropriations for its tenant loan program. At its annual meeting in December of that year, the powerful AFBF called for the abolition of the FSA and the transfer of federal loan programs to the Agricultural Extension Service, whose agents generally supported the interests of large producers. Although the FSA officially survived until its replacement by the Farmers' Home Administration (FaHA) in 1946, its activities were sharply curtailed after 1942 by further budget cuts and the shifting of many of its responsibilities to the Extension Service. After the reorganization of the government's farm credit agencies, assistance was denied the majority of poor farmers who applied for loans. The displacement of plantation workers continued with little to cushion the effect, relegating many people to the status of seasonal wage laborers forced to work for low pay during the harvest seasons and dependent on public welfare services at other times of the year.[87]

At around the same time, the fortunes of the LFU began to decline. After reaching a high point of about three thousand members in 1940, both membership and finances decreased dramatically over the next several years.[88] Organizing efforts had always been hindered by widespread poverty among the people the union sought to recruit. Most rural families could barely afford to spare even the meager amount it cost to join the union, and the LFU had many members who paid their dues irregularly, if at all. The union was therefore heavily dependent on donations from liberal sympathizers to finance its activities. Those funds became harder to obtain as the United States prepared to support the European democracies in World War II, a move that most liberals supported, while the Communist Party and union leaders advocated American neutrality and attempts to resolve European problems peacefully. In June 1941 one staff member wrote of the difficulties the LFU was experiencing in raising funds from former benefactors, saying, "the war has changed the attitudes of 'liberals' who once contributed liberally. . . . Try to appeal to the [deleted words] today! There's a red bogeyman hiding behind everything except a defense poster." Later that month Germany's invasion of the Soviet Union prompted an abrupt switch in the party line, but the transition to all-out support for the war only further weakened the LFU, as activists shifted their attention from the rural South to the fight against fascism overseas.[89]

The union also suffered from the loss of two of its most experienced organizers. Gordon McIntire contracted tuberculosis and was forced to give up work in January 1940. He left Louisiana six months later, and Peggy Dallet shortly followed. Two other staff members, Roald Peterson and Kenneth Adams, attempted to keep the New Orleans office functioning, but insufficient funds and continued repression by plantation owners hindered their efforts. Failure to collect annual dues in the fall, the only time most rural workers had any cash, left the LFU with only one paid-up member on record in 1941. Peterson and Adams found themselves in an impossible predicament, lacking money because they were unable to visit union locals to collect it and unable to visit locals because they had no money. The union's financial difficulties resulted in the suspension of its state charter by the NFU in December. Concordia Parish officials took advantage of the situation to arrest Adams and Clinton Clark for "collecting money under false pretenses" when they ventured into the parish on a fund-raising trip in January 1942. The two organizers were not released for three months.[90]

Meanwhile, the planter-dominated Louisiana Farm Bureau used its influence with the Agricultural Extension Service to encourage rural people to join the bureau instead of the LFU. Extension agents printed and distributed notices of farmers' meetings, promoting the Farm Bureau as an organization that had close ties with the government and could do more for farmers than other agricultural unions. An additional "advantage" for poor sharecroppers and tenants was that their landlords were often willing to pay Farm Bureau dues for them.[91]

Developments during World War II also contributed to the demise of the

LFU. New economic opportunities drew thousands of rural people to the cities, where they worked in factories for wages that were higher than they could ever hope to earn as farmers. Wartime prosperity and the increasing demand for labor offered an easier solution to farmworkers' problems than remaining on the land and fighting plantation owners. Many of the LFU's rural constituents drifted away, either migrating to urban areas or moving into nonagricultural employment.[92] In March 1942 Gordon McIntire wrote a circular letter to LFU members from a Denver sanatorium urging them to continue their union activities while organizers worked to collect enough dues to have the state charter restored, but his appeal failed to halt the disintegration of the union. Although a few locals continued to hold meetings and recruit members, the LFU was not rechartered, and there is no trace of official union activity after the mid-1940s.[93]

The New Deal era was a crucial point in the history of rural black political activism. The extension of federal influence into the South and agitation by farmers' unions like the LFU provided opportunities for African Americans to lift the freedom struggle to the level of organized politics. Plantation owners fought these efforts with intimidation, violence, and congressional action to limit social change. But even as elites appeared to preserve their power during this period, the New Deal precipitated changes in the region's economy that had profound consequences. Southern agriculture came increasingly to rely on seasonal wage labor instead of tenant families supported year-round by planters. At the same time, federal farm programs helped a few black people to achieve economic independence. As the nation prepared for war in the 1940s, these trends accelerated and resulted in even greater disruptions to the social order. Once again, African Americans took advantage of the situation to intensify their fight for equality.

6

I Am an American Born Negro:
Black Empowerment and White
Responses during World War II

Though studies of the civil rights movement generally acknowledge the ideological and economic significance of World War II, the early 1940s have not received nearly the same amount of attention from scholars as the postwar period. Existing histories mostly focus on the activities of national leaders and organizations and the ways they used the war to pressure the federal government to implement antidiscrimination measures.[1] Yet the actions of black activists in Louisiana reveal that the freedom struggle was just as intense at the local level.

The war brought dramatic changes to the rural parishes. Once again thousands of black people left the region to join the armed forces or to seek industrial employment in urban centers both within and outside the state. Higher incomes and liberation from the control of planters enabled African Americans to launch some powerful offensives against white supremacy during this period. Adopting the slogan of the "Double V" for victory over racism at home as well as abroad, black people worked to bring freedom, equality, and justice not only to the occupied nations but to their own country as well. Newspaper editors and civil rights groups highlighted the contradiction of fighting for democracy overseas while allowing segregation, disfranchisement, and violence against black people to continue in the United States. Soldiers and defense workers protested discrimination in the armed forces and war industry employment. White Louisianans responded by attempting to force their former farm laborers and domestics back into subservience, but they were unable to reverse the massive changes brought about by the war. After World War II, neither the South nor the nation would ever be the same.

As the threat of war in Europe loomed in the late 1930s, the Roosevelt administration worked to support the western democracies and prepare the United States for possible intervention. By this time many people, including former pacifists, were convinced that taking up arms was the only way to prevent the further expansion of Nazi Germany. But others remained un-convinced that events taking place in a far-off continent could have any relevance to themselves. Given their experiences in the aftermath of World War I, African Americans were understandably ambivalent. In 1936 a ten-ant farmer in St. Landry Parish expressed a common view among black people when he stated: "The only thing that made me sorry was when the world was in war before. They picked us up and registered us and sent us to war to fight for our country. Now the country is quieted down and steady and the government doing with us just like a man would do with an old poor dog. If they was going to fight again we would sit right here."[2]

Although many black Louisianans eventually supported the war effort, many also continued to voice suspicion and mistrust. In May 1940 a group of black newspaper editors and business leaders in New Orleans warned President Roosevelt that the "un-American practices against the Negroes of this state" were having a detrimental effect on black people's willingness to participate in defense preparations. Some African Americans had "shown evidences of revolt against anything sponsored by the officials of this state for the promotion of the Defense Program," they said, and were "advocating non-cooperation and rebuke to the fullest extent."[3] The federal government's own regional analyst in Louisiana, Edgar Schuler, also reported widespread dissatisfaction among the state's black residents. As he put it, "The dumbest plantation Negro can't see why he should fight to save Germans from Hitler when he has a Hitler right over him on his plantation."[4]

Accounts such as these caused much consternation at the Office of War Information (OWI) and other federal agencies responsible for monitoring and directing public opinion about the conflict. Throughout the war govern-ment officials kept a close watch on African Americans, assigning bureau-cratic armies to tasks such as scanning black newspapers and magazines, visiting the headquarters of civil rights groups, gathering and analyzing information from around the country, and conducting special investigations to assess the state of "Negro morale." The *Chicago Defender* did not exaggerate when it reported that administrators in Washington could hardly wait until Thursday of each week to "grab a 'Negro paper' and find out how the wind blows."[5] In June 1942 FBI director J. Edgar Hoover commissioned a special survey on racial conditions in the United States to assess the threat of subversive activity among the nation's black citizens.[6] The reports that resulted from these efforts often concluded the obvious: to gain African Americans' wholehearted support for the war, it was necessary to eliminate discrimination—at least in the armed forces, civilian defense training, and industrial employment, if not in all aspects of American life.[7]

African Americans did not wait patiently for state and national political leaders to grant them these things. As during World War I, hundreds of thousands of black people left the South to seek better jobs and living conditions elsewhere.[8] Louisiana's net gain in black population between 1940 and 1950 makes it difficult to tell exactly how many black Louisianans left the state during this period, but census data for individual parishes provide some indication of the extent of black migration from the various regions. All but four of the cotton plantation parishes reported decreases in their black populations ranging from 4 to 31 percent. Seven of the thirteen sugar parishes also lost some of their black residents, with the parishes located near Baton Rouge losing the most. At the same time, parishes with cities of ten thousand people or more gained in black population at an average rate of 26 percent, suggesting that many African Americans left the countryside to seek new jobs in urban areas. (See Table 6.1.) A notice that appeared in the *Madison Journal* in May 1943 is also revealing. Out of thirty-five local black men who were called to military service that month, only six still resided in Madison Parish. Nineteen of the missing men had moved to either California or Nevada, one had gone to Chicago, and the remaining nine were living in cities in Louisiana or in other southern states.[9]

The armed forces provided black Louisianans with another avenue of escape from the plantations. Reservations about sacrificing their lives for an imperfect democracy aside, joining the military offered opportunities for training and employment that few black people could have gained otherwise. In 1940 pressure from national civil rights groups persuaded Congress to include prohibitions on discrimination in the Selective Training and Service Act, raising hopes that African Americans might be treated equally in the selection and training of military personnel. In April the following year, the *Madison Journal* reported that many black men in the parish had eagerly signed up for service. "Several colored citizens here remarked during the week that if another trainload of negro soldiers passed through Tallulah, there would not be a young negro left," the article stated. So far the local draft board had managed to fill all of its black quotas with volunteers and had a waiting list of fifty men.[10]

With the creation of the Women's Auxiliary Army Corp (WAAC) in May 1942, the possibility of military service was also opened to black women. Recruitment officers for the WAAC and its successor, the Women's Army Corp (WAC), toured Louisiana in 1943 and 1944, encouraging women to join up through appeals to their pocketbooks as much as their patriotism. The WAC offered women a fifty-dollar-per-month salary plus free housing, meals, uniforms, and medical care, along with the chance to train in a variety of careers. Courses to prepare them for jobs as clerks, stenographers, bookkeepers, typists, airplane mechanics, radio operators, and chauffeurs were among those on a list that one officer stated "would fill a college catalogue."[11] African Americans who served in the military often achieved levels of education, skills, and economic security that were unheard of among rural black people, in addition to being exposed to new people, ideas, and social settings outside their home state.[12]

For black people who remained in Louisiana, defense preparations created new employment opportunities. Early in 1941 construction work began on several military training camps and airports in northern and southeastern Louisiana. In April, state employment analysts reported that landowners in the region were having difficulty finding tenants and day laborers, since many farmworkers had abandoned the plantations for the higher wages they could earn on construction projects. Only a handful of these people returned to their former employers when the building boom ended. J. H. Crutcher informed WPA officials in Washington that "because of the great difference between the rate paid farm labor, from $.75 to $1.50 a day, and that of $3.20 paid at the camps, many are putting off accepting employment or seeking reinstatement on W.P.A. because of their hope that further work, such as the cantonments, will develop." Over the next few years new shipbuilding and ordnance plants located in Baton Rouge, Shreveport, Lake Charles, and Erath continued to act as magnets for farmworkers from the surrounding parishes, exacerbating the problems of planters but greatly increasing the economic prospects of the African Americans employed in them.[13]

Black people who continued to work on the plantations also benefited from

Table 6.1 African American Migration in Louisiana during World War II

Parish	Number of African Americans in Parish		Percentage Change
	1940	1950	
Cotton Parishes			
Avoyelles	10,556	9,907	−6
Bossier	16,654	13,883	−17
Catahoula	5,345	4,145	−22
Claiborne	17,083	12,952	−24
Concordia	9,767	8,519	−13
De Soto	20,114	13,812	−31
East Carroll	12,784	9,936	−22
East Feliciana	11,649	11,137	−4
Franklin	12,628	10,770	−15
Madison	12,775	11,545	−10
Morehouse	16,129	15,418	−4
Natchitoches	19,946	17,048	−15
Red River	7,987	6,056	−24
Richland	13,057	10,926	−16
St. Landry	33,815	35,009	+4
Tensas	11,194	8,563	−24
Webster	14,246	13,018	−9
West Carroll	4,248	3,117	−27
West Feliciana	8,954	7,239	−19
Sugar Parishes			
Ascension	7,948	7,916	−(-)[a]
Assumption	7,530	7,226	−4
Iberville	14,171	13,049	−8
Lafourche	5,635	5,243	−7
Plaquemines	5,410	5,462	+1
Pointe Coupee	13,556	11,725	−14
St. Charles	3,909	4,349	+11
St. James	8,228	7,706	−6
St. John the Baptist	6,876	7,411	+8
St. Martin	9,651	9,734	+1
St. Mary	14,242	13,644	−4
Terrebonne	8,823	8,814	+(-)
West Baton Rouge	6,859	6,240	−9

Table 6.1 Continued

Parish	Number of African Americans in Parish		Percentage Change
	1940	1950	
Rice/Grain Parishes			
Acadia	8,319	8,994	+8
Allen	4,421	4,373	−1
Beauregard	2,593	3,023	+17
Cameron	670	583	−13
Jefferson Davis	6,015	5,683	−6
Vermilion	5,043	4,698	−7
Subsistence/Truck Parishes			
Bienville	11,491	9,407	−18
Caldwell	3,496	2,936	−16
Evangeline	6,999	7,553	+8
Grant	3,979	3,454	−13
Jackson	5,612	4,592	−18
La Salle	1,337	1,376	+3
Lincoln	11,239	10,362	−8
Livingston	2,639	2,951	+12
Sabine	4,760	4,291	−10
St. Bernard	1,405	1,614	+15
St. Helena	5,048	4,785	−5
St. Tammany	7,303	7,922	+8
Tangipahoa	15,042	16,589	+10
Union	7,259	6,623	−9
Vernon	2,420	2,216	−8
Winn	4,278	4,415	+3
Parishes with Cities of 10,000 People or More			
Caddo	63,793	66,361	+4
Calcasieu	14,952	20,563	+38
East Baton Rouge	33,634	52,262	+55
Iberia	13,447	12,965	−4
Jefferson	8,475	16,138	+90
Lafayette	14,098	15,727	+12
Orleans	149,034	181,775	+22

Table 6.1 Continued

	Number of African Americans in Parish		Percentage Change
Parish	1940	1950	
Ouachita	21,020	24,647	+17
Rapides	26,899	29,967	+11
Washington	10,814	12,064	+12
Total for Louisiana	849,303	882,428	+4

SOURCES: Bureau of the Census, *Sixteenth Census of the United States: 1940, Population, Volume 2: Characteristics of the Population, Part 3: Kansas–Michigan* (Washington, D.C.: GPO, 1943), 362–65, 421, 435, and *A Report of the Seventeenth Decennial Census of the United States, Census of Population: 1950, Volume 2: Characteristics of the Population, Part 18: Louisiana* (Washington, D.C.: GPO, 1952), 49–50, 78–81.

[a](-) indicates less than 0.5 percent.

the war. Competition for labor forced planters to raise wage rates and offer tenants more appealing work contracts. Anticipating as much, Congress extended the Sugar Act for three years past its initial expiration date of December 1941 and gave growers a 33.5 percent increase in subsidies to enable them to match the wage scales offered by other employers. Consequently, minimum wages for adult male sugarcane cutters rose from $1.50 per day in 1941 to $1.85 in 1942. The following year, many growers found it necessary for the first time to pay more than the minimum rate determined by the Department of Agriculture, increasing average wages during the harvest season by approximately 46 percent. Observers recorded similar increases for day laborers in the cotton parishes.[14] A study conducted in 1943 noted that because of the demand for personnel in industry and the armed forces, "Even the farm laborer and migratory worker are being comparatively well paid for the first time in their lives." In 1945 Louisiana reported a farm wage bill of $30,102,470, an increase of 107 percent over the $14,546,990 paid to agricultural workers in 1940.[15]

The need to raise agricultural production to levels sufficient for feeding

African American company of the Women's Auxiliary Army Corps in training at Fort Des Moines, Iowa, May 1943. Service in the armed forces and their auxiliaries did not insulate black military personnel from discrimination or persecution during World War II, but it did offer a measure of economic security as well as training opportunities that most African Americans had not previously had access to. RG 111-SC-238651, National Archives, Washington, D.C.

European allies as well as Americans once again resulted in the expansion of the Agricultural Extension Service. Funds allocated by the War Food Administration enabled the states to hire more African American agents to work with black farmers, and a nationwide "Food for Freedom" campaign exhorted all rural families to grow their own food so that more would be available for domestic and foreign consumers.[16] Louisiana administrators announced plans to contact every farmer in the state, promising to provide all the assistance that was available from the various farm agencies to those who agreed to cooperate with the program. Pointe Coupee Parish extension agent A. B. Curet declared, "This is the finest opportunity we have ever had to achieve a balanced agriculture, increase our income, improve our standard of living, make our farms better farms and at the same time aid national defense." After visiting Louisiana and several other states in 1942, two

Black laborers awaiting transport to a construction project in Camp Livingston, Louisiana, December 1940. Defense preparations created new jobs and lured thousands of rural people away from the plantations even before the United States officially entered World War II. LC-USF34-56690-D, Library of Congress, Washington, D.C.

officials from the Department of Agriculture reported that landlords who had formerly prevented workers from growing their own food were now "encouraging and occasionally requiring their tenants to grow a variety of foodstuffs."[17] Landowners risked being labeled unpatriotic if they refused to allow tenants and sharecroppers to cultivate "victory gardens." Wartime exigencies therefore forced planters to concede on issues that had long concerned black people in their struggle for economic independence.

African Americans' new prosperity fueled an increase in civil rights activity during the war. At the same time, wartime rhetoric and the government's need to unite people behind mobilization efforts provided black Americans with powerful leverage in the fight against injustice. A special issue of the black New Orleans newspaper *Sepia Socialite* published in 1942 was filled with references to the dual meaning of the war for African Americans. In one article, Bishop S. L. Green wrote, "the Negro marches on with America, but not blindly. When he defends the United States of America abroad, he does not want to be disenfranchised and unjustly treated at home." In a fore-word to the work, George Schuyler urged black Louisianans to take advantage of the war to demand equality. "Let them resolve that not only will they enjoy democracy and freedom AFTER this great world struggle is over, but that they must have them HERE and NOW," he wrote. "Let them insist with all the force and eloquence at their command that for them democracy must begin AT HOME, in Louisiana, and that they want it to begin AT ONCE."[18] Staff at the FBI's New Orleans Field Division reported that the state's other black newspapers had adopted a similar tone. According to these agents, African American editors and publishers were conducting "a militant campaign for equal rights as well as those against social, economic and political discrimination" and often exploited the war situation to threaten the withdrawal of black people's support if conditions did not change.[19]

Civil rights organizations like the Urban League, the NAACP, and the newly formed March on Washington Movement (MOWM) engaged in similar campaigns. The NAACP increased its presence in Louisiana during the war, with local activists managing to charter more than thirty branches by the end of 1946. The strongest chapters were in urban areas like New Orleans and Baton Rouge, but the organization also reached into Iberville, Concordia, Madison, St. Landry, and other rural parishes.[20] In the early 1940s the NAACP worked with the Louisiana Colored Teachers' Association (LCTA) and local civil rights groups to pressure school boards to equalize white and black teachers' salaries. African American leaders used the rhetoric of the nation's war propaganda to argue the case for justice. In April 1943 the Iberville Parish Improvement Committee presented a petition to school board officials that stated, "We approach this problem in the Democratic way—the way for which our sons and other loved ones are sacrificing their lives on foreign battle fields with the hope that this honorable body will deal with the matter in the American spirit of fair play, granting to the Negro teachers their appeal for equal pay for equal work." Two months later LCTA president J. K. Haynes warned Governor Sam Jones that the state might soon suffer from a shortage of black teachers unless they were treated fairly. "Many of our teachers are leaving the profession going to defense area and other high salaried positions due to inability to make a living wage teaching," he observed. "We humble urge that you use your influence to the realization of equalization of economic opportunity in the teaching profession in this state which is in keeping with the American ideal of democracy."[21]

Working-class black people made up a large proportion of the NAACP's membership, and they were also vital participants in the March on Washington Movement.[22] As government analysts noted, the MOWM's focus on gaining equal job opportunities for black people held enormous appeal to thousands of African Americans. One report explained: "It is in regard to job discrimination that Negroes feel the deepest rancor. They recognize that economic opportunity is the basic remedy for all of the injustices which they suffer. They are distressed by social discrimination, by segregation, by the unfortunate living conditions imposed upon them and by other disadvantages. But interviewing indicates that their prime concern at present is over their economic handicaps."[23] In war industry centers like California's East Bay area, migrants from the rural South strongly supported the NAACP's and the MOWM's organizing efforts. There and in other cities across the nation, former tenants and sharecroppers who joined the industrial working class continued their struggles for economic independence and political influence, pursuing long-standing goals in new contexts with new methods. The threat of mass demonstrations if the government failed to act against racism persuaded President Roosevelt to issue Executive Order 8802 in June 1941, banning discrimination against black workers by unions and employers who held government contracts and creating the President's Committee on Fair Employment Practice (FEPC) to monitor the hiring procedures of companies.[24]

Although lack of resources and opposition from business leaders and conservative politicians hindered the FEPC's work, the government's ostensible commitment to equality encouraged black people to assert their rights and made them more likely to protest discrimination. In February 1944 two thousand African Americans employed at the Delta Shipbuilding Company in New Orleans went on strike after some of the plant's white guards harassed and assaulted several black workers. The walkout lasted for a day and a half while FEPC staff members tried to negotiate a settlement to the dispute. The company's managers eventually agreed to fire those responsible for the attacks and to hold weekly meetings on racial issues with supervisors and superintendents in an attempt to avoid further conflict. An FEPC report on the incident noted that in this time of national crisis, it was becoming more difficult for white people "to terrorize and keep the Negro in his place, for his cooperative effort in the production of ships is vitally needed."[25]

Often, black Louisianans' petitions to the FEPC's office in New Orleans reflected a new sense of empowerment. Their letters expressed both indignation at the abuses they suffered and the belief that the government should and could do something about them. Laundry worker Lena Mae Gordon reported from Camp Claiborne in Rapides Parish that her supervisor had said that she would rather resign than recommend a black woman for a raise. Gordon stated, "I want to know why we don't get a raise? . . . I am willing to work on any defense job but I want to be treated justly. They say we are ignorant but this is not so. . . . I am an american born Negro and willing to do any thing to help my country but I WANT JUSTICE." Some letters slyly manipulated official concerns about maintaining black people's support for the war. For example, when clerical worker Edith Pierce wrote to complain of an "atmosphere of under-cover hostility" toward her and the other African American employees at the Port of Embarkation in New Orleans, she ended by saying, "This letter is written with the expectation that something might be done toward improving the morale of one who would enjoy all the privileges of American Citizenship in full."[26]

Being asked to contribute to the defense of democracy overseas while suffering decidedly undemocratic treatment in the United States naturally sharpened black Americans' resentment of injustice. Such feelings were especially intense among those who were drafted or chose to serve in the armed forces. As newspapers, government reports, and civil rights activists pointed out repeatedly, the treatment of black military personnel by their commanding officers and white civilians was a national disgrace. African Americans served in segregated units and were often assigned to unskilled work regardless of their qualifications. Dining and recreational facilities provided for black servicemen and women were invariably inferior to those of their white counterparts. Discipline was stricter on their side of the Jim Crow line, with African Americans routinely suffering harassment and sometimes violence at the hands of white military police and local law enforcement officers.[27]

Conditions for black personnel stationed in Louisiana were abysmal. African Americans at Camp Polk reported that the white civilians who ran the canteen refused to sell food to black people and stated, "Colored soldiers at this camp are treated like dogs." Black technicians assigned to Camp Claiborne spent most of their time performing menial tasks far below their skill level. Edgar Holt complained, "After spending months in school being trained to do specific jobs we land in labor battallions while our skills go to waste. Our assignments are permanent K.P., supply and other details." George Grant considered the treatment of African Americans at the camp to be "on a par with the worst conditions thru the south since eighteen sixty-five." White officers called them "niggers," their pay checks often arrived late, and they frequently suffered rough treatment by military police who resembled "nothing so much as a deputized Dixie mob." A resident of Camp Livingston expressed similar sentiments. In meting out punishment to black servicemen, he stated, white officers were "just like a lynch mob with a neggro to hang."[28]

Many African Americans did not suffer such treatment quietly. A group of WACs stationed at Camp Claiborne made their resentment known to their commander, who complained that the women seemed "dissatisfied with their assignments and treatment," that "most of them had a bad attitude," and that "they are race conscious and feel that they were being discriminated against."[29] Black servicemen and women petitioned federal agencies and civil rights organizations protesting discrimination and highlighting the contradictions between the government's war propaganda and its practice. Writing to the War Department about her experiences with white bus drivers in Alexandria who repeatedly refused to let her ride even though she "had on the same government uniform that the white soldiers wear," Dorothy Bray asked, "Why? Why are we here, I am sure none of us asked to be born but since we are born, don't we have the right to liberty and the pursuit of happiness, even when the color of our skin is dark?" A black man stationed at an army air base near Baton Rouge made a similar argument. "Owing to the fact that we are Negro soldiers of the American Army and fighting for the same cause as the White Soldiers," he wrote, "we expect and feel that we should have just treatment due an American Citizen and an American Soldier, who has sworn to protect and defend this country from such practices as are exercised in this particular camp."[30]

Both soldiers and civilians in Louisiana also engaged in direct action against injustice. Immediately after arriving at a train station in Sabine Parish, black sergeant Nelson Peery spat on the "White" and "Colored" signs that designated the separate waiting areas, and another member of his division knocked them down with his rifle butt. Segregated seating arrangements on public transportation provided one of the most frequent areas of contestation in Louisiana and other parts of the South. White bus drivers and riders were stunned to discover that African American servicemen and women believed that their uniforms gave them the right to sit anywhere they liked.[31] Altercations between white Louisianans and black military personnel became so frequent that the commanding officer at one camp issued a special memorandum reminding African Americans of their second-class status. "The Louisiana law prescribes that white people riding conveyances shall take seats from the front of conveyance toward the rear and colored people from rear of conveyance toward the front," the order stated. "This law also applies to Military Personnel. . . . In the event that operator of public conveyance request[s] Military Personnel to move toward the front or the rear they will occupy seats assigned to them by the operator without argument."[32]

The presence of black soldiers and defense workers from other parts of the country created opportunities for local black people to engage in their own subterfuges against the social order. An officer stationed at Harding Field near Baton Rouge told Edgar Schuler, "Sometimes you get a case like this: a boy who claimed he was from New York, after he had got into some difficulty, turned out to be from the South. They say they aren't used to conditions as they find them in the South." Some African Americans engaged unapologetically in blatant acts of defiance. "They think they're as good as we are right now," one white Louisianan complained. "Some of em don't even move off the banquette (sidewalk) to let you pass, or on the side even." Other white people cited the "high and mighty ways displayed by previously apparently docile colored girls and women" as a constant source of annoyance. Dozens of similar comments and quotations filled Schuler's weekly reports, indicating that many black people were no longer willing to conform to their expected roles. By April 1943 law enforcement officials in all but one Louisiana parish had reported having some kind of trouble with "uppity" African Americans.[33]

White people deeply resented the loss of servility that seemed to be infecting the state's black inhabitants. But it was not so much disrespectful behavior as the disappearance of their cheap labor supply that upset them the most. Many of the concerns they expressed about the impact of the war on black people centered on the economic gains that African Americans had made and their unwillingness to perform menial tasks now that alternatives were available. "This terrible war has made some big changes with us, and our mode of life will be even more changed before it is ended," a resident of Tangipahoa Parish fretted. "The negroes just won't do domestic work—so we are still without a cook, or servant of any kind." Analyzing the sources of increasing tension between white and black people in the state, Edgar Schuler noted that a major factor was the "improved economic status of Negroes . . . and resentment by whites at scarcity of domestic help." Most people recognized that even when the fighting was over, African Americans would not willingly return to the positions they had occupied before the war. The entire southern social order was being contested, and white people knew it. According to Schuler, local authorities avoided discussing or drawing people's attention to these matters, but there was "a great deal of private talk consisting of rumors, stories, gossip, threats, and boastings—all or largely from the point of view that 'we'll teach the damn' nigger to keep in his place.' "[34]

Throughout the war, white Louisianans made plain their unwillingness to tolerate attempts by African Americans to gain equality. During the initial phases of defense preparation, state and local officials made only token efforts to train black people for industrial jobs. Federal investigator John Beecher reported in March 1942 that Louisiana had a thriving defense training program that offered participants the chance to acquire, at public expense, the skills that would eventually enable them to obtain well-paid work in the region's new shipbuilding and munitions plants. However, he noted, "From this program of free public instruction Negroes have been excluded almost completely, and solely by reason of their race." Educators responsible for the programs said that they would gladly include African Americans but their local defense councils refused to provide the necessary funds; state and local officials argued that it was a waste of taxpayers' money to train black people for defense jobs because companies refused to hire them; and employers claimed that they were willing to hire black workers but feared strikes and other negative reactions by their white employees.[35] The arguments went around in a seemingly unbreakable circle, using the results of racist practices to justify perpetuating those same practices.

The efforts of the FEPC went a small way toward increasing black employment in defense industries, but African Americans did not gain access to these jobs in large numbers until the pool of white labor was exhausted. In the spring of 1942, two years after the defense program was established, black people represented only 2.5 percent of Americans employed in war production. By November 1944 the proportion had risen to 8.5 percent, with 1.25 million black workers finding jobs in defense industries. In Louisiana, the number of African Americans employed in all manufacturing occupations rose from 28,909 to 37,995 between 1940 and 1950.[36]

As some company owners had predicted, white workers did not easily accept the influx of African Americans into new positions perceived to be far above their rightful status. After one WPA administrator arranged employ-

National defense training program, Southern University, Baton Rouge, 1941. Defense training offered the chance to learn new skills and gain jobs in defense industries that sprang up throughout the state during World War II. RG 208-NP-2-R, National Archives, Washington, D.C.

ment for ten young black men at a small shipbuilding plant in St. Mary Parish, he learned that "white workers in the yard were bitterly hostile to the idea and were threatening to massacre the Negroes if they were put to work." Rather than risk their lives, the well-meaning official "whisked his charges unhurt but still unemployed back whence they had come." In July 1945 workers at the Todd-Johnson shipyard in Algiers went on strike after a black man was hired as a boilermaker's helper. Despite their desperate need for his skills, the company's owners fired the man and reassured white employees that they would not employ African Americans in any positions other than unskilled labor.[37]

Even when the entry of black people into formerly all-white workplaces was achieved peacefully, this did not imply acceptance of their right to equality. Complaints to the FEPC testify to the discrimination, harassment, and threats to their physical well-being that some African Americans faced every day on the job. Edith Pierce's official job title at the Port of Embarkation in New Orleans was "Junior Clerk Typist," but the amount of typing or other clerical tasks she received was "negligible." Instead, her supervisors assigned her to "messenger work and errands throughout the area of the Port." When Joseph Provost asked his foreman about obtaining a position as a tow-motor or tractor operator at the port, he was told that black people could not be employed in those jobs. Provost appealed to the officer in charge of his section, who agreed to allow several black workers to take the tests required for operating the machinery. In response, white operators recruited some white men from outside the port to learn the job and try out the same day. Subsequently, five of the new arrivals and none of the African Americans were hired. One of the white men later told Provost that they had decided to resign "rather than to have Negroes holding the same job as they and getting the same pay with them."[38]

While industrial workers sought to exclude African Americans from their terrain, plantation owners attempted to prevent black people from leaving theirs. In 1942 farmers and extension agents in the rural parishes complained of "serious and numerous" labor shortages during the harvest season because of the alternatives to cotton picking and cane cutting that were available.[39] As the demand for industrial workers increased, large numbers of black people abandoned rural areas for the army or defense jobs, and the money they sent home to their families enabled others to withdraw from the labor market as well.[40] For these reasons, white people in the plantation parishes resented the federal government's efforts to ensure equal opportunities for black people at least as much as those who lived in urban areas. In September 1942 the chairman of the Pointe Coupee Parish Civilian Defense Council complained to Governor Sam Jones that "from the very beginning of our preparedness move certain organized minorities have seized the opportunity to advance their causes, through unheard of wage rate increases and working conditions." He enclosed a resolution from the parish defense council suggesting that "the government in its struggle for existence should be less solicitous about the social gains made during recent years by a few groups, and exert its unhampered resources to the winning of the war."[41]

The same month, representatives of the nation's major agricultural organizations met in Washington, D.C., to devise a coordinated plan of attack against government intervention in the economy and new protections for the rights of workers. Leaders of the AFBF, the Grange, the National Coun-

Workers on a lunch break at Higgins shipyard, New Orleans, June 1943. African Americans were excluded from most defense industry jobs in the early phases of World War II, but once the pool of white workers was exhausted, employers were forced to hire black labor. LC-USW3-34429-D, Library of Congress, Washington, D.C.

cil of Farmer Cooperatives, and the National Cooperative Milk Producers' Federation discussed ways to defend the "business interests of farmers" from assaults by the Roosevelt "dictatorship." According to one source, "The general tone of the discussion was . . . that it is necessary for business men and 'business farmers' to block further administrative control of American business life whether in the farm, field or any other [area] and particularly to stop administration coddling of labor."[42]

Pressure from this powerful farm bloc persuaded Roosevelt to approve legislation in April 1943 that placed restrictions on the mobility of agricultural workers and empowered the Extension Service to assist in the recruitment of additional labor for those areas that were experiencing shortages. A labor stabilization plan went into effect in Louisiana at the end of that month. Under the new regulations, workers in "essential activities" like farming could not leave their jobs unless they obtained a "Statement of

Availability" from their employers, and they could not be hired for new positions unless they produced proof of their release. Though these obstacles were a potential hindrance to black migration, they were not entirely effective. Many farmworkers registered with employment services as truck drivers, mechanics, or other types of laborers without mentioning their agricultural backgrounds, enabling them to slip through the net. In addition, planters in northeastern Louisiana received a nasty shock when federal authorities designated their region a labor *surplus* area and began transporting workers to places deemed to be in greater need of their services. Congressman Charles McKenzie eventually managed to convince the meddling officials that his district could not spare any labor, and they agreed to stop encouraging workers to leave.[43]

At the same time, extension agents worked with parish advisory committees to devise local solutions to farm labor problems. Often these efforts involved encouraging or coercing black people to return to the plantations at harvest time to help gather the crops. Louisiana's state supervisor of extension work explained how the system worked in one rural community: county agents enlisted African American ministers to canvass

> every colored section of Monroe and West Monroe for six days.... The patriotic duty of every American to assist in the war effort was explained to each person visited, together with the need of getting this year's vitally important cotton crop out of the fields as quickly as possible. At first, many of the persons visited were reluctant to give their names as volunteer cotton pickers; others said they were willing to pick, although not physically able. Under the persuasive influence of their fellow-race members, however, reluctance was shortlived. Those who said they were not physically able to go to the fields, changed their minds.

One thousand cotton pickers, mostly women and children, eventually "volunteered" to help with the harvest.[44]

Although it is possible that the "persuasive influence" of extension agents and civic leaders inspired black workers to perform their patriotic duty, a more likely explanation was that they feared retaliation by white people if they did not comply. Local authorities who seemed unconcerned when white women declined to enter the workforce became incensed at the idea of black women doing the same. In April 1943 Alexandria mayor W. George Bowden invited employers to provide him with the names and addresses of black women who had quit their jobs "for no legitimate reason" and announced that he would force them back to work "or run them out of town personally." The same year, a report prepared by the Social Science Institute at Fisk University noted an increasing number of incidents of intimidation in the South, mostly involving agricultural and domestic workers. Its authors concluded that threats, violence, and the restrictive legislation embodied in the Farm Labor Program and local work-or-fight ordinances were aimed at forcing black people to continue working for "unwarrantedly low wages."[45]

In addition to seeking tighter control over the existing workforce, plantation owners initiated a campaign to import extra laborers into the state. In June 1943 Louisiana's Extension Service administrators reported that they had received "numerous requests as to the possibility of using war prisoners in the harvesting of crops," mostly from sugar growers. Local farm labor committees succeeded in gaining permission to set up prisoner-of-war camps in Calcasieu, Ouachita, Iberia, Ascension, Jefferson Davis, St. Charles, St. Mary, West Baton Rouge, and Madison Parishes, accommodating nearly four thousand workers. War prisoners were later brought into Pointe Coupee and St. Landry Parishes after extension agents concluded that labor shortages were likely. By 1944, twenty-six prisoner-of-war camps were operating throughout the state. Proponents of the camps insisted that the use of prisoners would not "impair wages, working conditions and employment opportunities or displace employed workers," but these claims were unrealistic. Planters' manipulation of the labor supply prevented farmworkers from increasing their bargaining power as much as they might have. As the county agent in Madison Parish reported, the prisoner-of-war camps "stabilized local labor considerably because the local labor knew that the p.ws. were available for farmers to use and if they did not do the job, farmers would get p.ws. to help them out."[46]

Though these actions went some way toward alleviating labor problems, agricultural employers remained dissatisfied. Ultimately, many planters adopted the more effective strategies of mechanization and crop diversification, enabling them to operate their plantations with fewer workers. Max McDonald reported from Madison Parish in 1945 that farmers were "becoming mechanical minded since there has been such a severe labor shortage." Farmers in the parish had not previously shown much interest in new machinery because of an abundance of cheap labor, McDonald explained, but with workers now in shorter supply they had "changed over rapidly from necessity." Newspapers and extension agents in other parishes noted that the use of tractors for plowing and planting cotton crops was spreading, and that many growers were experimenting with grain and livestock production, two enterprises that required less labor than cotton and were more easily mechanized. By 1950 cotton accounted for only 29 percent of the cropland harvested in the state, compared with 48 percent in 1930. In the following decade, the proportion fell to 20 percent, while hay crops, small grains, and legumes all increased their share.[47]

In the sugar parishes, planters began using weedkillers for cultivating and mechanical cane cutters for harvesting, greatly reducing their labor requirements. Sugar grower Arthur Lemann of Ascension Parish remembered the sweeping changes that occurred on his family's plantation during the war. Machines eliminated the need for one hundred workers who were normally hired during the harvest season, and the fifty people who had formerly been employed to weed grass from the cane gave way to chemical herbicides and aerial spraying. During the 1944 harvest season, Louisiana growers used 356 mechanical harvesters that did the work of 21,000 people. Department of Agriculture officials reported that the harvesters helped to ease the labor situation and eliminated the necessity of paying wages that were higher than the minimum required to receive federal subsidies. The next year, Iberville Parish extension agent R. J. Badeaux confirmed the trend toward mechanization, citing it as the "natural road" for plantation owners concerned with efficiency and economy.[48]

These developments accelerated the displacement of farm families from the land that had begun during the New Deal era. As in the decade from 1930 to 1940, the number of tractors in Louisiana almost doubled again between 1940 and 1945, increasing from 9,476 to 17,630. Correspondingly, the number of farm operators declined from 150,007 to 129,295, a decrease of 14 percent. The number of black farmers dropped by a slightly higher rate, from 59,584 to 49,131 (18 percent). As long as the armed forces and war industries stood ready to absorb these workers, the consequences were not catastrophic for African Americans (although they caused severe problems for many communities in later decades). Those who moved from farm to factory increased their incomes and achieved levels of independence from white people that most plantation workers could not hope to enjoy. Meanwhile, larger crop acreages and better prices for farm products meant that conditions for tenant families who remained on the land also improved. Between 1940 and 1945 black farm operators in the state increased the average value of their lands

Table 6.2 African American Farm Operators in Louisiana, 1940–1960

Tenure	1940		1950		1960	
	Number	Percentage	Number	Percentage	Number	Percentage
Owners	11,187	19	12,965	32	8,666	49
Managers	17	(-)ᵃ	22	(-)	13	(-)
Tenants	48,380	81	27,669	68	9,064	51
Total	59,584	100	40,656	100	17,743	100

SOURCE: Bureau of the Census, *United States Census of Agriculture: 1959, Volume 1: Counties, Part 35: Louisiana* (Washington, D.C.: GPO, 1961), 6.

ᵃ(-) indicates less than 0.5 percent.

and buildings by 38 percent, from $1,123 to $1,545. While tenancy declined, black farm ownership increased in the 1940s, reflecting the higher levels of prosperity that all farmers enjoyed during the war.[49] (See Table 6.2.)

As African Americans continued to gain economically, white Louisianans became increasingly alarmed. The sentiments expressed by many people revealed that their concerns stemmed from a much more complicated set of beliefs than the simple idea that black people were inferior. Some of the real fears underlying the commitment to white supremacy were voiced by a woman who complained about recent efforts to improve educational opportunities for African Americans, then stated, "I think they like to study; they're more ambitious than we are. . . . The government is giving 'em too much education. Builds 'em schools, colleges, and universities. They're supposed to be lower class than we are, aren't they? But they keep on educating them."[50] Government researchers investigating racial tensions in defense industries found white workers fearful that the war was "permanently destroying barriers against Negro competition" and likely to view the movement of African Americans into new occupations as a threat to their economic security.[51] Southern business owners who relied on racism to keep wages low for both white and black labor were among those who were most concerned about threats to the social order. Out of the various groups that made up the OWI's nationwide pool of correspondents, business leaders were the least supportive of equality. Their proposed solution to the problem of racial animosity was invariably to "*Keep the Negro in his place*, and, as a corollary, see that segregation is rigidly enforced."[52] These reports suggest that at least some people who sought to deny African Americans access to education, skilled jobs, and political participation did so not because they believed that black people lacked the requisite abilities, but because they knew the opposite to be true.

White insecurity frequently manifested itself in violence. In February 1943 white guards and workers at the Delta Shipbuilding Company in New Orleans dragged a black truck driver from his vehicle and beat him severely after he blew his horn at a group of white people who were obstructing his path. A year later the sheriff and deputies of New Iberia accorded similar treatment to a group of NAACP leaders who had helped to establish a black welding school in the town. Some of the worst attacks were directed against black people in the armed forces. In January 1942 twelve African Americans were shot during a riot that occurred near Camp Claiborne, and in August 1944 a soldier reported that local white people seemed determined to spark a repeat performance of that event. He had heard rumors that three black servicemen had recently been found dead in the area and stated, "Now right at this moment the woods surrounding the camp are swarming with Louisiana hoogies armed with rifles and shot guns even the little kids have 22 cal. rifles and B & B guns filled with anxiety to shoot a Negro soldier."[53] In 1943 a mob seized a soldier from his hospital bed in Camp Polk and hanged him for allegedly insulting a white woman. A few months later, in Beauregard Parish, four white men stopped to offer a black soldier a ride to the bus station, and when he got into their car they branded him on the face with a hot iron. One particularly disturbing incident occurred in March 1944, when Private Edward Green boarded a bus in Alexandria and sat down in the section reserved for white people. The bus driver told him to move to the back, and when Green refused, the white man pointed a gun at him and ordered him to get off the bus. Although Green complied with this request, the driver shot and killed him anyway. Members of the local branch of the NAACP reported to the national office that Green was the fourth or fifth black soldier killed by white people in the area since the beginning of the war.[54]

In some parishes, white civilians and officials openly prepared for a "race war." When Louisiana legislators authorized the formation of a state guard, the first places its chief officer decided to organize were areas "where there're lots of Negroes." G. P. Bullis, who represented Concordia Parish in the state legislature, wrote to the commander in January 1943 to request urgent action in establishing a company of the guard in Ferriday. "We feel that we especially need this guard, because we live in a section which has some sparcely settled areas; also four-fifths of our population are negroes," he explained. "This entire area is delta land, heavily populated with negroes, and a guard unit seems especially desirable here." A few months later, the mayor of Ferriday wrote to express similar sentiments, saying, "The state as a whole is going to need [the Home Guard] very badly, and especially will the sections having large negro populations, of which this community is one, need it." White people in several other parts of the state also believed violent uprisings by African Americans were imminent. "I think we're going to have race riots that are going to back everything else we've known off the board," and "I think our next war will be coming with the colored folks" were two of the comments noted by Edgar Schuler in his "Weekly Tensions Report" during March and April 1943.[55]

White Louisianans' fears were exaggerated but not completely unfounded. Between June 1942 and July 1943 their state was home to the "eighteen thousand bitter, frustrated, armed black men" who made up the U.S. Army's Ninety-third Division, the largest concentration of African American soldiers in the country. These troops were acutely aware of the lynchings, riots, and violent attacks on black people that were occurring throughout the nation, and they had experienced similar treatment themselves. During their stay in Louisiana Nelson Peery and a small group of other soldiers secretly obtained and stockpiled ammunition, intending to fight back against white violence. The men contemplated going to the assistance of African Americans in nearby Beaumont, Texas, when rioting broke out there in June 1943 but decided it was too risky. After intelligence agents in the War Department learned of the conspiracy, military commanders quickly decided to transfer the division out of the South. A few weeks after the Texas riots, the men of the Ninety-third left Louisiana bound for the isolated Mojave Desert in California.[56]

Based on reports that reached them from Louisiana and elsewhere, government researchers discerned the existence of a "growing and militant minority of Negroes" who were "increasingly talking of a resort to violent action to maintain their rights." The federal government had done nothing to prevent violence against African Americans, leaving many to conclude that their only recourse was to defend themselves.[57] The *Baltimore Afro-American* editorialized in 1944, "If the Army can't or won't protect soldiers in the Southern camps, has anybody objections to soldiers protecting themselves? . . . They practice with jiujitsu, knives, revolvers, machine guns, tanks and cannons, and then sit on a bus seat while a driver fills them full of lead."[58]

In the minds of most black people, fighting back against white violence had never entailed much moral anguish or required justification. In the 1940s, the fact that Americans had taken up arms to fight a racist regime in Germany that closely resembled the racist regime in Louisiana provided an even more powerful rationale for using armed self-defense. John Henry Scott of East Carroll Parish explained, "I do not consider violence protecting yourself, no more than the soldiers out there where they fighting war. . . . Christ say put your sword down if you're fighting for his cause but when you going to fight for democracy why you pick your gun up. So if I could pick my gun up to go across the ocean to fight for democracy naturally I could pick my gun up to protect my democracy at home. And I wouldn't call that violence."[59]

Other black Louisianans seem to have shared Scott's views. A young man who was attacked by a white soldier after refusing to give up his seat while waiting at a first-aid station shot his assailant in self-defense. In a letter to his mother, he declared: "I am not going to stand for any misstreatment. After all I didn't ask to come into the Army. And after I have been put here, I won't be treated like a dog." He had told officers who suggested he ought to show white people more respect, "If we were good enough to fight their war for them we were entitled to a littel respect too." In a similar incident, Private Oliver W. Harris Jr. of Tallulah was arrested for aggravated assault against a hardware store owner while on leave from the army shortly after the end of the war. An account given to the NAACP by his wife explained that Harris had ordered a piece of tubing from the store that he intended to use to wire their home so they could have electric lights installed. When he went to pick up the tubing, he found that it had been cut too long. The manager of the store, R. L. Betz, told him that he would have to pay for all of the tubing, and Harris argued with the man, saying that he did not think he should have to pay for all of it because the store had made the mistake. "Mr. Betz then became very angry and struck my husband," Cora Mae Harris stated. "My husband then picked up a shovel and proceeded to go to work on Mr. Betz, in the meantime, V. R. Dace, white clerk rushed up and struck my husband with a pipe. My husband managed to take the pipe away from Mr. Dace and work on him." The white men both received severe cuts in the head.[60]

Taking note of such incidents, government analysts, civil rights activists, and other observers warned that unless the federal government showed some willingness to eliminate racial discrimination and safeguard black people's citizenship rights, disaster could result. Early in the war a leader of the MOWM predicted, "We are slowly moving into one of the most bloody national race riots in history. If the administration doesn't give Negroes equal rights we are going to run into it sure as hell."[61] Throughout the conflict liberals in the Roosevelt administration repeatedly urged the president to take decisive action on civil rights, including better enforcement of Executive Order 8802, equal treatment in the armed forces, and the inclusion of African Americans in defense programs. Roosevelt heeded this advice to whatever extent seemed possible without unduly angering powerful southern Democrats in Congress. The result was a series of limited concessions designed to reassure black Americans while attempting to avoid interference with the South's cherished racial traditions.[62]

Roosevelt refused requests by civil rights groups to fully integrate the armed forces, but in March 1943 the army ended its practice of constructing separate facilities for white and black soldiers and issued directives prohibiting the designation of camp amenities by race. The following year, the president issued an executive order mandating the desegregation of all officers' clubs, service clubs, and other social facilities at army posts, although he modified it with a clause allowing individual commanders to disregard the order if they believed that its peaceful implementation was not possible. None of these measures succeeded in eliminating discrimination against African Americans in the camps. In addition, neither the federal government nor the army exercised much control over white civilians in the South, and violent attacks on black servicemen and women continued through the end of the war. As a "disgusted Negro Trooper" noted when African Americans at Camp Claiborne were threatened by white mobs in 1944, "This camp isn't run by government regulations its controlled by the state of Louisiana and white civilians."[63]

Though federal authorities had thus far failed to prevent violence against African Americans, there were indications that they were becoming more willing to intervene in this area. Since 1939 the Civil Liberties Unit within the Department of Justice had been working on developing ways of using the Constitution and other federal laws to better protect the civil rights of individuals. Through careful study of the legislation, prosecution of court cases, and development of legal precedents, its staff worked to strengthen the government's ability to bring southern lynch mobs and other offenders to justice. These efforts received further impetus when Roosevelt appointed Francis Biddle to the attorney general's office in August 1941. Biddle had expressed a commitment to upholding Americans' civil liberties, and the appointment received strong support from black leaders. In February 1942 the attorney general took the unprecedented action of ordering a federal investigation into the murder of a black man by a crowd of white people in Missouri. Three years later the Justice Department's civil rights section brought charges against law enforcement officers in Georgia who had administered a fatal beating to a black prisoner in their custody. Neither action resulted in convictions, but they revealed a change in attitude on the part of officials in Washington that seemed an encouraging sign.[64]

By far the most significant development of the war years was the Supreme Court's decision to outlaw the system of white-only primary elections in the South. In states where the Democratic Party was assured victory in any contest with Republicans, the only time voters had the opportunity to participate meaningfully in the political process was during the primary elections for Democratic candidates. Party officials argued that theirs was a private organization entitled to restrict its membership to white people. The Court's opinion in *Smith v. Allwright* (1944) rejected that view, stating that political parties were public entities and could not discriminate against African Americans. The decision removed a major obstacle to black voting in the South and encouraged mass voter registration efforts by the NAACP and other civil rights groups after the war.[65]

National political developments continued to favor African Americans through the end of the decade. The emerging Cold War with the Soviet Union and the need to seem credible as leaders of the "free" world meant that national elites remained susceptible to pressure from black Americans to ensure justice and equality within the United States. On taking office after Roosevelt's death in April 1945, President Harry Truman worked to maintain black people's support for his administration by taking several actions on civil rights. In the first year of his administration he advocated establishing a permanent FEPC, ordered the Justice Department to investigate the murders of several black people by white supremacists in Georgia, and appointed a committee to study the problem of racism. In October 1947 the President's Committee on Civil Rights presented its report, *To Secure These Rights*, urging the government to take sweeping measures to eliminate racial discrimination. Truman spoke on the issue of civil rights before Congress in January 1948, endorsing many of the committee's recommendations for action. He later issued executive orders to establish a Fair Employ-ment Board within the Civil Service Commission and to desegregate the armed forces.[66]

Truman's actions precipitated an open split within the Democratic Party between its northern liberal and southern reactionary wings. After a bitter struggle at the party's 1948 national convention over the adoption of a civil rights plank and the nomination of Truman as presidential candidate, dis-senting southern "Dixiecrats" organized the States' Rights Party to contest the coming elections. Their actions failed to prevent the reelection of the president, and Truman carried all the southern states except Louisiana, Mississippi, South Carolina, and Alabama. An NAACP newsletter stated optimistically that the election results proved that most white Americans supported civil rights and were prepared to see black people treated fairly at last.[67]

Whether or not this assessment was accurate, in the late 1940s African Americans were better placed than ever before to engage in organized, sustained attacks on white supremacy. The ideological implications of the war, increased economic opportunity and prosperity, and the federal govern-ment's gradual shift toward accepting its responsibility to ensure justice for all Americans suggested that the post–World War II era would bring important developments in the freedom struggle. Both white and black ana-lysts pointed to the gains African Americans had made and predicted far-reaching consequences. Quite simply, as one writer stated, the nation's black citizens were "not content to return to serfdom in the South, or to second-class social and economic status in the industrial North."[68] White Louisi-anans who viewed these developments with trepidation were right to be afraid. In the next two decades, many of their worst fears were realized.

7

The Social Order Have Changed:
The Emergence of the Civil
Rights Movement, 1945–1960

Nora Windon, the registrar of voters in Rapides Parish, must have been alarmed by the letter she received from the leaders of the Alexandria branch of the NAACP in August 1946. The petitioners pointed out that the recent Supreme Court decision in *Smith v. Allwright* allowed for federal charges to be brought against officials who interfered with the right of any person to register to vote and enclosed statements from several people accusing her of violating the law. "You do not seem to realize that the social order have changed," they stated. "Over ten thousand Negro men and women died in World War II for 'World Democracy,' when you are denying [it] at home. . . . This local branch of over five hundred members are requesting you to eliminate these practices when the books open again next month, when large number will appear to register."[1]

Encouraged by the federal government's tentative support for civil rights and empowered by their improved economic status, black activists in Louisiana launched their strongest assault yet on white supremacy in the postwar years. Local NAACP branches, fraternal orders, teachers' associations, voters' leagues, and labor unions worked together to demand an end to discrimination in education, voting, and employment. White opponents countered these efforts with state repression, economic reprisals, intimidation, and accusations that civil rights activity was communist-inspired. These attacks hindered but did not halt black people's march toward equality. In the late 1950s and early 1960s, sympathetic media coverage helped to elevate African Americans' battles against injustice to national prominence, transforming local struggles into a nationwide movement that had the support of thousands of white as well as black people.

There is some disagreement among historians concerning the impact of World War II on the freedom struggle. Scholars who see the 1940s as a turning point in African American history and the catalyst for the civil rights movement have recently been taken to task by analysts who point out continuities between the prewar and postwar decades.[2] White opposition to the struggle, for example, hardly abated at all, despite the discrediting of racist theories that resulted from the worldwide revulsion at Nazi atrocities. Racial violence in the United States intensified as white supremacists fought to maintain their dominant position in society, and reform efforts that had been gathering strength in the previous decade were stymied by resurgent conservatism during the early years of the Cold War.[3] The FEPC and the civil rights measures proposed by the Truman administration fell victim to the usual coalition of southern Democrats and business-oriented Republicans that, according to one congressman, had "been behind every reactionary movement, and . . . opposed to all liberal, forward-looking legislation" presented to lawmakers in previous decades.[4]

Cumulatively, however, the war brought changes to the nation and to the lives of its black inhabitants that should not be underestimated. This was especially the case in the rural South, where mechanization eroded the power relationships between white landlords and black tenants, in the process weakening one of the chief means of maintaining white supremacy. Although the ideological impact of the war on both white and black people has probably been too heavily emphasized, its economic effect on African Americans has not been emphasized enough. An examination of the early civil rights movement in Louisiana suggests that there were strong links between World War II and the emergence of an organized, mass protest movement in the 1950s and 1960s.

Significantly, in Louisiana and elsewhere, black war veterans played prominent roles in the freedom struggle in the second half of the twentieth century.[5] As African American leaders had predicted and white Louisianans had feared, black people's experiences in the armed forces broadened their horizons and made them less willing to accept discrimination. Many recalled military service as a defining moment in their lives. Harrison Brown was stationed overseas during the presidential election of 1944, when black as well as white soldiers received ballot papers allowing them the opportunity to participate. After mailing in his ballot, however, he received a letter from officials in Louisiana telling him that he was not allowed to vote. Disgusted by the hypocrisy of a nation that expected him to risk death to protect it but refused to treat him as a citizen, he returned home "determined to try to do something about it." A. Z. Young of Bogalusa experienced a similar revelation. After serving three and a half years in the U.S. Army and spending 168 days on the front line, he concluded that he should be entitled to the same rights as white Americans. "This is where the turning point actually came in my life," he stated, "where I was willing to stand up and to fight not only for myself, but for my people, wherever they be." Both these men and many others who shared their experiences became key participants in struggles against white supremacy in their communities.[6]

The heightened sense of injustice that infected thousands of black people as a result of their participation in World War II was an important factor in the 1940s and 1950s, but this alone could not have sparked the mass movement of the postwar period. African Americans had emerged from World War I feeling much the same way, but attempts to engage in organized protest activity following that war could not be sustained. An important difference between the 1920s and the 1940s was that the political economy of the South was fundamentally altered after World War II. Large numbers of black people had escaped or were displaced from agricultural labor, making them more independent of white people. By 1950 the proportion of black workers engaged in agriculture had dropped to 27 percent, and of those who were still farmers, a higher percentage owned their own land. At least a few observers realized that the demise of farm tenancy was likely to have significant consequences. In 1947 extension agent Norvel Thames of Tensas Parish wrote in his annual report: "As through the rest of the South . . . the agriculture of the parish is in the throes of revolution in its farming type and system. . . . Though the writer has no crystal it appears that this change will be far reaching in both its economical and social phases."[7]

Other white Louisianans also recognized that the dislodgment of thousands of black people from plantations where they had been under tight control had potentially serious implications. Early on, some analysts perceived the need to move the state away from its traditional focus on agriculture toward a more diversified economy so that surplus laborers could be absorbed. Chambers of commerce and civic leaders encouraged industri-

Cultivators with mules and drivers (above) and cultivating sugarcane with tractor and driver (below), Schriever, Louisiana, June 1940. These two photographs illustrate the dramatic reduction in labor needs that accompanied the mechanization of agriculture, which had important consequences for rural southern communities and for the black freedom struggle in the second half of the twentieth century. LC-USF34-55260-D and LC-USF34-54273-D, Library of Congress, Washington, D.C.

alization throughout the 1940s and 1950s, emphasizing the advantages of cheap utility rates, low wages, and tax exemptions to persuade investors to build factories and processing plants in their parishes.[8] In February 1948 a group of farmers and business owners from eleven plantation parishes formed the Louisiana Delta Council to develop collaboration between the agricultural and business interests of the region. Modeled on a similar organization created ten years earlier by Mississippi Delta planters, the council listed among its objectives "To cooperate with all interested groups in establishing uniform policies relating to labor and its costs" and "To jealously guard and protect our area from discriminatory and unfair legislation and from any predatory encroachment whatever." Council members aimed to perpetuate racial inequality in the new economy and to fight attempts by the federal government, labor unions, or civil rights groups to interfere with the social order.[9]

With northern workers rapidly unionizing and labor costs increasing, industrialists needed little persuasion to build new plants or relocate existing ones in the South. Between 1947 and 1954 Louisiana gained 632 new manufacturing establishments, increasing industrial employment for the state by 9 percent. The area around Baton Rouge became a center for chemical and petroleum processing plants owned by giant corporations like the Dow Chemical Company, providing employment opportunities for displaced farmworkers from nearby rural parishes. By 1954 East Baton Rouge Parish had 142 industrial enterprises that employed 18,882 people. Another 104 manufacturing plants located in neighboring Ascension, Iberville, Pointe Coupee, and Livingston Parishes provided nearly two thousand more jobs.[10]

New industries appeared in other rural areas as well. In 1942 the Illinois-based Princeville Canning Company began contracting with West Feliciana farmers to grow sweet potatoes, and three years later its owners decided to build a cannery in the parish that employed around 150 people during the peak season. These developments benefited black sharecroppers, who reportedly were "astonished to receive from sixty to eighty dollars from an average acre of sweet potatoes" after being accustomed to earning only twenty-five dollars an acre from cotton. In the 1950s the Crown-Zellerbach Corporation constructed a new paper mill in St. Francisville, giving an added boost to the economic life of the parish.[11]

Throughout the state, the lumber industry expanded rapidly both during and after World War II, fueled by the demand for new housing and other buildings. In 1954 every Louisiana parish except Cameron, Plaquemines, and West Baton Rouge had at least one enterprise producing lumber or wood products, with the northern parishes of Jackson, Ouachita, Rapides, and Winn each reporting more than forty. Although some of the smaller, family-owned operations remained, the trend after World War II was toward larger companies with their own sawmills and processing facilities. These mills were subject to federal minimum wage laws and other legislation protecting workers, offering employees a better chance of earning a decent living than had existed in the early twentieth century.[12]

Economic diversification had some positive effects for African Americans. The incomes of many black people increased in the decades after the war, with new nonagricultural industries contributing to higher living standards for rural families.[13] Yet the lower wages that black workers received compared with their white counterparts, lack of opportunities for promotion, and other discriminatory treatment revealed that most white Louisianans were prepared to allow only limited advancement for African Americans. The owners of newly established industries had as much to gain by perpetuating racism as did the older plantation elite, so they generally adapted willingly to traditional southern practices.[14] African American farmers who produced sweet potatoes for the Princeville Canning Company had their yields weighed on different scales from the white contractors, and the inaccurate readings taken from the Jim Crow apparatus meant that they consistently earned less from their crops. The company also gave first preference to white farmers in supplying the crates used for transporting potatoes during peak production times. As a result, black growers often missed their contracted delivery dates and were penalized accordingly. Princeville had a contract with the U.S. government to supply canned sweet potatoes to the army, and in 1958 its St. Francisville plant came under federal investigation for failing to pay workers the wages specified in its contract or to meet the required health and safety standards. Substandard and discriminatory conditions also prevailed at Crown-Zellerbach's paper-processing plants in Bogalusa and St. Francisville, where white and black workers had separate union locals; used segregated bathrooms, water fountains, and other facilities; and were promoted along separate lines of progression that ensured that African Americans were always confined to the lower-paying jobs. As a result of such practices, many black people failed to share in the increasing prosperity that other Americans enjoyed after World War II. Dilapidated houses, outdoor toilets, open sewers, and malnourished, poorly clothed children remained a feature of the landscape of rural Louisiana well into the second half of the twentieth century.[15]

A more encouraging postwar development was the implementation of the

Servicemen's Readjustment Act of 1944. The "GI Bill of Rights," as it came to be called, rewarded Americans who had served in the armed forces and their auxiliaries by granting them a wide range of benefits that included a weekly allowance to ease the transition back into civilian life, grants for education and training, preference for civil service jobs, and access to low-interest federal loans to buy houses, farms, or businesses. Government subsidies gave millions of working-class veterans opportunities that most could not have dreamed of before the war. A stipend of fifty dollars a month plus up to five hundred dollars a year to pay for tuition fees and books enabled many people to receive a college education that they would not otherwise have been able to afford. Better jobs and a higher standard of living followed, greatly enlarging the nation's middle class. By 1950 one-third of the population of the United States had benefited in some way from the GI Bill, with nearly eight million veterans taking advantage of the educational benefits alone.[16]

Civil rights leaders recognized the potential contribution that these programs could make to the freedom struggle and worked to ensure that black veterans knew of their rights under the act. African Americans often encountered the same kind of discrimination that local administrators of New Deal agencies had practiced in the 1930s.[17] To combat efforts by white officials to deny benefits to black veterans, the *Louisiana Weekly* suggested, "Our churches, schools, labor unions, civic organizations and press should keep abreast with veterans' information and provide means of getting it to the veteran." In March 1946 activists organized a two-day conference at Dillard University to focus on black veterans' problems. Speakers encouraged those in attendance to take advantage of the GI Bill, and a Citizens' Committee on Services to Veterans was created to provide follow-up advice and assistance to Louisiana's returning soldiers. The NAACP established a special Veterans Affairs division to make sure the leaders of local branches knew about the GI Bill and could tell members how to apply for aid. The Southern Regional Council, an organization of white and black liberals formed in 1944, also helped to disseminate information. In September 1946 the council had between eight and ten African American veterans traveling through the South, visiting the administrators of veterans' services in small towns and rural areas to ensure that black people received their fair share of benefits. According to the *Louisiana Weekly*, these efforts resulted in "a good many of the service officials opening up real opportunities to the increased applications submitted by Negro veterans."[18]

Those opportunities had profound consequences for black people who gained access to them. The experiences of Nelson Cyprian mirrored those of many others whose lives were changed by the GI Bill. Born in Tangipahoa Parish in 1912, Cyprian completed five grades of school and then had to give up his education so he could work and help support his family. He held various low-paying jobs ranging from farmhand to utility man before joining the army in 1942. After being discharged, he worked as a truck driver and warehouseman for a few years and in 1949 began attending night classes at a local high school. He earned his high school equivalency diploma in April 1951 and in June entered Southern University, graduating with a bachelor of arts degree three years later. Cyprian was then employed as an adult education teacher at his former high school. "My present income is more than twice the income before completing high school and college," he wrote in a letter to the state superintendent of education. "I can now provide a more wholesome life for my wife and children for the rest of my life."[19]

Harrison Brown's journey from a sharecropping home in Tensas Parish to ownership of a successful business in Tallulah also owed much to the GI Bill. Like Cyprian, Brown had only an elementary school education when he entered the army in 1942. He was trained for a clerical position and sent to Iran, an experience that enhanced both his knowledge about the world and his material wealth. Military service enabled him "to meet a lot of different people, and talk, and learn," he recalled. More importantly, the money he earned was deposited safely in an army bank account instead of being given over to a landlord. "It enabled me to see what it meant to be independent," he said. "And use my little earnings to my advantage." After leaving the army, Brown spent a year studying at Tyler Texas Barber College in Jackson, Mississippi, worked for another man for a while, and eventually established his own barber shop in Tallulah. Brown remembered how the opportunities provided by his veterans' benefits set him apart from the older barber who had employed him. After many years of working, the other man owned nothing, whereas Brown was just beginning his career and already he could afford to buy a house. The army and the GI Bill, he said, "enabled you to put your money where it would help you."[20]

Other federal programs also continued to have a positive impact on the lives of some African Americans. In 1949 a Department of Agriculture bulletin reported on the success of a family of tenant farmers in Washington Parish whose local extension agent had encouraged them to shift from cotton to dairy farming, and who now owned sixty acres of land, a new home, and twenty-four cows that brought in a gross income of five thousand dollars per year.[21] Extension work with three generations of farmers in the Elloise family of Pointe Coupee Parish yielded similar results. Income from the family farm provided Leroy Elloise with a good living in the 1950s, and it enabled his brother and two of his sisters to pursue careers in education while a third sister trained as a registered nurse. William Minor and his wife were tenant farmers in West Feliciana Parish in the 1930s and so poor, they said, that "when we were married in 1937 the preacher didn't charge us; and besides, took up a $6 collection for us." With the help of black extension agent Aldero Stevenson, the Minors increased their cotton and sweet potato yields and earned enough income to buy their own farm. By 1960 they owned 157 acres of land and were planning to purchase more.[22]

Martin Williams's economic progress was also linked to assistance provided by the federal government. After learning the drycleaning trade at a CCC camp in the 1930s, Williams moved to Tallulah and established his own business. In 1950 he took out a low-interest loan from the Federal Land Bank and used it to buy his first piece of land. With the help of a friend who worked for the Agricultural Soil Conservation Service (ASCS) (successor to the AAA), Williams improved the land and leased it to some of his employees. The income he earned from drycleaning and renting his farm enabled Williams to keep buying, improving, and selling land very profitably throughout the second half of the twentieth century.[23]

The significance of these stories is not just that they depict an enlarging middle class within the African American population. They also reveal a change in its nature. Unlike many members of the black elite in the early twentieth century, these people achieved economic success without the assistance of local planters and politicians. Although some of the older community leaders did become involved in the postwar freedom movement, most still preferred not to jeopardize their jobs or patronage. Neither could the dwindling number of black Louisianans who continued to live and work within the repressive confines of the plantations become involved in civil rights activity without risking eviction or other reprisals. However, very often it was *former* sharecropping and tenant families who led the struggle in Louisiana's rural communities. The life histories of individual activists like Harrison Brown and Martin Williams reflect transformative influences that were at work on a large scale. By 1950 black people were employed in a much more diverse range of occupations than they had held in the early twentieth century. Losses in agricultural and domestic employment were matched by almost identical gains in industrial employment, clerical and service jobs, and unskilled labor. (See Table 7.1.) Another important development was the decline in the number of women and children who had to work to help support their families. In 1910, 67 percent of African Americans over ten years old were in the labor force. Four decades later that figure had dropped to 41 percent.[24] Whether former plantation workers became farm owners, business owners, factory operatives, students, homemakers, or unemployed, their lives were no longer as tightly controlled by white people. In this development lay the seeds of a mass movement to demand social change.

The basis for unified, organized activity had long existed in African Americans' churches, fraternal orders, and societies. In the decades following World War II, these institutions were instrumental in providing financial support, publicity, volunteers, and meeting halls for civil rights groups throughout the state. East Carroll Parish activist John Henry Scott belonged to several fraternal orders and was encouraged to join the NAACP by the pastor of his church. Black lawyer A. P. Tureaud of New Orleans held administrative positions in both the Knights and Ladies of Peter Claver and the NAACP and used his contacts in the two organizations to encourage protest activity in some rural parishes. The Knights and other fraternal orders cooperated closely with the NAACP in its efforts to eliminate discrimination in education, voting, and employment. In Madison Parish, members of the Improved Benevolent Order of Elks of the World took the lead in establishing a local voters' league and an NAACP branch in the 1940s. Headed by Zelma Wyche, a war veteran and barber, the group included Martin Williams, Harrison Brown, and several others who had served in World War II and now owned businesses. Moses Williams joined both the Elks and the voters' league when he moved to Tallulah to take a job in a tire repair shop in 1952. After his employer fired him because of his civil rights activism, he built his own tire shop from scrap materials and went into business for himself.[25]

Higher incomes and payment in cash instead of scrip or "furnish" meant that many more people than previously could spare the few dollars a year that it cost to join civil rights organizations. But participation was not limited to those who were well off. Local activist Earnestine Brown remembered that all kinds of people became involved in the Madison Parish voters' league, including many who were poor and uneducated. Members might have lacked formal schooling, she said, but they "had some intelligence, you

Table 7.1 African American Employment in Louisiana, 1940–1960

Occupation	1940		1950		1960	
	Number	%	Number	%	Number	%
Farmers and farm managers	59,980	20	34,860	13	9,427	3
Farm laborers	42,498	15	24,875	9	17,069	6
Farm laborers (unpaid family members)	24,933	9	11,158	4	1,519	1
Domestic service workers	59,619	20	40,783	15	55,455	19
Service workers (outside private homes)	21,345	7	33,869	12	45,654	16
Nonfarm laborers	41,405	14	50,925	19	47,413	17
Clerical and sales workers	3,379	1	6,436	2	9,546	3
Operatives and kindred workers	23,453	8	39,639	15	51,164	18
Craft workers and supervisors	7,687	3	13,386	5	16,098	6
Professional and semi-professional workers	6,010	2	8,647	3	13,444	5
Nonfarm proprietors, managers, and officials	2,137	1	4,260	2	3,935	1
Occupation not reported	1,084	(-)[a]	3,782	1	13,700	5
Total	293,530	100	272,620	100	284,424	100

SOURCES: Bureau of the Census, *Sixteenth Census of the United States: 1940, Population, Volume 3: The Labor Force, Part 3: Iowa–Montana* (Washington, D.C.: GPO, 1943), 235–36, 239, *A Report of the Seventeenth Decennial Census of the United States, Census of Population: 1950, Volume 2: Characteristics of the Population, Part 18: Louisiana* (Washington, D.C.: GPO, 1952), 204–6, and *Eighteenth Decennial Census of the United States, Census of Population: 1960, Volume 1: Characteristics of the Population, Part 20: Louisiana* (Washington, D.C.: GPO, 1963), 378–80.

[a](-) indicates less than 0.5 percent.

know—they might not have been making a lot of money, but they had sense enough to be a member of an organization."[26]

The composition of local NAACP branches also reflected the participation of working-class and rural poor African Americans in the movement. Laborers made up the majority of those who belonged to an NAACP branch in the Iberville Parish town of Carville in 1946. Out of sixty-two people who established a branch in Pointe Coupee Parish in the 1950s, sixty gave their occupation as either "labor" or "house-wife." Other NAACP members in Louisiana worked as farmers, carpenters, mechanics, clerks, mill hands, service station attendants, bus drivers, and domestics. Such people were the driving force behind the organization at the local level. At a leadership training conference for Louisiana and Texas members that was held in 1945, one man stated, "I find that it is people who are *not* doctors, ministers, teachers and the other so-called 'big shots' are the ones who do the job. It's the masses who really work."[27]

At least a few NAACP members had been involved in the LFU in the 1930s, and those links might have been stronger were it not for the migrations and other disruptions that accompanied World War II.[28] Resolutions adopted at the state conference of branches in October 1947 reiterated and expanded on many of the demands made by the LFU a decade earlier. They included equal educational and employment opportunities for black people, federal protection of their civil rights, the extension of minimum wage and social security legislation to agricultural workers, rent controls to enable poor people to afford decent housing, and repeal of the antilabor Taft-Hartley Act.[29]

As in the past, one of the most important goals of Louisiana activists was gaining better educational facilities for black children. Throughout the 1940s local NAACP branches and citizens' groups supported the LCTA's efforts to force parish officials to pay African American teachers the same salaries as white teachers when their qualifications were comparable. The NAACP had been working on this issue since 1936, when its lawyers filed and won their first salary equalization case in Montgomery County, Maryland. It was a difficult task, hindered by the necessity of tackling each local school board individually, intimidation of plaintiffs and lawyers, and teachers' fears of losing their jobs if they became involved in lawsuits. Despite these obstacles, by 1941 the NAACP had succeeded in equalizing salaries throughout the state of Maryland and in several counties in Virginia and Kentucky. At the request of local teachers' associations in Georgia, Alabama, Texas, South

Carolina, and Louisiana, the organization extended the campaign to the Deep South.[30]

The black educators who led the struggle for equal pay in Louisiana were perhaps emboldened by a 1936 teacher tenure law that ensured their job security after a three-year probationary period.[31] In addition, other employment opportunities that were available in the 1940s may have lessened teachers' fears of being fired.[32] Strong support from community members who provided financial aid and the backing of a national organization like the NAACP also helped to strengthen the teachers' resolve.[33] For a brief period during this decade, some black teachers displayed considerable determination and courage in demanding an end to discrimination. Their efforts were eventually rewarded, but only after a long fight that brought much suffering and took many casualties. Not surprisingly, given the costs of the salary equalization campaign, in later decades black teachers were much more reluctant to become involved in civil rights work.

The NAACP won its first Louisiana case against the Orleans Parish school board in June 1942, and a few months later a group of parents and teachers in Iberville Parish enlisted A. P. Tureaud's help in gaining equal pay for black educators there. In February 1943 their leading organizer, W. W. Harleaux, informed Tureaud that the teachers were meeting that month and that they hoped to be ready to bring a lawsuit against the school board soon. Tureaud did not have to wait long. In April, after receiving no response from parish officials to a petition that the group had presented earlier in the year, the chairman of the citizens' committee wrote to Tureaud saying, "I think the School Board has had ample time for reply to the petition concerning the case. Please take necessary steps to prosecute our foe as soon as possible. WE WANT ACTION!"[34]

Soon after the Iberville activists decided to take legal action against the parish, there were some discouraging developments on the salary equalization front. A lawsuit filed against the Jefferson Parish school board resulted in the dismissal of its plaintiff for "willful neglect of duty," and in June 1943 the state board of education adopted a resolution authorizing school boards to establish salary schedules that considered the "merit" and "responsibility" of individual teachers, providing a loophole for continued discrimination even if the courts ruled in favor of equalization. Despite these setbacks, White Castle school principal Wiley B. McMillon agreed to act as lead plaintiff in a lawsuit against the Iberville Parish school board in March 1944.[35]

The school board's first response was to try to have the case dismissed.

Early in April its lawyers filed a brief claiming, among other things, that McMillon's motives were "'political' rather than 'personal,'" and that he had no more right to sue on behalf of all the teachers in the parish than he had to represent all the "Eskimos of the Arctic, or the Negroes of Africa." Federal district court judge Wayne G. Borah rejected the motion. When the school board failed to file a response to the judge's decision within the ten-day time limit, McMillon's attorneys claimed victory by default.[36] The school board indicated its intention to circumvent equalization in July 1944, when it announced new salary guidelines allowing for the assessment of teachers according to education, experience, merit, and responsibility. Under the merit system, administrators could consider factors such as "temperament," "character and dependability," "habits, and so on" in deciding the amount of remuneration. When the new schedule was implemented, not one of the forty-four black teachers in the parish was rated higher than a C, and only four achieved that level. Thirty received a rating of D, and the remaining ten were rated E. Conversely, all of the white teachers except one received an A or a B.[37]

Black teachers rejected the merit system, and negotiations began between the NAACP attorneys and the school board's lawyers to work out a settlement of the case that would satisfy both parties. White officials refused to abandon the merit system, however, and the teachers refused to accept it, leading to an impasse. In January 1945 African American leaders met with parish and state education officials in a series of conferences to discuss the equalization issue. Black representatives made clear their opposition to any system that allowed subjective judgments of "character" or "temperament" to affect teachers' salaries. Iberville Parish school superintendent Linus Terrebonne was unwilling to compromise, but his colleagues, fearing further lawsuits, were more amenable. On 23 January both sides agreed on a five-year plan to improve the quality of education for all children in Louisiana. The resolutions adopted included the equalization of salaries for all teachers for equal services rendered, the provision of adequate buildings and facilities, and a nine-month school term for every child. A. P. Tureaud agreed not to file any more salary equalization suits until the state legislature had had time to consider the group's proposals and to act on them. The resolutions were also to be submitted to the court in the McMillon case as the basis of an agreement for a consent decree.[38]

For a while it seemed that some real progress was being made, but at a meeting in February between the judge and lawyers for both sides in the

Iberville Parish case the defendants tried once again to have the merit system included in the proposed agreement. Tureaud rejected the idea, and when the teachers' final offer was in turn rejected by the school board, the matter was returned to the courts. A decision in favor of the school board seemed unlikely, so parish officials turned to intimidation of the plaintiffs in an attempt to prevent equalization. Toward the end of July, eleven junior teachers involved in the lawsuit received notice that their services were no longer needed. At the same time, the school board began proceedings to remove Wiley McMillon from his position as principal of White Castle School by charging him with incompetence, dishonesty, and willful neglect of duty. McMillon was later suspended after appearing before a hearing of the board.[39]

African Americans in Iberville Parish were outraged. Instead of being cowed by the reprisals, they responded by sending a petition to the school board demanding not just equal salaries for their teachers, but the equalization of all educational facilities for black children in the parish: the same quality of buildings that were provided for white children, the same kinds of courses in both elementary and high schools that were provided for white children, a school term of nine months as provided for white children, the same teacher-student ratios that existed in white schools, and bus transportation for black children as provided for white children. "This is the answer of the Negroes of that community to the reprisals taken by Terrebonne, the superintendent," wrote Tureaud in a letter to one of his colleagues.[40]

Black people from all over the parish attended a mass meeting held in September, where they listened to a speech by NAACP special counsel Thurgood Marshall. Arriving in cars, trucks, and wagons, they packed a local church and spilled out of its confines, leaving several hundred people standing outside listening at the windows. "The[y] all agreed to support the fight to have the teachers reinstated and are backing an action to be filed to compel the school board to equalize *all* facilities for education," Marshall reported later. "If the superintendent wants to fight we will give him one. Despite the fact that he fired teachers and threatened others all the older teachers still in his employ were present at our meeting last night . . . how is that?"[41]

Local and national civil rights organizations worked to find other employment for those who had lost their jobs while negotiating with the school board's lawyers to have the teachers reinstated. But progress was slow, and Tureaud was unable to provide much reassurance that justice would ultimately prevail. In April 1946 he told one of the fired teachers that the NAACP was doing its best but advised her not to be too hopeful and to take a job in another parish if she was offered one. In August, the judge in the McMillon case, Adrian Caillouet, suggested that Tureaud might have to find another plaintiff, since McMillon had been suspended from his position. Tureaud worried that replacing McMillon could present problems, because by this stage the Iberville teachers seemed thoroughly demoralized by the amount of time it was taking to get anything done. He doubted that any of them could be persuaded to file another lawsuit.[42]

When Caillouet died in January 1947, responsibility for the Iberville case passed to Judge Borah. At Tureaud's request, the judge agreed to make a decision based on the existing evidence and without hearing further testimony, since it was obvious that the arguments of both sides had been exhausted and that they would never reach an agreement. In November, Borah ruled in favor of the plaintiffs, declaring that the school board's practice of paying black teachers less than their white colleagues was unconstitutional. Louisiana officials eventually tired of the continuous stream of lawsuits that the NAACP seemed prepared to file, and in August 1948 the state board of education ordered all parishes to equalize teachers' salaries.[43]

After winning the salary equalization fight, the NAACP and local citizens' committees turned their full attention to the struggle for equal school facilities. Tureaud expressed optimism that they might encounter fewer difficulties here than in the salary cases "for the reason that we would not have the same problem as we experienced in trying to get teachers to file suits against their school board. All that is required in cases of this kind is some interested parents and this should not be any trouble at all because they do not have to fear the loss of their job." Subsequent events proved Tureaud tragically wrong, but in June 1948 thirty-six parents and guardians volunteered to sign their names to a lawsuit demanding equalization of school facilities in Iberville Parish. In March 1949 Judge Borah again ruled in the NAACP's favor, ordering the school board to provide the same quality of education to black children as was available to white children in the parish.[44]

The signs were encouraging, but achieving real equality was never as simple as winning legal cases or obtaining federal court orders to force an end to discrimination. White supremacists fought to maintain racial hierarchies at every step. Following Borah's decision in the Iberville case, the school board appointed a committee of local black people to advise it on how best to implement the judge's order. None of the original instigators of the lawsuit were asked to help, and W. W. Harleaux told Tureaud, "You can rest assured that if there is such a committee it is made up of hand pick *good 'N.'* They don't represent us." The school board's failure to adequately address inequality forced the NAACP to take further legal action in the 1950s.[45]

Officials in other parishes followed the example set by the Iberville board, harassing people who signed their names to NAACP lawsuits and using delaying tactics to postpone legal decisions for as long as possible. After agreeing to act as a plaintiff in a school equalization case in St. Landry Parish, Louis Thierry was arrested and charged with gambling when police raided his house and found him playing cards with some friends in July 1949. While imprisoned, he was beaten by his cellmates, who were acting under orders from the jailers. Shortly afterward, a prominent white lawyer arrived to offer his assistance. He advised Thierry to sign some documents indicating that he wished to withdraw his name from the lawsuit. Thierry at first refused and was returned to his cell with the warning that any harm that came to him was his own fault. Afraid for his life, Thierry finally signed the documents. The lawyer then drove him home, cautioning him not to tell anyone what had happened at the jail. By the end of the following month several more plaintiffs had been frightened into removing their names from the lawsuit. When the case eventually made it into court, the school board slowed its progress using the same tired arguments for dismissal that had proven useless in other school equalization suits.[46]

Black activists persevered, and ultimately their efforts yielded some significant gains. School boards in parishes where cases had been won by the NAACP grudgingly began to spend more on black education. Others attempted to avoid lawsuits and federal intervention by voluntarily improving facilities. In July 1952 NAACP field secretary Daniel Byrd reported that since the filing of a petition protesting the state of black education in St. Helena Parish, officials had decided to renovate a training school for African Americans and for the first time in the parish's history they contracted with a company to do the work. Previously, black people themselves had donated material and labor while school board members pocketed the funds allocated for such projects. In Ferriday, Robert Lewis's classes were relocated from a one-room building with no running water to a new high school constructed for black students in the 1950s. For the first time, he and his classmates experienced what it was like to attend a fully equipped school, complete with a gymnasium and cafeteria. Statewide, African Americans gained fourteen new trade schools and over one hundred new public schools, while spending on black colleges was multiplied by ten. Between 1948 and 1956 local governments in Louisiana floated bond issues amounting to $300 million, with much of the money going toward improving black schools. In 1955 state legislators approved $220 million in expenditures over the next five years for a school building program designed to equalize facilities in all parishes.[47] Although black schools never reached the same standards as white schools, the quality of education provided to African Americans was greatly enhanced during this period.

In addition to their attacks on educational inequalities, civil rights activists in Louisiana launched a powerful offensive against discrimination in voter registration. In May 1944 African Americans from throughout the state met in New Orleans to organize a branch of the National Progressive Voters' League (PVL). Encouraged by the Supreme Court's decision abolishing the white primary, they planned a statewide educational campaign to urge black people to register to vote. A. P. Tureaud told those present that *Smith v. Allwright* was "the Negro's Second Emancipation" and that the time had come to "effect this emancipation or return to slavery." African Americans were to visit their local registrars' offices and to file complaints with the NAACP if they were turned away. Attorneys could then bring lawsuits against officials who denied black applicants the right to register. The PVL viewed the mobilization of black voters as a crucial element in nationwide efforts to increase support for progressive causes. A speaker for the group urged African Americans to take their "rightful place by the side of liberal political groups irrespective of race or class" and to combine their political power with that of organized labor, sharecroppers' unions, taxpayers' associations, and other reformers.[48]

With the poll tax and white primary system no longer in effect, the main obstacles to black registration were the literacy test, a requirement that applicants show some understanding of the state constitution, and the complexities of the registration form itself. Officials were meticulous in checking the application forms of African Americans and often failed people on the basis of a misspelled word or failure to dot an *i* or cross a *t*. Martin Williams recalled that instead of requiring black people to interpret a section of the constitution, the registrar in Madison Parish asked them unanswerable questions like "How many bubbles are there in a bar of soap?" Prospective applicants could study for days or weeks before the test, but still they failed. As Williams explained, the aim was to make black people so frustrated or discouraged that they would stop trying to register.[49]

The NAACP and PVL worked through churches, fraternal orders, and labor unions to organize classes aimed at guiding black applicants through the registration process.[50] The instructional sessions were well attended in many parishes, and in one instance not even severe flooding prevented African Americans from traveling to a remote meeting place and going ahead with a scheduled class. Daniel Byrd reported: "On Sunday, June 16, 1946 in Hymel, Louisiana the Instructors from New Orleans put on hip boots and waded through water and mud in order to reach the place set aside for registration classes. More than 50 men and women pulled off their shoes, socks and stockings, the men rolled up their pants, the women pulled their dresses tightly around them and waded in water twelve inches deep in order to learn how to fill [out] the registration form." Similarly, when one observer visited a meeting of the NAACP branch in Iberville Parish, he found the local black people enthusiastic about voter registration and "determined to participate in their government."[51]

Throughout the 1940s and 1950s NAACP branches and other civil rights groups sent their members to attempt to register, with varying degrees of success. Black applicants registered with relatively little trouble in Orleans, East Baton Rouge, Ouachita, Iberville, and Ascension Parishes, and in some cases friendly white people assisted them in completing the forms. In St. John the Baptist Parish, the registrar developed the habit of becoming "conveniently sick" during the week and keeping his office closed; on weekends he could be seen out walking his dog. The *Louisiana Weekly* reported that local black people "put spotters on the registration office and whenever the registrar would show up the spotter would pass the word and shortly the office was continuously crowded. Apparently the registrar found that his illness spells did not work so now the office remains open, making registration possible."[52]

Officials in other parishes proved more recalcitrant. Members of the Madison Parish voters' league received no response to a petition they sent to the mayor of Tallulah demanding an end to discrimination in voter registration in 1947. Registrar Mary Ward later told an NAACP lawyer that in rejecting black applicants she had acted under the orders of the sheriff and district attorney; she also stated that an agreement existed between officials in Madison, Tensas, and East Carroll Parishes that they would never allow African Americans to vote. In St. Helena Parish, NAACP members who attempted to register were confronted by a white man wielding a gun. "Get out all of you 'n—s' before all of you get killed," he told them. "Nobody is going to let you vote. If you don't run, there'll be plenty more to shoot you down." Three black men who attempted to register in St. Landry Parish in June 1949 were violently attacked and chased from the registrar's office. They filed a complaint with the Department of Justice and FBI agents were supposedly sent to investigate, but early in 1950 the men reported that no one from the federal government had contacted them about the incident. Later that year Alvin Jones of the Orleans Parish PVL visited Opelousas and persuaded a group of African Americans to go with him to the courthouse to inquire about registering. Sheriff Clayton Guilbeau called the group into his office, where he and his deputies severely beat them. Jones died a few months later from injuries inflicted by the police officers.[53]

The uneven progress of voter registration reflected the absolute and arbitrary power that white elites exercised over local government. Black applicants' success or failure depended sometimes on the registrar, sometimes on more powerful parish officials who could dismiss registrars if they seemed too lenient, and almost never on the ability of individual African Americans to meet the voter registration requirements. In one case, nineteen people who went to register in Pointe Coupee Parish in November 1951 did not even have the opportunity to fail. The registrar told them that he had received no orders to register black people and suggested they talk to the district attorney about it instead. Reflecting the other side of the coin, when D. J. Doucet regained the sheriff's office in St. Landry Parish from Clayton Guilbeau, African Americans were suddenly able to register by the thousands. Realizing that NAACP lawsuits and federal intervention would ultimately enable black people to register in large numbers, Doucet ended police brutality in the parish and actively courted the black vote to keep himself in power for the next sixteen years.[54]

Local officials' attitudes toward black voter registration were shaped in part by the factional nature of state politics during this period. Huey Long's governorship had split Louisiana's Democratic Party into two fiercely opposing sides, forcing candidates to compete more intensely for votes. African Americans benefited from the social welfare measures introduced in the 1930s, and black voters generally supported Long and his successors. Members of the Long faction therefore had much to gain by protecting black people's voting rights, and for this reason officials in some parishes actually encouraged African Americans to register. Between 1948 and 1952 black Louisianans' postwar voter registration campaigns and the presence of Huey Long's brother Earl in the governor's office increased the number of black registered voters in Louisiana from 28,177 to 107,844. In parishes that were dominated by conservative, anti-Long politicians, however, strong opposition remained. As late as 1962, East Carroll, Madison, Tensas, and West Feliciana Parishes still had no black people registered.[55]

The NAACP's offensives against discrimination in education and voter registration were the most publicized aspects of the freedom struggle in this period. At the same time, many black Louisianans continued to fight for economic justice by becoming involved in the labor movement. Civil rights groups and labor unions often cooperated closely to advance progressive causes in the postwar period. Recognizing the importance of interracial solidarity to workers' struggles, the CIO had since the 1930s pursued a policy of nondiscrimination and encouraged black people's participation in unions. The nation's major civil rights organizations strongly supported these efforts. The National Negro Congress, the Urban League, and the NAACP all contributed to the CIO's general strike fund and encouraged union membership among black Americans. In return, the CIO supported African Americans' struggles for citizenship, including voting rights and equal employment opportunities.[56]

African Americans played prominent roles in the CIO's efforts to organize southern workers in the 1940s, often emerging as some of the most courageous and dedicated union leaders. After touring Mississippi, Arkansas, and Louisiana in 1945, CIO public relations officer Lucy Randolph Mason stated that one of the most encouraging aspects of her visit was seeing "the way Negroes have turned to the CIO unions and the great gains they have made thereby."[57] The CIO's southern staff found black workers much easier to organize than their white counterparts. One man recalled, "Oh, yeah! Blacks was right with ya! They were smarter than the whites, where the union was concerned. They had more to gain. And they knew that!"[58] As Barbara Griffith has noted, working-class African Americans were already "highly politicized," and they willingly seized the opportunities presented by the CIO. Many black members of CIO unions also belonged to the NAACP, suggesting that civil rights and economic rights were intricately connected in their minds.[59]

Louisiana's predominantly black lumber industry became the target of intensive organizing efforts by the CIO-affiliated International Woodworkers of America (IWA) in the early 1940s. Although many workers supported unionization, organizers encountered strong opposition from company owners and local officials. After spending three weeks in Tallulah working with employees at the Chicago Mill and Lumber Company, Morton Hobbs Davis was run out of town at gunpoint by three men who claimed to speak for the entire community when they told him: "We are not going to have the C.I.O. here. Understand? You come in here trying to stir up these niggers, and we're not going to have you organizing those damn niggers." Another IWA representative who spoke with white officials about the possibility of organizing a union local in the town was "frankly told . . . that they did not want any C.I.O. organization in the city and did not intend to have one."[60] Attempts to build unions at lumber mills located in Iberville, St. Landry, and West Feliciana Parishes provoked similar responses. A summary report of the IWA's activities in rural Louisiana from 1946 to 1948 observed that in most cases the workers had filed petitions requesting that elections be held to decide on union representation, but these were later withdrawn because of threats and intimidation by local citizens. "It seems the different towns that these plants are located in immediately formed vigilante committees or so-called citizens committees and immediately began to put pressure on the employees and threatened and in some cases did beat up some of our boys," the author wrote. "Quite a number of employees were fired during this drive and were never able to be reinstated."[61]

Nonetheless, the IWA continued its efforts into the next decade and eventually managed to establish union locals in Lake Charles, Zimmerman, Long Leaf, Castor, Clayton, Alexandria, Eunice, and Tallulah. In June 1952 union members at the Chicago Mill and Lumber Company in Tallulah opened negotiations with their employers, asking for a 9¢ wage increase, paid holidays, and insurance benefits. Receiving no relief from the company, they went on strike at the end of October and stayed out for two weeks. This action gained them a 2.5¢ wage increase, and further negotiations in September 1953 yielded another increase of 3.5¢.[62]

As small as such gains were, they were more than most business and political leaders were willing to concede. Throughout the decade employers, local officials, and state legislators discouraged unionization in Louisiana. Foremen at the Bentley Lumber mill in Zimmerman hired only those job applicants who agreed not to join the union. Lumber operators in Eunice and Winnfield threatened to fire workers or evict them from company-owned homes if they were spotted at union meetings. In 1953 plantation owners in southern Louisiana responded to a strike by sugar workers belonging to the National Agricultural Workers' Union (NAWU) by cutting off utility services to the ·homes of the families involved, issuing eviction notices, and (assisted by the police) violently attacking union members. The strike was crushed after planters obtained a court order preventing the union from picketing or any other activity.[63]

Plantation owners also lent their formidable organizational power to lobbying efforts to gain passage of a state right-to-work law. The AFBF had consistently opposed compulsory unionism, arguing that labor leaders were "more interested in a contest for personal and political power and a reckless race for dues" than in workers' welfare. In 1947 the Taft-Hartley Act weakened the labor movement by outlawing closed shops (workplaces where only union members could be employed), but the AFBF continued to push for the abolition of union shops (where employees were required to join a union after being hired) as well. A resolution adopted at its annual meeting in 1952 stated: "State laws guaranteeing the right to work should be enforced. States which have not done so should be encouraged to enact legislation guaranteeing the right to work."[64]

Following the 1953 sugar strike, the Louisiana Farm Bureau took over the state's right-to-work campaign "lock, stock, and money bag," according to one source.[65] Farm Bureau president Malcolm Dougherty assumed the chairmanship of the Louisiana Right to Work Council when it was formed in April 1954 and set about trying to convince legislators that the law was necessary to prevent "strikes and violence" from harming the state's industry, farming, and business interests. The right-to-work campaign received widespread support from planters and business owners, and police juries in several parishes endorsed the measure. A few months later, conservative governor Robert Kennon signed the legislation into law. Labor leaders led a successful campaign to repeal the act in 1956, but only after making a compromise with powerful senators from the sugar parishes that meant agricultural workers were not freed from its restrictions. At the same time that the state's politicians passed the bill repealing the original legislation, they enacted a separate right-to-work law covering agricultural workers only.[66]

Along with legislative attacks, opponents of the labor movement manipulated racism to discourage white workers from joining unions. Antiunion employers and politicians emphasized the CIO's support for black civil rights, arguing that the organization was as great a threat to southern racial hierarchies as the NAACP. After the Supreme Court's historic decision in *Brown v. Board of Education* (1954) declaring school segregation unconstitutional, it was not difficult to incite white southerners to a state of panic on the race issue. A CIO representative in Louisiana reported that "statements connecting us with the N.A.A.C.P. and the segregation fight in this state" were being used to divide white and black workers, adding to the already difficult task of union organizing.[67] Throughout the South in the 1950s employers and politicians used the race-baiting tactic very effectively to hinder unionization in their states.[68]

In a detailed analysis undertaken in 1956, agricultural union organizer H. L. Mitchell outlined the relationship between racism and antilabor elements in the South. Some of the strongest opposition to black civil rights and federal intervention came from the southern elite, including plantation owners, lawyers, bankers, industrialists, judges, and politicians. Many prominent segregationists were also active in efforts to prevent union organizing in their states. In Louisiana, former Right-to-Work Councils provided the basis for the formation of white supremacist groups like the White Citizens' Councils, the Southern Gentlemen, and the Ku Klux Klan. Racist rhetoric threatened to splinter the fragile coalitions that working-class white and black people had forged during the 1930s and 1940s. In areas where the Klan and Citizens Councils had established themselves, Mitchell noted, it was becoming increasingly difficult to organize unions. He concluded that white political and economic leaders aimed to destroy not just the civil rights movement, but the labor movement as well.[69]

In addition to exposing the connections between civil rights and labor organizations, conservatives sought to equate both of these social movements with communism. Opponents of the freedom struggle pointed out that some union organizers and civil rights activists were or had been members of the Communist Party, arguing that these people were taking their orders from Soviet leaders who aimed to foment civic unrest to prepare the United States for invasion. An editorial printed in two Louisiana newspapers explained that the best way to destroy a nation was to divide its people—by encouraging "racial controversy," for example, or attacking the Constitution "under the guise of protecting minorities."[70] Conservative propaganda conflated labor unions, the NAACP, and communism into one massive subversive threat, discouraging people who might otherwise have been sympathetic toward the struggle from lending their support.[71] Anticommunism also created dissension within the movement, as liberals tried to distance themselves from radicals whose presence made organizations vulnerable to attack. Unions and civil rights groups purged communists from their ranks in an effort to ensure respectability, leading to the loss of many dedicated and experienced members that progressive causes could ill afford.[72]

Southern segregationists capitalized on the repressive political climate to attack the NAACP. In 1956 Louisiana attorney general Fred LeBlanc charged that communists had infiltrated the organization and attempted to force local branches to make their membership lists public by invoking an old law that had been passed to combat Klan activity in the 1920s. NAACP leaders refused to reveal members' names for fear of making them vulnerable to reprisals by white supremacists. A state court then enjoined the NAACP from operating in Louisiana until the membership lists were disclosed. Though they could not meet openly, local people maintained support for civil rights activity by sending money to the national office and establishing alternative organizations to continue the struggle in their own communities. With the state threatening further legal action unless the NAACP filed its membership lists by 31 December, a few branches complied with the attorney general's request. Fear of reprisals caused many people to withdraw from open affiliation with the NAACP. Between 1955 and 1957 membership in Louisiana dropped from 13,190 to 1,698, and most branches outside of the major cities disintegrated. At the end of the decade one report stated that the NAACP had been "grievously injured to the extent of almost total extinction" by legislative proceedings, economic reprisals, and other forms of intimidation against its members and supporters.[73]

In the late 1950s and early 1960s white supremacists rolled back many of the gains in voter registration that black Louisianans had made in the postwar years. The Citizens' Councils began a campaign to purge African Americans from the rolls by challenging the registration of "unqualified" people, pressuring registrars to administer the literacy and constitutional interpretation tests more stringently, and intimidating black people to discourage them from attempting to register. In April 1956 Daniel Byrd reported: "Make no mistake about it the Citizen's Council[s] are following the pattern instituted by the White South during reconstruction. . . . Unless we can stop them, in the next several months almost all Negroes will be disfranchised in Louisiana." Byrd's prediction came close to being realized in East Feliciana Parish, where registrar Charles S. Kilbourne was ordered to join the local Citizens' Council or lose his job. Kilbourne resigned from the position rather than comply with the request, and in 1958 council leaders replaced him with Henry E. Palmer. The Citizens' Council then challenged the registration of every voter in the parish, forcing people to reregister. Many residents failed to pass the tests Palmer administered, and within two years the number of black people registered in East Feliciana dropped from 1,361 to 82. Statewide, the Citizens' Councils succeeded in removing more than 15,000 African Americans from the rolls between 1956 and 1959.[74]

The purges of black voters were part of the councils' campaign of massive resistance to school desegregation, an effort that received support from state and local officials as well as thousands of white activists across the state. Political leaders and newspaper editors condemned the Supreme Court's *Brown* decision, complaining that it violated the rights of state governments to manage their own internal affairs and predicting civil unrest if the federal government tried to force southerners to integrate. Louisiana congressman F. Edward Hebert stated: "The decision of the supreme court has set race relations back in the south 50 years and it is definitely a blow against those of us who sincerely believe in proper race relations. . . . Now a seed has been planted for the renewal of strife and which will generate unnecessary hatred and prejudice."[75]

Immediately after the Court's ruling was announced, Louisiana legislators indicated their intention not to comply with the law. House representatives voted 84–3 to continue segregation in the schools and created the Joint Legislative Committee on Segregation to study ways to circumvent *Brown*. Between 1954 and 1961, following suggestions by the committee, Louisiana officials enacted no fewer than eighty laws designed to prevent school desegregation. The new measures included a system of pupil placement by superintendents, educational grants for parents of children wishing to attend private academies, a requirement that all students entering public colleges and universities be certified as having "good moral character" by a principal or superintendent, and a law allowing parish authorities to close public schools to avoid integration. Perhaps the most ingenious piece of legislation was an act invoking the state's police power to maintain separate schools "to promote and protect public health, morals, better education, and peace and good order in the state and not because of race."[76]

The lengths that white people were prepared to go to protect their children's "health" and "morals" were made clear to African Americans in St. Helena Parish after the NAACP filed a school desegregation suit there in 1952. Officials first tried to persuade the plaintiffs to content themselves with the equalization of facilities instead of pushing for integration and offered five members of the group ten thousand dollars each to supervise the building of a new school. Lawyers for the school board then asked federal judge J. Skelly Wright to allow them extra time to file a reply to the suit while they waited to see how the Supreme Court ruled in the *Brown* case.

When no progress had been made by June 1955, A. P. Tureaud wrote to Attorney General LeBlanc requesting a move toward the desegregation of schools in St. Helena Parish in accordance with the federal law. No action was taken except that the Joint Committee on Segregation met to discuss ways to block the NAACP's efforts.[77]

Having failed to bribe the plaintiffs to abandon the lawsuit, the school board next tried intimidation. Parish officials rescinded black teacher Lucille Overton Johnson's appointment for the coming session because her father, Fred Overton, was a party to the lawsuit. The brother of another plaintiff was fired from his job as a janitor, and the superintendent visited others who were involved in the case and advised them to withdraw. In July, a group of white supremacists established a chapter of the Southern Gentlemen in St. Helena Parish, adding to the pressure on the black families who had instigated the suit. Southern Gentlemen chairman N. H. Singleton threatened Fred Overton, warning him that he might be physically harmed if he continued to press for school desegregation. Reminding Overton of the recent murders of some black activists in Mississippi, Singleton stated, "you know about the Ku Klux Klan well we are the same as the Klan." Daniel Byrd reported on these developments in August, concluding, "Some Negroes are in fear, great fear for their lives."[78]

Others, like black landowner John Henry Hall, were not so afraid. Several members of the Hall family remembered the night their father received a visit from some white men who wanted to know if it was true that he planned to send his children to St. Helena Parish's white schools. On learning that this was indeed the case, the men said, "We want you to know that we will wade neck-deep in blood before we see that." Hall replied, "Well, y'all get your wading boots 'cos mine's coming." Hall was an active member of the local NAACP branch and carried a loaded gun with him whenever he traveled to civil rights meetings. When white vigilantes shot into their home, the Halls returned their fire. Lawrence Hall explained, "We never was afraid because we knew how to use ammunition just like they did."[79]

For farmers like John Henry Hall, owning firearms had been a normal part of rural life throughout the twentieth century. After World War II, the practice spread, especially among people who were involved in the emerging civil rights movement. In 1950 LCTA president J. K. Haynes decided to purchase a weapon after a white service station owner beat him over the head for drinking at the wrong water fountain. Haynes recalled, "I was crazy, and I went to Monroe that day and bought the biggest pistol I could find to go back and shoot that sleazy white man." After calming down, he decided against the action, but he kept his .45 automatic in case of further trouble. Activists in Madison Parish also armed themselves in this decade, as did those in Pointe Coupee Parish. In 1956 the *Opelousas Daily World* reported that white people in one Baton Rouge neighborhood had announced their intention to shoot any black child who dared to enter their school, and that there had been "reports of Negroes storing guns and ammunition."[80]

The use of armed self-defense in the early civil rights movement was not unique to black activists in Louisiana. In her study of an averted lynching in Columbia, Tennessee, in 1946, Gail Williams O'Brien notes that one reason for the failure of mob violence in this case was that African Americans in the community organized and armed themselves to protect the young war veteran whose life was threatened. O'Brien suggests that increasing militancy among African Americans and a growing determination to defend themselves from violence contributed to the decline of lynching after World War II. Similarly, in the 1950s Robert Williams of North Carolina organized his local NAACP branch into an armed militia to deter attacks by the Ku Klux Klan. Though his actions brought him into conflict with the NAACP's national leadership and eventually led to his expulsion from the organization, Williams and many other local activists throughout the South remained convinced that armed self-defense was a legitimate tactic in the freedom struggle.[81]

Returning World War II and Korean War veterans contributed to the increasing use of armed self-defense in the postwar decades.[82] At the same time that former soldiers' economic resources helped to power the civil rights movement, their military expertise helped to protect participants from violence. Robert Lewis recalled that the first time he saw African Americans in Concordia Parish make a stand against injustice was in the 1950s, when the black citizens of Ferriday organized to defend themselves against a police attack on their community. They had angered a deputy by taking a flashlight he had broken on a black man's head, hiding it, and refusing to give it back to him since they planned to use it as evidence in a lawsuit against the policeman. According to Lewis, the deputy called the other members of the police force together and they went downtown to administer punishment, but when they got there, "On both sides of that street . . . it was loaded with blacks . . . and they didn't have sticks and bottles—they had guns." The law enforcement officers of Ferriday decided to leave the black people alone.[83]

Meanwhile, developments at the national level were moving in a somewhat different direction. In 1955 and 1956 a year-long boycott of segregated buses by African Americans in Montgomery, Alabama, received widespread publicity and resulted in the formation of a new organization, the Southern Christian Leadership Conference, led by the charismatic Martin Luther King Jr. Inspired by Mohondas Gandhi's use of "passive resistance" in the struggle to free India from British colonial rule, King articulated an approach to the problem of racism that he hoped would gnaw at the consciences of white Americans and force them to end discrimination. Taking as its motto "To Redeem the Soul of America," the SCLC aimed to expose the contradictions between the nation's expressed ideals of freedom, democracy, and equality and the actual treatment of black people in the United States.[84]

A key component of this strategy was nonviolent direct action, a technique that had been pioneered by CORE in the early 1940s. The Congress of Racial Equality grew out of the religious and pacifist Fellowship of Reconciliation, whose members remained opposed to violence for any reason even during the worldwide fight against Nazism. Arguing that the use of violence to solve social problems could only lead to more violence, CORE members attacked racist discrimination in northern cities by peacefully "sitting in" at segregated facilities. In the 1950s CORE worked with the SCLC to organize workshops that would teach nonviolence to black southerners. Veteran activist Bayard Rustin explained that the purpose of the training sessions was "to bring the Gandhian philosophy and tactic to the masses of Negroes in the South." Rustin perceived a growing tendency among African Americans to fight back against white supremacists' acts of aggression and feared that this might lead to "widespread racial conflict." He and other national spokespeople insisted that, for practical if not philosophical reasons, civil rights activists must remain nonviolent.[85]

The student sit-in movement of the late 1950s and early 1960s seemed to vindicate this approach. Well-dressed, educated young black people walked into "white only" lunch counters and restaurants and politely requested service, refusing to move until their requests were granted. Though they were insulted, spat upon, assaulted, and arrested, they did not respond aggressively to the actions of their tormentors. White proprietors in many cities eventually succumbed to the pressure to desegregate their facilities. CORE leader James Robinson stated that the sit-ins showed "the power of Satyagraha—soul force" and argued that the social order could be changed through "a spirit of good will and understanding."[86] Newspaper reporters, radio commentators, and television crews were fascinated by the extraordinary restraint shown by people involved in the sit-ins and other protests against discrimination that occurred throughout the nation in the years that followed. In 1963 the image of demonstrators in Birmingham, Alabama, refusing to fight back even after police attacked them with tear gas, fire hoses, clubs, and dogs was branded into the minds of TV viewers and became one of the most enduring symbols of African Americans' struggle for freedom and equality.

Media coverage brought these events to the attention of millions of white Americans, shocking them into recognizing the huge gulf between their professed values and actual practices. In the 1960s thousands of young white and black people volunteered to take part in the Southern Regional Council's Voter Education Project (VEP) to study the causes of low voter participation among black people in the South. The nation's major civil rights organizations each received grants to conduct voter registration drives in the southern states, working closely with local groups in the region. The project aimed to increase the number of African American voters and to gather evidence of the need for federal legislation to ensure black people's democratic rights by documenting incidents of discrimination, intimidation, and violence.[87]

The emergence of the national civil rights movement boosted morale and inspired renewed activity among local activists in Louisiana. Martin Williams remembered that by the late 1950s, repression by the state legislature and the Citizens' Councils had made speaking out against the system too dangerous for many people to contemplate, "but after the movement got started we had a little bit more protection, and we got a little bit more exposure through the news media, the TV media—that kind of educated a lot of people." The knowledge that people all over the nation supported the struggle strengthened activists' determination to continue the fight for equality, despite the risks. Williams stated, "When you get in that movement, you don't think about death. . . . Look like all that fear just leaves."[88]

These developments revitalized the freedom struggle, but they came at a price. In the 1930s and 1940s cooperation between labor unions and civil rights organizations had raised the possibility of poor white and black people joining together to demand political and economic rights. Federal intervention to protect the rights of workers to organize and the passage of legislation to ensure decent working conditions greatly strengthened the position of labor, creating a chance to build a mass movement around social issues that affected all Americans, such as job security, education, housing, and health care. Anticommunism and the racist rhetoric of southern segregationists in the 1950s destroyed these hopes. African American leaders became wary of addressing the class inequalities that lay at the base of the white supremacist social order for fear of being perceived as dangerous radicals. At the same time, union organizers shied away from advocating black equality to avoid losing white workers' support.[89]

When the black freedom movement captured the nation's attention in the 1960s, the economic agenda was pushed to the background. Key initiatives like the Montgomery bus boycott and the Birmingham protests had included demands for jobs, but these aspects of the struggle were overshadowed in media portrayals that preferred to emphasize more esoteric goals, like dignity or respect. National civil rights leaders at first did little to challenge the emerging consensus, which denied the need for fundamental restructuring of the social system to ensure black equality. The middle-class white and black activists who headed CORE and the students who joined the organization's Louisiana Freedom Task Force each summer tended to define racism as essentially a moral problem that could be eliminated by ending segregation, ensuring black voting rights, and encouraging interracial communication. At the local level, however, many black people continued to attach the greatest importance to removing economic obstacles to equality. It remained for them to remind a new generation of activists that civil rights were not enough.

8

To Provide Leadership and an Example:
The Congress of Racial Equality
and Local People in the 1960s

In August 1962 CORE received a grant from the Voter Education Project to conduct voter registration drives in seven parishes in Louisiana's Sixth Congressional District, located in the southeastern part of the state. The organization's Louisiana Freedom Task Force was active in the region for the next four years, conducting intensive voter registration drives during the summer months as well as working with local leaders on more long-term community organizing projects. In the mid-1960s CORE expanded its reach to include eight additional parishes in the northern Fourth and Fifth Congressional Districts.[1]

CORE began its work in rural Louisiana with three main objectives: increasing black voter registration, desegregating public facilities, and training local people in nonviolence. Volunteers aimed to encourage people to join the civil rights movement by educating them about the importance of voting and teaching them how to challenge segregation using nonviolent direct action. As time went on, CORE workers realized that not all of the black people they worked with shared their ideas about how best to overcome white supremacy. Voter registration provided a common goal that local people as well as outside activists embraced. But attempting to desegregate restaurants or public facilities did not seem as important to some black Louisianans as gaining fair treatment by employers, increases in pay, and access to decent jobs. Despite CORE's efforts to convert them to nonviolence, many local activists continued to carry guns to defend themselves. CORE workers eventually modified their own attitudes toward both these issues. By the mid-1960s most volunteers had accepted the practice of armed self-defense, and CORE as an organization began to emphasize economic inequality as the major problem facing African Americans. In the second half of the decade, the goals of the broader freedom struggle were revived and given new impetus by federal antipoverty programs that offered the possibility of real change. As in the 1930s, however, white political and economic leaders in rural Louisiana successfully resisted these threats to their power. At the end of the 1960s and well into the late twentieth century, the most fundamental problems of many black people remained unresolved.

Founded in 1942, CORE was one of the nation's oldest civil rights organizations. Its origins and development over the next two decades reflected many of the broader political trends of the post–World War II era. A small group of white and black young people in Chicago who were committed to pacifism, interracialism, and economic justice initiated the formation of CORE, conceiving it as a nationwide network of activists who were prepared to engage in direct action against racism.[2] Early CORE chapters concentrated mostly on attempting to desegregate restaurants and public facilities in northern cities, with a few chapters also trying to address discrimination in employment. Although CORE achieved some success against the most obvious forms of injustice, like segregation, activists found that pressuring business owners to hire more African Americans was much more difficult. Excluding black people from jobs did not violate northern civil rights statutes or offend white Americans' sensibilities in the same way that excluding them from dining and recreational facilities did, giving CORE no clear basis (in the eyes of the larger community) for its attacks on racist employers. Like many similar organizations, CORE also sought to avoid any association with leftists and radicals, adopting a resolution at its 1948 convention that prohibited communist-controlled groups from affiliating with it. Heavily dependent on white liberals for members and financial contributions, CORE narrowed its focus to those issues most likely to gain their support. When the organization expanded into the southern states in the late 1950s, its attention centered on direct action against segregation. In the 1960s the VEP provided the resources and incentive for CORE to include voter registration among its activities in the South.[3]

After receiving funding for VEP work in rural Louisiana, CORE's first task was to establish contact with local civil rights leaders in the region. Ronnie Moore, one of several black college students who had been expelled from Southern University in Baton Rouge for participating in protest marches and sit-ins, assumed responsibility for initiating these efforts.[4] For several months Moore worked virtually alone, surveying each parish and assessing the possibilities for civil rights work. He quickly discovered a group in Iberville Parish that was eager to cooperate with the voter registration drive and moved his headquarters to Plaquemine in October 1962. Veteran activist W. W. Harleaux recognized an opportunity to gain valuable assistance for the freedom struggle in his community. As was the case in many parishes, people wanted to participate, but they needed money for things like printing leaflets, making copies of registration application forms, and transport for canvassing and for bringing people to the registrar's office. Early in 1963 Harleaux wrote to VEP director Wiley Branton outlining the constraints that widespread poverty among African Americans in the parish placed on civil rights activity. Harleaux stated that black people in rural Louisiana needed outside help and asked Branton to allocate more resources to the region.[5]

Between October 1962 and May 1963 members of the Iberville Parish NAACP and the local voters' league assisted Moore in persuading several hundred African Americans to attempt to register in Iberville and the surrounding parishes. Participants filed more than three hundred complaints of discrimination with the Department of Justice, and these resulted in an investigation of voter registration records in Pointe Coupee, St. Helena, West Feliciana, Tangipahoa, and Iberville Parishes by federal agents. Meanwhile, CORE laid plans for its first summer project. Local activist Spiver Gordon helped Moore prepare for the influx of volunteers, and in July 1963 forty new workers arrived in Plaquemine for orientation and training.[6]

Most of these recruits were white, northern college students in their early to mid-twenties. Many had been involved in civil rights activities in their hometowns, working through church groups and youth organizations as well as CORE chapters, and they were often deeply religious and committed to pacifism. For some participants, the decision to become involved in the movement seemed the only possible response to reports of the injustice and brutality that black people suffered in the 1950s and 1960s. Former task force worker Ronnie Sigal Bouma recalled that, for her, it was simply a matter of right and wrong. "[In] the groups that I belonged to people were just aware of the fact that there were discriminatory practices going on, and they just wanted to end them, and we really didn't get into the psychology of the whole thing," she stated. "We were simply interested in taking a moral and an active stand to change the way that companies and society and government operated, and doing it in a nonviolent way."[7]

Activists Miriam Feingold, Bill Brown, and Mike Lesser shared a similar commitment to achieving racial equality. Feingold's belief that segregation was a fundamentally evil, sick, and irrational institution inspired her to participate in CORE's Freedom Ride to desegregate interstate travel facilities in 1960. Despite being arrested and serving a jail sentence in Mississippi's notorious Parchman Penitentiary as a result of that effort, Feingold once again put herself on the front line of the struggle by offering to help with the project in Louisiana. Bill Brown had been active in the movement for several years before applying as a task force worker, as had Mike Lesser. All three of these volunteers decided to stay in Louisiana for another year after CORE's initial voter registration drive ended. Their dedication and ability to empathize with local people made them some of CORE's most effective and respected organizers.[8]

The summer project of 1963 established the general pattern followed by CORE for the next several years. Volunteers gathered in Plaquemine, where they learned about such matters as state and local politics, the intricacies of Louisiana's complicated registration form, how to approach people when canvassing, what to do in case of harassment by the "po-lice," and how to organize demonstrations. After the initial training period, participants spread out into the surrounding rural areas. CORE workers and local activists went door-to-door, explaining to people the importance of registering to vote and inviting them to attend classes where they could learn how to fill out the application forms. When prospective voters were ready to take the test, task force workers transported them to the registrar's office and observed how they were received.[9] Intensive VEP work usually lasted from July through August. At the end of each summer, a few volunteers stayed on as full-time task force workers.

Although the main object of the VEP was to register as many African Americans as possible before the upcoming gubernatorial and presidential elections, volunteers also worked to train local people in nonviolence and to establish CORE-like groups to challenge racism through direct action. Encouraging awareness of and adherence to CORE's philosophy and ideals was a central goal of the organization in the early part of the decade. In 1960 one local activist in Baton Rouge who had received financial aid from CORE for his organizing efforts lost this support because he had "not really indicated much progress in forming a small, dedicated group of Satyagrahis."[10] When work began on the VEP, task force staff members were asked to report weekly on their success in developing CORE chapters as well as in voter registration. As Miriam Feingold noted during a staff meeting in December 1963, the national office considered chapter development *very imp[ortan]t*."[11]

Local people's responses to CORE's arrival varied. Task force volunteer John Zippert recalled, "The people who were most receptive to talk to us were small farmers, people who had some degree of independence." Several hundred black families in St. Helena and St. Landry Parishes owned farms, and African Americans in both parishes impressed CORE workers with their readiness to become involved.[12] After scouting St. Landry in December 1963, Bill Brown reported: "There is a large body of persons who can be moved for the cause of FREEDOM. . . . The Negro leaders are strong, militant and willing to work." Sharon Burger reached a similar conclusion about St. Helena Parish, stating, "The Negro community is sincerely interested in registration; many people left work in the fields during a busy season to attend the clinics, and several spent the entire day at the registrar's office even when it became obvious that there would not be time for them to get in." Another CORE worker noted that black people in the parish provided "very capable and competent leadership. CORE Task Force workers take advice rather than give it."[13] An analogous situation existed in Madison Parish, where CORE worked with Zelma Wyche's group to revitalize voter registration efforts after the local activists won a lawsuit they had filed against registrar Mary Ward in 1954. After eight years of procrastination and obstruction by parish officials, a federal court finally issued an injunction in 1962 prohibiting discrimination against black applicants.[14]

Self-employed farmers and business owners like those who led voter registration efforts in St. Landry, St. Helena, and Madison Parishes were still a minority in Louisiana. A much greater number of black people labored in jobs where they were subject to economic reprisals, and many were reluctant to become involved. Field reports from the rural parishes cited "apathy and fear" as major obstacles to black registration. According to one activist, civil rights work in the West Feliciana town of Hardwood was fruitless, for it was virtually owned by the King Lumber Company and closely resembled "company towns of the early 20th century" for levels of repression and for "rock-bottom conditions." Eighty-two percent of farmers in the parish labored as tenants or sharecroppers on plantations owned by white people, and the 1960 census listed only sixty black landowners. Miriam Feingold wrote that work in the plantation regions was "the hardest, because people have been beaten down for so many years that very few are willing to fight back. We've got to travel many miles, spend much time just talking, before we convince one Negro to go to the registrar's office." Fear of reprisals was so pervasive that when CORE workers first approached a group of ministers in West Feliciana Parish about registering, they were asked to leave. In neighboring East Feliciana Parish, a local man told activists that they might be able to work out of a house that belonged to his mother-in-law. Ed Vickery later reported, "When he approached her about renting it to us *she tore it down.*"[15]

In almost every parish, two groups seemed especially reluctant to become involved in civil rights work: teachers and preachers.[16] Black schoolteachers naturally feared losing their jobs, especially given the experiences of those in Iberville and other parishes who had been fired during the salary equalization struggles of the 1940s. The state had further undermined their security by passing legislation in 1956 that enabled school boards to dismiss any employee who advocated integration. Although most black educators adopted a position of cautious neutrality on civil rights, some of them actively discouraged others from joining the movement. In November 1963 East Feliciana principal W. W. Wilson suspended twenty-three students from West High School for wearing CORE buttons and refusing to take them off. He later called his teachers together and told them he would not allow such buttons in his school, adding that they could all join CORE and get fired if they wanted to, but he would not jeopardize his own position. Attempts by CORE workers and local activists to mobilize black people in Pointe Coupee Parish around plans to boycott Mardi Gras celebrations in January 1964 encountered strong opposition from school principals. Even in St. Helena Parish, where support for the movement was generally strong and several teachers did become involved, other teachers worked to undermine CORE. The principal of the local black high school tried to embarrass student civil rights leaders and warned others not to listen to them. According to task force member Fred Lacey, some teachers in the parish informed white people of everything that activists were doing and advised their students, "You better keep your minds on your grades and leave that freedom mess behind."[17]

Activists encountered similar problems with ministers. Robert Lewis believed that church leaders in Ferriday could have assisted greatly in the movement, "But instead, they refused because they were bought off by money, and worried about the building—that the church was going to be burned." With black churches and meeting halls in Louisiana regularly being burned to the ground by white vigilante groups in the 1960s, this was an understandable fear. At one point, white insurance companies canceled the policies of every black church in Concordia Parish to discourage civil rights activity. But as Lewis suggested, some ministers avoided becoming involved in the struggle because they did not want to lose the patronage of powerful white friends. In the summer of 1963 a local activist who was working with CORE in Iberville Parish reported: "Our greatest problem here now is the unwillingness on the part of the local ministers to take an active stand in this movement. It is our belief that the political figures of this parish have gained control of these ministers which inclines to slow the movement down." Task force workers' letters and field reports echoed these sentiments, citing multiple complaints about "Uncle Tom ministers."[18] Miriam Feingold wrote: "In my area I have a mess of them. One has refused to let us step beyond the doors of the church; another lets us speak for five minutes, and in his own speech undoes everything we did. As old-time community leaders, I think they are afraid of losing their position and power, but the way they're acting is not designed to win them perpetual support, that's for sure."[19]

Feingold's prediction turned out to be accurate. At a meeting of CORE workers and local activists in St. Francisville, someone stated that the group needed to gain the support of black community leaders. One of the local people, a Mr. Minor, asked, "But who are the leaders?" "The teachers and the ministers," came the reply. Minor pointed out: "They are way behind us— they should be walking in front of us, but they are not. So we'll have to find other leaders." Civil rights leadership eventually emerged not from the traditional black elite—teachers, ministers, and professionals whose positions of influence depended on the support of white people—but from an entirely different source. As Ronnie Moore later stated, in the little towns and farming hamlets of rural Louisiana "the poor, farmers, the unemployed, and young people led the struggle."[20]

Partly because CORE workers were youthful themselves and because activities such as demonstrations, picketing, and sit-ins held the most appeal to people their own age, high school students and other young adults were often the first to join the movement. Kenny Johnson estimated that around 90 percent of those who attended his high school in Plaquemine participated in some form of civil rights activity in the 1960s. A strike by approximately five hundred students to protest segregation, lack of employment opportunities, and the firing of a black cafeteria worker who had attended a recent demonstration closed down the school in October 1963. A CORE worker reported, "CORE has been enjoined from demonstrating, but the high school students have not, and they have been raising hell." Young people in East and West Feliciana Parishes seemed less timid than most others in the region, and activists wrote late in 1963 of plans to establish CORE chapters in both parishes. By January the following year, these groups were "raring to go sit-in."[21]

Such eagerness was not simply the result of youthful exuberance. It also reflected these participants' relative immunity from economic reprisals. Robert Lewis provided insight into why some people became involved in the civil rights movement while others did not when he described the members of the Ferriday Freedom Movement (FFM), a local group that CORE workers helped to establish in Concordia Parish in the summer of 1965. Asked what their occupations were, Lewis said that most of them "weren't doing anything"—they were unemployed people or homemakers who had some independence as well as the time to devote to the freedom struggle. At twenty-five, Lewis was one of the group's oldest members. He had attended college in Natchez, Mississippi, for two years on a basketball scholarship until an illness forced him to take a break from his studies. When CORE arrived in Ferriday, he and his wife were living on welfare payments and whatever other income they managed to scrape up. Other participants were students or young people like Mary Whatley (later Mary Boyd) and her nephew David who had both recently finished school and not yet found jobs. The two youths lived with an older relative, Alberta Whatley, who was retired. Lewis recalled Alberta Whatley's courage and dedication, saying, "I would consider her the mother of the freedom movement in Ferriday, because when no one else would allow the CORE person to come through their gates, she allowed them in her home. Her whole family became very involved in it."[22]

Women like Alberta Whatley played key roles in other parishes as well. Both Ronnie Sigal Bouma and another CORE activist, Meg Redden (formerly Peggy Ewan), vividly remembered Josephine Holmes, an outspoken woman in her seventies who lived in East Feliciana Parish. When ministers refused to allow CORE workers to use their churches for meetings or registration clinics, Holmes opened her home to the freedom fighters. "She was just . . . outrageous," Redden stated. "I mean, she was just willing to do anything." "Anything" included facing down the local sheriff with a loaded shotgun when he came to her home to harass the volunteers who were staying there. Holmes's actions inspired others to join the movement, and by the end of the first summer project a few ministers had agreed to allow civil rights activities in their churches. Eighty-two-year-old Charlotte Greenup was also a strong supporter of CORE. In 1964 the *Louisiana Weekly* described her as "one of the most gracious, articulate, vibrant, and militant Negroes" in Clinton. Though a native of East Feliciana Parish, Greenup had spent most of her life in Chicago, where she had worked as, among other things, a political secretary to black congressman Oscar DePriest. She returned to the parish in the 1960s to help manage the family homestead and to assist in civil rights work in her home state. As the owner of a 191-acre farm, Greenup was in a better position than most other African Americans in East Feliciana Parish to lend her support to the movement.[23]

Black landowners were central to civil rights work in neighboring West Feliciana Parish as well. Voter registration in the parish began in large part through the efforts of just one man, Joseph Carter, a minister, laborer, and owner of a small farm located about six miles from St. Francisville. Carter had heard that CORE was conducting voter registration drives in the region, and early in August 1963 he attended a meeting at a church in East Feliciana Parish where he met Ronnie Moore and two other task force workers.[24] A few days later Carter and another minister, Rudolph Davis, made their first attempt to register. Although registrar Fletcher Harvey knew both Carter and Davis well, he told them that they must each find two registered voters to verify their identities before he could allow them to take the registration test. Since no black people were registered in the parish and no white people were willing to vouch for them, meeting the identification requirement was impossible. Davis left, but Carter stayed and questioned Harvey further about how he might qualify to vote. This resulted in his being arrested for "disturbing the peace." CORE provided two hundred dollars in bond money to secure his release from jail and then helped him to file a lawsuit in federal court charging the registrar and sheriff with violating his civil rights.[25]

Carter was a member of the Knights of Pythias in addition to being a Baptist minister, and he used his church and fraternal order connections to bring other people into the movement. Farm owner and Knights of Pythias president Nathaniel Smith became a key participant in the struggle, along with William Minor and his son Raymond, members of a black farming family who had worked their way out of sharecropping with the help of the Agricultural Extension Service. Voter registration classes held at the Masonic Hall in September and October gradually increased in size, with even some tenant farmers braving the wrath of their employers to learn how to exercise their citizenship rights.[26]

Local activists and CORE workers in West Feliciana carefully formulated a plan to register black voters that they hoped would minimize the threat of violence or other reprisals. The group deliberately waited until after the farmers had sold their sweet potato crops to the local cannery to avoid the possibility of economic retaliation, and Ronnie Moore asked the Department of Justice to send federal agents to the parish on the day the black people planned to register. Early on the morning of 17 October 1963, forty-three African Americans met at the Masonic Hall and traveled from there to the courthouse in St. Francisville. Although they arrived almost as soon as Fletcher Harvey opened his office, the registrar told them that eight white people were ahead of them and made them wait. The group stood outside for almost six hours before the registrar finally called Joseph Carter into the building. With CORE workers, newspaper reporters, FBI agents, and Justice Department officials stationed around the courthouse, Carter took and passed the voter registration test, becoming the first African American to register in the parish since 1902. Four other applicants who tried to register that afternoon failed the test.[27]

Threats made against two black families by their landlord that night did not prevent thirty applicants from returning to the courthouse the following day. Harvey allowed seven people to take the test, and three of them passed. The next week the Justice Department filed suit against Harvey in the federal district court, charging him with discriminating against African Americans by requiring them to meet stricter requirements for proving their residence than he asked of white applicants and taking an excessively long time to process their applications. Federal intervention in addition to the lawsuit filed by Joseph Carter encouraged more people to join the movement. Early in November, Mike Lesser reported that African Americans in West Feliciana seemed much more confident and that white people in the region were beginning to realize that their black neighbors would no longer accept discrimination. He observed, "The social and political structure of the parish is being shaken to its roots."[28]

This assessment of events proved too optimistic. In reality, the pace of change was extremely slow. White supremacists in the plantation parishes responded to the civil rights movement with their usual tactics of intimidation, arrests, legal delays, economic reprisals, and violence.[29] In East and West Feliciana, CORE's work was obstructed by some of the most recalcitrant officials in the state. The two parishes made up Louisiana's Twentieth Judicial District, presided over by Judge John R. Rarick and District Attorney Richard Kilbourne, both staunch segregationists. Rarick was openly contemptuous of federal authority and given to ignoring court rulings that conflicted with his desire to uphold white supremacy. He ran for Congress in 1966 with strong support from the Ku Klux Klan. Kilbourne was secretary of the East Feliciana Citizens' Council and had been instrumental in purging African Americans from the parish voter registration rolls in the 1950s—this despite the fact that it involved removing his own cousin, Charles Kilbourne, from his position as registrar. In the 1960s CORE workers described him as a "vicious, coniving individual" who was prepared to do everything in his legal power, and a few things that were not, to destroy the civil rights movement in his district.[30]

Task force volunteers became aware of the strength of white resistance to their activities almost as soon as they arrived. Early in August 1963 Mike Lesser accompanied several black residents of East Feliciana Parish to the registrar's office and was ordered to remain outside. While sitting quietly on some stairs waiting for the registrar to admit him, Lesser was arrested and charged with disturbing the peace. Judge Rarick refused to accept a property bond that was offered to secure Lesser's release, setting the amount of bail at two thousand dollars in cash. This was an extraordinary action considering that the maximum fine for disturbing the peace was half that amount, but no less than CORE workers came to expect from local officials who repeatedly demonstrated their lack of respect for the law.[31]

Some scholars have noted changes in the composition of the dominant class of white people in the South after World War II, as urbanization and economic diversification diluted the influence of the rural plantation-owning elite. They suggest that the rise of a managerial and professional white middle class whose interests relied less heavily on maintaining overt racism—and who feared the negative publicity generated by protests and demonstrations—contributed to the success of the civil rights movement in the 1960s.[32] Although this was the case in some towns and cities of Louisiana (for example, Opelousas, where civic leaders self-consciously tried to maintain a "progressive" image and activists encountered little violent opposition), it was not a uniform pattern throughout the state. In the Felicianas, power remained with the same individuals and families who had ruled for generations and whose commitment to white supremacy was unshakable. Members of the Woods, Spillman, and Daniel families in West Feliciana Parish still owned most of the land, stores, and businesses in the parish and served in some of the same public offices they had held in the 1930s. At the time CORE arrived, Thomas E. Spillman had been a member of the school board for more than forty years. Similarly, Richard Kilbourne belonged to a family of East Feliciana planters and lawyers who had monopolized the offices of judge and district attorney in the Twentieth Judicial District since 1920.[33]

Powerful white Louisianans used familiar tactics to hinder civil rights work. In November 1963 the district attorney and sheriff harassed black voter registration applicants as they waited outside the registrar's office in East Feliciana Parish. Armed with a tape recorder, Richard Kilbourne asked people to tell him their names, why they wanted to register, and who had sent them. Police stationed themselves across the street from the building used for voter registration clinics in Clinton and wrote down the license plate numbers of all the cars parked nearby. Shortly afterward, African Americans who had never before had trouble at work began losing their jobs. Ester Lee Daniel's employer of fourteen years fired him after he tried to register. According to Daniel, the white man told him: "I will have to lay you off. We are going to have a meeting to put a stop to Negroes' registering to vote. I'll have to lay you off until things cool off."[34]

The following year, the Princeville Canning Company refused to grant contracts to more than 150 black sweet potato growers in West Feliciana Parish. Although many of the farmers had not attempted to register to vote and some of those who were registered received contracts, CORE workers and local activists believed the action was taken to punish black people for asserting their citizenship rights. Most of the farmers had grown potatoes for Princeville for many years and none of them had experienced problems gaining contracts before. Ronnie Moore argued that the company's owners avoided establishing a clear pattern of discrimination to evade prosecution and that they intended not so much to retaliate against individual African Americans but to warn the whole community. He stated, "The significance of Princeville's action as a threat against the community is clear when one learns that never before the onset of Negro voting had Princeville similarly c[u]t off contracts."[35]

Whether or not this analysis was correct, CORE's response to the incident revealed how valuable a national organization's contacts and resources could be to local people's struggles against oppression. Feeling partly responsible for what had happened, task force members worked to find alternative markets for the black farmers' sweet potatoes and researched the possibility of helping them form a cooperative to sell their own crops. In addition, CORE publicized Princeville's actions and urged a nationwide boycott of its canned products. Though the company's owners steadfastly denied that they had intended to discriminate against African Americans when they failed to renew the contracts, economic pressure forced them to modify their action. In September 1964 all the farmers who had been refused contracts received letters inviting them to sell their sweet potatoes to the Princeville Canning Company.[36]

CORE's presence helped cushion the effect of economic reprisals in other parishes as well. When local activist Corrie Collins was fired from his position at a hospital in East Feliciana Parish in October 1963, CORE's lawyers appealed to the Louisiana Civil Service Commission on his behalf. A few months later, Collins was reinstated. Civil rights workers established community relief programs in several parishes to assist people who lost their jobs because of their participation in the movement. Supporters of CORE's work across the country sent donations of money, food, and clothing, which were distributed to those in need by committees of local people.[37]

Access to these resources might have decreased some people's fears of eviction or unemployment, but those emboldened enough to attempt to register still had to contend with other obstacles. Parish officials limited the number of successful applicants by slowing down the application process, requiring multiple forms of identification, and strictly implementing the literacy and constitutional understanding tests. Under "Reason for Failure" on complaint forms sent to the Justice Department, black Louisianans wrote things like "I failed to dot the letter I in writing Plaquemine and the registrar said my writing was not clear enough" and "I didn't have sufficient identification to prove my age; even though I had in my possession a Social Security card and NAACP membership card, and besides this I am sixty years old and this should prove that I look over 21." Every day that black people visited Fletcher Harvey's office in West Feliciana Parish, he told them that there were white applicants who had to be processed first, yet activists there said they had never seen any white people in or around the building. In another parish, the registrar told an applicant who passed the test that before he could vote he would have to obtain a doctor's certificate proving that his "health would permit it."[38]

In addition to the machinations of local officials, vigilante groups like the Ku Klux Klan and other terrorists worked to discourage civil rights activity through intimidation and violence. White "friends" visited African Americans who attempted to register to vote and warned them that they risked harm to their homes and families if they continued with such behavior. On the night of 18 October 1963, five cars filled with armed white men circled the house of John Brannon, a bus driver who had transported people to the registrar's office in St. Francisville, and fired several shots into his home. Vandals threw rocks at the church that civil rights workers used as a meeting place in East Feliciana Parish, breaking all of the windows along one side. In January 1964 both East and West Feliciana were hit by a wave of cross burnings. The following month, arsonists attempted to burn down the Masonic Hall in West Feliciana Parish by disconnecting the gas heaters and leaving a lighted candle on the floor. Local black people who spotted the flames and rushed to put them out were shot at by a carload of white men as they drove along Highway 61. The hall was set alight a second time in December. African Americans who lived nearby once again saved the building while repeated calls to the fire department went unanswered for more than an hour.[39]

Under these circumstances, CORE's goal of changing the social order through nonviolence, love, patience, and appealing to the consciences of white southerners was unlikely to succeed. Local black people who had lived with violence and terror throughout their lives were aware of this fact, and many of them demonstrated early on their determination to defend themselves against the numerous crossburners, firebombers, thugs, and assassins who aimed to destroy the movement. In November 1963 Mike Lesser told a friend, "The really beautiful thing to see and be a part of is the movement—the spirit, the people, the courage *and the shotguns*." He reported that weekly voter registration clinics held at the Masonic Hall in West Feliciana Parish were protected by an armed guard, and any unwelcome intruders would be confronted with "15–20 highpowered, long-range shotguns before they got within 50 yards of the building."[40]

Although many rural black people who worked with volunteers shared their religious beliefs, few were willing to become pacifists in the absolutist sense initially advocated by CORE. Task force workers found that teaching nonviolence to local activists was far from easy. A field report from West Feliciana in 1964 observed: "A great deal of education is needed to cement the relation between CORE and the people of West Feliciana Parish. The idea of non-violence is a new one, and will require much discussion and training, especially for the older people." Another report from the same parish noted of one local leader that he was "young, extremely militant, with nothing to lose. . . . Will take some time for him to get used to non-violence." CORE worker Meldon Acheson arrived in Ferriday in the summer of 1965 to find that almost everyone in the town was "armed to the teeth." When the local student group that CORE worked with in Ferriday organized a march, Acheson opposed it, stating, "the people aren't prepared for NV (= non violence), they say they'll hit back if attacked."[41]

Most local people who became involved in the movement did accept the importance of remaining nonviolent during demonstrations, although they did not always succeed at doing so. A report on the picketing of a store in Pointe Coupee Parish in July 1965 stated that when the protesters were harassed and attacked, one local activist hit a white man, giving him several cuts in the face. In contexts where there were no news reporters or television cameras, black Louisianans were even more likely to depart from the teachings of CORE. FFM secretary Mary Boyd saw no reason to remain passive when group members were arrested and beaten by police while putting up posters to advertise a planned demonstration. Boyd attempted to stop the officers from dragging one of her friends along the ground by her feet; after one policeman slapped her in the face, she pulled off her shoe and hit him with it twice before being knocked down from behind by a man with a soda bottle.[42]

Activists frequently employed more lethal weapons than shoes against their attackers. The most common response of African Americans to the numerous drive-by shootings and bombings carried out by white supremacists in black neighborhoods was to reach for their firearms. The night after Joseph Carter registered to vote, he was awakened by shots fired at a neighbor's house. Carter immediately grabbed his gun and prepared to fight off the intruders. In July 1965 night riders shot into a black woman's house in Ferriday and she shot back, reportedly hitting the windshield of their car. A few months later, when police arrived at the home of Robert Lewis after it had been bombed, they found him standing on the lawn with a loaded shotgun. The bomber was perhaps fortunate that the gun was not loaded before the attack. Lewis had seen the man jump out of a truck and place the firebomb on the porch. He later stated, "I had enough time to blow his brain out, had I found some shells."[43]

Some activists preferred to head off trouble before it started. Returning home one day to find a local Klansman parked in front of his house, Frank Norman of Tallulah took his gun and fired a shot behind the man's vehicle, causing it to move off rapidly. Martin Williams kept firearms in his house and car just in case he ever needed them. Other black residents of Tallulah who were involved in the movement did the same. Williams said, "As far as I know, there wasn't nobody who was afraid—I don't know what they carried, but nobody was afraid back in them times. Nobody. And you could get on the phone and call one, in a few minutes you'd have a hundred to your rescue."[44]

Similarly, CORE worker Meg Redden remembered that most of the people she worked with in Pointe Coupee Parish were armed. Redden stayed at the home of Siegent Caulfield, a longtime activist and construction worker who had to leave his family for several months during the summer of 1964 to work in New Orleans. Caulfield taught his seventeen-year-old daughter Thelma how to use the family's shotgun, and after vigilantes shot into their house, Redden also learned how to handle the firearm.[45]

African Americans' use of armed self-defense cut across class, gender, and generational lines. The black men and women who carried guns and used them were farmers, homemakers, students, laborers, ministers, and small business owners who wanted only to be recognized as citizens and were forced to defend themselves from those who attempted to deny them that right. The civil rights movement provoked responses from white supremacists in Louisiana that rivaled the notorious and more widely publicized actions of their counterparts in Alabama and Mississippi. In Plaquemine, peaceful demonstrations held in August 1963 were broken up by law enforcement officials using tear gas, electric cattle prods, and clubs. On 1 September, after mounted police had dispersed a crowd of about one thousand African Americans who rallied to protest the earlier acts of brutality, more terror was unleashed on the black community. Police and vigilantes arrested or attacked any black people they found on the streets and forced others out of the homes and churches where they were hiding by throwing tear gas into the buildings. A twelve-year-old girl died after being trampled by a horse, 150 other people required hospitalization, and the church where the demonstrations had been based was virtually destroyed.[46]

As elsewhere in the South, CORE workers and local people who were involved in the Louisiana movement faced threats to their lives every day.

In 1964, at around the same time that national attention was focused on the disappearance of three civil rights activists in Mississippi, the bodies of two black men were found floating in a river near Tallulah. David Whatley reported in 1966 that several attempts had been made to destroy his grandmother's house "and us along with it," and that a reward of one thousand dollars had been offered for anyone who would kill him. In some places merely being black was reason enough to be afraid. The proprietor of a shoe repair shop in Ferriday was burned to death when vigilantes poured gasoline over the store and its owner, setting both alight. The incident perplexed civil rights workers because the man had never been involved in the movement. One writer concluded wearily, "He was a Negro, and someone found him guilty of breathing."[47]

Incidents of harassment and intimidation were routinely reported to local and federal authorities, and, almost as routinely, they were ignored. Around midnight on 19 January 1964, task force workers in East Feliciana Parish informed the fire chief that a cross was burning outside CORE headquarters in Clinton. He refused to do anything, saying, "We cain't be bothered with putting out fires in the middle of the night burning in the middle of the street." As in previous decades, parish officials often knew about, helped to plan, and participated in the violence. The day CORE volunteers arrived in Ferriday, the town sheriff drove his car up to where they were talking with a group of African Americans, let out two criminals he had brought with him from the jail, and watched as the men beat up the civil rights workers. Like the local black people, CORE members became accustomed to treatment that suggested police in Louisiana were not bound by national laws or statutes protecting citizens' constitutional rights. Bill Brown was once arrested for speeding while he was sitting on a front porch; another time he was jailed for "obstructing the highway" after the town marshal's car swerved off the road in an attempt to hit him. A discussion paper prepared for a CORE training session warned: "One does not 'reason' with a Southern cop . . . and 'laws of the land' do not apply to him. 'I[']m the law here' is a standard thing to hear—and the hardest thing to accept is its truth."[48]

Federal agencies also seemed reluctant to intervene. Civil rights workers rarely saw action on complaints sent to the FBI or the Department of Justice in Washington. Miriam Feingold observed, "The FBI snoops around, writes a lot, and sits on its rear ends as it were."[49] In a 1966 interview, Gayle Jenkins of the Bogalusa Voters League laughed when she was asked if activists had received much help from the federal government. "Mostly what they do is take notes," she said. "You have the FBI agents in here and they take notes and they say that's all they can do." When a group of African Americans attempted to integrate a city park, federal officials scribbled on notepads while local police and Klan members violently attacked the activists. Later the Klan killed a black deputy sheriff, and the authorities failed to apprehend anyone for the crime. Jenkins concluded: "I don't know what you would do to get protection from the federal government. . . . Even if somebody's killing you they can't stop [it], they can only take a note."[50]

No wonder, then, that local activists decided to take control of the situation themselves. In the northern Louisiana town of Jonesboro, a group of African Americans that included several war veterans founded the Deacons for Defense and Justice to protect civil rights workers from violence. They assigned CORE project director Charles Fenton his own bodyguard, provided armed escorts for activists traveling through and around the town, guarded meetings and demonstrations, and patrolled black neighborhoods at night to deter the Klan. The Deacons proved so effective that black people in other communities formed similar groups. Residents of Bogalusa, Ferriday, Tallulah, St. Francisville, Minden, Homer, Grambling, and New Orleans established their own chapters of the Deacons, and eventually the movement spread outside the state.[51] In June 1965 Deacons president Earnest Thomas told the *Louisiana Weekly* that the organization had over fifty-five chapters in various stages of development in Louisiana, Mississippi, and Alabama.[52]

Like other aspects of the freedom struggle in the 1960s, the spread of armed self-defense groups reflected a transition from the mostly unplanned, individual responses of the Jim Crow era to more organized forms of fighting back against white violence. It also indicated CORE's failure to convert the majority of rural black people into Gandhian Satyagrahis. Although nonviolence was an effective tactic for national civil rights organizations seeking to appeal to white Americans' sense of justice, in the context of many local activists' lives it seemed hopelessly irrelevant. CORE workers did what they could to persuade people otherwise, with only limited success. Just two days after FFM members voted in favor of requiring everyone who belonged to the organization to take an oath of nonviolence, they decided that this should only apply while members were participating in demonstrations. Task force volunteers soon realized that they could not prevent residents from taking up arms to protect their homes and families, and at least some of them were grateful that the local people were prepared to carry guns even if they refused to do so themselves. As Mike Lesser stated, "We cannot tell someone not to defend his property and the lives of his family, and let me tell you, those 15–20 shotguns guarding our meetings are very reassuring."[53]

Discussions within CORE about the commitment to nonviolence were frequent. National officers argued that the organization could not allow the use of violence to fight violence and urged volunteers to try to discourage people from carrying weapons. "This is our responsibility," CORE leaders asserted. "It is our responsibility to provide leadership and an example." But many workers in the field found the arguments of those who were directing operations from the safety of CORE's headquarters in New York unconvincing. In the summer of 1963 Miriam Feingold informed her family: "Most everyone, especially the kids who have been most active, are disillusioned with non-violence, & see the situation very much turning toward violence. They think that we must do as the masses feel—& if it means violence, then that's what we do." At a staff meeting a few months later she wrote in her notebook: "Jim McCain says CORE can't afford to advocate retaliation. But Dave Dennis, Jerome Smith say to hell w/ CORE, we're w/ the people!"[54]

Local black people's determination to fight back against violence was crucial to the survival of the civil rights movement in rural Louisiana. Activists struggled daily to overcome the fear of reprisals that prevented many African Americans from participating in voter registration efforts and demonstrations against segregation. The armed guards who watched over meetings and escorted civil rights workers safely through Klan territory offered the protection and security that law enforcement agencies had failed to provide. Significantly, voter registration clinics in West Feliciana Parish typically drew over one hundred people, whereas in neighboring parishes where there were no armed guards it was harder to persuade people to attend meetings. CORE worker Catherine Patterson remembered the difference that the Deacons made in Jonesboro. When she first visited the town in the spring of 1964, no African Americans would allow civil rights workers to stay with them, but the following spring local people were more willing to invite them into their homes. "I think it had a lot to do with the Deacons," she said. "And I think it had a lot to do with members of the community sensing their own capacity to protect themselves."[55]

Where African Americans showed their willingness to defend themselves, violence seems to have diminished. Mike Lesser reported that when black people first began registering to vote in West Feliciana, they were threatened and beaten, "But as soon as Neg[ro]es started carrying sho[t]guns and announced they would shoot any strange white face on their property the attacks stopped and haven't resumed."[56] In St. Helena Parish, black students attending a newly integrated high school hit back when they were tormented by white classmates. Task force workers there reported that "these episodes created something of a stir, but the Negro students have not been bothered since."[57] Bogalusa Deacons leader Charles Sims found that would-be harassers normally backed down once they realized he had a gun. "The showing of a weapon stops many things," he said. "Everybody want to live and nobody want to die."[58]

Partly in response to the use of armed self-defense by black people, federal officials finally began to crack down on white violence to avert what they feared could become a race war. The FBI initiated counterintelligence operations against the Ku Klux Klan in September 1964, and the evidence of illegal activity gathered by agents enabled the Justice Department to gain a court order in December 1965 that enjoined Klan members in Bogalusa from using threats, intimidation, and violence. The belated action failed to impress some local activists, however. Several members of the Bogalusa Voters League expressed the view that the presence of the Deacons for Defense and Justice was the only thing that enabled civil rights work to continue in their town. That belief was shared by Steven Rubin, of the Louisiana Civil Liberties Union, who stated in 1966 that he had "not the slightest doubt that the presence of the Deacons, rather than the police, has served as a deterrent to the Klan. But for the Deacons, there would have been a lot of dead Negroes in Bogalusa."[59]

Americans who remember the civil rights movement are likely to recall with reverence the inspiring speeches of Martin Luther King Jr. and his commitment to nonviolence. But in the minds of at least some who were there, a different image stands out: African Americans fighting back. Twenty-five years after he participated in the Plaquemine demonstrations, local activist Kenny Johnson still recalled the sense of empowerment he felt at the sight of black people refusing to remain passive when confronted by white violence. "I could look over and see my father also out there taking the tear gas canisters that were thrown and throwing them back toward the police," he said. "That's a real—a real high."[60]

The achievements of Dr. King and others who struggled to remain nonviolent under extremely trying circumstances deserve all of the recognition and respect they have received. But activists who rejected that strategy and took up arms to defend black communities were essential in helping to realize the goals that all participants were fighting for. Their insistence on protecting themselves and the young volunteers who had recently joined the freedom struggle was as important to the movement at the local level as nonviolence was to the national movement. African Americans who fought back against attempts to repress their demands for citizenship signaled to white and black southerners alike that they did not accept second-class status and helped to preserve the space for political action that had emerged as a result of developments at the national level.

The accounts of discrimination, threats, economic reprisals, and violent attacks that permeated civil rights workers' field reports provided ample evidence that federal intervention was necessary to protect black southerners' citizenship rights. As one study noted, the most important contribution of the VEP was "its demonstration, day by day for two and a half years, of the need for federal legislation if Negro enfranchisement were ever to be fully achieved for the present generations in the South." In 1964 Congress finally passed a comprehensive Civil Rights Act that outlawed discrimination in public accommodations, employment, and unions; created the Equal Employment Opportunity Commission; and authorized the government to withhold federal funds from public programs that were operated in a discriminatory manner. A year later the Voting Rights Act of 1965 abolished the literacy and constitutional understanding tests that had been used to prevent black southerners from registering to vote and provided for federal registrars to be sent to districts where patterns of discrimination had been clearly demonstrated.[61]

The removal of arbitrarily enforced testing and qualifications requirements led to a rapid increase in black voter registration. In West Feliciana Parish, for instance, CORE had managed to register fewer than one hundred African Americans before the Voting Rights Act was passed. By October 1965 almost seven hundred black people were listed on the parish registration rolls. One month later, after the arrival of a federal registrar, that number more than doubled with the addition of one thousand newly registered voters. A similar increase occurred in East Feliciana Parish, where over one hundred people lined up to be registered each day. Local activists James Bell and Laura Spears remembered African Americans' relief that the tests were no longer to be used. Bell stated, "The applications weren't any more long and drawn out, where you had to be a history student or a grad student to pass the exam." Two thousand black people registered in the parish in eighteen days. Statewide, the number of black voters grew from 153,781 to 243,000 in the first year after passage of the Voting Rights Act.[62]

Compared with the strong support that rural black people gave voter registration efforts, CORE's attempts to desegregate public facilities received only a lukewarm response in some communities. In July 1963 Miriam Feingold reported: "One lady told me yesterday that she didn't care if the lunch counters everywhere were opened—she couldn't buy anything with the money she had. All she wants is a good job for her husband, and the chance to bring up her kids like everyone else's kids." African Americans in Tallulah expressed similar sentiments. Early in the summer of 1965, CORE workers in cooperation with the local voters' league succeeded in desegregating the downtown restaurants and triumphantly advertised this "big step toward first class citizenship" in their weekly newsletter. Local black people do not seem to have rushed to take advantage of these new opportunities, however. A later issue of *CORE Freedom News* reminded readers that the restaurants were integrated and urged them to use the facilities that were now open to them. The following month CORE workers admitted that desegregation was "only a scratch" on the surface of problems facing the African American community. After canvassing the town to assess black people's needs, civil rights activists discovered that most of them were more concerned with things like the suspiciously high readings of gas and electricity meters, the poor condition of streets, and the lack of garbage service, street lights, and fire protection in black neighborhoods.[63]

CORE workers had only to look around them to understand why local people cared more about economic issues than desegregation. Writing home to her parents about the extreme poverty that many black Louisianans endured, Miriam Feingold must have realized that exclusion from white restaurants or public facilities was not the biggest problem these people had. "Some areas haven't changed much since slavery," she stated. "There is no running water, no indoor toilets, no street lights, no garbage collections, no paved roads. . . . The houses have holes in [the] walls and floor, and drainage ditches in the front." Feingold saw mothers and their children walking around with bare feet in the middle of winter and found one family living in a shack where "a fire in a fireplace barely heated a room with more holes than walls." By March 1964 the young civil rights worker had concluded, "What is needed, basically, are not desegregated libraries, but decent farm income and decent jobs for non-farm people."[64]

When black people did express interest in desegregation, they were not, as some white southerners believed, "begging for social acceptance." Robert Lewis stated that when FFM members began pushing for more than token integration of Concordia Parish schools, it was not because they wanted to go to school with white people, "but rather . . . to be able to have the same economic opportunity as white had." In his ranking of local activists' priorities, Lewis placed gaining access to those opportunities second only to ending police brutality in Ferriday. A notice announcing a boycott of white-owned stores in the town declared: "Too long we the Negro citizens of Concordia Parish have been treated like animals and second class citizens. . . . We are fighting for equal rights, better jobs, better schools, better streets, better garbage service, more street lights, more fire [plugs], better mail service, better jobs downtown where we spend our money, and a countless number of other things." The notice summarized the aims of the FFM as "Fir$t Cla$$ Citizen$hip [and] Fir$t Cla$$ Job$."[65]

By the mid-1960s CORE was redefining its own goals and programs to align more closely with the needs of the people its task force workers were trying to help. Plans for a "Louisiana Citizenship Program" drawn up by Ronnie Moore and his staff in September 1964 emphasized that it was necessary to survey local communities and ask people what issues were important to them rather than trying to impose a predetermined agenda. The group suggested combining voter registration with other activities like attacking discrimination in employment, building community centers, and establishing adult literacy programs. "In short," they stated, "our program will emphasize community demands rather than a program priority of our own." A discussion paper prepared for volunteers and supporters of CORE's 1965 summer projects made a similar point. "We have come to realize that voter registration and desegregation of public accommodations and facilities are not enough," its authors explained. "The problems are deeper than lack of the vote and legislated segregation, and many aspects must be tackled at the same time if the whole is to emerge sound and sensible."[66]

In the second half of the decade, CORE workers became involved in a broad range of activities designed to attack the root causes of poverty and racism. Volunteers assigned to Tallulah in the summer of 1965 worked with a group of black employees of the Chicago Mill and Lumber Company to press for equal employment opportunities in compliance with Title VII of the Civil Rights Act and attempted to reorganize the white-dominated union local.[67] They also helped the local voters' league to organize a selective buying campaign aimed at pressuring the owners of stores and businesses in the town to hire more black workers. Activists knew that change was much more likely to be achieved through exercising and enhancing their economic power than through moral persuasion. A flyer announcing the boycott stated that white people had not heeded the requests of civil rights groups, "but they will listen to the voices—and pocket books—of all Tallulah's Negroes speaking together." After resisting for several months, the town's stubborn employers finally capitulated. Local leader Earnestine Brown explained that by the 1960s, most white people owned cars and could afford to travel to larger cities to shop, leaving the economic life of small rural towns like Tallulah heavily dependent on black people's dollars. White merchants ultimately realized that "they had to do something, you know—couldn't just remain as it was, because this was a different day now, and [black people's] money was all spent just like the white man."[68]

Activists continued the struggle for better education by pressuring white officials to act more decisively on the issue of school desegregation. As a result of a CORE-sponsored lawsuit, federal district court judge E. Gordon West ordered that the first and twelfth grades of all public schools in West Feliciana Parish be desegregated in 1965 and formulated plans for the integration of the remaining grades over a two-year period.[69] More than a decade after the Supreme Court's ruling in *Brown v. Board of Education*, parish school boards in Louisiana finally accepted the inevitability of desegregation. Judge West was himself a segregationist who had strongly criticized the higher court's decision. Nevertheless, he cut short the hearing in the West Feliciana case, stating that school boards in Louisiana were tired of fighting lawsuits and wanted to be taken "off the hook." According to West, parish officials had to show some resistance to appease their white constituents, but ultimately they wanted "the Federal court to be their 'fall guy' and tell them this is what you will have to do."[70]

In St. Helena Parish, efforts to force school board officials to implement a desegregation order that had been handed down in 1960 as a result of an NAACP lawsuit were combined with pressure from a local student group to improve facilities at the black high school. Members of the Students' Association for Freedom and Equality (SAFE) organized a boycott of the school in January 1966, issuing those who participated in the protest absentee notes that read, "The reason I stayed out of school Friday is that I was sick . . . of second class education." In response to rumors that black students might have to start paying for their textbooks, SAFE demanded that the school board cease its practice of forcing the black community to finance construction projects and amenities that white students received without charge. A leaflet advertising a meeting to discuss the issue reminded African Americans in the parish of the injustices they had endured and how they had struggled to overcome them. "We have had to cut down trees for our light poles. We have had to pay for the football field fence, We have had to put up our football bleachers, We have had to pay for our piano, We have had to plant grass and carry dirt. . . . Whites had all this done for them by school board money and state workers. We are sick and tired of paying for things the whites get for free." Picketing, demonstrations, and the threat that newly enfranchised African Americans might vote them out of office forced school board members to give in to most of SAFE's demands in April 1966.[71]

In initiatives that were reminiscent of the LFU's efforts in the 1930s, CORE activists also worked with local people to increase black participation in federal farm programs. Many black farmers had been denied access to federal loans and ignored by their county agents after the demise of the New Deal in the 1940s, and CORE workers found that this was a major complaint of the African Americans they spoke with. They informed black farmers of government financial assistance that was available and attempted to gain representation for African Americans on local administrative committees of the Agricultural Soil Conservation Service. In rural communities, the decisions made by ASCS committees were as important to many people as those of police juries and school boards. Committee members ran the government's crop allotment and price support programs, and allocated federal funds to farmers who adopted agricultural conservation practices. According to one report, their power was such that "in many areas county government operations are dwarfed by ASC programs as measured in dollar expenditures or impact on residents or both."[72]

Not surprisingly, given what was at stake, the white men who controlled the ASCS committees were just as determined to prevent any African American influence here as in other areas. In West Feliciana Parish, officials had for years neglected to send ballots for ASCS elections to many eligible farmers, preventing them from participating. When CORE accused them of discriminating against black people, members of the all-white local committee drafted an integrated slate of candidates and agreed to mail ballots to every farm family in the parish. However, as was often the case when African Americans were finally included in the political process, the black candidates were handpicked by white administrators. The farmers CORE was working with chose their own representatives and attempted to elect them with write-in votes, but none of the candidates received enough support to make it onto the committee.[73]

In a similar initiative in Pointe Coupee Parish, seven black candidates contested the ASCS election. White committee leaders responded by placing the names of eight other African Americans on the ballot who were unqualified and had not expressed any interest in running, but who could be easily manipulated. CORE workers complained to the Department of Agriculture and an agent visited the parish to investigate. Yet according to Paul Kleyman, "His 'investigation' consisted of talking to the clerks in the ASC office. He wasn't interested in the list of complaints we had prepared nor in speaking with the Negro farmers and discussing their complaints about the unqualified Negroes put on the ballot without their knowledge." As in West Feliciana and seven other parishes where CORE tried to increase black representation on the agricultural committees, no African Americans were elected.[74]

A more promising development occurred in St. Landry Parish, where CORE worker John Zippert helped a group of white and black farmers to organize the Grand Marie Vegetable Producers' Cooperative (GMVPC). Small farmers in the region were finding it difficult to survive in the face of increasing competition from large-scale corporate farms that monopolized the processing and selling of sweet potatoes, their primary cash crop. Black farmers usually received between fifty cents and one dollar per fifty-pound crate of potatoes they sold to the larger growers, who were organized and sought to keep the prices they paid as low as possible.[75] In 1965 six farmers who had already joined together to purchase machinery began meeting with others and discussing the idea of forming a marketing cooperative. Interest in the project was strong, especially among African Americans, and membership in the GMVPC grew steadily after its official incorporation in February 1966.

Zippert assisted the group in gaining financial support from various sources, including the Scholarship, Education, and Defense Fund for Racial Equality (SEDFRE), the Office of Economic Opportunity (OEO), and the Farmers' Home Administration. After buying storage facilities and processing equipment, the GMVPC assumed control over the preparation, packaging, and marketing of its members' potatoes, offering them prices that were double or triple those they had received before. By providing an alternative market, the cooperative forced other buyers to compete with its prices and in this way benefited all the farmers in the community. In addition, the

GMVPC used some of its funds to launch an educational program that provided much-needed advice and assistance to rural poor people in St. Landry and three other parishes. Field workers for the GMVPC's Sweet Potato Alert Program renewed efforts to involve black people in government farm programs by visiting farmers and arranging lectures and seminars to explain the various types of aid that were available from federal antipoverty agencies.[76]

Community organizing efforts like the project in St. Landry became the primary focus of CORE's work after 1965, encouraged by President Lyndon Johnson's Great Society programs. The War on Poverty provided funding and technical assistance for local initiatives to supply needed services and employment opportunities for the nation's most impoverished citizens. Examples of the types of activities financed by the OEO in cooperation with local Community Action Programs (CAPs) included the construction of low-income housing and the establishment of early childhood education and day care programs (Head Start), health clinics, adult literacy classes, and community information centers where people could go for legal assistance and other aid.[77]

Guidelines for the antipoverty programs called for "maximum feasible participation" of the poor, a mandate that CORE workers and local people took seriously. In discussions about how to organize the Head Start program in East Feliciana Parish, for example, several local activists argued passionately that the opportunities for employment generated should be given to black people who were not college graduates or professionals. One woman expressed concern that if too much emphasis was placed on hiring people with educational qualifications, the jobs would go to teachers who did not need them; instead, administrators should hire "people who ain't got no jobs." At a similar meeting attended by representatives from several parishes, one person suggested that Head Start staff should have at least some college education. Bernice Noflin of West Feliciana Parish retorted that she thought the program was supposed to help poor people, and "in poor parishes you don't find many people running around w[ith] college degrees."[78]

Such comments reflected local activists' belief that the people most qualified to run antipoverty programs were those who were poor themselves. Only when they had experienced firsthand the kinds of problems created by desperate economic circumstances could administrators fully understand what was needed to solve them. In 1966 a group of rural farm women in St. Landry Parish gave eloquent expression to this idea in a grant proposal they submitted to the OEO. The women were members of a homemakers' club that had been established as part of the Home Demonstration Program (a branch of agricultural extension work) in the parish. They explained: "Our club is not very big because most of the people who really need to learn and get help do not come to our meetings. Most poor people have to work too hard and have too many children to be able to come to meetings." They wanted to organize a program that enabled volunteers to visit people in their own homes instead. "Most people don't have time to listen to small people, but we will take time and learn by what we hear," the women wrote. "We want to help poor people learn to stick together to fight for the things they really want. This is the only way we will change things for poor people. This is what we think 'community action' is all about. . . . We feel that the real purpose of the Anti-poverty program was to HELP THE POOR TO HELP THEM-SELVES and our own proposal was written by concerned poor people in our community through employing other poor people to bring this assistance to them."[79]

The idea of granting funds directly to poor people to enable them solve their own problems was a fundamentally different approach from traditional welfare systems that had kept thousands of displaced, unskilled, and uneducated black workers dependent on unemployment benefits and seasonal, low-wage jobs. It offered the possibility of breaking the cycle of poverty by providing access to job training, employment, loans, and other forms of assistance that could help people achieve economic independence. As in the 1930s, that possibility was anathema to many white political and business leaders in rural Louisiana. The threat to their power that antipoverty initiatives represented, as well as the thousands of dollars in federal grants that had suddenly become available, provided incentives for police juries and other administrative bodies to stake out their own claims on the Great Society. In almost every community where CAPs were established, local activists and CORE workers became embroiled in bitter struggles with parish officials over control of these programs.

Developments in East Feliciana Parish represented a typical scenario. In May 1965 a group of white residents organized a committee to work on setting up a CAP agency for the parish that consisted of twenty-five white and five black people. According to county agent Farrell Roberts, those behind the move included "bankers, education leaders, political leaders, and business men" who were interested in "promoting economic development in the parish." Many committee members openly opposed the civil rights movement. L. D. Peay, for instance, had assaulted two activists who picketed his store in December 1963. Others, including Roy Chaney and police jury president L. E. Brian, had held key positions in the East Feliciana Citizens' Council until the organization dissolved itself in June 1965 so that its members could help set up the CAP agency without being tainted by their segregationist affiliations. The CAP organizers held no public meetings to discuss their plans, nor did they consult African Americans in the community about who should represent them. The five black appointees to the committee, including extension agent Prince Lewis and school principal W. W. Wilson, had all distanced themselves from civil rights activity. CORE workers reported that these people were completely controlled by white officials.[80]

The CAP agency, Community Development Incorporated, was formed and its fourteen board members were chosen from among the thirty people who had served on the planning committee. The board then applied for and received an OEO grant of just over forty thousand dollars to establish a Head Start program in the parish. W. W. Wilson was appointed as director. Among the other paid staff were to be eighteen certified teachers and eighteen teachers' aides, two secretaries, two lunchroom workers, and five bus drivers. Wilson and a few other black community "leaders" then chose candidates for these positions. Little was done to publicize the jobs or encourage others to apply for them, and no African Americans who had been active in the civil rights movement were hired.[81]

A similar situation developed in St. Landry Parish. Black lawyer Marion Overton White reported in May 1966 that the directors of Acadiana Neuf, a CAP agency that had been formed to serve St. Landry and eight other parishes in southwestern Louisiana, were "in the truest sense racists and 'Nigger haters.'" White asked for help from the OEO in ensuring that antipoverty funds reached the poor people they were intended to help instead of being used by wealthy white people to further their own interests. The white administrators had wrested control of Acadiana Neuf from Southern Consumers' Cooperative (SCC), an organization based in Lafayette that had a strong history of working with poor black people. Its founder, Father Albert McKnight, told OEO staff members, "They used us . . . to get approved, and now since they are approved, we are not involved at all."[82]

The OEO received hundreds of identical complaints about CAPs that were dominated by white people who appointed "pet" African Americans to create the illusion that administrative boards were integrated and representative of everyone. Federal officials attempted to solve these problems by investigating the composition of CAP boards more closely and withholding funds from those that did not seem to genuinely represent their local communities. But even when federal intervention resulted in more participation by poor people, administrators still had to contend with opposition from local officials. In 1966 the OEO rejected an application from a conservative, segregationist, white-dominated CAP in St. Mary Parish and granted funding to operate Head Start programs in the region to SCC instead. The white people responded by persuading Governor John McKeithen to exercise his right to veto the project and putting pressure on administrators at the OEO's regional office in Austin, Texas, to support their own grant proposal. In Rapides Parish, African Americans on the board of directors of Total Community Action successfully handled the antipoverty program for a year, then split between members who strongly supported civil rights work and others who were indifferent. According to local activist Louis Berry, tensions resulted in the moderates leaving to set up a rival agency "with the tacit consent and blessing of the white power structure for the latent purpose of neutralizing our full participation in Poverty Projects." The new organization received funding to operate Head Start in the parish, and Berry's group was "rebuffed, thwarted and frustrated in project after project" that it submitted to the local CAP and the regional office.[83]

Such conflicts were a nationwide phenomenon that greatly hindered the effectiveness of antipoverty measures, provided ammunition for conservative opponents of the War on Poverty in Congress, and contributed to a growing public perception that millions of tax dollars were being wasted on useless projects.[84] In addition, many white Americans rejected the notion that economic equality for African Americans was necessary to eliminate racism. The Civil Rights and Voting Rights Acts were enough, they thought. Now that legalized segregation and disfranchisement had been abolished, black people's success or failure depended on their own abilities and actions, just like everyone else's. Affirmative action programs threatened white workers' economic security, intensifying opposition to the civil rights movement. These problems were compounded by the negative publicity surrounding the emerging Black Power movement and the rise to national prominence of black spokespeople who advocated a radical restructuring of society, if necessary through violent revolution.[85]

In the second half of the 1960s, thousands of Americans withdrew their support for the civil rights movement, leaving both local and national activists without the finances or other resources necessary to sustain the struggle for more meaningful social change. Limited funds had been a major hindrance to civil rights work in rural Louisiana since the beginning of the decade, and CORE's Freedom Task Force could not survive the dramatic losses in income that began to afflict the organization in 1964.[86] In a memorandum of April 1965, Ronnie Moore informed staff members that the project was more than $1,600 in debt and asked them to limit travel and long-distance telephone calls. The following month, CORE reported an excess of expenditures over income of $220,059 for the previous financial year. Most of the volunteers for the summer project of 1965 paid all of their own expenses because, as one worker put it, "CORE is broke."[87] At the same time, Black Power advocates within CORE made it clear that white people were no longer welcome in the organization. When Floyd McKissick took over from James Farmer as national director in 1966, several experienced staff members who still adhered to the ideal of integration were either fired by the national office or resigned, and thousands of rank-and-file members also left.[88] Greatly weakened both administratively and financially, CORE abandoned its projects in rural Louisiana after the summer of that year.[89]

Though they had not always agreed with task force workers, local activists deeply appreciated the assistance that CORE had provided to the freedom struggle. After recounting the history of violent repression that characterized Ferriday before 1965, Robert Lewis stated, "Then . . . CORE came to Ferriday, and Ferriday . . . hasn't been the same since." CORE workers informed black people of their legal rights, showed them how to organize demonstrations, and told them which federal agencies to contact to make complaints. "Once we found out what our rights were," Lewis said, "once we found out we had a legitimate right to assemble peacefully . . . to speak or say what we wanted to say . . . then we knew we didn't have any problems." Zelma Wyche told Miriam Feingold in 1966, "People need help at all times, local people, and had it not been for the civil rights groups throughout America I doubt if Madison Parish would really have started moving." In the face of Klan violence, police brutality, church burnings, and other efforts to stifle the movement, the members of Wyche's group kept struggling because they knew that "the federal government was finally moving into the South with force, only because they had been pushed by these national civil rights organizations." Moses Williams concurred, asserting, "CORE played a major, a *major* role, in helping us to move up the ladder, so to speak."[90]

As these statements attest, civil rights workers from outside rural Louisiana were vital and valued participants in the freedom movement. But those members of CORE who believed that they needed to provide local people with "leadership and an example" were mistaken. Moses Williams stated, "I came [to Tallulah] late, in the last part of '52, and I found in Madison Parish, some Roy Wilkinses, Martin Luther Kings, and James Farmers right here in Madison Parish—not in New York or Chicago, they were here." The desire to achieve first-class citizenship existed before the 1960s, but often the financial resources to sustain a powerful movement did not. As Martin Williams explained: "Nobody got no money, nobody got a lawyer to get nobody out of jail. . . . How can you do something when you ain't got nothing? And CORE had all kind of money and connection. We didn't have nothing."[91]

Black Louisianans looked to national civil rights groups not for inspiration or guidance, but as important means of support for their own agenda. When CORE's ideas or priorities differed from those of local activists, as was the case with the organization's emphasis on nonviolence and direct action against segregation, task force workers—not local people—ultimately adjusted their approach to the freedom struggle. As Charles Payne has argued and this study reiterates, rural black southerners were not passive recipients of the ideas or leadership of national civil rights groups. They were agents in their own right who helped shape the development and outcomes of the movement.[92]

Significantly, the issues that motivated black protest and political activity in the 1960s showed some continuity with earlier struggles: higher wages, access to good jobs and education, helping poor people to achieve economic independence, preventing white violence, and federal protection of African Americans' citizenship rights. These same concerns lay behind the broad range of methods that black Louisianans had used in their attempts to challenge white supremacy throughout the twentieth century. By leaving plantations in search of fair treatment, accepting advice and assistance from extension agents, participating in the labor movements of the 1930s and 1940s, fighting racism at home and abroad during World War II, establishing NAACP branches, and supporting CORE's efforts in the 1960s, African Americans signaled their rejection of the second-class status assigned them in the social order and pressured white Americans to accord them real freedom and equality. These activities should not be seen as separate and unrelated to each other. For black people who engaged in some or all of them, they were different parts of the same struggle.

Epilogue

Without minimizing the achievements of the civil rights movement, a recognition of its limits seems a standard lament among participants and historians.[1] Federal legislation abolished legalized discrimination and protected African Americans' voting rights, but the failure to redistribute economic power left some of the most important causes of inequality untouched. Political leaders and the majority of white Americans refused to acknowledge that ending racism required more far-reaching reforms. The backlash against civil rights initiatives and conservative dominance over national politics after 1970 ensured that subtle but powerful forms of discrimination and injustice would persist into the next century.

No one doubts that the events of the 1960s altered conditions in the South in important ways. Not least among the significant and lasting changes effected by the civil rights movement was the restoration of black southerners' ability to vote. African American voter registration in Louisiana increased dramatically after 1965, rising from rates as low as 2 percent of those eligible to more than 90 percent in some parishes. Statewide, the proportion of black voters who were registered doubled, rising from 31 percent in 1964 to 59 percent in 1967. By the end of the 1970s, close to 70 percent of black Louisianans were registered.[2]

African Americans' new voting strength opened the possibility of electing more sympathetic parish officials to replace the racist white men who had traditionally dominated police juries, school boards, town councils, and police forces in rural Louisiana. A fact sheet prepared by SEDFRE in October 1967 noted that African Americans in Louisiana seemed poised to greatly increase their political representation, with black candidates contesting almost every available elected position in some parishes.[3] The following year the U.S. Commission on Civil Rights counted thirty-seven black elected officials in Louisiana, including ten police jurors, four school board members, eight constables, one mayor, and one representative in the state legislature.[4]

Even after passage of the Voting Rights Act, however, white supremacists contested black political participation. Forced to accept the reality of mass voter registration by African Americans, opponents of the freedom struggle shifted their attention to minimizing the impact of black votes. In 1966 dubious electoral practices prevented African American candidates from winning office in several parishes. In Tallulah, during the Democratic primary elections in April, officials provided only one polling place in the precinct where Zelma Wyche was running for nomination as city alderman. Fourteen hundred voters had to wait in long lines, and weariness or other commitments caused many to leave without casting their votes. Harrison Brown won the nomination for school board member in his ward in the same primary, but he was defeated in the general election after parish officials solicited more than five hundred absentee ballots favoring his white opponent. In West Feliciana Parish, poll workers prevented several African Americans from voting in the Democratic primary by claiming that they were registered as members of other parties. One black woman who had registered as a Democrat several months earlier was stunned to discover that she was listed as a member of the segregationist States' Rights Party. Other subterfuges employed by opponents of the freedom struggle included switching from ward-based to at-large elections, gerrymandering electoral districts, denying black people assistance at the polls, vote buying, and the old methods of threats and intimidation.[5]

White recalcitrance was gradually overcome through the persistence of local activists, Justice Department lawsuits, and Supreme Court decisions that gave federal authorities the power to ensure not only that African Americans could vote, but also that their votes would mean something.[6] Redistricting plans and electoral laws that attempted to dilute black votes were challenged and struck down, opening the way for a significant increase in the number of black elected officials in Louisiana. In 1975 more than two hundred African Americans held political office in the state, and over the next decade that number doubled. By the 1990s twenty Louisiana towns had African American mayors, and black people filled more than six hundred other elected positions.[7]

With African Americans in office, Louisiana's rural communities became much safer places for black inhabitants. Local activists often made it a priority to elect black law enforcement officers to ensure an end to police brutality. With African Americans also filling positions as judges and serving on juries, Klan members and other perpetrators of violence could no longer rely on an all-white justice system to absolve them of their crimes, which helped to deter the attacks on black people that had been so common before the 1960s. Interviewed in 1984, Spiver Gordon stated: "I can see night and day difference in terms of the fear that was there. I can drive in West Feliciana and not worry about it, because I know there are black folk in office. . . . I can drive through these places and not be worried about whether somebody's gonna shoot me or whether or not I'm gonna get arrested or hauled off to jail for something."[8] Most activists counted the realization of black people's desire for political participation and protection from violence as the main achievements of the civil rights movement.

Changes in other areas proved more difficult. White officials countered the struggle for equal education with as much determination as they had fought black voting rights and with more success. Most school districts waited until lawsuits were filed against them before taking any action to end segregation and then adopted plans that ensured integration would be minimal. Under "freedom of choice" plans that placed most responsibility for integrating the schools on black parents and children, little progress was made in the civil rights era. Fear of reprisals and concerns about sending children into hostile environments discouraged many African American families from requesting transfers to white schools. In 1969 more than 90 percent of black children in Louisiana still attended all-black schools. When federal courts began pushing school boards to adopt more effective desegregation measures, such as zoning and busing, many white parents pulled their children out of the public schools rather than allow them to attend classes with African Americans. Private, all-white academies sprang up across the state, particularly in parishes that had black majorities. White people apparently feared predictions like that made in the *St. Francisville Democrat* by columnist Ben Garris, who claimed that schools could not withstand more than a 30 percent black enrollment without becoming "unstable" and experiencing a decline in the quality of education. In Concordia Parish, the Ku

Klux Klan issued a similar warning, portraying school desegregation as a communist plot to take over the country by ensuring the undereducation of American children.[9]

While white parents worried about the effect that attending classes with African Americans might have on their children, black families found that integrated schools did not necessarily afford black children a better education than they had received previously. Racist white teachers treated African American students with contempt, ignoring them when they asked questions, refusing to give them the same amount of attention that white students received, and in some cases physically abusing them. Administrators maintained segregation within integrated schools by partitioning facilities such as bathrooms, lunch tables, and play areas. Violent conflicts often erupted between white and black students, for which African Americans received a disproportionate amount of blame and punishment. Suspensions and expulsions of black students skyrocketed, with more than one hundred thousand occurring in the 1971–72 school year alone.[10]

The following decades saw a steady deterioration in conditions in the public schools of many parishes. In 1998 Eunice Hall Harris prepared a list of the shortcomings of the high school in St. Helena Parish that eerily echoed reports on black education from a century earlier: buildings that leaked, classes that were canceled in cold weather because of lack of heat, toilets and faucets that did not work, a gymnasium with no hot water, and a filthy cafeteria frequented by farm animals that wandered in through broken doors.[11] The parish's African American school superintendent seemed reluctant to do anything for fear of upsetting his white superiors. Most power in the parish still lay with the white families who had dominated the community in previous decades. Incumbent officials managed to fight off challenges from black candidates by bribing poor residents to vote for them and threatening to remove people from welfare rolls if they supported African Americans in elections. Although physical violence subsided after the 1960s, economic reprisals remained a powerful tool for maintaining white supremacy.[12]

In St. Helena Parish and elsewhere, persistent poverty hindered black people's efforts to translate their new voting strength into meaningful change. Political campaigns cost money, placing poor people at a disadvantage when it came to running candidates for office. Wealthy white people funded the campaigns of some black candidates, expecting them to maintain the status quo once they were elected.[13] In many communities black activists watched in anger as middle-class African Americans who had remained aloof from the movement in the 1960s became the chief beneficiaries of civil rights legislation. Working-class and rural poor people who had led the struggle in the early days were "suddenly unqualified to run for public office," reported Ronnie Moore in 1967, and were urged by college-educated professionals to leave such activities to them. Once hopeful that black votes could transform communities, civil rights lawyer Lolis Elie stated in 1988 that traditional electoral politics had done little to address the problem of poverty. "What I grossly misunderstood or overestimated was the nature of the black people who were going to seek political power," he said. "The same people who did nothing at all to change things, when things were changed . . . those were the ones who emerged and got the goodies—as a result of other people's efforts."[14]

Although some black politicians seemed more concerned with pleasing their white benefactors than bringing about changes to benefit black communities, many others were genuinely interested in solving social problems. But often their influence on local government was not enough to combat the power of more conservative politicians and businesspeople. In West Feliciana Parish, for example, African American representatives had to work with white officials who openly expressed their contempt for the idea of black people voting or holding office. When two black men who had been elected to the school board attended their first meeting, president Thomas Spillman demanded to see their commissions to office, claiming that he did not know who they were. West Feliciana was the only parish in the state by the late 1960s that still required its voters to reregister every few years. In December 1968 the six white police jurors voted down a suggestion by the three black jurors that the parish introduce a system of permanent registration. Responding to the suggestion that the necessity of periodically returning to the registrars' office might discourage many African Americans, particularly the elderly, from participating politically, white juror A. A. Wilkinson stated, "I was sorry when they cut the poll tax. . . . If a man can't register, then he doesn't need to vote."[15]

Even when black officials were in the majority, as eventually happened in Madison Parish, poverty remained an obstacle to progress. Rural communities often lacked the financial resources and tax base necessary to improve public services or initiate programs to provide employment for jobless people. With the resurgent conservatism of the 1970s and 1980s, federal support for antipoverty efforts declined. At the same time, continued displacement of agricultural workers from the plantations created an even greater need for jobs and housing in the rural parishes. Martin Williams recalled that in Tallulah, "The people on the plantations was moving into town, people didn't need them, getting modern equipment—these people didn't have any place to stay—some of the places you would see where they'd sleep at night, you would cry." Williams helped to finance and build two housing projects for low-income people in the town, but the lack of employment opportunities remained a problem in Madison Parish and elsewhere.[16]

In some parishes, white politicians and business leaders seemed to actively discourage any kind of economic development that could provide jobs for black people. According to black activist Wilbert Guillory, oil refineries and other industries that could have been located in St. Landry Parish were instead built in Lafayette, because local employers expressed concern that the new enterprises would "spoil the people . . . people was gonna get a job, and they would no longer work for four or five dollars a day." Of St. Helena Parish, Eual Hall observed: "There's no future here. White people are not going to let no industry come here, the affluent leaders, they're not gonna let no industry come into this parish unless they have the controlling interest." African Americans who aspired to occupations other than farming or low-paid wage work had to leave the parish. According to Clifton Hall, "If you were an aggressive individual, being a black man, you could not stay here in Greensburg. So their motive was to get you out of here and that was their way of doing it: if there's nothing here, you don't stay here."[17]

At the end of the twentieth century, poverty and inequality remained the dominant features of many rural parishes. In 1989, 46 percent of African Americans in Louisiana—more than half a million people—earned incomes below poverty level. Three decades after the civil rights movement, both former CORE workers and local people expressed disappointment in its outcomes and emphasized the limits that low incomes and poor education placed on efforts to eradicate discrimination and injustice. Rudy Lombard stated: "I think that there is a kind of slavery still exists, we call poverty. . . . If you're financially poor you're a slave pretty much and your life is circumscribed by people who control wealth, and government." Eual Hall raised the question that has plagued rural black people since the end of Reconstruction: "When everything is kept from you, how do you fight?"[18]

Yet, as most of these activists also emphasized, the freedom struggle continues. They work and put their children through college, remain active in their churches and lodges, support nonprofit organizations and other projects that aim to enhance economic opportunities for African Americans, lobby for improvements in the quality of education provided by the state's public schools, and vote in every election. Local black people draw strength from the knowledge that their ancestors endured conditions that were far worse and from the tradition of stubborn persistence that has characterized the centuries-long fight for equality. "The white man wonder how we still smile and go ahead on," says Clifton Hall. "Well, we grew up with it, and we've lived with it, so we know how to survive and still deal with it."[19]

Notes

Abbreviations

AESP	Agricultural Extension Service Papers, HML
APTP	Alexander Pierre Tureaud Papers, ARC
ARC	Amistad Research Center, Tulane University, New Orleans
BWEGM	*Black Workers in the Era of the Great Migration, 1916–1925*, edited by James R. Grossman (Frederick, Md.: University Publications of America, 1985), microfilm
CIR, RG 35	CCC Camp Inspection Reports, Records of the Civilian Conservation Corp, RG 35, NA
CLJP	Clyde L. Johnson Papers, in *The Green Rising, 1910–1977: A Supplement to the Southern Tenant Farmers Union Papers* (Glen Rock, N.J.: Microfilming Corporation of America, 1977), microfilm
CLMP	Charles Lewis Mathews Papers, HML
COREP	*The Papers of the Congress of Racial Equality, 1941–1967* (Sanford, N.C.: Microfilming Corporation of America, 1980), microfilm
CORE–SCDP	Congress of Racial Equality, Louisiana Sixth Congressional District Papers, SHSW
CORE–SHPP	Congress of Racial Equality, St. Helena Parish Papers, SHSW
CORE–SROP	Congress of Racial Equality, Southern Regional Office Papers, SHSW
CRS–SLU	Oral History Collection, Center for Regional Studies, Southeastern Louisiana University, Hammond

CSF, RG 60   Classified Subject Files—Correspondence, Central Files and Related Records, 1904–67, General Records, Records of the Department of Justice, RG 60, NA

CSJP   Charles S. Johnson Papers, Fisk University Library Special Collections, Fisk University, Nashville

DEBP   Daniel Ellis Byrd Papers, ARC

DTP   Daniel Trotter Papers, HML

FCC—NOPR   Friends of the Cabildo Collection, New Orleans Public Library

FDR   Franklin D. Roosevelt

FESR   Federal Extension Service Records, Extension Service Annual Reports, Louisiana 1909–44, microfilm, Historic New Orleans Collection, New Orleans

FFMP   Ferriday Freedom Movement Papers, SHSW

FRSD, RG 44   Field Reports of the Division, 1942–43, Records of the Surveys Division, Research Division, Bureau of Special Services, OWI, U.S. Information Service, Records of the Office of Government Reports, RG 44, NA

GCCO, RG 96   General Correspondence Maintained in the Cincinnati Office, 1935–42, Records of the Office of the Administrator, Records of the Central Office, Records of the Farmers' Home Administration, RG 96, NA

GCN, RG 16   General Correspondence, Negroes, 1909–23, Records of the Immediate Offices of the Commissioner and Secretary of Agriculture, Records of the Office of the Secretary of Agriculture, RG 16, NA

GCOS, RG 16   General Correspondence of the Office of the Secretary, 1929–70, Records of the Immediate Offices of the Commissioner and Secretary of Agriculture, Records of the Office of the Secretary of Agriculture, RG 16, NA

HML   Hill Memorial Library, LSU

HNLP   Harold N. Lee Papers, Manuscripts Division, HTL

HTL   Howard Tilton Library, Tulane University, New Orleans

IWAP   International Woodworkers of America Papers, Southern Labor Archives, Special Collections Department, Pullen Library, Georgia State University, Atlanta

JZP   John Zippert Papers, SHSW

LFU—FBI   File 100-45768, Louisiana Farmers' Union, FBI Headquarters, Washington, D.C.

LSFP   Lewis Stirling and Family Papers, HML

LSU   Louisiana State University, Baton Rouge

LWPA	Selected Documents from the Louisiana Section of the Work Projects Administration General Correspondence File ("State Series") 1935–43, microfilm, Historic New Orleans Collection, New Orleans
MAP	Meldon Acheson Papers, SHSW
MBP	Murphy Bell Papers, microfilm, SHSW
MFP	Miriam Feingold Papers, microfilm, SHSW
NA	National Archives, Washington, D.C.
ODP	*Operation Dixie: The CIO Organizing Committee Papers, 1946– 1953* ([Sanford, N.C.]: Microfilming Corporation of America, 1980), microfilm
OFWCL, RG 228	Office Files of Wilfred C. Leland Jr., Consultant, October 1943– August 1945, Records of the Division of Review and Analysis, Headquarters Records, Records of the Committee on Fair Employment Practice, RG 228, NA
OWI	Office of War Information
PFUS	*Peonage Files of the U.S. Department of Justice, 1901–1945* (Frederick, Md.: University Publications of America, 1989), microfilm
PNAACP– LC	Papers of the National Association for the Advancement of Colored People, Library of Congress, Washington, D.C.
PNAACP– Micro	*Papers of the NAACP* (Frederick, Md.: University Publications of America, 1982), microfilm
RCFT, RG 83	Records Relating to the President's Special Committee on Farm Tenancy, 1936–37, Division of Land Economics, Divisional Records, Records of the Bureau of Agricultural Economics, RG 83, NA
RFDRA, RG 228	Reference File, July 1941–April 1946, Records of the Division of Review and Analysis, Headquarters Records, Records of the Committee on Fair Employment Practice, RG 228, NA
RFEPC	*Selected Documents of Records of the Committee on Fair Employment Practice, 1941–1946* (Glen Rock, N.J.: Microfilming Corporation of America, [1970]), microfilm
RFP	Rosenwald Fund Papers, microfilm, ARC
RG	Record Group
RMRD, RG 44	Reports and Memoranda, 1942–46, Records of the Research Division, Records of the Bureau of Special Services, OWI, Records of the U.S. Information Service, Records of the Office of Government Reports, RG 44, NA
RSD, RG 44	Reports of the Division, 1942–44, Records of the Surveys Division, Records of the Bureau of Special Services, OWI, Records of the U.S. Information Service, Records of the Office of Government Reports, RG 44, NA
RTC	Robert Tallant Collection, microfilm, ARC

RWLP   Richard W. Leche Papers, HML

SEDFREP   Scholarship, Education, and Defense Fund for Racial Equality
              Papers, SHSW

SFDS,   Subject File of David Squire, 1965–66, Records of the Office of the
  RG 381   Director, Records of the Job Corps, Records of the Office of Eco-
              nomic Opportunity, RG 381, NA

SHJP   William Walter Jones Collection of the Papers of Sam Houston
              Jones, Manuscripts Division, HTL

SHSW   State Historical Society of Wisconsin, Madison

SNF,   Straight Numerical Files, 1904–37, Central Files and Related
  RG 60   Records, 1904–67, General Records, Records of the Department
              of Justice, RG 60, NA

SS, RG 453   Records Relating to Surveys and Studies, 1958–62, Records of
              the Commission on Civil Rights, RG 453, NA

STFUP   *Southern Tenant Farmers' Union Papers* (Sanford, N.C.: Micro-
              filming Corporation of America, 1971), microfilm

TAFP   Turnbull-Allain Family Papers, HML

THWC–   T. Harry Williams Center for Oral History, LSU
  LSU

WMRRD,   Weekly Media Reports, 1942–43, Records of the Research Divi-
  RG 44   sion, Records of the Bureau of Special Services, OWI, Records of
              the U.S. Information Service, Records of the Office of Govern-
              ment Reports, RG 44, NA

Introduction

1. A. Z. Young, Zelma Wyche, Harrison H. Brown, T. I. Israel, F. W. Wilson, and Moses Williams, Joseph Carter, interviews by Miriam Feingold, MFP.

2. See, e.g., Morris, *Origins of the Civil Rights Movement*; Brown, "Womanist Consciousness"; Lewis, *In Their Own Interests*; Honey, *Southern Labor and Black Civil Rights*; Woodruff, "African American Struggles for Citizenship"; Kelley, *Race Rebels*; Reich, "Soldiers of Democracy"; Hunter, *To 'Joy My Freedom*; and Fairclough, "'Being in the Field of Education.'" In *But For Birmingham: The Local and National Movements in the Civil Rights Struggle* (1997), Glenn Eskew challenges the emphasis on continuity by arguing that the civil rights movement represented a significant departure from black activism in earlier decades. Before the mid-twentieth century, he asserts, the "traditional Negro leadership class" accommodated the Jim Crow social order, rarely agitating for anything more than small improvements within the confines of segregation. The civil rights movement began "when local black activists in the South organized new indigenous protest groups in the 1950s and 1960s that demanded immediate and equal access to the system" (p. 15). Although Eskew's analysis offers some valuable insights into class conflict and other divisions that afflicted the black

community (which has too often been portrayed as monolithic), his account does not warrant rejection of the continuity thesis. Eskew conflates black activism in the early twentieth century with the black middle class, ignoring working-class and rural poor people's resistance to oppression. The agenda that Eskew associates with the "race men" who led the fight for civil rights reflected long-standing goals of many African Americans, not a new departure as he suggests. More than ideology, shifting political and economic contexts that allowed a change in tactics were what set the freedom movement of the 1950s and 1960s apart from earlier decades.

3. Wyche et al. interview.

4. Meier and Rudwick, *CORE*, 160.

5. Bureau of the Census, *Eighteenth Decennial Census . . . Population: 1960, Volume 1, Part 20*, 90–95.

6. Adam Fairclough's *Race and Democracy* provides a statewide study of the civil rights movement in Louisiana.

7. Writing in 1960, for instance, Elliott Rudwick (*W. E. B. Du Bois*, 118) suggested that the majority of African Americans in the first half of the twentieth century were "little interested in politics" and required exceptionally inspirational leadership to stir them to action. The almost exclusive focus on national civil rights organizations and leaders that characterized studies of the movement for the next three decades did little to refute this view, though this does not detract from the significant contributions these works have made to the field. The most useful and comprehensive accounts are Meier and Rudwick, *CORE*; Carson, *In Struggle*; Garrow, *Bearing the Cross*; Fairclough, *To Redeem the Soul of America*; Branch, *Parting the Waters*; and Goldfield, *Black, White, and Southern*.

8. McMillen, *Dark Journey*; Litwack, *Trouble in Mind*; Cecelski and Tyson, review of *Trouble in Mind*, 736.

9. Aptheker, *American Negro Slave Revolts*; Genovese, *Roll, Jordan, Roll*; Thompson, *Making of the English Working Class*; Levine, *Black Culture and Black Consciousness*.

10. James C. Scott, *Moral Economy of the Peasant* and *Weapons of the Weak*; Kelley, *Race Rebels*; Allen Isaacman et al., "'Cotton Is the Mother of Poverty'"; Stern, *Resistance, Rebellion, and Consciousness*; Hunter, *To 'Joy My Freedom*. See also Guha, *Subaltern Studies, Volume I*, and subsequent volumes in this series.

11. For a summary of the main issues in this debate and some helpful critiques, see the essays in *Journal of Peasant Studies* 13 (January 1986), a special issue devoted to studies of everyday forms of peasant resistance in Southeast Asia, especially those by James Scott, Christine Pelzer White, and Benedict J. Tria Kerkvliet. Another useful overview is O'Hanlon, "Recovering the Subject."

12. Woodruff, "African-American Struggles for Citizenship." Michael Honey (*Black Workers Remember*) provides further evidence that black activists viewed economic rights as an integral part of the fight for equality.

13. James C. Scott, *Domination and the Arts of Resistance*, 200–227. Steve Stern makes a similar point in his introduction and contribution to *Resistance, Rebellion, and Consciousness*, 9–10, 34–93. Stern suggests looking at "*preexisting* patterns of 'resistant adaptation'" as a way to understand peasant rebellions, arguing that open protests might not reflect a sudden awakening to political consciousness on the part of the oppressed (as is often supposed), but rather the continuation, in new contexts, of earlier efforts to overcome injustice.

14. Daniel, *Breaking the Land*; Kirby, *Rural Worlds Lost*.

15. Grubbs, *Cry from the Cotton*; Kelley, *Hammer and Hoe*. See also Foley, *White Scourge*, 163–82.

16. See, e.g., Kelley, *Hammer and Hoe*; Honey, *Southern Labor and Black Civil Rights*; and Sullivan, *Days of Hope*.

17. One exception is Jeannie M. Whayne's *New Plantation South*.

18. Harrison and Earnestine Brown, interview by author, THWC–LSU.

Chapter One

1. Vandal, *Rethinking Southern Violence*, 40–46.

2. Smith and Hitt, *People of Louisiana*, 47–49; "The Social Setting of the Louisiana Negro Schools," n.d. [ca. 1940], 2–3, file 8, box 226, CSJP.

3. Johnson, *Louisiana Educational Survey*, 13, 15.

4. Vandal, *Rethinking Southern Violence*, 52–53, 57; Hyde, *Pistols and Politics*, 186, 209.

5. Vandal, *Rethinking Southern Violence*, 50–51; Johnson, *Louisiana Educational Survey*, 5.

6. Du Bois, *Black Reconstruction*, 453; Sitterson, *Sugar Country*, 104–7; Hall, *African Americans in Colonial Louisiana*, 150; Hyde, *Pistols and Politics*, 180–212. See also Thomas Becnel's study of labor organizing efforts in the sugar parishes and plantation owners' responses in *Labor, Church, and the Sugar Establishment*. Becnel finds that most Catholic planters rejected the admonitions of priests who supported workers' struggles, acting according to their economic interests rather than their religious beliefs in refusing to give in to union demands.

7. This analysis is drawn from general works on the post–Civil War South and more specific studies of Louisiana itself. The best overviews of the period are Du Bois, *Black Reconstruction*; Woodward, *Origins of the New South* and *Reunion and Reaction*; Kousser, *Shaping of Southern Politics*; Powell, *New Masters*; and Foner, *Reconstruction*. For Louisiana, see Shugg, *Origins of Class Struggle*; Hair, *Bourbonism and Agrarian Protest*; Taylor, *Louisiana Reconstructed*; Vincent, *Black Legislators*; Tunnell, *Crucible of Reconstruction*; and Hyde, *Pistols and Politics*.

8. Reed, "Race Legislation," 380; General Assembly of . . . Louisiana, *Acts of the General Assembly . . . 1865*, 3–9.

9. U.S. Senate, *Report and Testimony*, 176–77, 192–211 (quotation, p. 176).

10. Engstrom et al., "Louisiana," 104; Prestage and Williams, "Blacks in Louisiana Politics," 293–96.

11. Reed, "Race Legislation," 381–84; Tunnell, *Crucible of Reconstruction*, 113–15, 117–18; Vincent, *Black Legislators*, 48–70.

12. Crouch, "Black Education," 289, 297–98; Anderson, *Education of Blacks in the South*, 21; Robert Dabney Calhoun, *History of Concordia Parish*, 136.

13. Foner, *Nothing but Freedom*, 44–45; Aiken, *Cotton Plantation South*, 17–21.

14. Shugg, *Origins of Class Struggle*, 228–29; Hair, *Bourbonism and Agrarian Protest*, 17–18, 56; Vandal, *Rethinking Southern Violence*, 34, 67–89.

15. Hyde, *Pistols and Politics*, 166–68; Taylor, *Louisiana*, 111–12; Tunnell, *Crucible of Reconstruction*, 173–209; Vincent, *Black Legislators*, 183–85, 202–17; Vandal, *Rethinking Southern Violence*, 24, 29, 102–3.

16. Vandal, *Rethinking Southern Violence*, 178, 10, 179; Warmoth, *War, Politics, and Reconstruction*, 67–68; Tunnell, *Crucible of Reconstruction*, 189–92.

17. Woodward, *Origins of the New South*, 23–51; Vandal, *Rethinking Southern Violence*, 189–91. Nell Irvin Painter (*Exodusters*) provides a detailed account of the Exodus of 1879.

18. Hair, *Bourbonism and Agrarian Protest*, 60–61, 142–233; Becnel, *Labor, Church, and the Sugar Establishment*, 7–8.

19. Hair, *Bourbonism and Agrarian Protest*, 234–67 (quotation, p. 260).

20. Dart, *Civil Code of . . . Louisiana*, 424–25; Act 50 of 1892, General Assembly of . . . Louisiana, *Acts Passed by the General Assembly . . . 1892*, 71–72; *Constitution of . . . Louisiana . . . 1898*, 77–87, 104.

21. Foner, *Nothing but Freedom*, 72.

Chapter Two

1. Field workers normally picked between one hundred and two hundred pounds of cotton per day. Taylor, *Louisiana*, 66–67. Tom Alexander therefore owed the men between seven and fourteen dollars each.

2. Bernice Wims to Attorney General Murphy, 25 October 1939, frames 0959–60, reel 9, *PFUS*.

3. O. John Rogge to Bernice Wims, 7 November 1939, frame 0958, and Wims to Rogge, 18 November 1939, frame 0957, ibid.

4. Key, *Southern Politics*, 664.

5. C. Vann Woodward first suggested that post–Civil War southern society was shaped chiefly by northern capitalists and southern converts to new ideologies that emphasized industrial development, profits, and progress. Jonathan Wiener presented a different view, arguing that conservative plantation owners retained control over the economic development of their states, allowing them to limit industrialization and ensure that the South remained a primarily agricultural region powered by cheap black labor. Yet as scholars such as Stanley Green-

berg, James Cobb, and Alex Lichtenstein have shown, the interests of planters and industrialists were not necessarily incompatible. Employers of all types of labor (in the North as well as the South) benefited from racist ideas and practices that originated in slavery and were perpetuated in the twentieth century. See Woodward, *Origins of the New South*; Wiener, *Social Origins of the New South*; Greenberg, *Race and State in Capitalist Development*; Cobb, *Industrialization and Southern Society*; and Lichtenstein, *Twice the Work of Free Labor*. Two other very useful works are Fields, "Ideology and Race," and Hale, *Making Whiteness*. Both argue persuasively that racism is not a static entity that has existed throughout time. Their analyses suggest that the twentieth-century southern social order did not necessarily have to be based on racist discrimination, and that these practices were perpetuated because they served the interests of powerful elites.

6. M. Buck to Sister, 20 February [1866], 2, file 187, box 8, CLMP; John T. Bramhall, "The Exploitation of Louisiana," *Country Gentleman*, 14 October 1909, 970; Nesom, "Louisiana Delta"; "Who's Who in the Making of Madison," *Madison Journal*, 26 October 1930, 3; Shannon, *Toward a New Politics*, 38–53; Hair, *Bourbonism and Agrarian Protest*, 35–39; Hyde, *Pistols and Politics*, 145–46, 194–98.

7. As Gavin Wright (*Old South, New South*, 47–50) points out, whether post–Civil War landowners had been members of the antebellum planter class or were northern immigrants is not as important as the changes in economic relationships that resulted from the abolition of slavery. *All* postbellum planters were members of a new class whose interests were different from those of Old South plantation owners.

8. "Who's Who in the Making of Madison," *Madison Journal*, 26 October 1930, 3.

9. Hyde, *Pistols and Politics*, 196–98. See also "Two Industries for Opelousas through Bureau," *St. Landry Clarion-Progress*, 10 March 1923, 1; "The Future of Opelousas," *St. Landry Clarion-Progress*, 17 October 1925, 6; "Louisiana Should Watch Her Step," *Madison Journal*, 30 June 1928, 1; and "Industries for Tallulah," *Madison Journal*, 29 November 1929, 1.

10. *Constitution of . . . Louisiana . . . 1898*, 94, 128–30 (quotation, pp. 129–30).

11. Reidy, "Mules and Machines and Men," 184; "Cotton Planters Organize," *Country Gentleman*, 2 July 1903, 575.

12. Hair, *Bourbonism and Agrarian Protest*, 35–39; Sitterson, *Sugar Country*, 262–63, 311–13; "Excerpt from Regional Director's Weekly Report, Region VI," 25 January 1937, 1, loose in box, box 4, RCFT, RG 83. Louisiana's "business plantations" closely resembled those described in studies of the Mississippi and Arkansas deltas by Robert Brandfon (*Cotton Kingdom of the New South*) and Jeannie Whayne (*New Plantation South*). Also useful for understanding the transformation of the plantation economy after the Civil War are Woodward, *Origins of the New South*, 178–85; Gaston, *New South Creed*; Powell, *New Masters*; Mandle, *Roots of Black Poverty*; and Woodman, *New South—New Law*.

13. Goins and Caldwell, *Historical Atlas of Louisiana*, 68–69; Bureau of the Census, *Eighteenth Decennial Census ... Population: 1960, Volume 1, Part 20*, 5, and *Census of Manufactures: 1947, Volume 3*, 251.

14. Bureau of the Census, *Thirteenth Census ... 1910, Volume 2: Population*, 778, and *Volume 4: Population, Occupation Statistics*, 465–66; John R. McMahon, "Scraping the American Sugar Bowl," *Country Gentleman*, 15 December 1917, 1958–59, 1994; Whayne, *New Plantation South*, 27; Hair, *Bourbonism and Agrarian Protest*, 51–55, 87; Sitterson, *Sugar Country*, 292–93.

15. Sitterson, *Sugar Country*, 221; Ferleger, "Problem of 'Labor,'" 146; "Labor Troubles in North Louisiana," *New Orleans Times-Democrat*, 26 April 1900, 4; Rodrigue, "'Great Law of Demand and Supply,'" 168; M. Buck to Sister, 20 February [1866], 1, file 187, box 8, CLMP; P[aul] L. DeClouet, Diary, 1869–70, entries for 1–3 January 1870, vol. 5, box 2, Alexandre Etienne DeClouet and Family Papers, HML; Jas Selby to P[enelope] Mathews, 2 February 1871, 2–3, file 193, box 9, CLMP; Peter [Henry M. Stewart] to Nance [Annie L. Allain], 27 December 1906, 1–3, file 19, box 8, TAFP.

16. Henry [M. Stewart] to Nan [Annie L. Allain], 29 November 1898, file 14, box 8, TAFP; Sarah T. Bowman to Nina Bowman, n.d. [1907], 7, file 7, box 2, Turnbull-Bowman-Lyons Family Papers, HML; "The Negro," *Madison Journal*, 28 April 1928, 2.

17. Bureau of the Census, *Sixteenth Census . . . 1940, Agriculture Crop-Sharing Contracts*, 14–16.

18. Alston and Kauffman, "Up, Down, and Off the Agricultural Ladder," 263–65; Bureau of the Census, *Fifteenth Census ... 1930, Agriculture, Volume 2, Part 2*, 2–3; Woodman, *New South—New Law*, 105–6. In this study, I have sometimes used "tenants" to refer to all those who labored in return for a portion of the crop, including sharecroppers. "Sharecroppers" refers more specifically to those workers who owned no farm animals or implements, and "renters" is used to distinguish cash tenants from those farming on shares.

In a recent review essay, Alex Lichtenstein ("Was the Emancipated Slave a Proletarian?") questioned whether sharecroppers should really be categorized as wage laborers, as Woodman and others have suggested. Highlighting some important distinctions between sharecropping and free labor as it existed elsewhere (e.g., year-long contracts that bound workers to the plantations, the use of family labor, and the illusion of autonomy gained from working individual plots of land), Lichtenstein argued that until the 1930s, southern sharecroppers constituted an American peasantry, not a displaced rural proletariat. Although Lichtenstein's approach might be useful for analyzing farm tenancy in some parts of the South, Woodman's wage labor thesis seems more appropriate for the region under study here. As is noted in Chapter 3, most African Americans who worked on plantations in rural Louisiana viewed themselves as exploited laborers, not semi-independent farmers.

19. After 1920 agricultural censuses grouped African Americans, Native

Americans, and Asian Americans together in the category of "nonwhite" farmers. Between 1900 and 1960 the vast majority of people in this category were African American, with other groups never making up more than 0.5 percent of the total nonwhite population in Louisiana. See Bureau of the Census, *Census of the Population: 1970, Volume 1, Part 20,* 42. In the agricultural statistics cited in this study, the terms "black" and "African American" correspond to the census category of "nonwhite."

20. Ramsey and Hoffsommer, *Farm Tenancy in Louisiana,* 7–8, 11–17. My interviews with civil rights activists who grew up on Louisiana plantations also suggest the prevalence of closely supervised tenancy arrangements. See, e.g., Harrison and Earnestine Brown, Moses Williams, and Robert and Essie Mae Lewis, interviews by author, THWC–LSU.

21. Aiken, *Cotton Plantation South,* 97–100.

22. Byron A. Case, "In the Mississippi Delta–II," *Country Gentleman,* 28 March 1907, 322–23; "The Problem," n.d., 3–4, file "LU-1 184-047, Farm Tenancy," box 1, RCFT, RG 83; Hair, *Bourbonism and Agrarian Protest,* 51–52; Taylor, *Louisiana Reconstructed,* 401–3; Mertz, *New Deal Policy,* 8–9; Brown interview.

23. Sitterson, *Sugar Country,* 240–41, 389–90.

24. Ibid., 114–33; Reidy, "Mules and Machines and Men," 185–94.

25. Sugar wage rates fluctuated from year to year and during different times of the season, according to prices, market conditions, and the labor supply. Workers had some leverage during the harvest season, as planters could not afford to allow the cane to spoil. In the decades following the Civil War, field hands used that power to gain a few concessions from planters (like monthly instead of yearly payments) while plantation owners explored ways to undermine workers' bargaining power. By adopting labor-saving cultivating methods and implements, agreeing among themselves not to pay more than a certain wage rate each season, and using violence and intimidation to crush strikes, sugar growers in Louisiana gradually brought their workforce under control. In the early 1890s wages stabilized at around 75¢ per day during the cultivating season and $1.00 per day during harvesting, rising slightly in the early twentieth century because of competition from the lumber industry. Sitterson, *Sugar Country,* 318–22; Reidy, "Mules and Machines and Men"; Rodrigue, "'The Great Law of Demand and Supply.'"

26. Laws, "Negroes of Cinclare Central Factory," 107–12; Sitterson, *Sugar Country,* 391; Gordon McIntire to Miss La Budde, 12 October 1937, 3–4, file 3, reel 13, CLJP.

27. Hair, *Bourbonism and Agrarian Protest,* 48–49; Mary White Ovington, *Bogalusa* (New York: NAACP [1920]), frames 0002–5, reel 10, part 10, *PNAACP*–Micro; Dinwiddie, "International Woodworkers of America," 4–5; John C. Howard, *Negro in the Lumber Industry,* 3–4, 7–8, 12, 26–28.

28. "Abolish the Commissaries," *Louisiana Farmers' Union News,* 1 March

1938, 2; "Madison Parish; Its Customs—Yesterday and Today," *Madison Journal*, 27 March 1926, 1.

29. Act 50 of 1892, General Assembly of . . . Louisiana, *Acts Passed by the General Assembly . . . 1892*, 71–72.

30. "Negroes in Keen Demand," *New York Sun*, 30 January 1904, item 295, frame 30, *Hampton University Peabody Newspaper Clipping File*, microfiche; "Planters Resist Exodus of Labor," *New Orleans Daily Picayune*, 25 March 1914, 7. William Cohen (*At Freedom's Edge*) provides a useful analysis of plantation owners' attempts to control workers and African Americans' ability to move about in the late nineteenth and early twentieth centuries. Cohen argues that peonage and restrictive labor practices were not constant elements but related to specific times and places—plantation owners were most likely to resort to such methods during labor shortages, and when labor was plentiful they allowed workers to leave. In addition, the conflicting interests of different classes of white people in the South, combined with periods of intense planter competition for labor, enabled a certain amount of worker mobility.

31. F. M. Tatum to FDR, 9 September 1903, frames 0224–0025, reel 2, *PFUS*; H. M. A. [Henry M. Stewart] to Annie [L. Allain], 15 December 1905, 5, file 17, box 8, TAFP. For more reports of peonage in Louisiana, see Walter L. Jones to Department of Justice, 1 June 1903, frame 0045, reel 2, *PFUS*; Fred R. Jones to Attorney General, 23 January 1909, frames 0542–44, reel 13, *PFUS*; B. F. Wilmer to Attorney General, 24 October 1929, frames 0689–91, reel 11, *PFUS*; and J. A. Persons to Richard Leche, 4 August 1938, file "Labor Miscellaneous," box 39, RWLP. At least sixty-seven cases of peonage in Louisiana were reported to the U.S. Department of Justice between 1901 and 1945, providing another indication of the extent of this practice. See Schipper, *Guide to the Microfilm Edition*, 1–59.

32. Act 50 of 1892, which prevented workers who were indebted to their employers from leaving, was modified slightly in 1906 and declared unconstitutional in 1918. See Act 54 of 1906 in Louisiana Department of Labor, *Compilation of General Labor Laws*, 188–89, and *State v. Oliva* 144 La. 51 (1918). The federal government's efforts to eradicate peonage are discussed in Daniel, *Shadow of Slavery*.

33. Clark M. Votaw to S. T. Early, 23 November 1937, file "[080] V," box 10, General Correspondence, 1937–42, Records of the Farm Ownership Division, Records of the Central Office, Records of the FaHA, RG 96, NA.

34. Galarza, *Louisiana Sugar Cane Plantation Workers*, 27.

35. "The Bill against Illiterate Immigrants," *New Orleans Daily Picayune*, 7 February 1914, 6 (first quotation); Unidentified school superintendent quoted in Johnson, *Louisiana Educational Survey*, 14 (second quotation).

36. Martin Williams, interview by author, THWC–LSU; Johnnie Jones Sr., interview by Mary Hebert, 6, 19, THWC–LSU; Rovan W. Stanley Sr., interview by Janie Wilkins, 1, CRS–SLU; "Official Proceedings of the School Board," *St. Francisville Democrat*, 11 July 1936, 2; "Farmers' Union Asks Federal Aid for

Rural Schools," *Louisiana Farmers' Union News*, 1 June 1938, 1. Even when schools were open for longer periods of time, poverty forced some black parents to send children to the fields instead of to class for much of the year. As late as 1967, the NAACP field director for Louisiana expressed concern that a campaign to enforce the state's compulsory school attendance laws might create "severe economic hardships" for families who relied on the labor of younger members to survive. "Field Director Newsletter, Louisiana N.A.A.C.P.," March 1967, 1, file 3, box 2, NAACP Louisiana Field Director Papers, ARC.

37. Louisiana Education Association Department of Retired Teachers, *We Walked Tall*, 38–40; "Want Adequate Schools, Equal Salaries; State Parent-Teachers Association Is Planning Action," *Louisiana Weekly*, 4 January 1941, 1; Anderson, *Education of Blacks in the South*, 190; "Public High Schools (Negro)," n.d. [ca 1940], file 4, box 227, CSJP; State Department of Education of Louisiana, *Ninety-Second Annual Report*, 109.

38. H. H. Long, "Washington Parish," n.d. [ca. 1940], 8–20, 22–23, file 8, box 225, CSJP; Johnson, *Louisiana Educational Survey*, 14–15, 38–39, 69; Leo M. Favrot to Francis W. Shepardson, 27 May 1923, file 5, box 339, RFP; T. H. Harris to Parish Superintendents and Parish School Board Members, Circular No. 1017, 2 April 1938, file "Cases Supported—Teachers Salary Cases—Louisiana 1938–1940," box 88, ser. D, pt. 1, PNAACP—LC.

39. Leo M. Favrot to Francis W. Shepardson, 27 May 1923, file 5, box 339, RFP.

40. Statement on Sugar Cane Wages by Gordon McIntire, Federal Hearing, 16 June 1939, 4, file 3, reel 13, CLJP.

41. "Ecological Description of Concordia Parish, Louisiana," n.d. [ca. 1940], 17, file 5, box 225, CSJP.

42. Johnson, *Louisiana Educational Survey*, 35; T. H. Harris to Parish Superintendents and Parish School Board Members, Circular No. 1017, 2 April 1938, 2, file "Cases Supported—Teachers Salary Cases—Louisiana 1938–1940," box 88, ser. D, pt. 1, PNAACP—LC.

43. Jones interview, 65; Palmer, "Evolution of Education," 116.

44. Brundage, *Lynching in the New South*, 103–60; Finnegan, "'At the Hands of Parties Unknown'"; Moses Williams interview; "Elstner Reviews Joel Johnson Case," clipping, *Shreveport Journal*, n.d. [ca. 1909], frames 0038–39, reel 17, *PFUS*; Report of George R. Faller, FBI, 13 August 1942, frame 0525, reel 20, *PFUS*.

45. See, e.g., Moses Williams, Martin Williams, and Lewis interviews.

46. Malcolm E. Lafargue to Attorney General, 21 July 1944, 2, file "144-33-17," box 17589, Classified Subject Files—Correspondence, Central Files and Related Records, 1904–67, General Records, Records of the Department of Justice, RG 60, NA (first quotation); Martin Williams interview.

47. Report of George R. Faller, FBI, 13 August 1942, frame 0551, reel 20, *PFUS*.

48. Report of T. F. Wilson, FBI, 1 August 1939, 16, file "144-32-2," box 17587,

CSF, RG 60. Sheriff Andrew Sevier of Madison Parish, e.g., began his career as a bookkeeper and manager of several plantations and, according to one account, "soon his personality and ability at leadership caused him to be offered the position of sheriff." He served the parish for thirty-seven years, from 1904 until his death in 1941. "He Was Her Sheriff," *Madison Journal*, 12 September 1941, 2; "Madison Loses Dean of Peace Officers," *Madison Journal*, 29 August 1941, 1, 6.

49. "Woman Witness Tells of Burning of Aged Negro," *New Orleans Times-Picayune*, 23 December 1914, 9; "Ignores Charges in Lynching Cases," *New Orleans Times-Picayune*, 9 April 1915, 9.

50. J. Leo Hardy to [John] Shillady, 5 April 1918, file "Shreveport, La.," box 357, ser. C, pt. 1, PNAACP—LC.

51. Benjamin J. Stanley to Walter White, 7 March 1935, frame 0322, reel 12, ser. A, pt. 7, *PNAACP*—Micro.

52. A. C. Rutzen to Director, FBI, 6 September 1940, 1–2, file "144-32-5," box 17588, CSF, RG 60; "A. P. LeBlanc," *St. Francisville Democrat*, 7 May 1954, 2. For more evidence of elite white people's complicity in violence, see "Coroner Names Four Men in Caddo Lynching Probe," *New Orleans Times-Picayune*, 31 December 1914, 1; John R. Shillady to R. G. Pleasant, 15 February 1919, frame 0031, reel 12, ser. A, pt. 7, *PNAACP*—Micro; C. S. Hebert to Joseph E. Ransdall, 7 January 1923, file "198589 Sec 4," box 3033, SNF, RG 60; "Sol Dacus Loses Heavy Damage Case in United States Court; Foremost Whites Joined Mob," newspaper clipping, source unknown, 9 March 1925, frame 0307, reel 14, ser. A, pt. 12, *PNAACP*—Micro; "Kill Innocent Colored Men in Louisiana," clipping, *Philadelphia Tribune*, 16 June 1928, frame 1152, reel 11, ser. A, pt. 7, *PNAACP*—Micro; Report of T. F. Wilson, FBI, 1 August 1939, 26, 28, file "144-32-2," box 17587, CSF, RG 60; Report of P. M. Breed, FBI, 9 December 1932, frames 0447–48, reel 22, *PFUS*; George A. Dreyfous and M. Swearingen, "Report to the Executive Committee of the L.P.C.R. on Investigations in West Feliciana Parish," n.d. [1937], 7, file 19, box 2, HNLP.

53. "Sheriff Holds Off Lynchers," clipping, *Savannah Tribune*, 11 February 1926, frame 1150, reel 11, ser. A, pt. 7, *PNAAC*—Micro. Similar incidents are reported in "Scott Is Convicted Johnson Acquitted in Assault Case," *New Orleans Times-Picayune*, 3 July 1915, 16; "Sheriff Saves Negro Threatened by Mob," *New Orleans Times-Picayune*, 26 September 1915, 12; and "Negro Taken to Pen via Eunice," *St. Landry Clarion-Progress*, 20 February 1926, 11; Jones interview, 62. See also Brundage, *Lynching in the New South*, 26–28.

54. Fred R. Jones to Attorney General, 23 January 1909 and 6 July [1909], frames 0542–44 and 0525–27, reel 13, *PFUS* (quotation, frame 0543).

55. Martin Williams interview. See also unsigned letter to Charles Houston, 15 October 1938, frames 0191–92, reel 21, part 10, *PNAACP*—Micro.

56. Brown interview. See also Jones interview; Report of T. F. Wilson, FBI, 1 August 1939, 25, file "144-32-2," box 17587, CSF, RG 60; Louisiana Education Association Department of Retired Teachers, *We Walked Tall*, 39; Ezekiel C.

Smith to A. H. Rosenfeld, memorandum, 23 May 1960, 4, file "General—Louisiana—BBS," box 2, SS, RG 453.

57. Lumber camps were often located in isolated areas and existed only as long as it took to clear all of the surrounding timber. Peonage and other abuses were usually discovered too late, if at all, making it difficult to deter operators from using such practices. Russell, *Report on Peonage*, 17–18; Cobb, *Industrialization and Southern Society*, 69; Dinwiddie, "International Woodworkers of America," 7.

58. Quoted in Fairclough, *Race and Democracy*, 346.

59. See, e.g., Stephen Norwood's ("Bogalusa Burning") account of union organizing efforts in Bogalusa after World War I.

60. Notes on NAACP Training Conference, 6 October 1945, 6, file "Leadership Training Conference, Louisiana-Texas (Conference) Correspondence 1945," box 375, ser. C, pt. 2, PNAACP—LC; J. E. Clayton to H. L. Mitchell, 23 September 1941, reel 19, *STFUP*; Edgar A. Schuler, Weekly Tensions Report, 20 March 1943, 7, file "Edgar Schuler—Field Reports," box 1824, FRSD, RG 44; H. A. Douresseau to A. P. Tureaud, 8 September 1949, file 28, box 9, APTP. Black lawyer and civil rights activist J. L. Chestnut Jr. outlines a similar phenomenon in another Deep South state in *Black in Selma*, 22–23, 114, 154. See also Zora Neale Hurston, "The Pet Negro System," *Folklore*, 914–21.

61. See, e.g., the portrait of the black landowning community in Washington Parish given in Bond and Bond, *Star Creek Papers*, esp. 11, 23. Mark R. Schultz ("The Dream Realized?," 305) makes a similar observation about black landowners in Georgia.

62. Jones interview, 11–12.

63. J. H. Scott to Walter White, 9 December 1940, frames 0340–41, reel 1, ser. A, pt. 13, *PNAACP*—Micro.

64. Carr, *Federal Protection of Civil Rights*, 77–84, 122–46; Daniel, *Shadow of Slavery*, 19–64. During the peonage trial of Joel Johnson in 1909, a U.S. attorney outlined the difficulties involved in prosecuting at the local level. A conviction in the case was unlikely, he reported, given the power and influence of the plantation owner. "Joel F. Johnson is . . . a man totally without respect for any consideration except his individual will," he stated, "and . . . will not hesitate to resort to any methods to circumvent the ends of justice. Johnson is a man of means and will employ the very best of counsel to aid him in his defense. . . . Besides, I am sure, he will try and enlist the services of some persons selected by him for that purpose to tamper with witnesses and jurors. . . . During the investigation of the cases before the Grand Jury it became necessary for me to have Joel F. Johnson arrested to prevent his interference with the Government witnesses." M. C. Elstner to Attorney General, 24 September 1909, frames 0042–0043, reel 17, *PFUS*.

65. Key, *Southern Politics*, 9; Zangrando, *NAACP Crusade against Lynching*, 15–19.

66. Milburn Calhoun, *Louisiana Almanac*, 385; Fairclough, *Race and Democracy*, 31, 168; H. L. Mitchell, Statement on Senator Allen J. Ellender prepared for International Free Trade Union News, n.d., 2, filed at n.d. [1955], reel 39, *STFUP*.

67. Brown interview; Moses Williams interview.

Chapter Three

1. Levine, *Black Culture and Black Consciousness*, xiii.

2. Saxon, Dreyer, and Tallant, *Gumbo Ya-Ya*, 450.

3. Hurston, *Folklore*, 77; Levine, *Black Culture and Black Consciousness*, 239–70.

4. Oliver, *Story of the Blues*, 11–25, 85–91, and *Conversation with the Blues*, 125 (J. D. Miller).

5. "Lafourche Parish Ecology," n.d., 5–6, box 225, file 6, CSJP; Oliver, *Conversation with the Blues*, 180 (Willie Thomas).

6. For more on the ways African Americans have used entertainment and culture to assert their independence from white control, see Hunter, *To 'Joy My Freedom*, 168–86, and Kelley, *Yo' Mama's Disfunktional!*, 43–77. The role that religion played in the lives of rural black people is discussed in more detail later in this chapter.

7. Thomas quoted in Oliver, *Conversation with the Blues*, 22.

8. Saxon, Dreyer, and Tallant, *Gumbo Ya-Ya*, 374.

9. Black Ace (B. K. Turner) quoted in Oliver, *Conversation with the Blues*, 53.

10. Government researchers found that in the spring of 1935, more than one-third of all sharecroppers and tenants in the nation had been on their present farms for less than one year. Report of the President's Committee on Farm Tenancy: Findings and Recommendations, February 1937, 19, file "Tenancy (Jan 1–Feb 1)," box 2661, GCOS, RG 16.

11. Entries for Affy Gilstan and Henry Haldman, 1915, Share Croppers' Record Book, 1904–8, 1914–18, box 16, LSFP; Report of William H. Pokorny, FBI, 1 December 1942, frames 0869–70, 0872 (quotation), reel 23, *PFUS*; "The Negro," *Madison Journal*, 28 April 1928, 2.

12. Statement of John Pickering, 8 April 1926, frame 0633, reel 12, *PFUS*.

13. Harrison and Earnestine Brown, interview by author, THWC–LSU; W. C. Brown to NAACP, n.d. [ca. 1920s], frame 0683, reel 14, ser. A, pt. 12, *PNAACP–Micro*; James Willis, interviewer unknown, transcript, 20 July 1939, 176, file 20-16, reel PP2.9, RTC.

14. "Runaway Negroes Again," *New York Sun*, 2 February 1912, item 295, frames 27–28, *Hampton University Peabody Newspaper Clipping File*, microfiche. The story was written by the *Sun*'s Louisiana correspondent, based on local newspaper accounts. According to these reports, plantation owners in Louisiana had customarily allowed indebted sharecroppers and tenants to leave if another

employer agreed to pay their debts. A growing tendency among planters not to allow families to move under any circumstances precipitated the migration of thousands of black people to Arkansas.

15. Peter [Henry M. Stewart] to Annie [L. Allain], 31 March 1907, 6–7, file 20, box 8, TAFP.

16. Robert H. Stirling to Sarah, 22 August 1910, 2, file 28, box 3, LSFP; "Trespass Notices," every issue of *St. Francisville Democrat*, 1929–70.

17. Vandal, "Property Offenses," 129–30; Peter [Henry M. Stewart] to Old Girl [Annie L. Allain], 17 June 1906, 7, file 19, box 8, TAFP; Sarah T. Bowman to Nina Bowman, n.d. [1907], 7, file 7, box 2, Turnbull-Bowman-Lyons Family Papers, HML (owner of Hazelwood); [J. S. McGehee] to G. A. Marsh, 22 August 1916, 1, file *M*, letter file box 1, John Burrus McGehee Papers, HML.

18. Jones, *Labor of Love*, 129 (quotation), 132; Aunt Ollie to Hattye, 3 March 1942, 3, file 2, box 1, John Hamilton and Harriet Boyd Ellis Papers, HML (white Louisianan); Saxon, Dreyer, and Tallant, *Gumbo Ya-Ya*, 501–3 (domestic worker); Kelley, *Race Rebels*, 18–20; Hunter, *To 'Joy My Freedom*, 132–34.

19. S. M. Kilgore to [Henry] Wallace, 18 September 1933, file "Negro," box 90, Subject Correspondence Files, 1933–38, General Records of the Agricultural Adjustment Administration, Records of the Predecessor Agencies, Records of the Agricultural Stabilization and Conservation Service, RG 145, NA. For the antebellum origins of black people's notions of economic justice and their belief in the right to take from white employers what they needed to survive, see also Genovese, *Roll, Jordan, Roll*, 599–612.

20. Elizabeth Ross Hite, interview by Robert McKinney, n.d. [ca. 1930s], in Clayton, *Mother Wit*, 110; Martin Williams, interview by author, THWC–LSU; Joseph Carter, interview by Miriam Feingold, MFP.

21. George E. Lewis to Miss Ovington, n.d. [ca. 1918], 3, file "Shreveport, La. 1918–1919," box 83, ser. G, pt. 1, PNAACP–LC; "Notes on NAACP Regional Training Conference," 6 October 1945, 6, file "Leadership Training Conference, Louisiana-Texas (Conference) Correspondence 1945," box 375, ser. C, pt. 2, ibid.

22. Clifton and Eual Hall, Lorin Hall, interviews by author, THWC–LSU; Lemke-Santangelo, *Abiding Courage*, 40 (Willa Suddeth).

23. Andrews, *To Tell A Free Story*, 13; Gates, introduction to *Classic Slave Narratives*, ix; Cornelius, *"When I Can Read My Title Clear,"* 1–4, 59–84, 142–50; Wilkie, *Ethnicity, Community and Power*, 317; Robert and Essie Mae Lewis, interview by author, Baton Rouge; Brown interview. This belief in the importance of education was universal among the participants in the freedom struggle who were interviewed for this book. Many of the older people had sent some or all of their children to college, and this was among their proudest achievements. Asked whether other black people in his community shared his emphasis on education, Martin Williams of Madison Parish stated, "There's any number of them, and more of them would do it if they had the support."

24. William Adams, Anthony Rachel, and Frank Wilderson, interview by Linda

Jules Adams, Friends of the Cabildo Collection, New Orleans Public Library; Palmer, "Evolution of Education," 230, 35, 232, 412; Wilkie, *Ethnicity, Community, and Power*, 83; Johnnie Jones Sr., interview by Mary Hebert, 10, Baton Rouge; State Department of Education of Louisiana, *Organizational Study*, 2.

25. Leo M. Favrot to Julius Rosenwald, 17 May 19[31], file 5, box 339, RFP; Embree, *Julius Rosenwald Fund*, 23.

26. Palmer, "Evolution of Education," 240–43; "Negro Education in Louisiana," n.d. [ca. 1940s], 2, file 5, box 4, SHJP. See also Kevin K. Gaines, *Uplifting the Race*, 32–34, and Anderson, *Education of Blacks in the South*, 33–147.

27. Collins, "Community Activities of Rural Elementary Teachers," 6 (President of Grambling College); State Department of Education of Louisiana, *State Course of Study*, 64; Lewis interview.

28. Lewis and Martin Williams interviews; Bond and Bond, *Star Creek Papers*, 43 (Willie Crain). The accommodationist approach had its drawbacks and has been rightly criticized, but many black people who were labeled "Uncle Toms" by more militant activists were not the obliging accomplices in white supremacy that they appeared to be. While preaching self-help and acceptance of inequality to black people in the late nineteenth century, Booker T. Washington covertly lent financial assistance to lawsuits that challenged segregation and disfranchisement, fought the exclusion of African Americans from the southern Republican Party, and supported efforts to end peonage. Similarly, Adam Fairclough's study of southern black teachers in the Jim Crow era (for whom some accommodation to the social order was necessary for survival) suggests that these educators made subtle but valuable contributions to the freedom struggle in the long term. See Meier, "Toward a Reinterpretation"; Harlan, *Booker T. Washington*, 288–303; and Fairclough, "'Being in the Field of Education,'" 73–75.

29. "Ecology of East Feliciana Parish," n.d. [ca. 1940], 7, file 5, box 225, CSJP (quotations); Neyland, "Negro in Louisiana," 78; Anderson, *Education of Blacks in the South*, 153–56.

30. Palmer, "Evolution of Education," 29.

31. Laws, "Negroes of Cinclare Central Factory," 117; Lemke-Santangelo, *Abiding Courage*, 138 (Ruth Cherry); James C. Scott, *Moral Economy of the Peasant*, 240. See also Thompson, *Making of the English Working Class*, 189–212, 418–29, and "Moral Economy of the English Crowd."

32. "Some Cultural Traits of Louisiana Families," n.d. [ca. 1940], 15, file 8, box 226, CSJP.

33. Frazier, *Negro Church in America*, 46; Johnson, *Louisiana Educational Survey*, 26; E. W. Grant, "Social Agencies," n.d. [ca. 1940], 3–5, file 8, box 226, CSJP.

34. Levine, *Black Culture and Black Consciousness*, 326–28; Saxon, Dreyer, and Tallant, *Gumbo Ya-Ya*, 483–84 (quotation).

35. "Some Cultural Traits of Louisiana Families," n.d. [1940], 14–17, file 8, box 226, CSJP; E. W. Grant, "Social Agencies," n.d. [ca. 1940], 3–5, ibid. For a useful

discussion of the black church's dual role as an agent of social control and social change, see Williams, "A Mighty Fortress."

36. Wilkie, *Ethnicity, Community, and Power*, 83; Sepia Socialite, *Negro in Louisiana*, 89; "Women's 4th Dist. Home Mission Baptist Association," 26 July 1938, 148, file 11-6, reel PP2.9, RTC; "50 Year History of the Knights and Ladies of Peter Claver," *Claverite*, November–December 1959, 12, file 38, box 6, APTP.

37. "Types of Organizations Engaging Interest and Participation of Rural Negro Families in Louisiana," n.d. [ca. 1940], file 10, box 226, CSJP (quotation, p. 12).

38. Muraskin, *Middle-Class Blacks*, 123–32; Levine, *Black Culture and Black Consciousness*, 268; Lewis, *In Their Own Interests*, 70–73; Higginbotham, *Righteous Discontent*, 4–13; Beito, "Black Fraternal Hospitals," 112–13; [Constitution], St. Mary Parish Benevolent Society, [23] October 1891, file 1, box 1, DTP; Oshinsky, "*Worse Than Slavery*," 127, 131; Rebecca Field, Promissory Note, 5 September 1898, file 1, box 1, DTP; Record Book, 1922–24, Bethel Baptist Church Records, HML.

39. "The Negro," *Madison Journal*, 28 April 1928, 2.

40. W. T. Meade Grant Jr. to FDR, 20 March 1934, and enclosed petition, file "158260 Sub 10, 2-12-34-4-15-34," box 1278, SNF. These connections are discussed in more detail in Chapters 5 and 7. See also Speech Delivered by Daniel E. Byrd at the [NAACP] National Convention, 27 June 1946, 5, additions file, box 8, DEBP; Fairclough, *Race and Democracy*, 69–72; Beito, "Black Fraternal Hospitals," 123–24; and Muraskin, *Middle-Class Blacks*, 219–36.

41. Unknown author to NAACP, n.d. [ca. 1921], frame 0418, reel 12, ser. A, pt. 7, *PNAACP*—Micro.

42. Walter White to John Garibaldi Sargent, 26 January 1926, frames 0755–56, reel 11, *PFUS*.

43. D. W. Taylor to NAACP, 11 August 1934, frames 0096–98, reel 12, ser. A, pt. 7, *PNAACP*—Micro; Bond and Bond, *Star Creek Papers*, 122–26.

44. Similar incidents are reported in "Man Hunt Starts for Negro Slayer," *New Orleans Times-Picayune*, 4 July 1914, 1; "Tie Negro to Auto, Then Throw on Speed," ibid., 6 August 1914, 7; "Two More Deaths Added to Long List," ibid., 10 August 1914, 12; "I. H. Cain Stabbed by Negro," *Pointe Coupee Banner*, 9 April 1921, 3; "C. E. Speed Is Shot by Negro," *Madison Journal*, 15 March 1924, 1, 4; "Bad Negro Captured," *St. Francisville Democrat*, 1 December 1934, 3; "Negro Attacks White Farmer of Woodside in Palmetto Friday," *Opelousas Clarion-News*, 1 August 1935, 3; "Four Negroes Convicted," newspaper clipping, source unknown, n.d. [January 1936], frame 0013, reel 12, ser. A, pt. 7, *PNAACP*—Micro; "Negro Evades Arrest," *St. Francisville Democrat*, 10 September 1938, 3; and "I. E. Darnell's Head Cut Open by Negro," *Madison Journal*, 3 March 1939, 1. Violent attacks on white people might have occurred more often than this list suggests. Black newspapers suppressed news of these events for fear of causing the culprits to be lynched, and white newspapers usually reported them only after the attacker had been caught and punished. See Bond and Bond, *Star Creek Papers*, 126.

45. Jones interview, 63; Lolis Elie, interview by Kim Lacy Rogers, 23 June 1988, ARC.

46. Walter White to FDR, 12 January 1935, file "15820, Sub 26, Jan 1935 Only," box 1280, SNF, RG 60; Bond and Bond, *Star Creek Papers*, 126; "Negro Taken to Pen via Eunice," *St. Landry Clarion-Progress*, 20 February 1926, 11; James A. Ray to President [Woodrow Wilson], 27 February 1912, file "158260, Section 1, #3," box 1276, SNF, RG 60; John R. Shillady to R. G. Pleasant, 25 June 1918, frame 0319, reel 12, ser. A, pt. 7, *PNAACP*—Micro; "Kill Innocent Colored Men in Louisiana," clipping, *Philadelphia Tribune*, 16 June 1928, frame 1152, reel 11, ser. A, pt. 7, *PNAACP*—Micro; "Somebody Ought to Pay These Mob Bills," clipping, *Chicago Defender*, 26 May 1928, frame 0436, reel 12, ibid.

47. Guzman, *Negro Yearbook*, 308.

48. See, e.g., [Henry M. Stewart] to [Annie L. Allain], letters dated n.d. [November 1898], 3; 29 November 1898, 4; 18 April 1900, 2; 8 February 1906, 7; 30 March 1906, 4; 26 June 1906, 4; and 27 December 1906, 1–3, files 14–19, box 8, TAFP. (No wonder she never married him.)

49. Peter [Henry M. Stewart] to Annie [L. Allain], 21 January 1908, file 21, 3, box 8, ibid.

50. Notes on Home Visits of Lucille Cook Watson, 6 November 1933, file 11, box 5, ser. 1, Cross Keys Plantation Records, Manuscripts Division, HTL.

51. Bond and Bond, *Star Creek Papers*, 91–94.

52. Ibid., 77–79 (quotation, p. 79); H. H. Long, "Washington Parish," n.d. [ca. 1940], 21–22, file 8, box 225, CSJP.

53. Wells-Barnett, *Southern Horrors*, 42; [W. E. B. Du Bois], "Cowardice," *Crisis*, October 1916, 270–71; "Tulsa—A Horror and a Benediction," *Baltimore Afro-American*, 10 June 1921, 2.

54. "Straight Talk," *Louisiana Weekly*, 15 March 1930, sec. 1, 6.

55. "Signs of the New Negro," ibid., 29 August 1931, sec. 1, 6.

56. Rogers, "'You Came Away with Some Courage,'" 179; Elie (Rogers) interview; Jerome Smith, interview by Kim Lacy Rogers, ARC.

57. Lewis interview.

Chapter Four

1. See, e.g., Gottlieb, *Making Their Own Way*; Grossman, *Land of Hope*; Marks, *Farewell—We're Good and Gone*; and Sernett, *Bound for the Promised Land*.

2. U.S. Department of Labor, Division of Negro Economics, *Negro at Work*, 10.

3. "Labor Agents Warned," *Madison Journal*, 26 December 1914, 4; Untitled article, ibid., 2 June 1917, 4; Grossman, "Black Labor Is the Best Labor," 51–52.

4. Charles S. Johnson, "Negro Migration," n.d. [ca. 1930s], file 31, box 167, CSJP (quotations, pp. 6–8). More recent scholarship on black migration to the North supports Johnson's analysis. See, e.g., Gottlieb, *Making Their Own Way*,

1–11; Grossman, *Land of Hope*, 66–97; and Sernett, *Bound for the Promised Land*, 36–86.

5. Unknown writers, 24 April 1917 (p. 296) and 18 April 1917 (p. 330), in Emmett J. Scott, "Letters of Negro Migrants"; Unknown writer, 30 April 1918, in Scott, "Additional Letters of Negro Migrants," 448.

6. Unknown writers, 13 May 1917 (p. 417), 6 June 1917 (p. 413), 12 August 1916 (p. 423), in Emmett J. Scott, "Additional Letters of Negro Migrants."

7. A. G. Smith, "Holding Labor on the Farms in the South," n.d. [ca. 1918–19], frame 00075, reel 22, *BWEGM*.

8. Unknown writers, 23 April 191[7] (p. 434), 5 May 1917, (p. 433), in Emmett J. Scott, "Additional Letters of Negro Migrants."

9. Unknown writers, 20 May 1917 (p. 450—first quotation), 23 May 1917 (p. 449—second quotation), ibid.; John R. Shillady, Address Delivered at the Tenth Anniversary Conference of the NAACP, 23 June 1919, frame 0504, reel 8, pt. 1, *PNAACP*—Micro; Scherer, *Nation at War*, 66–67; Tolnay and Beck, "Rethinking the Role of Racial Violence," 29–30.

10. Marks, *Farewell—We're Good and Gone*, 138; Tindall, *Emergence of the New South*, 541; Weiss, *Farewell to the Party of Lincoln*, 78–95; Sitkoff, *New Deal for Blacks*, 88–101.

11. Grossman, *Land of Hope*, 3–4.

12. Shillady, Address Delivered at the Tenth Anniversary Conference of the NAACP, frames 0499–0500, reel 8, pt. 1, *PNAACP*—Micro. See also Garfinkel, *When Negroes March*, 31, and Finch, *NAACP*, 24–27.

13. Fairclough, *Race and Democracy*, 8; Bureau of the Census, *Thirteenth Census . . . 1910, Volume 2: Population*, 790, and *Fourteenth Census . . . 1920, Volume 3: Population*, 399; A. W. Hill to NAACP, 1 June 1914, file "Shreveport, La. 1914–1917," box 83, ser. G, pt. 1, PNAACP—LC; Application for Charter, Alexandria Branch, 27 November 1918, file "Alexandria, La. 1918–1930," box 79, ser. G, pt. 1, PNAACP—LC; Application for Charter, Baton Rouge Branch, 10 March 1919, frames 0194–95, reel 13, ser. A, pt. 12, *PNAACP*—Micro; Application for Charter, Monroe Branch, 18 November 1927, frames 0651–53, reel 13, ser. A, pt. 12, *PNAACP*—Micro.

14. Application for Charter, St. Rose Branch, 15 July 1918, file "St. Rose, La. 1918," box 83, ser. G, pt. 1, PNAACP—LC; Application for Charter, [Clarence Branch], n.d. [ca. 1922], file "Clarence, La. 1922," box 79, ibid.

15. Shreveport Branch, NAACP, to Luther E. Hall, 11 August 1914, file "Louisiana—1914," box 357, ser. C, pt. 1, PNAACP—LC. As mentioned in Chapter 2, the governor finally sent investigators to Caddo Parish after several more lynchings occurred there toward the end of the year, but this action failed to persuade local authorities to punish those responsible for the murders.

16. George E. Lewis to [John] Shillady, 17 February 1919, 2, file "Shreveport, La. 1918–1919," box 83, ser. G, pt. 1, PNAACP—LC; Forest Trottie to [Robert] Bagnall, 13 January 1922, file "Clarence, La. 1922," box 79, ibid.

17. George G. Bradford, "Save," *Crisis*, May 1918, 7; Marks, *Farewell—We're Good and Gone*, 95; Henri, *Bitter Victory*, 88.

18. [W. E. B. Du Bois], "The Black Soldier," *Crisis*, June 1918, 60, and "Close Ranks," *Crisis*, July 1918, 111; "The Negro's Reward," *Vindicator*, 3 September 1918, frame 0212, reel 14, ser. A, pt. 12, *PNAACP*—Micro.

19. T. G. Garrett to [NAACP], [September] 1917, file "Shreveport, La. 1914–1917," box 83, ser. G, pt. 1, PNAACP—LC.

20. Emmett J. Scott, *American Negro*, 93, 103–4; Marks, *Farewell—We're Good and Gone*, 97; Henri, *Bitter Victory*, 47–51; Reich, "Soldiers of Democracy," 1485.

21. James B. Aswell, Entry for 25 September 1918, Diary, September 23–October 4 [1918], MS vol. 3, James B. Aswell and Family Papers, HML.

22. Henri, *Bitter Victory*, 38, 44; Tuttle, *Race Riot*, 208–41; Seligmann, *Negro Faces America*, 56.

23. Ray C. Burrus to Arthur Woods, 3 May 1919, frame 00366, reel 21, *BWEGM*.

24. "Planters Resist Exodus of Labor," *New Orleans Daily Picayune*, 25 March 1914, 7.

25. "Exodus of Negroes," *New Orleans Times Democrat/Daily Picayune*, 12 April 1914, 8 (reprinted from *Houma Courier*); "Labor Agents Warned," and "Notice to Labor Agents," *Madison Journal*, 26 December 1914, 4.

26. House of Representatives of . . . Louisiana, *Official Journal . . . May 13, 1918*, 136–37; Louis Posby to T. W. Gregory, 17 October 1916, frames 09948–50, reel 19, *BWEGM*; Henderson, *Negro Migration*, 45–46; Grossman, "Black Labor Is the Best Labor," 57–58; Wayne G. Borah to Attorney General, 3 February 1925, frame 1083, reel 9, *PFUS* (quotation).

27. State of Louisiana, Act No. 139, 9 July 1918, frame 0382, reel 23, pt. 10, *PNAACP*—Micro; Walter F. White, "'Work or Fight' in the South," *New Republic*, 1 March 1919, 144; Winn Parish Police Jury Resolution, 2 July 1918, reprinted in Louisiana Historical Records Survey, *Inventory of the Records*, 19; Lafayette Parish Police Jury Resolution, 1 August 1918, reprinted in Louisiana Historical Records Survey, *Inventory of the Records*, 15; Louisiana State Council of Defense, *Minutes of the Meeting . . . September 24, 1918*, 8.

28. Louisiana State Council of Defense, *Minutes of the Meeting . . . September 24, 1918*, 11–12; George E. Haynes to Felix Frankfurter, 21 August 1918, frame 00505, reel 19, *BWEGM*; [Frankfurter] to Haynes, 28 August 1918, frame 00507, ibid. (quotation).

29. White, "'Work or Fight,'" 144–46; [Walter White], "Louisiana," [16 December 1918], frames 0332–33, reel 23, pt. 10, *PNAACP*—Micro; George E. Haynes to Secretary, Department of Labor, 20 March 1919, frame 00004, reel 14, *BWEGM*.

30. U.S. Department of Labor, Division of Economics, *Negro Migration*, 32.

31. H. George Davenport to Roy Nash, 5 May 1917, frame 0143, reel 14, ser. A, pt. 12, *PNAACP*—Micro.

32. Shillady, Address Delivered at the Tenth Anniversary Conference of the NAACP, frame 0504, reel 8, pt. 1, ibid.; Francis Williams, "Louisiana's Sugar

Industry Revives," *Country Gentleman*, 3 November 1917, 1696; Henderson, *Negro Migration*, 49; Tolnay and Beck, "Rethinking the Role of Racial Violence," 29–30.

33. Leo M. Favrot, "Some Problems in the Education of the Negro in the South and How We Are Trying to Meet Them in Louisiana," n.d. [June 1919], frames 0597–0603, reel 8, pt. 1, *PNAACP*—Micro (quotation, frame 0599).

34. Daniel, *Breaking the Land*, 3–22.

35. Cotton, *Lamplighters*, 12; Crosby, "Building the Country Home," 59–64.

36. "T. J. Jordan Ag. Extension Leader Retires after 34 Years of Service," *Louisiana Weekly*, 2 October 1948, 12; J. S. Clark, "A Supplement to the Annual Report of the Agricultural Extension Service as Performed by Negroes," 1920, 3, 2 (last quotation), reel 5, FESR; Oscar G. Price, Annual Narrative Report, County Agent, St. Helena Parish, 1921, reel 8, FESR (first quotation).

37. Mason Snowden, Annual Narrative Report, State Agent, 1916, 348, reel 1, FESR. See also Baker, *County Agent*, 191–206; Daniel, *Breaking the Land*, 9–12; Crosby, "Building the Country Home," 9, 104, 165; and Cotton, *Lamplighters*, 89–100.

38. Higginbotham, *Righteous Discontent*; Kevin K. Gaines, *Uplifting the Race*. Glenda Elizabeth Gilmore (*Gender and Jim Crow*) provides another very useful account of black middle-class activism.

39. Adolph B. Curet, Annual Narrative Report, County Agent, Pointe Coupee Parish, 1919, reel 4; O. G. Price, Annual Narrative Report, County Agent, St. Helena Parish, 1919, reel 5; T. J. Watson, Annual Narrative Report, County Agent, Madison Parish, 1921, reel 7; State Agent's Report, Louisiana, 1922, 7, reel 8—all in FESR.

40. Harrison and Earnestine Brown, interview by author, THWC–LSU.

41. "T. J. Jordan Ag. Extension Leader Retires after 34 Years of Service," *Louisiana Weekly*, 2 October 1948, 12; Leon Robinson, Annual Narrative Report, Negro Agent, St. Landry Parish, 1938, 23, reel 49, FESR.

42. S. W. Vance, Annual Narrative Report, County Agent, South Madison and Tensas Parishes, 1915, reel 1, and 1917, reel 3, FESR.

43. Cotton prices increased from 7¢ per pound in 1914 to 36¢ per pound in 1919, then dropped to 14¢ per pound in 1920. Similarly, the average price per pound for raw sugar rose from 4¢ in 1914 to 13¢ in 1920, then fell to 5¢ in 1921. U.S. Department of Agriculture, *Yearbook of Agriculture 1930*, 680, 703. For some narrative accounts of economic conditions in the rural South during and after World War I, see Barton W. Currie, "Sky-High Cotton," *Country Gentleman*, 17 February 1917, 310–11; Francis Williams, "Louisiana's Sugar Industry Revives," *Country Gentleman*, 3 November 1917, 1696; and Mertz, *New Deal Policy*, 1–15.

44. J. E. Ringgold, Annual Narrative Report, Negro Agent, West Feliciana Parish, 1925, 1–2, reel 15, FESR.

45. Nine parishes (Bienville, Caddo, Claiborne, East Baton Rouge, East Feliciana, Lincoln, St. Landry, Washington, and West Feliciana) had extension agents

working with black farmers between 1925 and 1930. The increases in black farm ownership in those parishes ranged from 10 to 71 percent and averaged 33 percent. In the same period, black farm ownership in the state increased by 10 percent. But at the same time, the number of tenants in each parish and in the state increased at a much greater rate than landowners. Between 1925 and 1930 the proportion of black farmers who were tenants rose by 7 percent for the state and by an average of 5 percent for the parishes with extension agents. T. J. Jordan, Annual Narrative Report, Assistant State Agent, Negro Extension Work, 1931, 10, reel 29, FESR; Bureau of the Census, *Fifteenth Census . . . 1930, Agriculture, Volume 2, Part 2*, 1219–23, 1275–80.

46. L. W. Wilkinson, Annual Narrative Report, State Agent, Negro Extension Work, Louisiana, 1931, 9, reel 29, FESR.

47. J. E. Ringgold, Annual Narrative Report, Negro Agent, West Feliciana Parish, 1921, reel 8, FESR.

48. Myrtis A. Magee, Annual Narrative Report, Negro Agent, Washington, Tangipahoa, St. Tammany, and St. Helena Parishes, 1936, 12, vol. 510, AESP. See also L. J. Washington, Annual Narrative Report, Assistant State Agent for Work with Negroes, Franklin, Richmond, and Tensas Parishes, 1934, vol. 499, AESP, and T. J. Jordan, Annual Narrative Report, Assistant State Agent for Work with Negroes, 1945, 8, vol. 484, AESP.

49. O. G. Price, Annual Narrative Report, County Agent, St. Helena Parish, 1918, reel 4, and 1921, reel 8, FESR; J. E. Ringgold, Annual Narrative Report, Negro Agent, West Feliciana Parish, 1920, reel 6, FESR; "Extension Agent, M. Magee, Dies," *Louisiana Weekly*, 17 February 1940, 6.

50. Crosby, "Building the Country Home," 35; "Negro Work in Louisiana, 1920–21," n.d. [1921], 1, filed with State Administration Reports, reel 6, FESR; Cotton, *Lamplighters*, 102, 13. For a detailed study outlining the unequal allocation of federal funds and the poor quality of service provided to black farmers, see Wilkerson, *Agricultural Extension Services among Negroes*.

51. "Negro Work in Louisiana, 1920–21," n.d. [1921], 1, filed with State Administration Reports, reel 6, FESR; Annual Narrative Report, State Agent, Louisiana, 1924, 10, reel 13, FESR; Baker, *County Agent*, 198–99; W. B. Mercier to J. A. Evans, 10 March 1930, file "Director La. 1929–1930," box 193, General Correspondence of the Extension Service and its Predecessors, June 1907–June 1943, Correspondence, Records of the Federal Extension Service, RG 33, NA.

52. Brunner and Yang, *Rural America and the Extension Service*, 68–70; "Minority Report of W. L. Blackstone, Special Statements by Individual Members of the Special Committee on Farm Tenancy," n.d. [February 1937], 1–2, file "Tenancy (Jan 1–Feb 1)," box 2661, GCOS, RG 16.

53. Henri, *Bitter Victory*, 112–13, 115–17; Gottlieb, *Making Their Own Way*, 89–116; Cohen, "Great Migration," 73, 76; Matthews, "American Negro Leadership," 72; Emmett J. Scott, *American Negro*, 465.

54. Kellogg, *NAACP*, 235.

55. John R. Shillady to R. G. Pleasant, 15 February 1919, frame 0031, reel 12, ser. A, pt. 7, *PNAACP*—Micro; "Discharged Soldier Lynched and Burned," clipping, *Brooklyn Standard Union*, 1 September 1919, frame 0027, ibid.; Ernest J. Gaines, *Gathering of Old Men*, 104. For references to similar incidents in real life, see Henri, *Bitter Victory*, 113–14; Matthews, "American Negro Leadership," 73; and Reich, "Soldiers of Democracy," 1485.

56. Anonymous to Mr. Officer of Bigness [President], 18 March 1919, file "158260, Section 1, #1," box 1276, SNF; Anonymous to White House (via Dearborn Supply Co.), 15 September 1921, file "158260, Section 3, #2," SNF.

57. Green, *Grass-Roots Socialism*, 345–408; Dawley, *Struggles for Justice*, 254–94; MacLean, *Behind the Mask of Chivalry*; Tuttle, *Race Riot*, 3–31. For federal agencies' efforts to curtail the activities of black civil rights organizations during and after the war, see Kornweibel, *"Seeing Red."*

58. Mary White Ovington, *Bogalusa* (New York: NAACP [1920]), frames 0002–5, reel 10, pt. 10, *PNAACP*—Micro; Frank Duffy to District Councils and Local Unions of the United Brotherhood of Carpenters and Joiners of America, 9 January 1920, frames 0007–10, ibid.; Norwood, "Bogalusa Burning."

59. Report of the Secretary, December 1920, frame 0120, reel 4, pt. 1, *PNAACP*—Micro; Robert Bagnall, Report of Field Work, 9 May 1921, frame 0171, ibid.; "Parker and the Klan," *Madison Journal*, 2 December 1922, 2; "Comparative Statements of July 31, 1920 and August 31, 1920," frame 0102, reel 4, pt. 1, *PNAACP*—Micro (quotation); Record, *Race and Radicalism*, 31–33, 44. See also Reich, "Soldiers of Democracy," 1498–1504.

60. Director of Branches to B. V. Jennings, 11 August 1924, frame 0202, reel 13, ser. A, pt. 12, *PNAACP*—Micro; H. C. Hudson to Robert W. Bagnall, 27 March 1923, 1–2, file "Shreveport, La. 1920–1927," box 83, ser. G, pt. 1, PNAACP—LC (quotation); O. B. F. Smith to Robert Bagnall, 3 May 1926, file "Alexandria, La. 1918–1930" (box 79), "Shreveport Branch N.A.A.C.P. Sleeping," 7 April 1928, file "Shreveport, La. 1928–1932" (box 83), and N. H. Baker to Walter White, 3 February 1933 (box 83)—all in ser. G, pt. 1, PNAACP—LC.

Chapter Five

1. Baldwin, *Poverty and Politics*, 32; Mertz, *New Deal Policy*, 1–15; Holley, *Uncle Sam's Farmers*, 10–14; Moses Williams, interview by author, THWC—LSU.

2. Taylor, *Louisiana*, 149–66; Brinkley, *Voices of Protest*, 15–35. T. Harry Williams (*Huey Long*) offers a sympathetic account of Long's regime, arguing that his ruthless tactics were necessary to oust the reactionaries from power. More critical assessments are given in Sindler, *Huey Long's Louisiana*; Hair, *Kingfish and His Realm*; and Jeansonne, *Messiah of the Masses*.

3. "Huey Long Is Dead," *Louisiana Weekly*, 14 September 1935, 8; Sepia Socialite, *Negro in Louisiana*, 2. Like most of his southern white contemporaries, Long commonly referred to black people as "niggers."

4. Daniel, *Breaking the Land*, 65–68; Sullivan, *Days of Hope*, 3. See also Piven and Cloward, *Poor People's Movements*, 12.

5. Olson, *Historical Dictionary of the New Deal*, 177–78, 549; Leuchtenburg, *Roosevelt*, 118–42.

6. Douty, "FERA and the Rural Negro," 215; Sitkoff, *New Deal for Blacks*, 59–75; Weiss, *Farewell to the Party of Lincoln*, 220–21; Sullivan, *Days of Hope*, 41–67; Barnard, *Outside the Magic Circle*, 127; Willie Dixon to U.S. Attorney General, 24 April 1939, frame 0987, reel 9, *PFUS* (quotation).

7. "Final Enrolling of State CCC Begins July 6th," *Madison Journal*, 3 July 1936, 1–2; "Tells of Work CCC Boys Have Done in State," *Madison Journal*, 6 October 1939, 2; Martin Williams, interview by author, THWC–LSU (first quotation); CCC, Office of the Director, *The Civilian Conservation Corps and Colored Youth* (Washington, D.C.: [CCC], 1939), frames 0530–33, reel 1, pt. 10, *PNAACP*–Micro; Gordon P. Hogan and John Percy Bond, Monthly Educational Report, June 1935, 1, file "La. L-72, New Roads," box 89, CIR, RG 35; "Youth Impressions (Regarding Negroes)," 27 September 1941, 1, file "Special Reports Re: Negroes," box 4, Project Files, 1940–45, Records of the Division of Program Surveys, Divisional Records, Records of the Bureau of Agricultural Economics, RG 83, NA (second quotation).

8. Douty, "FERA and the Rural Negro," 215; James H. Crutcher, "Prosperity Returns to Louisiana," *Work*, October 1936, 3; "Chicago Mill Veneer Plant Burns Monday," *Madison Journal*, 4 December 1936, 1. In 1930 African Americans made up 71 percent of workers employed in sawmills and planing mills in Madison Parish. Bureau of the Census, *Fifteenth Census . . . 1930, Population, Volume 3, Part 1*, 999.

9. "Chicago Mill Is Operating under NRA Agreement," *Madison Journal*, 25 August 1933, 1. The rate works out at $1.92 per day or $38.40 per month, compared with an average wage rate of $17.31 per month (without board) for Louisiana farm laborers in 1933. U.S. Department of Agriculture, *Crops and Markets*, 119.

10. Martin Williams interview; Harrison and Earnestine Brown, interview by author, THWC–LSU. Between 1930 and 1940 Tallulah grew in population from 3,332 to 5,712. African Americans comprised 86 percent of the increase, numbering 2,043. Bureau of the Census, *Fifteenth Census . . . 1930, Population, Volume 3, Part 1*, 992, and *Sixteenth Census . . . 1940, Population, Volume 2, Part 3*, 419.

11. Sepia Socialite, *Negro in Louisiana*, 74, 79; "Literacy," *Work*, February 1937, 18 (first quotation); George Washington, "Adult Education among Negroes in Louisiana," *Louisiana Colored Teachers' Journal*, February–March 1939, frame 0322, reel 3, LWPA; "Adult Classes Proving Popular," *Work*, October 1936, 6 (second quotation); "School Days," *Work*, April 1938, 4 (last quotation).

12. J. H. Chapmon to FDR, 12 April 1938, frame 0665; Leola Dishman to FDR, 18 February 1939, frame 0794; and Annette Nelson to Harold S. Hopkins, 29 May 1936, frame 0430—all in reel 29, LWPA.

13. In its second year of operation, e.g., the FSA received 147,972 applications

for the 7,000 loans that were available. In 1940 the 6,678 families who were receiving help from the agency's tenant purchase program represented only 2 percent of tenants in the United States. Baldwin, *Poverty and Politics*, 199.

14. "Works Progress Administration of Louisiana," *Pointe Coupee Banner*, 23 July 1936, 1.

15. Charlie Young to Richard Leche, 15 December 1936, file "Public Welfare (T–Z)," box 36; Lillie Pearl Jackson to Leche, 15 December 1936, file "Public Welfare (J–L)," box 36; and Charlie Hines et al. to Leche, 23 March 1938, file "A," box 7—all in RWLP.

16. Weiss, *Farewell to the Party of Lincoln*, 50–59; Daniel, *Breaking the Land*, 80–81; Baldwin, *Poverty and Politics*, 196–97, 200–201, 279–80; "The Differential Labor Policy," *Louisiana Weekly*, 7 October 1933, sec. 1, 8 (first quotation); Louis Israel to A. P. Tureaud, 11 December 1933, file 6, box 1, APTP; "WPA Chief Tells of Racial Problem in U.S. Relief Work," *Louisiana Weekly*, 7 December 1935, 1, 7.

17. "Personnel of West Feliciana Parish Board of Public Welfare Selected by Police Jury at Meeting," 6 January 1937, file "Public Welfare Personnel—Parish Directors and Staff," box 36, RWLP; M. L. Wilson to W. W. Alexander, 10 December 1938, 15, file "Tenancy 2.1 (County Committee)," box 2902, GCOS, RG 16; "Personnel of Pointe Coupee Parish Board of Public Welfare Selected by Police Jury at Meeting," 4 January 1937, file "Public Welfare Personnel—Parish Directors and Staff," box 36, RWLP; Gordon McIntire, Statement on Sugar Cane Wages, Federal Hearing, 16 June 1939, 7, 11–12, file 3, reel 13, CLJP; Clyde Johnson, interview by Bob Dinwiddie, transcript, 4 April 1976, 46, file 1, reel 13, CLJP; Daniel, *Breaking the Land*, 91–109; Conrad, *Forgotten Farmers*, 39–42.

18. Clay Jackson to Alfred Edgar Smith, 11 March 1938, frame 0386, reel 29, LWPA (first quotation); C. L. Kennon to Richard Leche, 15 February 1936, file unlabeled [5], box 60, RWLP; Fritz Falcon to Henry Wallace, 23 March 1936, file "AD 510 Appeals for Aid, Louisiana Counties," box 193, GCCO.

19. W. F. Oakes to Alfred Edgar Smith, 2 November 1937, frame 0095, reel 5, LWPA; Cornelia Edge to Howard Sinclair, memorandum, 17 December 1941, frames 0316–17, reel 7, LWPA (first quotation, by Walter F. Craddock); J. B. Garrett, Annual Narrative Report, County Agent, West Feliciana Parish, 1940, 21, reel 56, FESR (second quotation); Guy Campbell to Allen J. Ellender, 8 August 1941, frame 0453, reel 7, LWPA.

20. "Cooperation," *Work*, September 1936, 4; Frank H. Peterman to Harry L. Hopkins, 10 August 1935, frame 0059, reel 1, LWPA (first quotation); Mildred Taylor, Narrative Report—Monroe District, Sewing Projects, 15 September 1936, frame 0818, reel 26, LWPA; Clay Jackson to Alfred Edgar Smith, 11 March 1938, frame 0386, reel 29, LWPA; Edgar A. Schuler, Weekly Tensions Report, 20 March 1943, 5, file "Edgar Schuler—Field Reports," box 1824, FRSD, RG 44.

21. Anonymous letter, no addressee (referred to Department of Justice), n.d. [ca. December 1933–January 1934], file "158260, Sub 46, 12/20/33–1/10/34," box 1291, SNF; Neill McL. Coney Jr., Camp Report, 11 September 1933, 2, file "La.

L-61, Krotz Springs, Co. #1481," box 88, CIR, RG 35; John P. Davis to Robert H. Jackson, 11 March 1940, 1, file "198589, Section 8," box 3034, SNF, RG 60.

22. N. Watts Maddux to Lewis B. Hershey, 30 September 1941, frame 0464, reel 7, LWPA; W. D. Haas to A. Leonard Allen, 21 October 1942, frame 0470, LWPA; "Resolution of Caddo Parish Police Jury," 24 September 1942, file 5, box 9, SHJP.

23. W. F. Oakes to David K. Niles, 14 May 1937, frames 0864–65, reel 4, LWPA.

24. C. C. Huffman to Sam H. Jones, 27 October 1942, file 5, box 9, SHJP. As Cindy Hahamovitch ("Standing Idly By," 16) has noted, decisions about whether or not labor shortages really existed were "inherently political" and rested on subjective judgments more than empirical measurements. Planters who were accustomed to a large and therefore cheap supply of workers were likely to perceive labor "shortages" whenever competition between employers caused wage rates to rise, regardless of the actual number of farmworkers who were available.

25. J. H. Crutcher to District Directors, memorandum, 26 August 1936, file "Federal–Public Works Administration," box 34, RWLP; "Workers Told by WPA Chief to Take Jobs," *Opelousas Clarion-News*, 19 November 1936, 8; Weekly News Letter, WPA of Louisiana, 23 August 1938, frames 0816–18, reel 1, LWPA; "WPA Will Guard against Scarcity of Farm Labor," *Madison Journal*, 9 September 1938, 1; "Welfare Office to Co-operate with Farmers," *Pointe Coupee Banner*, 3 September 1942, 1.

26. Aiken, *Cotton Plantation South*, 100–104; Sitterson, *Sugar Country*, 386–87; Bureau of the Census, *Sixteenth Census . . . 1940, Agriculture, Volume 1, Part 5*, 121; Wright, *Old South, New South*, 234.

27. Bureau of the Census, *Census of Agriculture: 1954, Volume 1, Part 24*, 11; Conrad, *Forgotten Farmers*, 58–82; Grubbs, *Cry from the Cotton*, 23–25; Mertz, *New Deal Policy*, 23; Tensas Parish Department of Public Welfare, "For the Welfare of Tensas Parish," 15 March 1937, 7, Tensas Parish Scrapbook, 1937–75, MS vol. 9, Gladys Means Loyd and Family Papers, HML (quotation); Maude Barrett to Loula Dunn, 11 September 1935, frames 0015–16, reel 1, LWPA.

28. Conrad, *Forgotten Farmers*, 50–63; Grubbs, *Cry from the Cotton*, 21–23; Clyde Johnson interview, 47; Brown interview.

29. Kelley, *Hammer and Hoe*; Grubbs, *Cry from the Cotton*; Flamm, "National Farmers Union"; Kirby, *Rural Worlds Lost*, 151–52; Holley, *Uncle Sam's Farmers*, 82–104; Mertz, *New Deal Policy*, 20–44. For a firsthand account of these struggles, see Rosengarten, *All God's Dangers*.

30. Clyde Johnson interview, 48, 29; Kelley, *Hammer and Hoe*, 168–69, 63, 172; Tom [Clyde Johnson] to H. L. Mitchell, 31 January [1936], reel 1, *STFUP* (quotation); Rosen, "Alabama Share Croppers Union," 89, 138–39; C. L. Johnson, "The Sharecroppers Union," *Louisiana Weekly*, 16 May 1936.

31. Johnson later became involved in organizing beet workers in Colorado, pecan shellers and oil workers in Texas, and electrical workers in Pittsburgh before taking a job as a carpenter and union official in California in the 1950s.

According to Robin Kelley, after his election as business agent for Local 550 of the Carpenters' and Millmen's Union, Johnson turned the local into "a powerful force for civil rights, trade union democracy, and antipoverty work in the Bay Area." Kelley, *Hammer and Hoe*, 63, 169, and "Lifelong Radical," 254–58 (quotation, p. 257).

32. Rosen, "Alabama Share Croppers Union," 4, 89, 138–39; Reuben Cole, "Southern Farm Students Praise College for Workers," *Southern Farm Leader*, February 1937, 2; Tex [Gordon McIntire] to Clyde and Anne [Johnson], 13 April 1956, file 3, reel 13, CLJP; Johnson, "Brief History," 18; FBI, "Louisiana Farmers' Union (Farmers' Educational and Cooperative Union of America, Louisiana Division)," 27 September 1941, 8, file 100–45768, LFU, FBI Headquarters, Washington, D.C.

33. "Southern Farm Leader," *Southern Farm Leader*, May 1936, 1; Rosen, "Alabama Share Croppers Union," 89 (Johnson).

34. "Share Croppers Union Expresses Its Thanks to Secretary Johnson," *Southern Farm Leader*, August 1936, 5; "Your Paper—Our Bow," *Louisiana Union Farmer*, November 1939, 4 (McIntire).

35. "For Unity in the South," *Southern Farm Leader*, May 1936, 4; Rosen, "Alabama Share Croppers Union," 99–106. Noncommunist contemporaries as well as many historians of New Deal era social movements viewed the part that communists played in these struggles with ambivalence. Communist Party members received funding and direction from the Soviet Union for their activities, raising concerns about their underlying motives and goals. Rigid adherence to the party line and the efforts of some members to gain control over the noncommunist organizations they belonged to antagonized more moderate activists and contributed to the weakening of the American left in the 1940s. On the other hand, the party provided many of the most dedicated and effective organizers in the labor movement, and its members were among the few white people who openly supported racial equality in the decades before World War II.

H. L. Mitchell's and others' suspicions notwithstanding, the organizers of the SCU and LFU bore little resemblance to the uncompromising ideologues depicted in some accounts of communist activity. The decision to seek alliances with other liberal and left-wing organizations was reached independently of Soviet influence and antedated the Communist International's formal proclamation of the Popular Front by more than a year. Although they might have started out with the goal of transforming southern sharecroppers and tenants into the vanguard of an American workers' revolution, organizers ultimately became more concerned with helping rural people to achieve a measure of comfort and security in their daily lives. By early 1935, Johnson stated, "all of the pretense of running party units á la New York was given up," and union organizers' contacts with the Communist Party leadership were minimal. Rosen, "Alabama Share Croppers Union," 3–4, 95–96 (quotation, p. 96). For some historical analyses of the role of communists in the freedom struggle, see Kelley, *Hammer and Hoe*; Record, *Race and Radicalism*; Naison, *Communists in Harlem*; Honey, *Southern Labor and Black Civil Rights*; and Horowitz, *"Negro and White, Unite and Fight!."*

36. Kelley, *Hammer and Hoe*, 169–72; Rosen, "Alabama Share Croppers Union," 86–87, 99–107, 112–13.

37. A union newsletter explained, "The charter gives the local the legal right to hold closed meetings and it is unlawful for anyone who is not a member to break in a meeting." "Organization Information," *Union News*, 30 April 1937, 2, file 2, reel 13, CLJP.

38. Clyde Johnson to J. M. Graves, 15 May 1937, 1, ibid.; "S.C.U. Locals Transferring to Farmers' Union," *Southern Farm Leader*, February 1937, 2.

39. Clyde Johnson interview, 48; [Clyde Johnson] to G. S. Gravlee, 23 September 1936, file 2, ibid.

40. SCU leaders strongly supported working with organized labor, encouraging members to form local farmer-labor cooperatives and to support candidates of the Farmer-Labor Party when they ran for political office. In return, leaders of the AFL and the CIO promised support for the struggles of rural people in the South. At its annual convention in April 1937, the Louisiana State Federation of Labor endorsed the LFU's efforts. The editor of the state AFL's newspaper, William L. Donnells, provided office space for LFU organizers and helped produce the *Southern Farm Leader* for more than a year before the farm union's failure to pay its bills caused him to withdraw this support. "Farmers' Union National Convention," *Louisiana Farmers' Union News*, 1 December 1937, 1–2; Farmers' Educational and Cooperative Union of America, National Program, December 1937, file 3, reel 13, CLJP; "Washington Hears Farm Workers' Plea for Recognition," *Southern Farm Leader*, May 1936, 1; "A New Party Is Needed to Battle for Justice," *Southern Farm Leader*, August 1936, 5; "Louisiana Labor Pledges Support for Farm Union," *Southern Farm Leader*, April–May 1937, 1; "New Office for Louisiana Farmers' Union," *Louisiana Farmers' Union News*, 15 January 1938, 1; Gordon McIntire to Mack, Bob, and Clyde [Johnson], 23 June [1938], file 3, reel 13, CLJP.

41. "For Unity in the South," *Southern Farm Leader*, May 1936, 4.

42. Although UCAPAWA represented agricultural workers at federal hearings and before government agencies concerned with labor, most of its organizing activity centered on the processing industries. [Clyde Johnson], "Activities in United Cannery, Agricultural, Packing and Allied Workers of America, 1938," 3 July 1976, 1–2, file 4, reel 13, CLJP; Kelley, *Hammer and Hoe*, 172; *UCAPAWA Yearbook*, December 1938, 8, 14, file 5, reel 13, CLJP; Rosen, "Alabama Share Croppers Union," 113–15.

43. Gordon McIntire to Miss La Budde, 12 October 1937, 3, file 3, reel 13, CLJP.

44. "S.C.U. Locals Transferring to Farmers' Union," *Southern Farm Leader*, February 1937, 2; "Organization Information," *Union News*, 30 April 1937, 2, file 2, reel 13, CLJP; Rosen, "Alabama Share Croppers Union," 91; Whayne, *New Plantation South*, 194. Women and girls typically spent less time working in the

fields than men and boys, so they could attend school for a greater part of the year. Stephanie J. Shaw provides additional insight into rural black people's determination to educate their daughters, particularly, in *What a Woman Ought to Be and to Do*, 13–16.

45. "Women Delegates Discuss Schools, Adopt Program," *Southern Farm Leader*, August 1936, 1; "Women Are Entitled to Free Medical Aid," ibid., 4.

46. The literature on this topic is extensive. White and black southerners were certainly capable of overcoming mutual suspicion and mistrust to form strong interracial alliances, but these organizations always remained vulnerable. If the racism of individual members did not weaken or destroy them, racist and sometimes violent attacks by members of the larger community often did. See, e.g., Honey, *Southern Labor and Black Civil Rights*, 93–173; Griffith, *Crisis of American Labor*, 62–105; Arnesen, *Waterfront Workers of New Orleans*, 74–118; Letwin, "Interracial Unionism"; and Norwood, "Bogalusa Burning."

47. Rosen, "Alabama Share Croppers Union," 90, 92 (quotation).

48. In the same article McIntire asserted: "The Farmers' Union is proud of its large colored membership. But just as America has more white farmers than colored so has the Union." It is (perhaps intentionally) unclear whether "Farmers' Union" meant the LFU or the NFU, but it is likely that he was referring to the predominantly white national membership, not the state union. Gordon McIntire, "Between the Plow Handles," *Southern Farm Leader*, December 1936, 4.

49. "Simmesport Hoodlums Drive Organizer Moore out of Town," *Southern Farm Leader*, August 1936, 2; Rosen, "Alabama Share Croppers Union," 90, 139–40; "Resolutions of Sharecroppers' Convention—A Call to Action," *Southern Farm Leader*, August 1936, 3–4.

50. "First Louisiana Union Label Farm Produce for Maritime Strikers" (p. 1) and "St. Landry Farmers Need Corn Relief" (p. 2), *Southern Farm Leader*, November 1936.

51. Gordon McIntire and Clyde Johnson, "Statement on the St. Landry Farm Case," n.d., 1–2, file 3, reel 13, CLJP (quotation, p. 2).

52. Ibid.; "Editorial Notes," *Southern Farm Leader*, December 1936, 4; McIntire and Johnson, "Statement on the St. Landry Farm Case," 2–3; Mercer G. Evans to Clyde Johnson, 24 December 1936, and Johnson to Louis Fontenot, 4 January 1937, file 3, reel 13, CLJP; "St. Landry Farm Tenants Getting Teams and Tools," *Southern Farm Leader*, January 1937, 1.

53. LFU news release, 29 November 1939, 1, file "Southern Tenant Farmers' Union Jan 23–Dec 20," box 406, ser. A, pt. 1, PNAACP—LC (quotation); "Cotton Tenants Win Rent Victory," *Louisiana Farmers' Union News*, March 1939, 1–2.

54. Sugar Act of 1937, in Lynsky, *Sugar Economics*, 215–16.

55. Although it is likely that some of the planters did have genuine financial difficulties, most were not as poverty-stricken as they claimed. Between 1930 and 1936 gross income from the Louisiana sugar crop more than doubled (increasing from $15 million to $33 million), while wages remained relatively static. Godchaux

Sugars, a company that owned a dozen plantations in seven parishes, reported a net income of $858,000 in 1936. At the 1937 hearings, when the owner of Burgaires Sugar stated, "It is not a question of how we are going to divide the profits but how we will share the losses," a small grower from his parish pointed out that the company had made $500,000 in profits the previous winter. In any case, plantation owners derived great benefits from the government's subsidy program, and it was not unreasonable to require them to share part of their increased earnings with their workers. Lynsky, *Sugar Economics*, 23, 93; Gordon McIntire to Miss La Budde, 12 October 1937, 1, file 3, reel 13, CLJP.

56. Gordon McIntire to Miss La Budde, 12 October 1937, 3–7, file 3, reel 13, CLJP (quotation, p. 5); Godfrey G. Beck and Gordon McIntire to Sugar Cane Cutters and Friends of Field Labor in the Sugar Industry, n.d. [October 1937], ibid.

57. U.S. Department of Agriculture, "Determination of Fair and Reasonable Wage Rates for Harvesting the 1937 Sugar Crop of Louisiana Sugarcane, Pursuant to the Sugar Act of 1937," 12 November 1937, in Lynsky, *Sugar Economics*, 233. This did not mean that all planters had to provide such benefits, only that those who had always done so could not withdraw these privileges in an effort to reduce wages. In a setback for the LFU, the Sugar Section later determined that growers could deduct pay for board if this was agreed to in advance with their laborers. Gordon McIntire called the new ruling "simply a loophole" that allowed planters to pay less than the minimum wage. "The Check-up on Cane Cutting Wages," *Louisiana Farmers' Union News*, 1 March 1938, 5; Tex [Gordon McIntire] to Clyde Johnson, 14 September 1939, 1, file 3, reel 13, CLJP.

58. "Farmers' Union Asks Wage Increases for Sugar Workers," *Louisiana Farmers' Union News*, 1 March 1938, 1–3; "Increased Wages for Sugar Cane Workers Specified in Rules," *Opelousas Clarion-News*, 28 July 1938, 3; Bernhardt, *Sugar Industry and the Federal Government*, 208.

59. LFU organizers and members attended additional hearings in August 1938 (to establish rates for the 1938 harvest season) and June 1939 (to establish rates for the 1939 planting and cultivation seasons, and the 1940 harvest season), but the union was unable to gain further wage increases. With the start of World War II, however, wages rose to almost $3.00 per day and continued to climb after the war, reaching up to $3.70 per day or $1.74 per ton during the 1949 sugar harvest. "Cane Grower Denies Labor Intimidated," clipping, *New Orleans Item*, n.d. [6 August 1938], and Tex [Gordon McIntire] to Clyde [Johnson], 20 June 1939, file 3, reel 13, CLJP; Bernhardt, *Sugar Industry and the Federal Government*, 224–25, 242, 251–52, 266, 272, 275–76; Sitterson, *Sugar Country*, 393–94.

60. "The Check-up on Cane Cutting Wages," *Louisiana Farmers' Union News*, 1 March 1938, 5; "Action on Cane Wages," ibid., August 1939, 3; "The Sugar Battle Still Rages," ibid., September 1939, 3; B. E. Sackett to Director, FBI, 7 September 1939, file "144-32-2," box 17587, CSF, RG 60; "Sharecroppers and Tenants Hold Convention," LFU news release, 4 November 1939, 2, file 3, reel 13, CLJP.

61. [Clyde Johnson] to G. S. Gravlee, 23 September 1936, file 2, reel 13, CLJP; FBI, "Louisiana Farmers' Union (Farmers' Educational and Cooperative Union of America, Louisiana Division)," 27 September 1941, 6–7, LFU–FBI. There were 206,719 farm operators and laborers (excluding unpaid family labor) in Louisiana in 1940. Bureau of the Census, *Census of Agriculture: 1945, Volume 1, Part 24*, 4, 10.

62. "Sharecroppers and Tenants Hold Convention," LFU news release, 4 November 1939, 1, file 3, reel 13, CLJP; "Negro Conference in Baton Rouge," *Louisiana Union Farmer*, November 1939, 1; Tex [Gordon McIntire] to Clyde [Johnson], 11 November 1939, 1, file 3, reel 13, CLJP.

63. FBI, "Louisiana Farmers' Union (Farmers' Educational and Cooperative Union of America, Louisiana Division)," 27 September 1941, 18, LFU–FBI; "Communism and the Negro Tenant Farmer," *Opportunity*, August 1931, 234.

64. A New Member, "Slavery," *Southern Farm Leader*, October 1936, 3; "Sharecroppers and Tenants Hold Convention," LFU news release, 4 November 1939, 1, file 3, reel 13, CLJP (second quotation).

65. Clyde Johnson interview, 45 (first quotation); Gordon McIntire and Clyde Johnson, "Statement on Farm-Tenancy," n.d. [ca. January 1937], 3, file "Extra Copies Briefs from Hearings on Farm Tenancy, Dallas, Texas, Jan. 4, 1937," box 1, RCFT, RG 83; "The Sharecrop Contract," *Southern Farm Leader*, April–May 1937, 3; Mertz, *New Deal Policy*, 202; "F.S.A. News," *Pointe Coupee Banner*, 8 June 1939, 1 (second quotation); "FSA Insists on Written Farm Lease," *St. Francisville Democrat*, 1 October 1938, 2 (last quotation); "FSA Farm News," *Pointe Coupee Banner*, 2 October 1941, 1.

66. C. L. Johnson, "The Sharecroppers' Union," *Louisiana Weekly*, 16 May 1936, 6; "Local No. 2 Resolution," *Southern Farm Leader*, December 1936, 3; "Mother's Club Gets Toilets for School," *Southern Farm Leader*, January 1937, 1.

67. "Want School Bus First," *Southern Farm Leader*, April–May 1937, 3 (first quotation); "Farmers' Union Asks Federal Aid for Rural Schools," *Louisiana Farmers' Union News*, 1 June 1938, 1; "Some Letters from the Field," *Louisiana Farmers' Union News*, 20 August 1938, 3 (last quotation).

68. "Unions Ask Land for Landless at Texas Meeting," *Southern Farm Leader*, January 1937, 1; "Your County Agent," ibid., June 1936, 4 (quotation); "Resettlement," ibid., May 1936, 4.

69. Pete Daniel has shown that government farm policies continued to favor large, corporate landowners over small farmers while accommodation to southern traditions and prejudices allowed racism to become institutionalized within the Department of Agriculture. As late as 1992, only 417 African Americans served on county committees of the FaHA (successor to the FSA) out of a total of 6,611 potential members. Discrimination was so prevalent that black farmers filed a class-action lawsuit against the government, winning a settlement in January 1999 that promised hundreds of millions of dollars in back payments to Afri-

can Americans who had wrongfully been denied credit, grants, and other benefits. See Daniel, "Legal Basis of Agrarian Capitalism" (statistic, p. 100), and Jenkins, "See No Evil," 16.

70. This was a much larger percentage than was typical for the South as a whole, where discrimination against black farmers kept the number of successful FSA applicants low. In 1939, e.g., only 722 loans were granted to African Americans in fourteen southern states, representing 23 percent of the loans that were available in those states. (Black people made up 35 percent of the tenant farmers in the same states.) African Americans constituted 70 percent of tenants in Pointe Coupee Parish in 1935. "Good Record for Pointe Coupee's FSA Farmers," *Pointe Coupee Banner*, 20 January 1938, 1, 4; *Report of the Administrator of the Farm Security Administration 1939* (Washington, D.C.: GPO, 1939), 15–16, file "183-04 Annual Report 1937," box 27, General Correspondence, 1935–42, Records of the Resettlement Division, Records of the Central Office, Records of the FaHA, RG 96, NA; Bureau of the Census, *Census of Agriculture: 1935, Volume 1*, 703.

71. Douglas Robinson to Steve Barbre, 18 March 1941, and E. C. McInnis to A. M. Rogers, 31 January 1942, both in file "Pointe Coupee Parish, La. AD-510," box 193, GCCO, RG 96.

72. See, e.g., L. I. Billingsley to Secretary of Agriculture, n.d. [ca. February 1934], 1, file "Bero to Bill," box 3, Correspondence with the General Public to Which Individual Replies Were Made, 1933–35, Records of the Division of Subsistence Homesteads, Records of the Central Office, Records of the FaHA, RG 96, NA; Willie Bates to FDR, December 1934, folder "Bas to Beat," box 2, ibid.

73. Statement of Harry Jack Rose, 7 December 1936, file 3, reel 13, CLJP.

74. "First Negro Farmer Pays Off FSA Farm Ownership Loan," *Louisiana Weekly*, 27 February 1943, 12; Arthur Hatfield, "Farmers Able to Buy Farms under Bankhead-Jones Farm Tenant Act," *Louisiana Weekly*, 9 August 1941, 7; [Statistics on African American Gains under FSA Programs], n.d. [ca. between 1937 and 1942], 1–2, file "Investigation of Clients Preference (Veterans, Indians, etc.)," box 43, General Correspondence, 1937–42, Records of the Farm Ownership Division, Records of the Central Office, Records of the FaHA, RG 96, NA.

75. "Good Record for Pointe Coupee's FSA Farmers," *Pointe Coupee Banner*, 20 January 1938, 1, 4. Statewide, the 6,899 farm families who had FSA loans in 1937 increased their net worth from an average of $213 when they received the loans to $418 at the end of the year. See "FSA Farmers Improve Net Worth in '37," *St. Francisville Democrat*, 2 April 1938, 2.

76. Arthur Hatfield, "FSA Performing Miracle for Low-Income Farmers, Says Writer after Tour," *Louisiana Weekly*, 2 August 1941, 7 (first quotation); Bureau of the Census, *Census of Agriculture: 1959, Volume 1, Part 35*, 6; J. A. M. Lloyd, Annual Narrative Report, Negro Agent, Tensas Parish, 1939, 2, reel 53, FESR. Between 1935 and 1940 the number of black landowners in the parish increased

from 88 to 159, raising the proportion of farm operators they represented from 5 to 9 percent. Bureau of the Census, *Sixteenth Census . . . 1940, Agriculture, Volume 1, Part 5*, 143.

77. "Some Letters from the Field," *Louisiana Farmers' Union News*, 20 August 1938, 3.

78. "Is Communism in Our Midst?," *Opelousas Clarion-News*, 3 December 1936, 4; Statement by Gordon McIntire, 9 December 1936, 1–2, file 3, reel 13, CLJP; "The Farmers' Union and the Negro," *Louisiana Farmers' Union News*, 15 February 1938, 1; "Some Letters from the Field," *Louisiana Farmers' Union News*, 20 August 1938, 3. Some planters honestly believed that union organizers were taking advantage of their black laborers for mercenary reasons. Numerous references to the poverty of the New Orleans staff members in the papers of the LFU show that this was not the case. Organizers received no regular salaries and depended on donations from northern supporters in addition to some limited funds allocated by the NFU. When they traveled out to the rural parishes to visit union locals, they relied on members to feed and house them. "Racketeers Said to Be Robbing Poor as Alleged RA Workers," *Opelousas-Clarion News*, 2 January 1936, sec. 2, 4; George A. Dreyfous and M. Swearingen, "Report to the Executive Committee of the LLPCR on Investigations in West Feliciana Parish," n.d. [1937], 6, file 19, box 2, HNLP; Tex [Gordon McIntire] to Clyde [Johnson], 17 February, 16 April, 22 May 1937, 22–23 June 1938, all in file 3, reel 13, CLJP.

79. Report of T. F. Wilson, FBI, 1 August 1939, 25, file "144-32-2," box 17587, CSF, RG 60; Elma Godchaux to LLPCR, 17 October 1937, 2, file 7, box 1, HNLP.

80. Report of T. F. Wilson, FBI, 1 August 1939, 28, file "144-32-2," box 17587, CSF, RG 60; "Natchitoches Farmers Rally to Defend Clark," *Louisiana Weekly*, 17 August 1940, 5; "Trouble with Checks," *Southern Farm Leader*, January 1937, 3 (quotations). Similar complaints were made by farmers in Alabama and Arkansas as well as other parishes in Louisiana. See "Resettlement," *Southern Farm Leader*, May 1936, 4.

81. Gordon McIntire to Gardner Jackson, 17 July 1939, 1, file 3, reel 13, CLJP.

82. Report of J. O. Peyronnin, FBI, 6 September 1939, 2–3, file "144-32-2," box 17587, CSF, RG 60 (first and last quotations); "Statement of Terror against Farmers' Union Leaders in West Feliciana Parish Louisiana," 2 July 1937, 1–3, file 3, reel 13, CLJP.

83. Report of T. F. Wilson, FBI, 1 August 1939, 28, file "144-32-2," box 17587, CSF, RG 60; Gordon McIntire [to St. Landry Farm LFU Members], February 1937, 3, file 2, reel 13, CLJP. See also Johnson, "Brief History," 11–12, and Rosen, "Alabama Share Croppers Union," 92.

84. George A. Dreyfous and M. Swearingen, "Report of the Executive Committee of the LLPCR on Investigations in West Feliciana Parish," n.d. [1937], 3, file 19, box 2, HNLP (1937 report); "Union Men Don't Scare," *Louisiana Farmers' Union News*, 15 February 1938, 1–2.

85. Gordon McIntire to Gardner Jackson, 17 July 1939, and to Clyde Johnson, 19

July 1939, both in file 3, reel 13, CLJP; Report of T. F. Wilson, FBI, 1 August 1939, and Report of J. O. Peyronnin, FBI, 6 September 1939, both in file "144-32-2," box 17587, CSF, RG 60. The FBI's involvement was reluctant, and its agents showed more sympathy with plantation owners than with sugar workers. In his final report, the bureau's special agent in charge in New Orleans dismissed McIntire's complaints, saying: "The Bureau's attention is invited to the fact that McIntire is a labor union organizer who is trying to organize the negro workers in the cane fields and he, of course, is meeting with the usual opposition any such movement would have, especially in this part of the country, in connection with attempts to organize negro workers. His interests in the whole matter are purely mercenary, in attempts to secure members for his organization." B. E. Sackett to Director, FBI, 7 September 1939, 2, file "144-32-2," box 17587, CSF, RG 60.

86. "The Sugar Battle Still Rages," *Louisiana Farmers' Union News*, September 1939, 3; Margery Dallet, "Case of Clinton Clark, Natchitoches, La.," 17 August 1940, 1–2, file 15, box 3, HNLP.

87. H. L. Mitchell to Members of Executive Council of the STFU, memorandum, 7 March 1941, 1, reel 18, *STFUP*; "Farm Bureau Advocates Abolition of Tenant Program," *Tenant Farmer*, 15 July 1941, 1, file "Southern Tenant Farmers' Union 1940–1941," box 527, ser. A, pt. 3, PNAACP—LC; H. L. Mitchell, "The People at the Bottom of Our Agricultural Ladder," 7 October 1952, 1, reel 36, *STFUP*; Baldwin, *Poverty and Politics*, 335–62; Holley, *Uncle Sam's Farmers*, 174–278; Mertz, *New Deal Policy*, 218–20; Daniel, *Breaking the Land*, 91–109; Kirby, *Rural Worlds Lost*, 51–79.

88. FBI, "Louisiana Farmers' Union (Farmers' Educational and Cooperative Union of America, Louisiana Division)," 20 February 1943, 1, LFU—FBI. The figure of 3,000 members was an estimate given to an FBI agent by a former member of the LFU. It is unclear whether it refers to the union's total membership or only dues-paying members—if there were 3,000 dues-paying members, then the union's total membership would have been several times that number.

89. Gordon McIntire, "Dear Friends," n.d. [1938], file 3, reel 13, CLJP; FBI, "Louisiana Farmers' Union (Farmers' Educational and Cooperative Union of America, Louisiana Division)," 20 February 1943, 1, LFU—FBI; Letter from unknown author to Peggy and Gordon [McIntire], 9 June 1941, excerpted in FBI, "Louisiana Farmers' Union (Farmers' Educational and Cooperative Union of America, Louisiana Division)," 27 September 1941, 22, LFU—FBI; Rosen, "Alabama Share Croppers Union," 122.

90. Gordon McIntire to Members and Friends of the Farmers' Union in Louisiana, 10 March 1942, 1, file 3, reel 13, CLJP; Fred Kane, "Clinton Clark Threatened with Mob Violence," *Louisiana Weekly*, 31 January 1942, 1, 7; "Farm Union Organizers Are Freed," *Louisiana Weekly*, 11 April 1942, 2.

91. Gordon McIntire to G. Warburton, 14 November 1939, 1–3, file 3, reel 13, CLJP; "Pointe Coupee Farmers Organize," *Pointe Coupee Banner*, 13 June 1940, 1; M. L. Wilson to H. C. Sanders, 9 June 1943, 1–3, file "Dir. La. 1.43–6.43," box

886, General Correspondence of the Extension Service and Its Predecessors, June 1907–June 1943, Correspondence, Records of the Federal Extension Service, RG 33, NA; Rosen, "Alabama Share Croppers Union," 79.

92. "Memorandum concerning Economic and Employment Conditions in Louisiana, Notes on Individual WPA Districts," June 1941, frames 0753–55, reel 6, LWPA; "Louisiana and National Defense, Second Report," 30 April 1941, 3, file 3, box 13, SHJP; Bureau of the Census, *Census of Agriculture: 1945, Volume 1, Part 24*, 4, 10. Approximately 60,000 rural people, representing more than one-quarter of Louisiana's farm population, left the land between 1940 and 1945.

93. Gordon McIntire to Members and Friends of the Farmers' Union in Louisiana, 10 March 1942, 4–5, file 3, reel 13, CLJP; FBI, "Louisiana Farmers' Union (Farmers' Educational and Cooperative Union of America, Louisiana Division)," 6 August 1943, 1, LFU–FBI.

Chapter Six

1. See, e.g., Garfinkel, *When Negroes March*; Finkle, *Forum for Protest*; Buchanan, *Black Americans*; and Wynn, *Afro-American*.

2. "No Crooked Talk in Such a Fix Says St. Landry Tenant," *Southern Farm Leader*, December 1936, 3.

3. Sepia Socialite, *Negro in Louisiana*, 50.

4. Edgar A. Schuler, "Weekly Report," 5 April 1943, 5, file "Edgar Schuler—Field Reports," box 1824, FRSD, RG 44.

5. *Chicago Defender*, 11 April 1942, quoted in "Weekly Media Report No. 11," 18 April 1942, 46, loose in box, box 1720, WMRRD, RG 44. Hundreds of documents in the record collections of wartime agencies held at the National Archives testify to the government's concern about African American attitudes toward the war.

6. Hill, *FBI's RACON*, xvii.

7. See, e.g., "Preliminary Appraisal of the Present Negro Situation," 9 March 1942, 2–4, 6, file "Surveys Div. Rep. No. 7," box 1786, Reports of the Division, 1942–44, RMRD, RG 44; "Current Problems of Negro Morale," 16 May 1942, 8, file "Sur. Div. Sp. Rep. No. 10," box 1784, ibid.; and "The Grievance Pattern: Elements of Disunity in America," 25 June 1942, 28, file "Sur. Div. Sp. Rep. No. 15a," box 1786, ibid.

8. FEPC, *First Report*, 96; Hill, *FBI's RACON*, 34. See also Lemke-Santangelo, *Abiding Courage*, and Lemann, *Promised Land*.

9. "Negroes Called from Here Going to Armed Forces," *Madison Journal*, 28 May 1943, 6.

10. "Many Volunteer after Colored Soldiers Pass," *Madison Journal*, 11 April 1941, 3.

11. "Courses in Many Subjects Offered WAAC Trainees," *Madison Journal*, 5

March 1943, 1. See also "Booths Provided Here to Recruit Women for WAAC," ibid., 12 February 1943, 1; "Special Effort Will Be Made to Recruit WAC's," ibid., 1 October 1943, 1; "WAC Anniversary" and "WACs to Stage Recruiting Drive in Louisiana," ibid., 12 May 1944, 2. Nationwide, approximately 6,500 African American women served in the WAC during the war. Martha S. Putney (*When the Nation Was in Need*) provides a useful account of the experiences of black women in the auxiliary corps.

12. Brown interview; Young interview; Veterans' Administration News Release, 14 March 1945, 2–3, file "Negro Problems—Misc. Material," box 386, OFWCL, RG 228; Wynn, *Afro-American*, 28.

13. "Army to Continue Use of WPA Aid, Says Gen. Hodges," *Madison Journal*, 14 February 1941, 4; "Louisiana and National Defense, Second Report," 30 April 1941, 2, file 3, box 13, SHJP; J. H. Crutcher to Malcolm J. Miller, 2 June 1941, frame 1092, reel 6, LWPA; "Memorandum concerning Economic and Employment Conditions in Louisiana," March–April 1942, frame 0956, reel 6, LWPA; Leon Robinson, Annual Narrative Report, Negro Agent, St. Landry Parish, 1943, 24, vol. 509, AESP; J. B. Garrett and H. B. Fairchild, Annual Narrative Report, County Agents, West Feliciana Parish, 1943, 9, reel 64, FESR. In the 1940s Baton Rouge became the state's fastest-growing city, reporting an increase in the number of manufacturing establishments from thirty-one in 1939 to sixty-two in 1947 and an increase in population from 34,719 to 125,629 between 1940 and 1950. Shreveport's population increased by 30 percent, from 98,167 to 127,206, and the city gained eighteen new industries. Rapides Parish experienced a similar boom, stimulated by the location of a military training center (Camp Claiborne) near Alexandria. Bureau of the Census, *Census of Manufactures: 1947, Volume 3*, 252, and *Seventeenth Decennial Census . . . Population: 1950, Volume 2, Part 18*, 7; Hill, *FBI's RACON*, 326.

14. Bernhardt, *Sugar Industry and the Federal Government*, 263, 275–76; "1942 Sugar Cane Wage Rates," *Pointe Coupee Banner*, 29 October 1942, 1; U.S. Department of Agriculture, "Digest of Clippings on Agriculture from the Negro Press," 13–20 June 1943, 2, file "Publications 1-1, Negro Press," box 25, General Correspondence, March–July 1943, Correspondence, Records of the Office of Labor (War Food Administration), RG 224, NA. Wage rates (without board) for farmworkers in Louisiana for 1941–42 averaged $25.79 per month, compared with $21.72 per month for the years 1935–40. U.S. Department of Agriculture, *Crops and Markets*, 119.

15. Bartlow, *Louisiana Study*, 61. The higher wage bill was also shared among fewer laborers—18,954 in 1945 compared with 56,712 in 1940. Bureau of the Census, *Census of Agriculture: 1945, Volume 1, Part 24*, 4.

16. "Food for Freedom Program," *Pointe Coupee Banner*, 6 November 1941, 1; "Farmers Hold Annual State Convention," *Louisiana Weekly*, 8 November 1941, 2.

17. "Pointe Coupee Parish U.S.D.A. Defense Board," *Pointe Coupee Banner*, 6 November 1941, 1, 8 (first quotation); Claude A. Barnett and F. D. Patterson to Claude R. Wickard, 26 June 1942, 2, file "Negroes," box 3, GCN, RG 16.

18. Sepia Socialite, *Negro in Louisiana*, 143, 16.

19. Hill, *FBI's RACON*, 315.

20. Ibid., 320–25, 462, 464; Louisiana State Conference of NAACP Branches, "Proposed Yearly Budget for State Office," 4 January 1947, file 1, box 9, APTP.

21. Iberville Parish Improvement Committee, "Petition to Iberville Parish School Board," 21 April 1943, 1–2, file 1, box 35, APTP; J. K. Haynes to Sam H. Jones, telegram, 15 June 1943, file 6, box 4, SHJP.

22. "Current Problems of Negro Morale," 16 May 1942, summary page, file "Sur. Div. Sp. Rep. No. 10," box 1784, RSD, RG 44; "March on Washington Movement among Negroes," 12 May 1942, 7, ibid.; Finkle, *Forum for Protest*, 90, 96–97.

23. Office of Facts and Figures, Bureau of Intelligence, "Survey of Intelligence Materials No. 25," 27 May 1942, 9, file "Negroes," box 3, GCN, RG 16.

24. Lemke-Santangelo, *Abiding Courage*, 76–78, 153–77; Buchanan, *Black Americans*, 15–27; Sitkoff, *Struggle for Black Equality*, 11; Finkle, *Forum for Protest*, 96–97.

25. Winn, *Afro-American*, 49–54; John A. Davis to Malcolm Ross, 29 February 1944, file "New Orleans," reel 76, Tension File, July 1943–October 1945, Headquarters Records, *RFEPC*.

26. Lena Mae Gordon to Civil Service Commission, 2 February 1943, 1–2, file "Q.M. Laundry, Camp Claiborne, La. 10-GR-148," reel 100, Closed Cases, August 1941–March 1946, Field Records, *RFEPC*; Edith A. Pierce to FEPC, 6 November 1944, file "Port of Embarkation 10-GR-433," ibid.

27. Finkle, *Forum for Protest*, 163–82; Wilson, *Jim Crow Joins Up*, 7–9, 11, 99; Treadwell, *Women's Army Corps*, 589–601; Putney, *When the Nation Was in Need*, 4, 50.

28. Samuel Bonery to Gloster B. Currant, 19 August 1942, frame 0442, reel 11, ser. B, pt. 9, *PNAACP*—Micro; Edgar B. Holt to Mr. Gibson, 14 October 1943, in McGuire, *Taps for a Jim Crow Army*, 66; George V. Grant to NAACP, 4 May 1943, frames 0242–45, reel 12, ser. B, pt. 9, *PNAACP*—Micro; Milton Adams to W. H. Hastie, 13 May 1942, in McGuire, *Taps for a Jim Crow Army*, 149.

29. Quoted in Putney, *When the Nation Was in Need*, 81.

30. Dorothy C. Bray to War Department, 4 October 1944, frames 0467–70, reel 1, ser. C, pt. 9, *PNAACP*—Micro; Darnell Harris to Walter White, 3 May 1942, frame 0344, reel 12, ser. B, pt. 9, ibid.

31. Peery, *Black Fire*, 173; Edgar A. Schuler, "Weekly Report," 5 April 1943, 1, 3, file "Edgar Schuler—Field Reports," box 1824, FRSD, RG 44. See also Kelley, *Race Rebels*, 55–75.

32. "Memorandum from Office of Commanding Officer, Headquarters Polk Louisiana," n.d. [ca. 1940s], frame 0440, reel 11, ser. B, pt. 9, *PNAACP*—Micro.

33. Edgar A. Schuler, "Weekly Report," 5 April 1943, 1–2, file "Edgar Schuler—

Field Reports," box 1824, FRSD, RG 44; Schuler, "Weekly Report," 3 April 1943, 5, ibid.; Schuler, "Tension Area Analysis: Racial Problems," 22 January 1943, 2, ibid.; Schuler, "Weekly Report," 5 April 1943, 4, ibid.

34. Edgar A. Schuler, "Summary of Tension Area Analysis: Racial Problems," 22 January 1943, ibid.; Aunt Ollie to Hattye, 3 March [1942], 2, file 2, box 1, John Hamilton and Harriet Boyd Ellis Papers, HML (resident of Tangipahoa Parish); Schuler, "Summary of Tension Area Analysis: Racial Problems," 22 January 1943, and "Tension Area Analysis: Racial Problems," 22 January 1943, 1, file "Edgar Schuler—Field Reports," box 1824, FRSD, RG 44. Howard Odum of the University of North Carolina collected hundreds of similar reports from across the South in his wartime study, *Race and Rumors of Race*.

35. John Beecher to Lawrence W. Creamer, memorandum, 7 March 1942, 7, file "1-1 Reports—John Beecher," reel 48, Central Files of the FEPC, August 1941–April 1946, Headquarters Records, *RFEPC*; Beecher to Creamer, memorandum, n.d. [ca. March 1942], 1, ibid. (quotation); Beecher to Creamer, memorandums, 16 March 1942, 2, n.d. [ca. March 1942], 1–2, and 7 March 1942, 6—all in ibid.

36. FEPC, *First Report*, 65; Peery, *Black Fire*, 154; Hill, *FBI's RACON*, 34; Bureau of the Census, *Sixteenth Census . . . 1940, Population, Volume 3, Part 3*, 264, 357, and *Seventeenth Decennial Census . . . Population: 1950, Volume 2, Part 18*, 225.

37. John Beecher to Lawrence W. Creamer, memorandum, 7 March 1942, 7, file "1-1 Reports—John Beecher," reel 48, Central Files of the FEPC, August 1941–April 1946, Headquarters Records, *RFEPC* (quotation); Clarence M. Mitchell to George Johnson, memorandum, 24 July 1945, file "Tension Report Region XIII," reel 63, ibid.

38. Edith A. Pierce to War Department, 6 November 1944, 1, file "Port of Embarkation 10-GR-433," reel 100, Closed Cases, August 1941–March 1946, Field Records, *RFEPC*; Joseph A. Prevost to FEPC, 13 October 1942, file "Port of Embarkation 10-GR-147," ibid.

39. "Louisiana and National Defense, Second Report," 30 April 1941, 3, file 3, box 13, SHJP; S. S. McFerrin, Annual Narrative Report, County Agent, St. Helena Parish, 1942, 10, reel 62, FESR; A. B. Curet, Annual Narrative Report, County Agent, Pointe Coupee Parish, 1942, 9, reel 61, FESR; "Every Citizen Is Asked to Aid in Harvesting Crops," *Madison Journal*, 9 October 1942, 6.

40. Edgar Schuler, "Tension Area Analysis: Racial Problems," 22 January 1943, 2, file "Edgar Schuler—Field Reports," box 1824, FRSD, RG 44; "Crops and Labor," *Pointe Coupee Banner*, 12 August 1943, 3; "Tax Losses," *Madison Journal*, 19 March 1943, 2. See also Woodruff, "Pick or Fight," 75.

41. A. J. Bouanchard to Sam Houston Jones, 14 September 1942, file "Pointe Coupee," box "Governor's File, New Orleans-St. Mary," SHJP.

42. Philleo Nash to Eugene Katz, memorandum, 3 October 1942, 1–2, file "Groups and Organizations Section, Bureau of Intelligence, OWI," box 1788, RSD, RG 44.

43. Woodruff, "Pick or Fight," 78–80; "Labor Freezing Covers Agriculture," *Pointe Coupee Banner*, 20 May 1943, 1 (quotations); "McKenzie Says Farm Labor Cannot Migrate," *Madison Journal*, 17 September 1943, 1.

44. C. E. Kemmerly Jr., Annual Narrative Report, Extension Farm Labor Program, Louisiana, 1943, 9, vol. 589, AESP.

45. "Nazi-Like Interpretation Given to 'Work or Fight Order' by City Official," *Louisiana Weekly*, 24 April 1943, 1 (first quotation); Social Science Institute at Fisk University, "A Monthly Summary of Events and Trends in Race Relations," September 1943, 3, file "Tension Areas Reports," box 389, OFWCL, RG 228.

46. C. E. Kemmerly Jr. to Meredith C. Wilson, 18 June 1943 (consolidated with Wilson to Kemmerly, 26 June 1943), file "La. K–O," box 887, General Correspondence of the Extension Service and Its Predecessors, June 1907–June 1943, Correspondence, Records of the Federal Extension Service, RG 33, NA (Extension Service administrators); "State Summary of County Statistical Reports, Louisiana," 1943, 4, vol. 589, AESP; A. B. Curet, Annual Narrative Report, County Agent, Pointe Coupee Parish, 1944, 5, reel 66, FESR; G. B. Martin, Annual Narrative Report, County Agent, St. Landry Parish, 1944, 5, reel 67, FESR; "Annual Report of Farm Labor Program, Louisiana," 1944, 4, vol. 589, AESP; "Eight Camps Set for Sugar Areas," *New Orleans Times-Picayune*, 9 October 1943, 16 (proponents of the camps); Max McDonald, Annual Narrative Report, County Agent, Madison Parish, 1944, 25, reel 66, FESR.

47. Max McDonald, Annual Narrative Report, County Agent, Madison Parish, 1945, 25, vol. 245, AESP; "Rapid[e]s Parish Points the Way," *Madison Journal*, 15 September 1944, 2; Farrell M. Roberts, Annual Narrative Report, County Agent, East Feliciana Parish, 1945, 4, vol. 146, AESP; "The Big Shift," *Pointe Coupee Banner*, 16 December 1948, 2; Bureau of the Census, *Census of Agriculture: 1959, Volume 1, Part 35*, 11–16.

48. Arthur Lemann, interview by Bernard Lemann, FCC–NOPL; "Mechanization Spreads," *Madison Journal*, 19 January 1945, 2; Bernhardt, *Sugar Industry and the Federal Government*, 282; R. J. Badeaux, Annual Narrative Report, County Agent, Iberville Parish, 1945, 18, vol. 181, AESP.

49. Bureau of the Census, *Census of Agriculture: 1959, Volume 1, Part 35*, 7, 6, *Sixteenth Census . . . 1940, Agriculture, Volume 1, Part 5*, 138, and *Census of Agriculture: 1945, Volume 1, Part 24*, 10; B. B. Jones, "Weekly Market News Letter," *St. Francisville Democrat*, 27 December 1946, 1; C. P. Seab, Annual Narrative Report, County Agent, Concordia Parish, 1949, 4, vol. 119, AESP.

50. Edgar A. Schuler, "Weekly Report," 3 April 1943, 5, file "Edgar Schuler–Field Reports," box 1824, FRSD, RG 44.

51. C. L. G. and J. A. D., "The Fair Employment Practice Committee and Race Tensions in Industry," n.d. [ca. 1940s], 8, file "The FEPC and Race Tensions in Industry," box 426, RFDRA, RG 228.

52. "Opinions about Inter-racial Tension," Division of Research Report No. C12, 25 August 1943, 13, file unlabeled, box 1719, RMRD, RG 44.

53. John A. Davis to Malcolm Ross, 29 February 1944, 1, file "New Orleans," reel 76, Tension File, July 1943–October 1945, Headquarters Records, *RFEPC*; Copy of article from *Sepia Socialite*, 27 May 1944, file "New Iberia," ibid.; "A Disgusted Negro Trooper" to *Cleveland Call & Post*, 16 August 1944, in McGuire, *Taps for a Jim Crow Army*, 196. On the January 1942 riot, see Sepia Socialite, *Negro in Louisiana*, 30–31, 33; Hill, *FBI's RACON*, 326–27; and Finkle, *Forum for Protest*, 106.

54. Prentice Thomas to Nora Williamson, 14 January 1943, frame 0485, reel 14, ser. B, pt. 9, *PNAACP*—Micro; Fred Hoord to *Chicago Defender*, n.d. [ca. June 1943], frames 0241–42, reel 13, ibid.; Francis Biddle to Mrs. Roosevelt, 17 May 1944, 1, file "144-33-14," box 17589, CSF, RG 60; George M. Johnson and S. Bradley to National Legal Committee, NAACP, 17 March 1944, frame 0548, reel 14, ser. B, pt. 9, *PNAACP*—Micro.

55. Edgar A. Schuler, "Weekly Tensions Report," 20 March 1943, 5–6 (quotation, p. 5), and 3 April 1943, 5, file "Edgar Schuler—Field Reports," box 1824, FRSD, RG 44; G. P. Bullis to Perry Cole, 21 January 1943, file "Request for Organizing," and A. B. Crothers to Cole, n.d. [June 1943], file "Ferriday, La.," Louisiana State Guard Records, Louisiana State Archives, Baton Rouge.

56. Peery, *Black Fire*, 170, 173–218.

57. R. Keith Kane to Reginald Foster, memorandum, 25 November 1942, 10, file "Civilian Problems," box 1790, Special Memoranda of the Division, 1942–44, RMRD, RG 44 (quotation); Thurgood Marshall to Tom C. Clark, 5 May 1944, frame 0556, reel 14, ser. B, pt. 9, *PNAACP*—Micro.

58. Quoted in "Information Roundup, No. 7," 24 April 1944, 23–24, loose in box, box 1712, RMRD, RG 44.

59. Transcript of Oral History Interview, Addendum, [Spring 1967], 55, file "Oral History Interview with John H. Scott and Related Material," John Henry Scott Papers, Archives, Manuscripts, and Special Collections Department, Earl K. Long Library, University of New Orleans, New Orleans.

60. Arthur to Mother, 18 November 1943, file 18, box 8, APTP; "R. L. Betz Assaulted by a Negro Soldier," *Madison Journal*, 8 February 1946, 1; Statement of Cora Mae Harris, n.d. [February 1946], frames 0222–23, reel 20, ser. C, pt. 9, *PNAACP*—Micro.

61. "March on Washington Movement among Negroes," 12 May 1942, 7, file "Sur. Div. Sp. Rep. No. 8," box 1784, RSD, RG 44.

62. "Preliminary Appraisal of the Present Negro Situation," 9 March 1942, 2–4, 6, file "Surveys Div. Rep. No. 7," box 1786, RSD, RG 44; "Current Problems of Negro Morale," 16 May 1942, 8, file "Sur. Div. Sp. Rep. No. 10," box 1784, RSD, RG 44; "The Grievance Pattern: Elements of Disunity in America," 25 June 1942, 28, file "Sur. Div. Sp. Rep. No. 15a," box 1786, RSD, RG 44; Hill, *FBI's RACON*, 3.

63. Buchanan, *Black Americans*, 76; Wilson, *Jim Crow Joins Up*, 125; "A Disgusted Negro Trooper" to *Cleveland Call & Post*, 16 August 1944, in McGuire, *Taps for a Jim Crow Army*, 196.

64. Carr, *Federal Protection of Civil Rights*, 163–76; Buchanan, *Black Americans*, 9–10, 125–26; Hill, *FBI's RACON*, 8–9; Goldfield, *Black, White, and Southern*, 33; Brundage, *Lynching in the New South*, 251.

65. Darlene Clark Hine, *Black Victory*, 212–42; Goldfield, *Black, White, and Southern*, 33–34.

66. Von Eschen, *Race against Empire*, 109–13; Wynn, *Afro-American*, 117–20; Finch, *NAACP*, 116–18. See also Berman, *Politics of Civil Rights*.

67. Southwest Region NAACP Newsletter, 20 November 1948, 1, file 26, box 15, APTP.

68. William A. Caudill, "Negro GI's Come Back," n.d., 2, file "Negro GI's Come Back," box 426, RFDRA, RG 228. See also Edgar A. Schuler, "Weekly Report," 5 April 1943, 2, file "Edgar Schuler—Field Reports," box 1824, FRSD, RG 44, and Albert Anderson, "Reactionaries and Progressives in Showdown Fight," *Louisiana Weekly*, 2 February 1946, 12.

Chapter Seven

1. Alexandria Branch of the NAACP to Nora Windon, August 1946, frame 0592, reel 8, pt. 4, *PNAACP*—Micro.

2. See, e.g., Wynn, *Afro-American*, 129–36. Wynn suggests that scholars have overstated the significance of World War II and that "some views may now need modification and qualification" (p. 129). David H. Onkst ("'First a Negro'") reaches a similar conclusion.

3. Burran, "Racial Violence in the South"; Norrell, "One Thing We Did Right," 68–70.

4. Arthur G. Klein, quoted in Ruchames, *Race, Jobs, and Politics*, 95.

5. For participation by black war veterans in the civil rights movement in other states, see Mills, *This Little Light of Mine*, 27; Dittmer, *Local People*, 1–18; Payne, *I've Got the Light of Freedom*, 24, 29–31, 47–49, 56–61, 66, 136–37, 181–82, 299, 404; and Tyson, "Robert F. Williams," 547–48.

6. Zelma Wyche, Harrison H. Brown, T. I. Israel, F. W. Wilson, and Moses Williams, interview by Miriam Feingold, MFP; Harrison and Earnestine Brown, interview by author, THWC—LSU; A. Z. Young, interview by Miriam Feingold, MFP; Fairclough, *Race and Democracy*, 395–98. See also Dittmer, *Local People*, 1–18, and Payne, *I've Got the Light of Freedom*, 29–66.

7. Bureau of the Census, *Seventeenth Decennial Census . . . Population: 1950, Volume 2, Part 18*, 225, and *Census of Agriculture: 1959, Volume 1, Part 35*, 6; Norvel E. Thames, Annual Narrative Report, County Agent, Tensas Parish, 1947, 2, vol. 392, AESP. See also "The Problem," n.d. [ca. 1930s], 1–3, file "LU-1 184-047 Farm Tenancy," box 1, RCFT, RG 83.

8. Bartlow, *Louisiana Study*, 50; "Louisiana Ideal for Many Industries, States Gov. Davis," *Madison Journal*, 27 June 1947, 4; "La. Industrial Leaders to Meet in New Orleans on December 16th," *Pointe Coupee Banner*, 4 December 1952, 1;

"La. Matching Agricultural with Industrial Expansion," *Opelousas Daily World*, 1 April 1955, 3; "Third Annual La. Industrial Development Conference Slated November 17th," *Pointe Coupee Banner*, 27 October 1955, 13.

9. "President's Message," *La. Delta Council News*, October 1948, 2; "Objectives of the Louisiana Delta Council," ibid., October 1948, 3. For analyses of the Mississippi Delta Council and its efforts to preserve white supremacy in the face of the economic transformation of the South, see Woodruff, "Mississippi Delta Planters," and Woods, *Development Arrested*, 121–82.

10. Bureau of the Census, *Census of Manufactures 1954, Volume 3*, 117-3, 117-4; Myrtle D. Anderson, Annual Narrative Report, Home Demonstration Agent, Iberville Parish, 1956, 2, vol. 184, AESP; LeRoy Barton, Annual Narrative Report, Negro Agent, Iberville Parish, 1957, 1, vol. 184, AESP; Prince H. Lewis, Annual Narrative Report, Negro Agent, East Feliciana Parish, 1957, 1, vol. 149, AESP.

11. "Sweet Potato Becomes an Industry," *St. Francisville Democrat*, 27 March 1942, 1; "Canning Plant to Locate Here," ibid., 23 March 1945, 3; "Paper Mill to Build Plant Here," ibid., 28 December 1956, 1, 4; W. D. Magee, Annual Narrative Report, County Agent, West Feliciana Parish, 1957, 4, vol. 457, AESP.

12. "Lumber and Logging Industry Increases," *Madison Journal*, 24 May 1946, 2; "Louisiana's Timber Industry Ranks High in Nation," ibid., 12 March 1948, 6; Bureau of the Census, *Census of Manufactures 1954, Volume 3*, 117-12–117-14; John C. Howard, *Negro in the Lumber Industry*, 12–13.

13. R. J. Courtney, Annual Narrative Report, Assistant State Agent for Work with Negroes, 1959, 3, vol. 525, AESP.

14. Accommodation to white supremacy was a feature of industrial development throughout the South. See Cobb, *Industrialization and Southern Society*, 83–85, and Greenberg, *Race and State in Capitalist Development*, 209–35.

15. Ronnie M. Moore to National CORE, memorandum, n.d. [ca. September 1964], 2, file 9, box 7, CORE–SROP; "St. Francisville Yam Canning Plant Charged by Labor Dept.," *Opelousas Daily World*, 14 December 1958, 44; "West Feliciana (St. Francisville)," [Summary Report, April 1965], file 10, box 7, CORE–SROP; Fairclough, *Race and Democracy*, 349; Miriam Feingold to Parents, 3 December 1963, frame 00738, reel 25, *COREP*.

16. State Department of Education of Louisiana, *Facilities for Veterans' Education*, 9; "G.I. Bill of Rights and What It Means," *Louisiana Weekly*, 16 September 1944, 10; Wynn, *Afro-American*, 15.

17. "G.I. Bill of Rights Amounts to Nothing More Than So [Many] Empty Words in Louisiana," *Louisiana Weekly*, 27 July 1946, 1. See also Onkst, " 'First a Negro,' " 519–23.

18. "The Veteran's Institute," *Louisiana Weekly*, 16 March 1946, 12; Secretary, Veterans Affairs, to Alphonce Williams, 23 May 1947, frame 0214, reel 1, ser. C, pt. 9, *PNAACP*—Micro; Record, *Race and Radicalism*, 137; "SRC Pushing 3 Point Program to Aid Veterans," *Louisiana Weekly*, 7 September 1946, 7.

19. "GI Education Bill Key to La. Vet's Success Story," *Louisiana Weekly*, 7 August 1954, 7.

20. Statement of Harrison H. Brown in "Trial Fact Book, Hearing on Voting, Shreveport, La., July 13, 1959," file "Trial Fact Book, Louisiana Hearings," box 7, SS, RG 453; Brown interview.

21. U.S. Department of Agriculture, *Parade of Progress*, 6.

22. "Louisiana's Farm Family Pioneer Vegetable Growers," *Louisiana Weekly*, 24 January 1959, 12; "Louisiana Man Top Sweetpotato Farmer," ibid., 5 November 1960, 12.

23. Martin Williams, interview by author, THWC-LSU.

24. Bureau of the Census, *Thirteenth Census . . . 1910, Volume 2*, 774, *Thirteenth Census . . . 1910, Volume 4*, 465–66, and *Seventeenth Decennial Census . . . Population: 1950, Volume 2, Part 18*, 28, 35.

25. Transcript of Oral History Interview, spring 1967, 43, file "Oral History Interview with John H. Scott and Related Material," John Henry Scott Papers, Archives, Manuscripts, and Special Collections Department, Earl K. Long Library, University of New Orleans, New Orleans; Roland Prejean to A. P. Tureaud, 7 April 1942, file 15, box 3, APTP; Dugas Theirry to Tureaud, 22 September 1943, and Tureaud to Theirry, 2 October 1943, both in file 18, box 8, APTP; Speech Delivered by Daniel E. Byrd at the [NAACP] National Convention, 27 June 1946, 5, additions file, box 8, DEBP; Fairclough, *Race and Democracy*, 69–71; Martin Williams interview; Brown interview; Moses Williams, interview by author, THWC-LSU; Fairclough, *Race and Democracy*, 395–98.

26. Brown interview.

27. Application for Charter, Carville Branch, 10 March 1946, file "Charter Applications, Louisiana A–J" (box 242), Application for Charter, Pointe Coupee Parish Branch, n.d. [ca. February 1954], file K–W (box 242), "Notes on NAACP Regional Training Conference," 6 October 1945, 6–7, file "Leadership Training Conference, Louisiana-Texas (Conference) Correspondence 1945" (box 375)—all in ser. C, pt. 2, PNAACP—LC. See also Bates, "New Crowd."

28. A comparison of names that appear in the records of the LFU and the NAACP suggests that several residents of Pointe Coupee Parish who were active in the 1930s were also involved in civil rights work in the 1950s (e.g., Siegent Caulfield and Leon Lafayette). Members of this group also assisted CORE workers in the 1960s. LFU leader Abraham Phillips later became involved in the Deacons for Defense and Justice, an armed self-defense group that was formed to protect civil rights activists in Louisiana. See Abraham Phillips, Siegent Caulfield, Leon Lafayette, and J. C. Prater to Mr. Baldwin, 21 October 1941, file "Pointe Coupee Parish, La. AD-510," box 193, GCCO; Application for Charter, Pointe Coupee Parish Branch, n.d. [ca. February 1954], file K–W, box 242, ser. C, pt. 2, PNAACP—LC; "Told 'No Order' Received Yet to Register Negroes," *Louisiana Weekly*, 26 January 1952, 1–2; Mimi Feingold, "Parish Scouting Report—Summer Project, Pointe Coupee Parish," 14 April 1964, 2, file 20, box 1, CORE—

SCDP; "Report for Pointe Coupee Parish," n.d. [11 October 1963], 1, file 3, box 6, CORE–SROP; and Kelley, *Hammer and Hoe*, 169. Similar connections between the rural unions of the 1930s and civil rights organizations in the 1950s and 1960s are noted in Couto, *Ain't Gonna Let Nobody Turn Me Round*, 101–2, and Payne, "The Lady Was a Sharecropper," 24.

29. "Statewide Drive for Full Citizenship Launched by La. Branches of NAACP," *Louisiana Weekly*, 25 October 1947, 1, 3.

30. NAACP, *Teachers' Salaries in Black and White: A Pamphlet for Teachers and Their Friends* (New York: NAACP, 1941), frames 0397–0404, reel 7, ser. B, pt. 3, *PNAACP*—Micro.

31. Memorandum, n.d. [ca. 1936], 2, file "Education—La. State Department of Education," box 3, RWLP; Lola Stallworth, interview by author, THWC—LSU.

32. See, e.g., J. K. Haynes to Sam H. Jones, 15 June 1943, file 6, box 4, SHJP. Haynes informed Governor Jones that many black teachers were abandoning their poorly paid profession to take higher-paying jobs in defense industries.

33. A. P. Tureaud to J. K. Haynes, 12 May 1943, file 19, box 34, APTP.

34. W. W. Harleaux to A. P. Tureaud, 12 February 1943, file 18, ibid.; W[illie] Franklin to A. P. Tureaud, 10 May 1943, file 19, ibid.

35. "The Teachers' Salary Issue," *Louisiana Weekly*, 10 July 1943, 10; "Principal Brings Suit to Equalize Salary; Paid $500 a Year by Board," newspaper clipping, source unknown, n.d., 8, file 27, box 35, APTP; Fairclough, *Race and Democracy*, 99–100.

36. "School Board Files Brief in Salary Suit," *Louisiana Weekly*, 8 April 1944, 1–2; "Iberville School Board Loses Teacher's Salary Case in Federal Court," *Shreveport Sun*, 29 April 1944, 7, file 27, box 35, APTP; "The Iberville School Board Fails to File Answer; NAACP Seeks Judgment by Default," *Louisiana Weekly*, 20 May 1944, 11.

37. "Salary Schedule for Teachers and Principals," Iberville Parish School Board Circular No. 776, n.d. [ca. July 1944], file 4, box 35, APTP; "Memorandum for Plaintiff, Civil Action No. 212, Baton Rouge Division, United States Court for the Eastern District of Louisiana, Wiley Butler McMillon vs. Iberville Parish School Board," n.d., 1, file 19, ibid.; Fairclough, *Race and Democracy*, 102.

38. H. E. Jarvis to A. P. Tureaud, 4 December 1944, and Thurgood Marshall, Tureaud, and Joseph A. Thornton to Ferdinand C. Claiborne and J. Studebaker Lucas, 6 December 1944, file 22, box 34, APTP; Claiborne and Lucas to Marshall, 13 December 1944, and Tureaud to Claiborne and Lucas, 27 December 1944, ibid.; Marshall [to NAACP], memorandum, 23 January 1945, file "Teachers Salaries Louisiana Iberville Parish Correspondence 1943–45," box 177, ser. B, pt. 2, PNAACP—LC; Tureaud to Marshall, 23 January 1945, file 23, box 34, APTP; "Meeting of Special Committee on Educational Planning," 23 January 1945, 1, file 6, box 35, APTP.

39. A. P. Tureaud to Thurgood Marshall, 25 February 1945, file 23, box 34, APTP; Tureaud to J. K. Haynes, 6 April 1945, file 24, ibid.; "11 Dismissed Iberville

Parish Teachers Express Confidence in Lawyers," *Louisiana Weekly*, 25 August 1945, 1, 7; L. P. Terrebonne to Wiley McMillon, 19 July 1945, and McMillon to Tureaud, 30 July 1945, file 25, box 34, APTP; Tureaud to Harold N. Lee, 17 October 1945, file 32, box 8, APTP.

40. A. P. Tureaud to Iberville Parish School Board, 13 August 1945, and Tureaud to Edward Dudley, 14 August 1945, file 26, box 34, APTP.

41. Thurgood [Marshall] to NAACP Office, 11 September 1945, frame 0482, reel 8, pt. 4, *PNAACP*—Micro.

42. A. P. Tureaud to Willie Franklin, n.d. [September 1945], file 27, Tureaud to Edith M. Jones, 13 April 1946, file 28, and Tureaud to Thurgood Marshall, 29 [August], 30 August 1946, file 28—all in box 34, APTP.

43. A. P. Tureaud to Thurgood Marshall, 14 March 1947, file 29, box 34, APTP; "Rules Dual Teacher Pay Is Illegal," newspaper clipping, no source, 7 November 1947, 14, file 27, box 35, APTP; "Federal Judge Orders Jefferson Parish School Board Stop Salary Bias," *Louisiana Weekly*, 7 August 1948, 1, 3.

44. A. P. Tureaud to J. K. Haynes, 19 June 1948, file 16, box 19, APTP; "New Suit Charges School Inequality," clipping, *New Orleans Times-Picayune*, 4 June 1948, 3, file 10, box 36, APTP; "Equal Facilities Suit Brings More Problems to Louisiana School Boards," *Louisiana Weekly*, 2 April 1949, 1, 8.

45. W. W. Harleaux to A. P. Tureaud, 1 August 1951, file 2, box 36, APTP; "Iberville Parish School Equalization Case to Be Tried May 1, 1952," [news release], n.d., file 30, box 19, APTP.

46. A. P. Tureaud to Thurgood Marshall, 4 August 1949, file 27, box 9, APTP; B. D. Donatto to Tureaud, 2 September 1949, file 15, box 56, APTP; "St. Landry School Board Asks Dismissal of Suit for Equal Facilities," *Louisiana Weekly*, 21 January 1950, 1–2.

47. Glenn Douthit, "Battles for Better Schools," clipping, *New Orleans Item*, 17 November 1949, file 19, box 76, APTP; Daniel E. Byrd, Activity Report, July 1952, 1, file 1, box 4, DEBP; Robert and Essie Mae Lewis, interview by author, THWC—LSU; Kurtz and Peoples, *Earl K. Long*, 198; Cline, "Public Education in Louisiana," 267; Clipping, *Southern School News*, 3 March 1955, 11, file 53, box 556, Russell B. Long Papers, HML.

48. "Louisiana Branch of National Progressive Voters League Organized as South Plans Mobilization of an Intelligent Negro Vote," *Louisiana Weekly*, 20 May 1944, 9.

49. Lewis interview; Meg Redden (formerly Peggy Ewan), interview by author, THWC—LSU; Martin Williams interview.

50. Speech Delivered by Daniel E. Byrd at the [NAACP] National Convention, 27 June 1946, 5, file "Additions," box 8, DEBP; "Longshoremen to Compel Applicants to Register, Vote," *Louisiana Weekly*, 12 July 1947, 4; "NAACP Drive Moves into High Gear," *Louisiana Weekly*, 29 April 1950, 1, 3; Fairclough, *Race and Democracy*, 69–71.

51. Byrd speech at the [NAACP] National Convention, 6; Ernest J. Wright, "Negroes Seek Ballot in Iberville Parish," *Louisiana Weekly*, 9 August 1947, 10.

52. "NAACP Survey Reveals Negroes Registered in Many Louisiana Parishes," *Louisiana Weekly*, 23 September 1944, 1, 8; "Enthusiasm High All over State in Registration Drive," ibid., 30 August 1947, 1–2.

53. Wyche et al. interview; [Report of Field Agents, Louisiana], 22–27 June 1959, 5, file "Louisiana Voting Case," box 4, SS, RG 453; "Pistol-Packing Politician Terrorizes Negroes at Poll," *Louisiana Weekly*, 9 August 1952, 1, 6; S. E. Briscoe to A. P. Tureaud, 28 July 1949, file 26, and Tureaud to M. O. Mouton, 12 December 1949, file 31, box 9, APTP; Junior Antoine to Tureaud, 20 February 1950, Hayward Dupre to Tureaud, 20 February 1950, and Carlton N. Frank to Tureaud, 20 February 1950, file 3, box 10, APTP; "Mob Slugs Educator," *Pittsburgh Courier*, 17 June 1950, 1, 5; "FBI Probing La. Vote Case," *Pittsburgh Courier*, 24 June 1950, 5; *OPPVL's Silver Anniversary Celebration*, 7–8 July 1974, 3, file 26, box 18, APTP; "Beating in Registrar's Office Thought to Be a 'Contributing Factor,'" *Louisiana Weekly*, 3 November 1951, 1, 8.

54. "Told 'No Order' Received Yet to Register Negroes," *Louisiana Weekly*, 26 January 1952, 1–2; Wheaton, "Sheriff D. J. 'Cat' Doucet."

55. Perry H. Howard, *Political Tendencies in Louisiana*, 275–77; Kurtz and Peoples, *Earl K. Long*, 151, 197–98; Wheaton, "Sheriff D. J. 'Cat' Doucet," 6–7; "Suit May End 36 Year Old Vote Drought," *Louisiana Weekly*, 4 November 1961, 1, 7; Fairclough, *Race and Democracy*, 303, 306.

56. Griffith, *Crisis of American Labor*, 64–66; Record, *Race and Radicalism*, 88–91; "Resolutions, National CIO," 1950, frame 0354, reel 58, *ODP*.

57. Griffith, *Crisis of American Labor*, 63–64, 72–74, 81; Honey, *Southern Labor and Black Civil Rights*, 135–41; Lucy Randolph Mason to E. T. Mollegen, 11 May 1945, frame 0110, reel 63, *ODP*.

58. Quoted in Griffith, *Crisis of American Labor*, 72.

59. Ibid., 72, 74.

60. Percy Wyly II to Director, FBI, 29 December 1942, 3, 5, file "144-33-7," box 17588, CSF, RG 60.

61. John A. Ritter, [Notes on Past Organizing Efforts in Louisiana], n.d. [1953], file 298, box 196, IWAP.

62. J. L. Baughman to R. W. Starnes, 3 March 1953, file 5, box 184, IWAP; "Officer's Report, Sixth Annual Convention, District Council No. 4 IWA-CIO," 12 September 1953, 16, file 1648, box 255, IWAP; William O. Jones to E. L. Luter, 10 November 1952, file 1094, box 231, IWAP.

63. A. C. Hudson, Weekly Report, 25 July 1953, 2, file 205, box 192, IWAP; A. M. Collins to Scott, 18 August 1953, file 1634, box 254, IWAP; A. M. Collins to Elizabeth H. Foster, 25 February 1956, file 1050, box 229, IWAP. The NAWU was the descendant of the Southern Tenant Farmers' Union, which changed its name to the National Farm Labor Union in 1946 and became the National Agricultural Workers' Union in the 1950s. The name changes reflected both an expansion in regional scope and the change in status of many agricultural workers in the South from tenant farmers to wage laborers after World War II. For more on the NAWU's organizing efforts in Louisiana's sugar parishes and planter reactions,

see Galarza, *Louisiana Sugar Cane Plantation Workers*, 43–72, and Becnel, *Labor, Church, and the Sugar Establishment*, 43–48, 93–159.

64. "Labor Relations," *AFBF News Letter*, 14 December 1943, 3; "Union and Closed Shop," ibid., 4 August 1952; "Labor Management Relations," ibid., 22 December 1952, 5.

65. H. L. Mitchell, Draft of pamphlet on Louisiana State Labor Council of the AFL-CIO's role in repeal of Louisiana Right-to-Work Law, 4, enclosed in Mitchell to Fay Bennett, 5 September 1956, reel 39, *STFUP*. The AFBF's weekly newsletter also credited the Louisiana Farm Bureau with spearheading the right-to-work effort and ensuring passage of the legislation. See "Dougherty Retains LFBF Post, Wins Acclaim of Press," *AFBF News Letter*, 16 August 1954, 1, 4.

66. "La. Farm Bureau Prexy to Lead Move for 'Right to Work' Law," *Pointe Coupee Banner*, 15 April 1954, 12; "Farm Bureau Prexy Says 'Right-to-Work' Bill Response 'Wonderful,'" ibid., 29 April 1954, 14; "Two Police Juries Endorse 'Right to Work' Legislation," ibid., 29 April 1954, 19; Kurtz and Peoples, *Earl K. Long*, 184–85; "Comments on the 'Special Convention Program' of the Louisiana State Labor Council AFL-CIO, Baton Rouge, August 4–5, 1956," 20 August 1956, reel 39, *STFUP*.

67. John A. Ritter, Weekly Report, 17 July 1954, file 297, box 196, IWAP.

68. Thurman Sensing, "Unionization in the South," *Opelousas Daily World*, 24 February 1957, 25; Griffith, *Crisis of American Labor*, 62–87. One reason for the success of this technique was that large numbers of white workers were deeply racist. Many resented their union leaders' support for black civil rights, and thousands of white members defected from their union locals in the wake of antiracism initiatives undertaken at the state and national levels. See Draper, *Conflict of Interests*, esp. 15–40, 105, and Halpern, "CIO and the Limits of Labor-Based Civil Rights Activism."

69. H. L. Mitchell, "On the Rise of the White Citizens Council and Its Ties with Anti-Labor Forces in the South," 30 January 1956, frames 0324–31, 0334, reel 13, part 20, *PNAACP*—Micro. See also "Labor and the Southern Negro," *The Nation*, 27 September 1952, 261, and Griffith, *Crisis of American Labor*, 62–87. For reports on the spread of white supremacist organizations in Louisiana, some of which also indicate the links between antilabor and segregationist leaders, see "Candidates Say 'No Comment' on Secret 'Ku Klux,'" *Opelousas Daily World*, 25 October 1955, 2; "Southern Gentlemen Group Formed in Lakeland," *Pointe Coupee Banner*, 27 October 1955, 1; "Group Promises Legislation to Strengthen Segregation Barriers," *Opelousas Daily World*, 26 April 1956, 31; "'Klan' Reborn in Louisiana," *Opelousas Daily World*, 3 June 1956, 1, 40; and "State Klan Leader Announces Plans for Organization," *Opelousas Daily World*, 28 April 1957, 1.

70. "How Might Communism Attack the United States?," *St. Francisville Democrat*, 15 August 1957, 2 (reprinted from *Clinton Citizen-Watchman*).

71. See, e.g., "Segregation Rule Based on Reds, Claims Perez," *Opelousas Daily World*, 19 February 1956, 3; Robert M. Stewart, "States' Rights Party

Held Last Hope of This Country," ibid., 22 July 1956, 31; and W. M. Rainach, "Communist-Front NAACP Leadership," ibid., 26 May 1957, 31.

72. Record, *Race and Radicalism*, 162–64; Egerton, *Speak Now against the Day*, 443–48; Fairclough, *Race and Democracy*, 137–47; Griffith, *Crisis of American Labor*, 139–60. See also Penny M. Von Eschen's illuminating study of the anticolonialist movement in the 1940s and 1950s, *Race against Empire*, esp. 96–166. As she notes, anticommunism weakened civil rights groups ideologically as well as organizationally by making them less willing to highlight the economic and political roots of inequality. An internationalist approach that had located the origins of racism in the economic exploitation of black people across the globe was replaced in the postwar decades by psychological explanations that portrayed discrimination as the result of individual prejudices.

73. Morris, *Origins of the Civil Rights Movement*, 30–35; Daniel Byrd to Fay O. Wilson, 28 May 1956, file 10, box 2, DEBP; "Desire for Freedom Indestructible," *Louisiana Weekly*, 12 May 1956, 3B; Fairclough, *Race and Democracy*, 208; Arthur J. Chapital Sr., Affidavit, 24 November 1959, file 12, box 68, APTP; Fairclough, *Race and Democracy*, 196–97, 207–11.

74. Daniel E. Byrd, Activity Report, April 1956, 3, file 3, box 4, DEBP (quotation); E. C. Smith to A. H. Rosenfeld, memorandum, 16 March 1961, 8–9, file "Louisiana," box 6, SS, RG 453; "Dissolution of the Citizens' Council of East Feliciana," clipping, *Clinton Watchman*, 11 June 1965, 7, file 7, box 1, CORE–SCDP; Ward E. Bonnell and Raymond H. Miller to A. H. Rosenfeld, memorandum, 29 June 1959, 1, file "Louisiana," box 6, SS, RG 453; Nils R. Douglas, "The United States Supreme Court and Clinton, Louisiana," n.d., frame 01068, reel 20, *COREP*; Kurtz and Peoples, *Earl K. Long*, 207.

75. "Supreme Court's Unequivocal Ruling Is Hailed as Second Emancipation," *Louisiana Weekly*, 22 May 1954, 1, 8.

76. "Segregation Fading, 'Diehards' Die Hard," ibid., 29 May 1954, 4B; "Statesmanship in Legislature," ibid., 5 June 1954, 4B; "Louisiana," n.d., file "Desegregation: Schools Branch Action—Louisiana 1954–55," box 227, ser. A, pt. 2, PNAACP–LC; Southern Educational Reporting Service, *A Statistical Summary, State by State, of Segregation-Desegregation Activity Affecting Southern Schools from 1954 to Present* (n.p.: Southern Education Reporting Service, 1961), 19–22, file 9, box 1, CORE–SROP ("good moral character"); William L. Taylor to Robert L. Carter, memorandum, 28 March 1955, 1, file "Schools—Louisiana 1943–54," box 143, ser. B, pt. 2, PNAACP–LC ("to promote and protect").

77. "2 Suits Ask Right to Attend White Schools," *Louisiana Weekly*, 13 September 1952, 1, 6; Daniel Byrd to Thurgood Marshall, 9 April 1953, file 3, box 1, DEBP; Byrd to Marshall, memorandum, 23 August 1955, 1, file 26, box 10, APTP; "Tureaud Starts Legal Action in St. Helena Parish," *Louisiana Weekly*, 11 June 1955, 1.

78. Daniel Byrd to Thurgood Marshall, memorandum, 23 August 1955, 3, file 26, box 10, APTP.

79. Lorin Hall, interview by author, THWC—LSU; Eunice Hall Harris and Lawrence Hall, interviews by author, THWC—LSU.

80. J. K. Haynes, interview by Miranda Kombert, Baton Rouge; Martin Williams interview; Redden interview; Walt Benton, "Louisiana's Top News Story: Segregation," *Opelousas Daily World*, 30 December 1956, 4.

81. O'Brien, *Color of the Law*, 3, 12–19, 89–108; Tyson, "Robert F. Williams." See also Umoja, "Eye for an Eye."

82. Lewis interview. See also Tyson, "Robert F. Williams," 547–48.

83. Lewis interview.

84. Goldfield, *Black, White, and Southern*, 92–106.

85. Bayard Rustin to Carroll G. Bowen, 21 February 1956, frame 00553, reel 20, Rustin Papers, ARC; William K. Hefner to A. J. Muste, 17 June 1963, frames 00667–68, ibid.; Dean B. Hancock, "Between the Lines," *Louisiana Weekly*, 9 April 1960, 10; "Violence Makes Non-Violent Stronger," *Louisiana Weekly*, 28 May 1960, 11; "Dr. King Deplores Move to 'Violence,'" *Louisiana Weekly*, 17 July 1965, 1, 11; Farmer, *Lay Bare the Heart*, 11, 94, 155–56.

86. "CORE Says Greensboro Shows that Nonviolence Can Change Society," *Louisiana Weekly*, 6 August 1960, 7.

87. "First Status Report, Voter Education Project," 20 September 1962, frames 00662–63, reel 26, *COREP*; "Voter Education Project Launched to Stir Interest," *Louisiana Weekly*, 7 April 1962, 2. The liberal foundations and government officials who helped to organize the VEP saw that increasing black political participation could strengthen the national Democratic Party; they also aimed to divert civil rights organizations away from direct action initiatives that too often resulted in violence, forcing federal authorities to choose between antagonizing white southerners by acting to protect activists or angering African Americans by failing to intervene. See Meier and Rudwick, *CORE*, 172–76, and Branch, *Parting the Waters*, 479–82.

88. "The Montgomery Story Inspiring," *Louisiana Weekly*, 3 March 1956, 3B; "Patience Beginning to Wear Thin," ibid., 20 February 1960, 10; Martin Williams interview.

89. Korstad and Lichtenstein, "Opportunities Found and Lost"; Bartley, *New South*, 64–69; Draper, *Conflict of Interests*, 17–40; Von Eschen, *Rage against Empire*, 7–21, 96–121.

Chapter Eight

1. Wiley Branton to James Farmer, 15 August 1962, frame 00930, reel 5, *COREP*; "Task Force: Freedom," 13 November 1962, frame 00445, reel 26, *COREP*; Meier and Rudwick, *CORE*, 160, 176–78; Fairclough, *Race and Democracy*, 294–96.

2. The six founding members of CORE were James Farmer, George Houser, Bernice Fisher, Homer Jack, Joe Guinn, and James Robinson. Two of the group

(Farmer and Robinson) were African American, and the remainder were white. All were students except for Farmer, who had graduated from Howard University in 1941 and was a field worker for the Fellowship of Reconciliation. Meier and Rudwick, *CORE*, 5–8.

3. Ibid., 26–27, 31, 63, 145, 163–65.

4. "Summary of the Testimony of Ronnie Moore," 25 May 1962, frame 00419, reel 17, *COREP*. For more on the student movement in Baton Rouge, see Meier and Rudwick, *CORE*, 107–8, 166–69, and Fairclough, *Race and Democracy*, 289–94.

5. Ronnie Moore to Barbara Whitaker, 21 May 1964, file 6, box 2, CORE–SROP; Meier and Rudwick, *CORE*, 177; Fairclough, *Race and Democracy*, 302; W. W. Harleaux to Wiley Branton, date unreadable [ca. February–March 1963], and Branton to Moore, 7 March 1963, box 2, file 6, CORE–SROP.

6. James Farmer to James McCain, 9 May 1963, frame 00694, reel 26; Marvin Rich to Wiley Branton, 10 May 1963, frame 00696, reel 26; Richard K. Parsons to McCain, 7 June 1963, frame 00853, reel 25; and "File 318 Voter Complaints in 5 Louisiana Parishes," *Core-lator*, July 1963, frame 00164, reel 49—all in *COREP*; Ronnie Moore to Barbara Whitaker, 21 May 1964, file 6, box 2, CORE–SROP; Meier and Rudwick, *CORE*, 261; Fairclough, *Race and Democracy*, 297.

7. "Task Force, Applications," frames 00744–00813, reel 44, *COREP*; Ronnie Sigal Bouma and Meg Redden (formerly Peggy Ewan), interviews by author, Baton Rouge. The papers of activists Meldon Acheson and Miriam Feingold held at the State Historical Society of Wisconsin, Madison, also provide a good sense of the background, religious beliefs, and outlook of task force workers.

8. Miriam Feingold, Speech, n.d. [ca. 1961], frames 0292–96, reel 2, MFP; Jim McCain to Mary Hamilton, 16 October 1963, frame 00672, reel 36, Bill Brown, Task Force Application, frame 01368, reel 44, Mike Lesser, Task Force Application, frame 01211, reel 44, Lesser to Gordon Carey, 27 April 1963, frame 01207, reel 44, Evert Makinen to Carey, 21 May 1963, frame 01209, reel 44, and Jim McCain to Mary Hamilton, 16 October 1963, frame 00672, reel 36—all in *COREP*; Meier and Rudwick, *CORE*, 288; Fairclough, *Race and Democracy*, 300.

9. Bouma interview; Redden interview; "Assorted Papers Prepared for Use in Informal Discussion Workshops for Volunteers and Supporters of CORE's Southern Summer Projects 1965," frames 00479–83, reel 26, *COREP*; Meier and Rudwick, *CORE*, 176.

10. Major Johns, a black student at Southern University, had instead organized a Student Welfare Committee to protest legislation passed by state lawmakers that made illegitimate children ineligible for public support. Johns to Gordon Carey, 22 August 1960, frame 01187, reel 36, *COREP*; Carey to Johns, 12 September 1960, frame 01188, ibid. For more on the welfare legislation and the black community's interpretation of the action as retaliation for civil rights activity, see "Welfare Cut Hits All Parts of La." (30 July 1960, 1, 7), "Example of States Rights . . . Southern Style" (17 September 1960, 11), "Starving Tots No Distortion

of Fact—Kerns" (1 October 1960, 1, 7), and "Child Welfare League Asks Probe of La. Welfare Laws" (1 October 1960, 2), *Louisiana Weekly*.

11. Miriam Feingold, Notes on CORE Staff Meeting, 6 December 1963, frame 0802, reel 1, MFP.

12. John Zippert, interview by author, THWC—LSU. St. Helena Parish had 351 black landowners in 1960, and St. Landry had 642. Bureau of the Census, *Census of Agriculture: 1959, Volume 1, Part 35*, 172.

13. Bill Brown, Field Report, 6–15 December 1963, frame 01378, reel 44, *COREP*; Sharon Burger, Field Report—St. Helena Parish, 18–24 June 1964, file 6, box 6, CORE—SROP; "St. Helena," n.d. [early 1964], 3, file 13, box 1, CORE—SROP.

14. Court Docket, Zelma C. Wyche, Ike Oliver, Martin Williams, Earl M. Thomas, Harrison Brown, Willie Haynes, Willie Mitchell and T. I. Israel vs. Mary K. Ward, Registrar of Voters for Madison Parish, La., 1954–55, file "Louisiana Exhibits AA26-R4," box 5, SS, RG 453; "Suit May End 36 Year Old Vote Drought," *Louisiana Weekly*, 4 November 1961, 1, 7; Moses Williams, interview by author, THWC—LSU; Fairclough, *Race and Democracy*, 395.

15. Ronnie [Moore] to Jim [McCain], [ca. March] 1963, frame 00737, reel 25, *COREP*; Moore, Field Report, 1–25 June 1964, frames 00754–56, ibid.; Jim Peck, *Louisiana—Summer 1964: The Students Report to Their Home Towns* (New York: CORE, 1964), frame 00465, reel 26, *COREP*; Parish Scouting Report, West Feliciana, n.d. [ca. 1964], 1, file 20, box 1, CORE—SCDP (town of Hardwood); Bureau of the Census, *Census of Agriculture: 1959, Volume 1, Part 35*, 173; Miriam Feingold to Parents, 3 December 1963, frame 00738, reel 25, *COREP*; Ronnie Moore, "The West Feliciana Story" *Core-lator*, November 1963, frame 00167, reel 49, *COREP*; Vick [Ed Vickery] to [Moore], 18 September 1963, 4, file 13, box 4, CORE—SROP.

16. There were some outstanding exceptions to this rule. W. W. Harleaux in Iberville Parish, Eunice Paddio-Johnson and Lola Stallworth in St. Helena Parish, and Hazel Matthews in East Feliciana Parish were all teachers who openly supported the movement. Black ministers Joseph Carter in West Feliciana Parish and Jetson Davis in Iberville Parish were key activists in their communities. In general, though, CORE workers found that members of these two professions preferred not to become involved in civil rights activity. Those who did usually were not solely dependent on a single source of income—female teachers were often married; Harleaux was a war veteran with access to GI benefits; and some rural ministers (like Carter) were farm owners and laborers in addition to heading their churches. Miriam Feingold, Parish Scouting Report—Pointe Coupee Parish, 14 April 1964, 1, file 20, box 1, CORE—SCDP; Feingold, Field Report—St. Helena, East Feliciana and West Feliciana Parishes, 28 June–5 July 1964, frame 00778, reel 25, *COREP*; *FFM Newsletter*, 15 August 1965, 1, MAP; "Morning Session—Saturday," [notes for meeting], n.d., CORE—SHPP.

17. Southern Educational Reporting Service, *A Statistical Summary, State by*

State, of Segregation-Desegregation Activity Affecting Southern Schools from 1954 to Present (N.p.: Southern Education Reporting Service, 1961), 20, file 9, box 1, CORE–SROP; Miriam Feingold, Notebook, 19, 21 November 1963, frames 0781–82, reel 1, MFP; Field Report, Pointe Coupee Parish, January 1964, frame 00578, reel 38, *COREP*; Fred Lacey, "Student Movement on the Schools," 15 February 1966, 2, 6, CORE–SHPP.

18. Robert and Essie Mae Lewis, interview by author, THWC–LSU; "Negro Gas Station Burned after Insurance Canceled; Violence Continues in Ferriday, La.," news release, 19 December 1965, file 1, box 1, FFMP; James Williams to Clarence A. Laws, 17 June 1963, file 11, box 36, APTP (activist in Iberville Parish); Notebook entry, 12 July 1963, frame 0772, and Miriam Feingold to Parents, 15 October 1963, frame 0327, reel 1, MFP; Feingold, Scouting Report, Pointe Coupee Parish, 14 April 1964, 1, file 20, box 1, CORE–SCDP; Feingold, Field Report, St. Helena, East Feliciana, and West Feliciana Parishes, 28 June–5 July 1964, frame 00778, reel 25, *COREP*; *FFM Newsletter*, 15 August 1965, 1, MAP; Spiver Gordon, Field Report, Iberville Parish, n.d. [May 1964], 1, file 3, box 5, CORE–SROP; [Wats Line Report], St. Landry Parish, 15 August 1965, file "Reports—St. Landry," Additions, CORE–SROP; David Whatley to Zelma Wyche and Willie Johnson, 29 December 1965, file 1, box 1, FFMP; Special Report, Madison Parish, n.d. [1965], 2, file "Tallulah (Madison)," Additions, CORE–SROP.

19. Miriam Feingold to Parents, 15 October 1963, frame 0327, reel 1, MFP.

20. Miriam Feingold, Notes on Meeting, n.d. [July 1964], frame 0145, reel 2, MFP (Mr. Minor); Ronnie M. Moore, "Evaluation of the Citizenship Education Workshop, Plaquemine, Louisiana, December 16–18th, 1966," 17 February 196[7], 4, file 4, box 23, SEDFREP.

21. Kenny Johnson, interviewer unknown, ARC; "Student Civil Rights Strike Closes School," news release, 7 October 1963, frame 00573, reel 31, *COREP*; Miriam Feingold to Parents, 15 October 1963, frame 0327, reel 1, MFP (CORE worker); Louisiana Field Report, 1 October–7 November 1963, frame 00542, reel 38, *COREP*; Bill Brown, Field Report, Sixth Congressional District, 6–15 December 1963, frame 01379, reel 44, *COREP*; Feingold to Maman, 5 January 1964, frame 0378, reel 1, MFP (last quotation).

22. Lewis interview.

23. Redden interview; Bouma interview; "Registration Drive in Rural Louisiana," *Core-lator*, September 1963, frame 00166, reel 49, *COREP*; Meier and Rudwick, *CORE*, 262; Fairclough, *Race and Democracy*, 304; "'Grand Lady' of Clinton CORE Unit," *Louisiana Weekly*, 18 January 1964, 13.

24. Notes on Carter v. Percy, 1963, reel 1, MBP; Weekly Report, [East Feliciana Parish], 5–11 August 1963, 1, file 14, box 1, CORE–SCDP.

25. Ronnie Moore, "The West Feliciana Story," *Core-lator*, November 1963, frames 00167–68, reel 49, *COREP*; Carter v. Percy, Complaint, 1963, reel 1, MBP; Field Report, n.d. [ca. August 1963], frame 00666, reel 36, *COREP*; "Sheriff and Registrar Are Named in Suit," *Louisiana Weekly*, 28 September 1963, 1, 8.

26. Carter v. Percy, 1963, rough notes, reel 1, MBP; Mary Hamilton to James McCain, report, 14 October 1963, frame 00671, reel 36, *COREP*; John W. Roxborough, Julius J. Hollis, and Ezekiel C. Smith to A. H. Rosenfeld, memorandum, 8 August 1960, 6, file "Louisiana," box 6, SS, RG 453; Parish Scouting Report, West Feliciana, n.d. [1964], 4, file 20, box 1, CORE–SCDP; "V.R. Meeting, Masonic Temple, Laurel Hill, (West Feliciana), La.," 24 September, 1 October 1963, file 3, box 2, CORE–SCDP; "Louisiana Man Top Sweetpotato Farmer," *Louisiana Weekly*, 5 November 1960, 12; Ronnie Moore, "The West Feliciana Story," *Core-lator*, November 1963, frames 00168–69, reel 49, *COREP*.

27. Bob Adelman, "Birth of a Voter," n.d., frame 00193, reel 49, *COREP*; Ronnie Moore, "The West Feliciana Story," *Core-lator*, November 1963, frames 00167–68, *COREP*; James Farmer, *Louisiana Story 1963* (New York: CORE, 1963), frame 00251, *COREP*.

28. Ronnie Moore, "The West Feliciana Story," *Core-lator*, November 1963, frames 00167–68, *COREP*; James Farmer, *Louisiana Story 1963* (New York: CORE, 1963), frame 00251, *COREP*; "Four Negroes Register as CORE Drive Begins," *St. Francisville Democrat*, 24 October 1963, 1; "Justice Department Files Suit against Registrar," *St. Francisville Democrat*, 31 October 1963, 1; Mike Lesser to Terry Perlman, 4 November 1963, frame 00185, reel 5, *COREP*.

29. Useful summaries of these incidents are given in "Intimidations and Harassment against Negroes and CORE Workers Summer 1963 to Summer 1964," n.d. [ca. July 1964], frames 00530–33, and Judy Rollins, "CORE's Chronological Listing of Intimidations and Harassments in Louisiana from December, 1961 to August 1, 1964," n.d. [16 October 1964], frames 00534–39, reel 20, *COREP*.

30. Fairclough, *Race and Democracy*, 326, 373, 465; "The Citizens' Council of East Feliciana," *St. Francisville Democrat*, 28 March 1957, 3; E. C. Smith to A. H. Rosenfeld, memorandum, 16 March 1961, 8–9, file "Louisiana," box 6, SS, RG 453; Parish Scouting Report, East Feliciana, n.d. [1963], 1, file 20, box 1, CORE–SCDP.

31. On 20 August 1963, at the request of some white citizens and without notice to civil rights workers or a court hearing, Judge Rarick issued a temporary restraining order against CORE that prohibited the group from operating in the parish. The order was supposed to last only ten days, until a hearing on a preliminary injunction could be held, but when CORE's attorneys attempted to have the case removed to federal court Rarick kept extending it while postponing setting a date for a trial. The day before the case was finally to be tried, CORE obtained a stay order from the Fifth Circuit Court of Appeals that should have automatically stopped proceedings until a decision could be made about whether the hearing should be held in state or federal court. Ten days later Rarick went ahead with the trial anyway, denouncing the stay order as "officious intermeddling designed to obstruct justice." Lawyers for the prosecution accused CORE of being a communist front that aimed to "foster and promote civil disturbances, racial tension, and lawlessness by mobs of emotionally aroused misled people." More hearings fol-

lowed, and Rarick continued to defy the ruling of the Fifth Circuit Court by renewing his restraining order every ten days for several months. Nils R. Douglas, "The United States Supreme Court and Clinton, Louisiana," n.d., frames 01068–70, reel 20, *COREP*; Meier and Rudwick, *CORE*, 262.

32. See, e.g., Black and Black, *Politics and Society in the South*, 23–49; Greenberg, *Race and State in Capitalist Development*, 235–42; and Jacoway and Colburn, *Southern Businessmen and Desegregation*.

33. "Segregationists Meet Opposition in Opelousas," *Louisiana Weekly*, 20 June 1959, 1–2; [Bill] Brown and [Brendan] Sexton, Parish Scouting Report, Opelousas, St. Landry Parish, 22 November 1963, 2, file 1, box 7, CORE–SROP; "Opelousas Group Issues Civil Rights Statement," *Louisiana Weekly*, 11 July 1964, 9; Mimi Feingold, Field Report, St. Helena, East Feliciana, and West Feliciana Parishes, 6–12 July 1964, frame 00790, reel 25, *COREP*; Parish Scouting Report, East Feliciana, n.d. [1963], 1, file 20, box 1, CORE–SCDP; "Negroes Seated on Parish School Bd. at Tuesday Meet," *St. Francisville Democrat*, 12 January 1967, 1, 4; East Feliciana Parish Sesquicentennial Committee, *East Feliciana Parish*, section on "The Kilbourne Family."

34. Weekly Report, [East Feliciana Parish], 5–11 August 1963, 6, file 14, box 1, CORE–SCDP; Miriam Feingold to Family, 19 August 1963, frame 0308, reel 1, MFP; "Intimidations and Harassment against Negroes and CORE Workers Summer 1963 to Summer 1964," n.d. [ca. July 1964], frame 00530, reel 20, *COREP*; Notebook entry, 18 November 1963, frame 0780, reel 1, MFP; Ester Lee Daniel, Affidavit, 4 August 1963, file 13, box 4, CORE–SROP.

35. Miriam Feingold to Fay Bennett, 3 March 1964, file 12, box 11, ibid.; Joseph Carter, interview by Edward Hollander, SHSW; Ronnie M. Moore to National CORE, memorandum, n.d. [September 1964], 2, file 9, box 7, CORE–SROP.

36. Miriam Feingold, "The West Feliciana Sweet Potato Story," 18 August 1964, 2–3, file 12, box 11, CORE–SROP; Princeville Canning Co. to CORE, 3 September 1964, file 12, box 11, CORE–SROP; J. Truitt to James Farmer, 7 September 1964, frames 01052–53, reel 20, *COREP*; Gordon R. Carey to Ronnie Moore, 9 September 1964, file 12, box 11, CORE–SROP; "Louisiana Canning Firm Relents—CORE Boycott Ended," *Core-lator*, September–October 1964, frame 00182, reel 49, *COREP*.

37. Collins—Louisiana Civil Service, Request for Appeal, 1963, reel 2, MBP; "Jailed CORE Leader Wins Reinstatement," *Core-lator*, February 1964, frame 00170, reel 49, *COREP*; Miriam Feingold, "East Feliciana Community Relief Fund," 19 August 1964, frames 0412–13, reel 2, MFP; Feingold, Field Report, West Feliciana Parish, 1–31 March 1964, frame 00279, reel 36, *COREP*; "Assorted Papers Prepared for Use in Informal Discussion Workshops for Volunteers and Supporters of CORE's Southern Summer Projects," 1965, frame 00479, reel 26, *COREP*; "CORE Sponsors Drive to Aid Evicted Families," *Louisiana Weekly*, 8 January 1966, sec. 2, 5.

38. Gertru[d]e Felton, Complaint Information, n.d., frame 00866, and Carrie

Robinson, Complaint Information, n.d., frame 00850, reel 25, "Louisiana Field Report for CORE," 1 October–7 November 1963, frame 00542, reel 38, Miriam Feingold, Field Report, St. Helena, East Feliciana, and West Feliciana Parishes, 27 July–5 August 1964, frame 00788, reel 25—all in *COREP*.

39. Judy Rollins, "CORE's Chronological Listing of Intimidations and Harassments in Louisiana from December, 1961 to August 1, 1964," [October] 1964, frame 00534–35, reel 20, *COREP*; Spiver Gordon to Burke Marshall, n.d. [ca. 28 February 1964], file 8, box 1, CORE–SCDP; Field Report, West Feliciana Parish, 10–29 February 1964, 2, file 15, box 1, CORE–SCDP; "Sheriff's Office Investigating Arson Attempt," *St. Francisville Democrat*, 5 March 1964, 1; Statements by Nathaniel Smith, Mrs. Nathaniel Smith, and Vincent Smith, n.d. [December 1964], file 10, box 7, CORE–SROP.

40. Mike Lesser to Terry Perlman, 4 November 1963, frame 00185, reel 5, *COREP* (my emphasis).

41. Field Report, West Feliciana Parish, 13–26 January 1964, 2, file 15, and Parish Scouting Report, West Feliciana Parish, n.d. [1964], 4, file 20, box 1, CORE–SCDP; Meldon Acheson to Parents, 10 July 1965, 2, and 13 August 1965, 2, MAP.

42. Wats Line Report, Pointe Coupee Parish, 9 July 1965, 2, file 4, box 2, CORE–SCDP; Statement by Mary Boyd, n.d. [ca. 17 March 1966], file 12, box 1, FFMP.

43. Bob Adelman, "Birth of a Voter," n.d., frame 00193, reel 49, *COREP*; [Wats Line Report], Concordia Parish (Ferriday), 21 July 1965, file 7, box 4, CORE–SROP; Statement of Robert Lewis, n.d. [ca. 20 November 1965], file 14, box 1, FFMP.

44. [Wats Line Report], Madison Parish (Tallulah), 18 July 1965, file "Tallulah (Madison)," Additions, CORE–SROP; Martin Williams, interview by author, THWC–LSU. Lance E. Hill ("Deacons for Defense and Justice," 36, 134, 270) cites several instances when groups of armed African Americans mobilized quickly in response to threats to local activists in Louisiana.

45. Jim Peck, *Louisiana—Summer, 1964: The Students Report to Their Home Towns* (New York: CORE, 1964), frame 00465, reel 26, *COREP*; Redden interview.

46. "The Story of Plaquemine," n.d., frames 00967–70, reel 20, *COREP*; Miriam Feingold to Danny, 5 September 1963, frame 0315, reel 1, MFP; Farmer, *Lay Bare the Heart*, 246–54.

47. Peck, *Louisiana—Summer, 1964*, frame 00459; Dittmer, *Local People*, 251; David Whatley, Field Report, Concordia Parish, n.d. [ca. February 1966], file 5, box 1, FFMP; Lewis interview; *News-Gazette*, 7 October 1965, 6, MAP.

48. Field Report, East Feliciana Parish, 13–26 January 1964, frame 00571, reel 38, *COREP* (fire chief); Wats Line Report, Concordia Parish, 3 July 1965, file 4, box 2, CORE–SCDP; Lewis interview; "Registration Drive in Rural Louisiana," *Core-lator*, September 1963, frame 00166, reel 49, *COREP*; Field Report, East Feliciana Parish, 13–26 January 1964, frame 00570, reel 38, *COREP* (Bill Brown);

"Assorted Papers Prepared for Use in Informal Discussion Workshops for Volunteers and Supporters of CORE's Southern Summer Projects," 1965, frame 00480, reel 26, *COREP*.

49. Miriam Feingold to Family, 5 August 1963, frame 0296, reel 1, MFP. The federal government's failure to protect civil rights workers has been well documented by historians and participants in the movement. See, e.g., Carson, *In Struggle*, 83–89, 121–22; Moody, *Coming of Age in Mississippi*, 367; Fairclough, *Race and Democracy*, 93–94; Mills, *This Little Light of Mine*, 27, 67; Farmer, *Lay Bare the Heart*, 243; and Gitlin, *The Sixties*, 136–46.

50. Gayle Jenkins, interview by Miriam Feingold, SHSW.

51. Bims, "Deacons for Defense"; Fairclough, *Race and Democracy*, 342–43, 357–58; Lewis interview; Minutes of Meeting of Legislative Campaign Steering Committee, 6 May 1967, 3, file 9, box 7, SEDFREP; Hill, "Deacons for Defense," 264.

52. "Deacons Spread Forces to Combat Terrorism," *Louisiana Weekly*, 19 June 1965, 4. It is difficult to say for sure how many people joined the Deacons because the organization was very secretive about its membership. But Lance Hill recently concluded that if informal groups as well as official chapters are counted, Earnest Thomas's claim to the *Louisiana Weekly* was not far off. Hill's research unearthed a total of sixty-four cities where Deacons chapters were reported or rumored to have been formed. Charles Sims, a founding member of the Deacons in Bogalusa who helped to organize chapters in other states, later said to an interviewer, "I won't tell you how many members we had, but I'll tell you this: if push hada come to shove, we were well covered." See Strain, "'We Walked Like Men,'" 48–49; Hill, "Deacons for Defense," 263; and Raines, *My Soul Is Rested*, 421.

53. Minutes of Meetings, 23 and 25 October 1965, Minute Book 25 July–October 25, 1965, file 2, box 1, FFMP; Mike Lesser to Terry Perlman, 4 November 1963, frame 00185, reel 5, *COREP*.

54. "Louisiana Summer Task Force Staff Meeting," 15 July 1964, frame 00052, reel 45, *COREP*; Miriam Feingold to Family, 14 July 1963, frame 0271, reel 1, MFP; Feingold, Notes on Staff Meeting, 24 November 1963, frame 0789, reel 1, MFP.

55. Field Report, East and West Feliciana Parishes, 30 December 1963–12 January 1964, frames 00565–66, reel 38, *COREP*; Catherine Patterson, quoted in Hill, "Deacons for Defense," 106.

56. Mike Lesser to Terry Perlman, 4 November 1963, frame 00185, reel 5, *COREP*.

57. Fred Lacey and Chuck Lawson, Field Report, St. Helena Parish, 17–28 August [1965], 3, CORE–SHPP. Parents of the black students who integrated the schools in St. Helena Parish instructed them not to start any trouble and not to respond to name-calling, but to fight back if they were physically attacked. Eunice Hall Harris recalled that her father's philosophy "was different from

Martin Luther King's in that area. Defend yourself, that's what he told us." Eunice Hall Harris, Lorin Hall, Clifton and Eual Hall, and Eunice Paddio-Johnson and Clarence Reed, interviews by author, all at Baton Rouge.

58. Charles Sims quoted in Strain, " 'We Walked Like Men,' " 60.

59. F. J. Baumgardner to W. C. Sullivan, 22 September 1964, file 157–9, Disruption of White Hate Groups, Records of the COINTELPRO Program, FBI Headquarters, Washington, D.C.; Fairclough, *Race and Democracy,* 371–74; Bims, "Deacons for Defense," 26; Royan Burris, Robert Hicks, and Gayle Jenkins, interviews by Miriam Feingold, Madison; " 'Police Brutality Creates Deacons'— LCLU Pres.," *Louisiana Weekly,* 29 January 1966, 2 (Steven Rubin).

60. Johnson interview.

61. Watters and Cleghorn, *Climbing Jacob's Ladder,* 50 (quotation); *Civil Rights Act, U.S. Code,* vol. 21, secs. 2000a–2000e-17 (1964); *Voting Rights Act, U.S. Code,* vol. 21, secs. 1973–1974e (1965).

62. Meier and Rudwick, *CORE,* 353; Bernice [Noflin] to Miriam Feingold, 20 October 1965, frame 0494–95, reel 1, MFP; "Negroes Evicted from Plantations for Registering to Vote in West Feliciana, La.," news release, 20 December 1965, file 6, box 1, FFMP; James Bell and Laura Spears, interview by Miriam Feingold, SHSW; Untitled document, n.d., file 2, box 4, CORE–SROP.

63. Southern Regional Council, press release, 5 August 1966, file 10, box 18, SEDFREP; Miriam Feingold to Family, 23 July 1963, frame 0278, reel 1, MFP; *CORE Freedom News,* 29 May 1965, 1, 13 June 1965, 2, and 14 July 1965, 1, file "Tallulah (Madison) 1965," Additions, CORE–SROP.

64. Miriam Feingold to Parents, 3 December 1963, frame 00738, reel 25, *COREP;* Feingold to Family, 1 January 1964, frame 0377, and 10 March 1964, frame 0412, reel 1, MFP.

65. Ben Garris, "Hooks and Shells," *St. Francisville Democrat,* 14 July 1960, 1 (first quotation); Lewis interview; Draft of notice, n.d. [ca. November–December 1965], 3, file 8, box 1, FFMP.

66. Ronnie Moore, "Louisiana Citizenship Program," September 1964, frame 00542, reel 20, *COREP;* "Assorted Papers Prepared for Use in Informal Discussion Workshops for Volunteers and Supporters of CORE's Southern Summer Projects," 1965, frame 00479, reel 26, *COREP.*

67. Wats Line Report, Madison Parish, 10 July 1965, 1–2, file 4, box 2, CORE–SCDP; [Wats Line Report], 15 and 17 July 1965, file "Tallulah (Madison) 1965," Additions, CORE–SROP; "CORE Worker Beaten Handing Out Leaflets," *Louisiana Weekly,* 24 July 1965, 2.

68. [Draft of flyer], n.d. [November 1965], file 19, box 1, FFMP; Moses Williams interview; Harrison and Earnestine Brown, interview by author, THWC–LSU; Zelma Wyche, Harrison H. Brown, T. I. Israel, F. W. Wilson, and Moses Williams, interview by Miriam Feingold, SHSW.

69. H[enry] Brown, M[iriam] Feingold, M[arty] Goldstein, and C[hristine] White, Field Report, West Feliciana Parish, 14–21 July [1965], 1, file 15, box 1,

CORE—SCDP; "School Desegregation Suit Hearing Slated Friday," *St. Fran-cisville Democrat*, 29 July 1965, 1; "Judge Orders West Feliciana to Desegregate Schools," *Louisiana Weekly*, 7 August 1965, sec. 1, 4; "School Suit Won by CORE," news release, 13 September 1965, frame 00235, reel 31, *COREP*.

70. Fairclough, *Race and Democracy*, 318, 334; "Federal Court Orders Grades 1 & 12 Mixed," *St. Francisville Democrat*, 5 August 1965, 1.

71. Freedom Day Action Committee of St Helena Parish circular, n.d. [January 1966], SAFE, "Refuse to Pay!" 22 March 1966, and Fred Lacey, "Student Movement on the Schools," 15 February 1966, 5—all in CORE—SHPP; Lacey, Field Report, St. Helena Parish, 22 April 1966, 1, file "Reports—'65—St. Helena," Additions, CORE—SROP.

72. "Agricultural Stabilization and Conservation Service: A Report of the United States Commission on Civil Rights," 1965, 1–2, file 5, box 1, CORE—SCDP (quotation); National Sharecroppers' Fund, "Statement on Discriminatory Practices Affecting Programs of the U.S. Department of Agriculture," 29 August 1963, frames 01228–31, reel 38, *COREP*; Wilbert Guillory, interview by author, THWC—LSU; Zippert interview.

73. H[enry] Brown, M[iriam] Feingold, M[arty] Goldstein, and C[hristine] White, Field Report, West Feliciana Parish, 14–21 July [1965], 1, file 15, box 1, CORE—SCDP; Henry Brown, Mimi [Miriam] Feingold, Marty Goldstein, and Christine Wright, Field Report, West Feliciana Parish, 28 July–3 August [1965], ibid.; Meier and Rudwick, *CORE*, 351.

74. Wats Line Report, Pointe Coupee Parish, 4 July 1965, file 4, box 2, CORE—SCDP; [Wats Line Report], Pointe Coupee Parish, 3 and 6 August 1965, file 24, box 52, SEDFREP; Meier and Rudwick, *CORE*, 351.

75. Zippert interview; Guillory interview.

76. Zippert interview; "History of Grand Marie Co-op," n.d., file 3, box 1, JZP; John Zippert to Marvin Rich, 2 August 1966, file 11, box 23, SEDFREP; Sweet Potato Alert Proposal, Progress Report, 30 May–3 July 1966, 2, file 3, box 1, JZP.

77. OEO, "The War on Poverty—A Hometown Fight," n.d., frames 00453–55, reel 26, *COREP*.

78. Notes on Meeting, n.d. [ca. July 1965], frame 0878, reel 1, MFP; [Notes on Interparish Antipoverty Meeting], n.d., [August 1965], frame 0923, ibid.

79. Notre Nouveau Jour A Commence, Inc., "Rural Community Visitors Proposal," n.d. [1966], 1, 4, 8–9, file 6, box 1, JZP.

80. "Parish Anti-Poverty Underway," clipping, *Clinton Watchman*, 11 June 1965, file 11, box 1, CORE—SCDP; "Community Action Program (CAP) Committee," n.d., [ca. June 1965], ibid.; Farrell M. Roberts, Annual Narrative Report, County Agent, East Feliciana Parish, 1965, 4, vol. 470, AESP; Statements by George Perry, 5 December 1963, and J. C. Sanders, 7 December 1963, file 18, box 1, CORE—SCDP; "The Citizens' Council of East Feliciana," *St. Francisville Democrat*, 28 March 1957, 3; "Dissolution of the Citizens' Council of East Feliciana," clipping, *Clinton Watchman*, 11 June 1965, 7, file 7, box 1, CORE—SCDP;

"East Feliciana Parish," n.d. [ca. July 1965], file 7, box 1, CORE—SROP; Parish Scouting Report, East Feliciana Parish, n.d. [1963], 5, file 20, box 1, CORE—SCDP; Notebook entries for 19, 21 November 1963, frames 0781–82, reel 1, MFP.

81. "Parish Anti-Poverty Underway," clipping, *Clinton Watchman*, 11 June 1965, "272 Children Will Participate in First Head Start Program," clipping, *Clinton Watchman*, n.d. [11 June 1965], and "Additional Notes on Operation Head Start in East Feliciana," n.d. [June 1965]—all in file 11, box 1, CORE—SCDP; Notebook entry, [22] June [1965], frames 0096–0100, reel 2, MFP.

82. Marion Overton White to Gregory Coronado, 12 May 1966, 1, file "Lafayette, Louisiana (Acadiana-Neuf)," box 31, Records Relating to the Administration of the Civil Rights Program in the Regions, 1965–66, Records of the Special Assistant to the Director for Civil Rights, Records of the Office of the Director, Records of the OEO, RG 381, NA; Samuel F. Yette to Theodore Berry, 13 April 1965, file "Lafayette, Louisiana (Acadiana-Neuf)," ibid. (Father McKnight).

83. Sargent Shriver to Gordain Sibille, 30 August 1965, 1–2, file "Lafayette, Louisiana (Acadiana-Neuf)," Hamah R. King to W. Astor Kirk, n.d. [ca. May 1966], 1–5, file "Louisiana—CAP," "Governor Explains Reason for Veto," newspaper clipping, no source, n.d., consolidated with Bill Crook to [Sargent Shriver], telegram, 23 March 1966, all in ibid.; Louis Berry to Derrick Bell, 18 April 1966, 1–2, file "Admin. Confidential," box 34A, Local Problem Areas File, 1966, Records of the Special Assistant to the Director for Civil Rights, Records of the Office of the Director, Records of the OEO, RG 381, NA.

84. "Summary Report of the Investigative Task Force of the Ad Hoc Subcommittee on the War on Poverty Program," 1 March 1966, 29, enclosed in Adam C. Powell to [David] Squire, 19 September 1966, file "Congressional," box 800, SFDS, RG 381. For accounts of attacks on antipoverty programs in other states, see Dittmer, *Local People*, 363–88; Aiken, *Cotton Plantation South*, 229–56; and Kiffmeyer, "From Self-Help to Sedition."

85. John C. Satterfield, "The Worker Looks to His Rights," *Pointe Coupee Banner*, 16 January 1964, 6; Rieder, "Rise of the 'Silent Majority'"; Payne, *I've Got the Light of Freedom*, 376–80; Goldfield, *Black, White, and Southern*, 223–24; Bouma interview.

86. CORE worker Verla Bell provided an indication of the problems presented by insufficient finances when she signed a field report from West Feliciana, "P.S. Could have gotten MUCH MORE work done, but without a car BOSS I was HELPLESS." Verla Bell, East Feliciana Field Report, September–October 1964, file 13, box 4, CORE—SROP. See also Shirley Thompson, Weekly Report, n.d. [October/November 1963], 2, file 3, box 6, ibid.; Field Report, Pointe Coupee Parish, January 1964, frame 00578, reel 38, *COREP*; Notes on Staff Meeting, 30 April 1964, frame 0028, reel 2, MFP; Ronnie Moore to Barbara Whitaker, 21 May 1964, 1, file 6, box 2, CORE—SROP; and Judy Rollins, "Report on Attempted Purge in St. Francisville," n.d. [October–November 1964], file 9, box 7, CORE—SROP.

87. Ronnie Moore to Louisiana Staff, memorandum, 1 April 1965, file 16, box 1, CORE–SCDP; "Report of the Convention Fund Raising Committee," n.d. [1965], 4, file 1, ibid.; Geraldine Maddocks to Miriam Feingold, 11 May 1965, frame 0470, reel 1, MFP (quotation). See also Meldon Acheson to Mother and Dad, 22 July [1965], 2, MAP.

88. Bouma interview; Clipping, *New York Times*, 24 July 1966, reprinted on NAACP flyer, file 9, box 1, NAACP Louisiana Field Director Papers, ARC; Meier and Rudwick, *CORE*, 407–8, 419–20; Fairclough, *Race and Democracy*, 381–82.

89. Meier and Rudwick, *CORE*, 338.

90. Lewis interview; Wyche et al. interview; Moses Williams interview.

91. Wyche et al. interview; Martin Williams interview.

92. Payne, *I've Got the Light of Freedom*, 180–206.

Epilogue

1. See, e.g., Sitkoff, *Struggle for Black Equality*, 210–35; Morris, *Origins of the Civil Rights Movement*, 286–90; Dittmer, *Local People*, 427–30; Eskew, *But for Birmingham*, 326–31; Lolis Elie, interview by Kim Lacy Rogers, ARC; Rudy Lombard, interview by Kim Lacy Rogers, ARC; and Clifton and Eual Hall, interview by author, THWC–LSU.

2. U.S. Commission on Civil Rights, *Political Participation*, 240–43; Engstrom et al., "Louisiana," 109.

3. Miriam Feingold to Russell [Gilmore], 12 August [1966], frames 0532–33, reel 1, MFP; Scholarship, Education and Defense Fund for Racial Equality, "Fact Sheet: Civil Rights Breakthrough in the Deep South," October 1967, file 9, box 7, SEDFREP.

4. U.S. Commission on Civil Rights, *Political Participation*, 217–18.

5. Ibid., 64–66, 79–80; 115–17; Engstrom et al., "Louisiana," 109–12; Eunice Paddio-Johnson and Clarence Reed, interview by author, THWC–LSU; Lorin Hall, interview by author, THWC–LSU; Clifton and Eual Hall interview.

6. The evolution of voting rights law after 1965 in response to efforts to dilute black votes is discussed in Lawson, *In Pursuit of Power*; Parker, *Black Votes Count*; and Davidson, "Recent Evolution of Voting Rights Law."

7. Engstrom et al., "Louisiana," 109; Fairclough, *Race and Democracy*, 466.

8. Robert and Essie Mae Lewis, interview by author, THWC–LSU; Spiver Gordon, interviewer unknown, ARC.

9. Ben Garris, "Hooks and Shells," *St. Francisville Democrat*, 5 June 1969, 1; Knights of the Ku Klux Klan, "Citizens of Concordia Parish!," n.d., file 24, box 34, NAACP Louisiana Field Director Papers, ARC.

10. Ellis Howard, Percy Gordon, and Charles Hall to John Doar, 19 January 1965, file 8, box 1, CORE–SCDP; Gerald Moses, "La. Civil Rights Arm Opens 2-day Hearing," news clipping, source unknown, n.d. [ca. 1965–66], CORE–

SHPP; Daniel Byrd, Special Report, 24 March 1973, 2, file 9, box 4, DEBP; "The Louisiana Education Association's Legal Plan of Action," n.d., 2, file 6, box 6, DEBP.

11. Eunice Hall Harris to Mary L. Landrieu, 22 April 1998, vertical file, THWC–LSU.

12. Paddio-Johnson interview; Lorin Hall interview; Lawrence Hall, interview by author, THWC–LSU.

13. Lolis Elie, interview by Langston Reid, FCC–NOPL; Lombard interview; Lorin Hall interview; Clifton and Eual Hall interview. See also Chestnut and Cass, *Black in Selma*, 375–76; Dittmer, *Local People*, 426–28; and Couto, *Ain't Gonna Let Nobody Turn Me Round*, 76.

14. Ronnie M. Moore, "Evaluation of the Citizenship Education Workshop, Plaquemine, Louisiana, December 16–18th, 1966," 17 February 196[7], 4, file 4, box 23, SEDFREP; Elie interview (Rogers).

15. "Negroes Seated on Parish School Bd. at Tuesday Meet," *St. Francisville Democrat*, 12 January 1967, 1, 4; "Periodic Voter Registration Wins by 6–3 PJ Vote," ibid., 12 December 1968, 1, 4.

16. Berman, *America's Right Turn*, 18, 92, 95; Walton, *African American Power and Politics*, 131, 337–39; Naples, *Grassroots Warriors*, 20, 60–61; Martin Williams, interview by author, THWC–LSU.

17. Wilbert Guillory, interview by author, THWC–LSU; Clifton and Eual Hall interview. See also Woods, *Development Arrested*, 183–84, 203–4, 269–70. According to Woods, white civic leaders' preferred solution to the problems caused by the demise of the plantation system was to encourage black people to leave. Thus, in the decades after the civil rights movement, state and local governments in the South kept welfare benefits low, cut back or eliminated social services, and rejected job creation efforts to provide African Americans with few reasons for staying in the region.

18. Bureau of the Census, *1990 Census of Population, Social and Economic Characteristics, Louisiana, Section 1*, 93; Lombard interview; Clifton and Eual Hall interview.

19. Martin Williams interview; Paddio-Johnson and Reed interview; Lewis interview; Guillory interview; Lorin Hall interview; Eunice Hall Harris interview; Lola Stallworth and Moses Williams, interviews by author, THWC–LSU; Clifton and Eual Hall interview.

Bibliography

Manuscript Collections

Atlanta, Ga.
   Southern Labor Archives, Special Collections Department, Pullen Library,
      Georgia State University
    International Woodworkers of America Papers
Baton Rouge, La.
   Hill Memorial Library, Louisiana State University
    Agricultural Extension Service Papers
    James B. Aswell and Family Papers
    Bethel Baptist Church Records
    Alexandre Etienne DeClouet and Family Papers
    John Hamilton and Harriet Boyd Ellis Papers
    Richard W. Leche Papers
    Russell B. Long Papers
    Gladys Means Loyd and Family Papers
    Charles Lewis Mathews Papers
    John Burrus McGehee Papers
    Lewis Stirling and Family Papers
    Daniel Trotter Papers
    Turnbull-Allain Family Papers
    Turnbull-Bowman-Lyons Family Papers
   Louisiana State Archives
    Louisiana State Guard Records

Charlottesville, Va.
   Special Collections Department, Alderman Memorial Library, University of
       Virginia
       Papers of Jackson Davis
Madison, Wis.
   State Historical Society of Wisconsin
       Meldon Acheson Papers
       Murphy Bell Papers, microfilm
       Congress of Racial Equality, Louisiana Sixth Congressional District Papers
       Congress of Racial Equality, Southern Regional Office Papers
       Congress of Racial Equality, St. Helena Parish Papers
       Miriam Feingold Papers, microfilm
       Ferriday Freedom Movement Papers
       Scholarship, Education, and Defense Fund for Racial Equality Papers
       John Zippert Papers
Nashville, Tenn.
   Fisk University Library Special Collections, Fisk University
       Charles S. Johnson Papers
New Orleans, La.
   Amistad Research Center, Tulane University
       Daniel Ellis Byrd Papers
       National Association for the Advancement of Colored People, Louisiana
           Field Director Papers
       Rosenwald Fund Papers, microfilm
       Bayard Rustin Papers, microfilm
       Robert Tallant Collection, microfilm
       Alexander Pierre Tureaud Papers
   Archives, Manuscripts, and Special Collections Department, Earl K. Long
       Library, University of New Orleans
       John Henry Scott Papers
   Historic New Orleans Collection
       Federal Extension Service Records, Extension Service Annual Reports,
           Louisiana 1909–44, microfilm
       Selected Documents from the Louisiana Section of the Work Projects
           Administration General Correspondence File ("State Series") 1935–43,
           microfilm
   Manuscripts Division, Howard Tilton Library, Tulane University
       Cross Keys Plantation Records
       William Walter Jones Collection of the Papers of Sam Houston Jones
       Harold N. Lee Papers
Washington, D.C.
   Federal Bureau of Investigation Headquarters
       File 100-45768, Louisiana Farmers' Union
       Records of the COINTELPRO Program

Library of Congress
  Farm Security Administration/Office of War Information Collection
  National Association for the Advancement of Colored People Papers
National Archives
  Records of the Agricultural Stabilization and Conservation Service, Record
    Group 145
  Records of the Bureau of Agricultural Economics, Record Group 83
  Records of the Civilian Conservation Corps, Record Group 35
  Records of the Commission on Civil Rights, Record Group 453
  Records of the Committee on Fair Employment Practice, Record Group 228
  Records of the Department of Justice, Record Group 60
  Records of the Farmers' Home Administration, Record Group 96
  Records of the Federal Extension Service, Record Group 33
  Records of the Office of Economic Opportunity, Record Group 381
  Records of the Office of Government Reports, Record Group 44
  Records of the Office of Labor (War Food Administration), Record Group
    224
  Records of the Office of the Secretary of Agriculture, Record Group 16

Microform Collections

Black Workers in the Era of the Great Migration, 1916–1925. Edited by James
    R. Grossman. Frederick, Md.: University Publications of America, 1985.
    Microfilm.
The Green Rising, 1910–1977: A Supplement to the Southern Tenant Farmers
    Union Papers. Glen Rock, N.J.: Microfilming Corporation of America, 1977.
    Microfilm.
Hampton University Peabody Newspaper Clipping File. Alexandria, Va.:
    Chadwyck-Healey, 1988. Microfiche.
Operation Dixie: The CIO Organizing Committee Papers, 1946–1953. [Sanford,
    N.C.]: Microfilming Corporation of America, 1980. Microfilm.
The Papers of the Congress of Racial Equality, 1941–1967. Sanford, N.C.:
    Microfilming Corporation of America, 1980. Microfilm.
Papers of the NAACP. Frederick, Md.: University Publications of America,
    1982. Microfilm.
Peonage Files of the U.S. Department of Justice, 1901–1945. Frederick, Md.:
    University Publications of America, 1989. Microfilm.
Selected Documents of Records of the Committee on Fair Employment
    Practice, 1941–1946. Glen Rock, N.J.: Microfilming Corporation of America,
    [1970]. Microfilm.
Southern Tenant Farmers' Union Papers. Sanford, N.C.: Microfilming
    Corporation of America, 1971. Microfilm.

Government Documents

Bureau of the Census. *Twelfth Census of the United States Taken in the Year 1900, Population, Part 2*. Washington, D.C.: GPO, 1902.

——. *Thirteenth Census of the United States Taken in the Year 1910, Volume 2: Population, Reports by States, Alabama—Montana*. Washington, D.C.: GPO, 1913.

——. *Thirteenth Census of the United States Taken in the Year 1910, Volume 4: Population, Occupation Statistics*. Washington, D.C.: GPO, 1914.

——. *Thirteenth Census of the United States Taken in the Year 1910, Volume 6: Agriculture*. Washington, D.C.: GPO, 1913.

——. *Fourteenth Census of the United States Taken in the Year 1920, Volume 3: Population*. Washington, D.C.: GPO, 1922.

——. *Fifteenth Census of the United States: 1930, Agriculture, Volume 2: Reports by States, Part 2: The Southern States*. Washington, D.C.: GPO, 1932.

——. *Fifteenth Census of the United States: 1930, Population, Volume 3: Reports by States, Part 1: Alabama—Montana*. Washington, D.C.: GPO, 1932.

——. *United States Census of Agriculture: 1935, Volume 1: Reports for States*. Washington, D.C.: GPO, 1936.

——. *Sixteenth Census of the United States: 1940, Agriculture, Volume 1: First and Second Series State Reports, Part 5: Statistics for Counties*. Washington, D.C.: GPO, 1942.

——. *Sixteenth Census of the United States: 1940, Population, Volume 2: Characteristics of the Population, Part 3: Kansas—Michigan*. Washington, D.C.: GPO, 1943.

——. *Sixteenth Census of the United States: 1940, Population, Volume 3: The Labor Force, Part 3: Iowa—Montana*. Washington, D.C.: GPO, 1943.

——. *Sixteenth Census of the United States: 1940, Agriculture Crop-Sharing Contracts, Appendix to Section of Special Study—Plantations*. Washington, D.C.: GPO, 1943.

——. *United States Census of Agriculture: 1945, Volume 1, Part 24*. Washington, D.C.: GPO, 1946.

——. *Census of Manufactures: 1947, Volume 3: Statistics by States*. Washington, D.C.: GPO, 1950.

——. *A Report of the Seventeenth Decennial Census of the United States, Census of Population: 1950, Volume 2: Characteristics of the Population, Part 18: Louisiana*. Washington, D.C.: GPO, 1952.

——. *United States Census of Agriculture: 1954, Volume 1: Statistics for Parishes, Part 24: Louisiana*. Washington, D.C.: GPO, 1956.

——. *United States Census of Manufactures: 1954, Volume 3: Area Statistics*. Washington, D.C.: GPO, 1957.

——. *United States Census of Agriculture: 1959, Volume 1: Counties, Part 35: Louisiana*. Washington, D.C.: GPO, 1961.

——. *Eighteenth Decennial Census of the United States, Census of Population:*

1960, Volume 1: Characteristics of the Population, Part 20: Louisiana.
Washington, D.C.: GPO, 1963.

——. *Census of Population: 1970, Volume 1: Characteristics of the Population,*
Part 20: Louisiana. Washington, D.C.: GPO, 1973.

——. *1990 Census of Population, Social and Economic Characteristics,*
Louisiana, Section 1. Washington, D.C.: GPO, 1993.

Constitution of the State of Louisiana, Adopted in Convention at the City of
New Orleans, May 12, 1898. New Orleans: H. J. Hearsey, 1898.

Fair Employment Practice Committee. *First Report, Fair Employment*
Practice Committee, July 1943–December 1944. Washington, D.C.: GPO, 1945.

General Assembly of the State of Louisiana. *Acts of the General Assembly of*
Louisiana, Regulating Labor, Extra Session, 1865. New Orleans: J. O. Nixon,
1866.

——. *Acts Passed by the General Assembly of the State of Louisiana at the*
Regular Session Begun and Held in the City of Baton Rouge on the Ninth
Day of May, 1892. Baton Rouge: Advocate, Official Journal of Louisiana, 1892.

House of Representatives of the State of Louisiana. *Official Journal of the*
Proceedings of the House of Representatives of the State of Louisiana at the
Second Regular Session of the First General Assembly under the Adoption of
the Constitution of 1913, Begun and Held in the City of Baton Rouge, May 13,
1918. Baton Rouge: Ramires-Jones Printing Co., 1918.

Louisiana Department of Labor. *A Compilation of General Labor Laws of*
Louisiana with Citations. Baton Rouge: Department of Labor, 1945.

Louisiana Historical Records Survey, Division of Community Service Programs,
Work Projects Administration. *Inventory of the Records of World War*
Emergency Activities in Louisiana, 1916–1920. Baton Rouge: Department of
Archives, Louisiana State University, 1942.

Louisiana State Council of Defense. *Minutes of the Meeting of the Louisiana*
State Council of Defense Held in the State House, Baton Rouge, Louisiana,
September 24, 1918. Baton Rouge: Ramires-Jones Printing Co., 1918.

State Department of Education of Louisiana. *Facilities for Veterans' Education*
and Training in Louisiana. State Department of Education of Louisiana
Bulletin No. 607. Baton Rouge: State Department of Education of Louisiana,
1946.

——. *Ninety-Second Annual Report for the Session, 1940–1941.* State
Department of Education of Louisiana Bulletin No. 458. Baton Rouge: State
Department of Education of Louisiana, 1941.

——. *Organizational Study, St. Helena Parish, Section II—Negro Schools.* State
Department of Education of Louisiana Bulletin No. 549. Baton Rouge: State
Department of Education, March 1945.

——. *State Course of Study for Negro High Schools and Training Schools.* State
Department of Education of Louisiana Bulletin No. 212. Baton Rouge: State
Department of Education, September 1931.

U.S. Commission on Civil Rights. *Political Participation: A Study of the*

Participation by Negroes in the Electoral and Political Processes in 10 Southern States since Passage of the Voting Rights Act of 1965. Washington, D.C.: GPO, 1968.

U.S. Department of Agriculture. *Yearbook of Agriculture 1930.* Washington, D.C.: GPO, 1930.

———. *Crops and Markets, Volume 19, Number 5.* Washington, D.C.: GPO, 1942.

———. *Parade of Progress: Negro Farm Families.* U.S. Department of Agriculture Production and Marketing Division Bulletin No. 5. December 1949.

U.S. Department of Labor, Division of Economics. *Negro Migration in 1916–1917.* Washington, D.C.: GPO, 1919.

U.S. Department of Labor, Division of Negro Economics. *The Negro at Work during the World War and during Reconstruction.* Washington, D.C.: GPO, 1920.

U.S. Senate. *Report and Testimony of the Select Committee of the United States Senate to Investigate the Causes of the Removal of the Negroes from the Southern States to the Northern States.* 46th Cong., 2d sess., 1880. S. Rept. 693.

Work magazine. Baton Rouge: Louisiana Works Progress Administration, various dates, 1930s.

Interviews

Baton Rouge, La.

T. Harry Williams Center for Oral History, Louisiana State University

Ronnie Sigal Bouma, interview by author, tape recording, 24 October 1998

Harrison and Earnestine Brown, interview by author, tape recording, 25 November 1996

Wilbert Guillory, interview by author, tape recording, 25 June 1998

Clifton and Eual Hall, interview by author, tape recording, 21 June 1998

Lawrence Hall, interview by author, tape recording, 20 June 1998

Lorin Hall, interview by author, tape recording, 20 June 1998

Eunice Hall Harris, interview by author, tape recording, 6 June 1998

J. K. Haynes, interview by Miranda Kombert, tape recording, 15 March 1995

Johnnie Jones Sr., interview by Mary Hebert, transcript, 1 September 1993

Robert and Essie Mae Lewis, interview by author, tape recording, 25 November 1996

Eunice Paddio-Johnson and Clarence Reed, interview by author, tape recording, 26 June 1998

Meg Redden (formerly Peggy Ewan), interview by author, tape recording, 8 December 1996

Lola Stallworth, interview by author, tape recording, 24 June 1998

Martin Williams, interview by author, tape recording, 24 November 1996

Moses Williams, interview by author, tape recording, 24 November 1996

John Zippert, interview by author, tape recording, 28 June 1998

Hammond, La.

Oral History Collection, Center for Regional Studies, Southeastern Louisiana University

Rovan W. Stanley Sr., interview by Janie Wilkins, transcript, 19 March 1978

Madison, Wis.

State Historical Society of Wisconsin

James Bell and Laura Spears, interview by Miriam Feingold, tape recording, 1966

Royan Burris, interview by Miriam Feingold, tape recording, 1966

Joseph Carter, interview by Miriam Feingold, tape recording, 1966

Joseph Carter, interview by Edward Hollander, tape recording, n.d. [1966]

Robert Hicks, interview by Miriam Feingold, tape recording, 1966

Gayle Jenkins, interview by Miriam Feingold, tape recording, 1966

Zelma Wyche, Harrison H. Brown, T. I. Israel, F. W. Wilson, and Moses Williams, interview by Miriam Feingold, tape recording, 1966

A. Z. Young, interview by Miriam Feingold, tape recording, 1966

New Orleans, La.

Amistad Research Center, Tulane University

Lolis Elie, interview by Kim Lacy Rogers, tape recording, 23 June 1988

Spiver Gordon, interviewer unknown, tape recording, 14 January 1984

Kenny Johnson, interviewer unknown, tape recording, 1988

Rudy Lombard, interview by Kim Lacy Rogers, tape recording, 7 June 1988

Jerome Smith, interview by Kim Lacy Rogers, tape recording, 8 July 1988

Friends of the Cabildo Collection, New Orleans Public Library

William Adams, Anthony Rachel, and Frank Wilderson, interview by Linda Jules Adams, tape recording, 28 February 1988

Lolis Elie, interview by Langston Reid, tape recording, 29 October 1988

Arthur Lemann, interview by Bernard Lemann, tape recording, January 1991

Newspapers and Magazines

AFBF News Letter

Baltimore Afro-American

Country Gentleman

Crisis

La. Delta Council News

Louisiana Farmers' Union News

Louisiana Union Farmer

Louisiana Weekly

Madison Journal
The Nation
New Orleans Daily Picayune
New Orleans Times-Democrat
New Orleans Times-Picayune
New Republic
Opelousas Clarion-News
Opelousas Daily World
Opportunity
Pittsburgh Courier
Pointe Coupee Banner
Southern Farm Leader
St. Francisville Democrat
St. Landry Clarion-Progress
Survey

Books

Aiken, Charles S. *The Cotton Plantation South since the Civil War*. Baltimore: Johns Hopkins University Press, 1998.

Anderson, James D. *The Education of Blacks in the South, 1860–1935*. Chapel Hill: University of North Carolina Press, 1988.

Andrews, William L. *To Tell a Free Story: The First Century of Afro-American Autobiography, 1760–1865*. Urbana: University of Illinois Press, 1986.

Aptheker, Herbert. *American Negro Slave Revolts*. New ed. New York: International Publishers, 1969.

Arnesen, Eric. *Waterfront Workers of New Orleans: Race, Class, and Politics, 1863–1923*. New York: Oxford University Press, 1991.

Baker, Gladys. *The County Agent*. Chicago: University of Illinois Press, 1939.

Baldwin, Sidney. *Poverty and Politics: The Rise and Decline of the Farm Security Administration*. Chapel Hill: University of North Carolina Press, 1968.

Barnard, Hollinger F., ed. *Outside the Magic Circle: The Autobiography of Virginia Foster Durr*. Tuscaloosa: University of Alabama Press, 1985.

Bartley, Numan V. *The New South, 1945–1980*. Baton Rouge: Louisiana State University Press, 1995.

Bartlow, John D. *Louisiana Study of Rural War Production Training*. State Board for Vocational Education Bulletin No. 510. Baton Rouge: [State Department of Education of Louisiana], 1943.

Becnel, Thomas. *Labor, Church, and the Sugar Establishment: Louisiana, 1887–1976*. Baton Rouge: Louisiana State University Press, 1980.

Berman, William C. *The Politics of Civil Rights in the Truman Administration*. Columbus: Ohio State University Press, 1970.

——. *America's Right Turn: From Nixon to Bush*. Baltimore: Johns Hopkins University Press, 1994.

Bernhardt, Joshua. *The Sugar Industry and the Federal Government: A Thirty Year Record, 1917–47*. Washington, D.C.: Sugar Statistics Service, 1948.

Black, Earl, and Merle Black. *Politics and Society in the South*. Cambridge: Harvard University Press, 1987.

Bond, Horace Mann, and Julia W. Bond. *The Star Creek Papers*. Edited by Adam Fairclough. Athens: University of Georgia Press, 1997.

Branch, Taylor. *Parting the Waters: America in the King Years, 1954–63*. New York: Simon and Schuster, 1988.

Brandfon, Robert L. *Cotton Kingdom of the New South: A History of the Yazoo Mississippi Delta from Reconstruction to the Twentieth Century*. Cambridge: Harvard University Press, 1967.

Brinkley, Alan. *Voices of Protest: Huey Long, Father Coughlin, and the Great Depression*. First Vintage Books ed. New York: Random House, Vintage Books, 1983.

Brundage, W. Fitzhugh. *Lynching in the New South: Georgia and Virginia, 1880–1930*. Urbana: University of Illinois Press, 1993.

Brunner, Edmund deS., and E. Hsin Pao Yang. *Rural America and the Extension Service: A History and Critique of the Cooperative Agricultural and Home Economics Extension Service*. New York: Columbia University Teachers College, Bureau of Publications, 1949.

Buchanan, A. Russell. *Black Americans in World War II*. Santa Barbara, Calif.: Clio Books, 1977.

Calhoun, Milburn, ed. *Louisiana Almanac, 1988–89*. Gretna, La.: Pelican Publishing Co., 1988.

Calhoun, Robert Dabney. *A History of Concordia Parish, Louisiana*. New Orleans: Robert Dabney Calhoun, 1932.

Carr, Robert K. *Federal Protection of Civil Rights: Quest for a Sword*. Ithaca, N.Y.: Cornell University Press, 1947; reprint, 1964.

Carson, Clayborne. *In Struggle: SNCC and the Black Awakening of the 1960s*. Cambridge: Harvard University Press, 1981.

Chestnut, J. L., Jr., and Julia Cass. *Black in Selma: The Uncommon Life of J. L. Chestnut, Jr.* New York: Farrar, Straus and Giroux, 1990.

Clayton, Ronnie W., ed. *Mother Wit: The Ex-Slave Narratives of the Louisiana Writers' Project*. New York: Peter Lang, 1990.

Cobb, James C. *Industrialization and Southern Society, 1877–1984*. Lexington: University Press of Kentucky, 1984.

Cohen, William. *At Freedom's Edge: Black Mobility and the Southern White Quest for Racial Control, 1861–1915*. Baton Rouge: Louisiana State University Press, 1991.

Conrad, David Eugene. *The Forgotten Farmers: The Story of Sharecroppers in the New Deal*. Urbana: University of Illinois Press, 1965.

Cornelius, Janet Duitsman. *"When I Can Read My Title Clear": Literacy, Slavery, and Religion in the Antebellum South*. Columbia: University of South Carolina Press, 1991.

Cotton, Barbara R. *The Lamplighters: Black Farm and Home Demonstration Agents in Florida, 1915–1965.* Tallahassee: U.S. Department of Agriculture in Cooperation with Florida Agricultural and Mechanical University, 1980.

Couto, Richard A. *Ain't Gonna Let Nobody Turn Me Round: The Pursuit of Racial Justice in the Rural South.* Philadelphia: Temple University Press, 1991.

Daniel, Pete. *Breaking the Land: The Transformation of Cotton, Tobacco, and Rice Cultures since 1880.* Urbana: University of Illinois Press, 1985.

——. *The Shadow of Slavery: Peonage in the South, 1901–1969.* Illini Books ed. Urbana: University of Illinois Press, 1990.

Dart, Benjamin Wall, ed. *Civil Code of the State of Louisiana, Revision of 1870, Volume 2.* 2d ed. Indianapolis, Ind.: Bobbs-Merrill, 1945.

Dawley, Alan. *Struggles for Justice: Social Responsibility and the Liberal State.* Cambridge: Harvard University Press, Belknap Press, 1991.

Dittmer, John. *Local People: The Struggle for Civil Rights in Mississippi.* Urbana: University of Illinois Press, 1994.

Draper, Alan. *Conflict of Interests: Organized Labor and the Civil Rights Movement in the South, 1954–1968.* Ithaca, N.Y.: ILR Press, 1994.

Du Bois, W. E. Burghardt. *Black Reconstruction: An Essay toward a History of the Part Which Black Folk Played in the Attempt to Reconstruct Democracy in America, 1860–1880.* 1935. Reprint, New York: S. A. Russell Co., Harbor Scholars' Classics, 1956.

East Feliciana Parish Sesquicentennial Committee. *East Feliciana Parish, 1824–1974: Land of Seven Springs and Seven Pastures.* [Clinton, La.: East Feliciana Parish Sesquicentennial Committee, 1974].

Egerton, John. *Speak Now against the Day: The Generation before the Civil Rights Movement in the South.* New York: Knopf, 1994.

Embree, Edwin R. *Julius Rosenwald Fund: A Review of Two Decades, 1917–1936.* Chicago: Julius Rosenwald Fund, 1936.

Eskew, Glenn T. *But for Birmingham: The Local and National Movements in the Civil Rights Struggle.* Chapel Hill: University of North Carolina Press, 1997.

Fairclough, Adam. *To Redeem the Soul of America: The Southern Christian Leadership Conference and Martin Luther King, Jr.* Athens: University of Georgia Press, 1987.

——. *Race and Democracy: The Civil Rights Struggle in Louisiana, 1915–1972.* Athens: University of Georgia Press, 1995.

Farmer, James. *Lay Bare the Heart: An Autobiography of the Civil Rights Movement.* New York: Arbor House, 1985.

Finch, Minnie. *The NAACP: Its Fight for Justice.* Metuchen, N.J.: Scarecrow Press, 1981.

Finkle, Lee. *Forum for Protest: The Black Press during World War II.* Cranbury, N.J.: Associated University Presses, 1975.

Foley, Neil. *The White Scourge: Mexicans, Blacks, and Poor Whites in Texas Cotton Culture.* Berkeley: University of California Press, 1997.

Foner, Eric. *Nothing but Freedom: Emancipation and Its Legacy*. Baton Rouge: Louisiana State University Press, 1983.

——. *Reconstruction: America's Unfinished Revolution, 1863–1877*. New York: Harper and Row, 1988.

Frazier, E. Franklin. *The Negro Church in America*. New York: Schocken Books, 1963.

Gaines, Ernest J. *A Gathering of Old Men*. New York: Knopf, 1983.

Gaines, Kevin K. *Uplifting the Race: Black Leadership, Politics, and Culture in the Twentieth Century*. Chapel Hill: University of North Carolina Press, 1995.

Galarza, Ernesto. *The Louisiana Sugar Cane Plantation Workers vs. the Sugar Corporations, U.S. Department of Agriculture, et al.: An Account of Human Relations on Corporation-Owned Sugar Cane Plantations in Louisiana under the Operation of the U.S. Sugar Program, 1937–1953*. Washington, D.C.: Inter-American Educational Association, Inc., 1954.

Garfinkel, Herbert. *When Negroes March: The March on Washington Movement in the Organizational Politics for FEPC*. Glencoe, Ill.: Free Press, 1959.

Garrow, David J. *Bearing the Cross: Martin Luther King, Jr., and the Southern Christian Leadership Conference*. New York: William Morrow and Co., 1986.

Gaston, Paul M. *The New South Creed: A Study in Southern Mythmaking*. New York: Knopf, 1970.

Gates, Henry Louis Jr., ed. *The Classic Slave Narratives*. New York: Penguin Books, 1987.

Genovese, Eugene D. *Roll, Jordan, Roll: The World the Slaves Made*. New York: Random House, Pantheon Books, 1974.

Gilmore, Glenda Elizabeth. *Gender and Jim Crow: Women and the Politics of White Supremacy in North Carolina, 1896–1920*. Chapel Hill: University of North Carolina Press, 1996.

Gitlin, Todd. *The Sixties: Years of Hope, Days of Rage*. Rev. ed. New York: Bantum Books, 1993.

Goins, Charles Robert, and John Michael Caldwell. *Historical Atlas of Louisiana*. Norman: University of Oklahoma Press, 1995.

Goldfield, David R. *Black, White, and Southern: Race Relations and Southern Culture, 1940 to the Present*. Baton Rouge: Louisiana State University Press, 1990.

Gottlieb, Peter. *Making Their Own Way: Southern Blacks' Migration to Pittsburgh, 1916–1930*. Urbana: University of Illinois Press, 1987.

Green, James R. *Grass-Roots Socialism: Radical Movements in the Southwest, 1895–1943*. Baton Rouge: Louisiana State University Press, 1978.

Greenberg, Stanley B. *Race and State in Capitalist Development: Comparative Perspectives*. New Haven: Yale University Press, 1980.

Griffith, Barbara S. *The Crisis of American Labor: Operation Dixie and the Defeat of the CIO*. Philadelphia: Temple University Press, 1988.

Grossman, James R. *Land of Hope: Chicago, Black Southerners, and the Great Migration*. Chicago: University of Chicago Press, 1989.

Grubbs, Donald. *Cry from the Cotton: The Southern Tenant Farmers' Union and the New Deal*. Chapel Hill: University of North Carolina Press, 1971.

Guha, Ranajit, ed. *Subaltern Studies: Writings on South Asian History and Society, Volume I*. Delhi: Oxford University Press, 1982.

Guzman, Jessie Parkhurst, ed. *Negro Yearbook: A Review of Events Affecting Negro Life, 1941–1946*. Tuskegee, Ala.: Tuskegee Institute Department of Records and Research, 1947.

Hair, William Ivy. *Bourbonism and Agrarian Protest: Louisiana Politics, 1877–1900*. Baton Rouge: Louisiana State University Press, 1969.

——. *The Kingfish and His Realm: The Life and Times of Huey P. Long*. Baton Rouge: Louisiana State University Press, 1991.

Hale, Grace Elizabeth. *Making Whiteness: The Culture of Segregation in the South, 1890–1940*. New York: Pantheon Books, 1998.

Hall, Gwendolyn Midlo. *Africans in Colonial Louisiana: The Development of Afro-Creole Culture in the Eighteenth Century*. Baton Rouge: Louisiana State University Press, 1992.

Harlan, Louis R. *Booker T. Washington: The Making of a Black Leader, 1856–1901*. New York: Oxford University Press, 1972.

Henderson, Donald H. *The Negro Migration of 1916–1918*. Washington, D.C.: Association for the Study of Negro Life and History, 1921.

Henri, Florette. *Bitter Victory: A History of Black Soldiers in World War I*. New York: Zenith Books, Doubleday, 1970.

Higginbotham, Evelyn Brooks. *Righteous Discontent: The Women's Movement in the Black Baptist Church, 1880–1920*. Cambridge: Harvard University Press, 1993.

Hill, Robert A., ed. *The FBI's RACON: Racial Conditions in the United States during World War II*. Boston: Northeastern University Press, 1995.

Hine, Darlene Clark. *Black Victory: The Rise and Fall of the White Primary in Texas*. Millwood, N.Y.: KTO Press, 1979.

Holley, Donald. *Uncle Sam's Farmers: The New Deal Communities in the Lower Mississippi Valley*. Urbana: University of Illinois Press, 1975.

Honey, Michael Keith. *Southern Labor and Black Civil Rights: Organizing Memphis Workers*. Urbana: University of Illinois Press, 1993.

——. *Black Workers Remember: An Oral History of Segregation, Unionism, and the Freedom Struggle*. Berkeley: University of California Press, 1999.

Horowitz, Roger. *"Negro and White, Unite and Fight!": A Social History of Industrial Unionism in Meatpacking, 1930–1990*. Urbana: University of Illinois Press, 1997.

Howard, John C. *The Negro in the Lumber Industry*. Racial Policies of American Industry Report No. 19. Philadelphia: Industrial Research Unit, Department of Industry, University of Pennsylvania, 1970.

Howard, Perry H. *Political Tendencies in Louisiana*. Rev. exp. ed. Baton Rouge: Louisiana State University Press, 1971.

Hunter, Tera W. *To 'Joy My Freedom: Southern Black Women's Lives and Labors after the Civil War*. Cambridge: Harvard University Press, 1997.

Hurston, Zora Neale. *Folklore, Memoirs, and Other Writings*. Edited by Cheryl A. Wall. New York: Library of America, 1995.

Hyde, Samuel C., Jr. *Pistols and Politics: The Dilemma of Democracy in Louisiana's Florida Parishes, 1810–1899*. Baton Rouge: Louisiana State University Press, 1996.

Jacoway, Elizabeth, and David R. Colburn, ed. *Southern Businessmen and Desegregation*. Baton Rouge: Louisiana State University Press, 1982.

Jeansonne, Glen. *Messiah of the Masses: Huey P. Long and the Great Depression*. New York: HarperCollins Publishers, 1993.

Johnson, Charles S. *Louisiana Educational Survey, Volume 4, Section 8—The Negro Public Schools*. Baton Rouge: Louisiana Educational Survey Commission, 1942. (In file 5, box 182, Charles S. Johnson Papers, Fisk University Library Special Collections, Nashville.)

Jones, Jacqueline. *Labor of Love, Labor of Sorrow: Black Women, Work, and the Family from Slavery to the Present*. New York: Basic Books, 1985.

Kelley, Robin D. G. *Hammer and Hoe: Alabama Communists during the Great Depression*. Chapel Hill: University of North Carolina Press, 1990.

——. *Race Rebels: Culture, Politics, and the Black Working Class*. New York: Free Press, 1994.

——. *Yo' Mama's Disfunktional! Fighting the Culture Wars in Urban America*. Boston: Beacon Press, 1997.

Kellogg, Charles Flint. *NAACP: A History of the National Association for the Advancement of Colored People, Volume I: 1909–1920*. Baltimore: Johns Hopkins Press, 1967.

Key, V. O., Jr. *Southern Politics in State and Nation*. New ed. Knoxville: University of Tennessee Press, 1984.

Kirby, Jack Temple. *Rural Worlds Lost: The American South, 1920–1960*. Baton Rouge: Louisiana State University Press, 1986.

Kornweibel, Theodore Jr. *"Seeing Red": Federal Campaigns against Black Militancy, 1919–1925*. Bloomington: Indiana University Press, 1998.

Kousser, J. Morgan. *The Shaping of Southern Politics: Suffrage Restriction and the Establishment of the One-Party South, 1880–1910*. New Haven: Yale University Press, 1974.

Kurtz, Michael L., and Morgan D. Peoples. *Earl K. Long: The Saga of Uncle Earl and Louisiana Politics*. Baton Rouge: Louisiana State University, 1990.

Lawson, Steven F. *In Pursuit of Power: Southern Blacks and Electoral Politics, 1965–1982*. New York: Columbia University Press, 1985.

Lemann, Nicholas. *The Promised Land: The Great Black Migration and How It Changed America*. Vintage Books ed. New York, Random House, Vintage Books, 1992.

Lemke-Santangelo, Gretchen. *Abiding Courage: African American Migrant*

Women and the East Bay Community. Chapel Hill: University of North Carolina Press, 1996.

Leuchtenburg, William E. *Franklin D. Roosevelt and the New Deal, 1932–1940*. New York: Harper and Row, 1963.

Levine, Lawrence W. *Black Culture and Black Consciousness: Afro-American Folk Thought from Slavery to Freedom*. New York: Oxford University Press, 1977.

Lewis, Earl. *In Their Own Interests: Race, Class, and Power in Twentieth-Century Norfolk, Virginia*. Berkeley: University of California Press, 1991.

Lichtenstein, Alex. *Twice the Work of Free Labor: The Political Economy of Convict Labor in the New South*. London: Verso, 1996.

Litwack, Leon F. *Trouble in Mind: Black Southerners in the Age of Jim Crow*. New York: Knopf, 1998.

Louisiana Education Association Department of Retired Teachers. *We Walked Tall*. N.p.: Louisiana Education Association, 1979.

Lynsky, Myer. *Sugar Economics, Statistics, and Documents*. New York: U.S. Cane Sugar Refiners' Association, 1938.

MacLean, Nancy. *Behind the Mask of Chivalry: The Making of the Second Ku Klux Klan*. New York: Oxford University Press, 1994.

Mandle, Jay R. *The Roots of Black Poverty: The Southern Plantation Economy after the Civil War*. Durham, N.C.: Duke University Press, 1978.

Marks, Carole. *Farewell—We're Good and Gone*. Bloomington: Indiana University Press, 1989.

McGuire, Phillip, ed. *Taps for a Jim Crow Army: Letters from Black Soldiers in World War II*. Santa Barbara, Calif.: ABC-Clio, 1983.

McMillen, Neil R. *Dark Journey: Black Mississippians in the Age of Jim Crow*. Urbana: University of Illinois Press, 1989.

Meier, August, and Elliott Rudwick. *CORE: A Study in the Civil Rights Movement, 1942–1968*. New York: Oxford University Press, 1973.

Mertz, Paul E. *New Deal Policy and Southern Rural Poverty*. Baton Rouge: Louisiana State University Press, 1978.

Mills, Kay. *This Little Light of Mine: The Life of Fannie Lou Hamer*. New York: Penguin Books, 1993; reprint, Plume Books, 1994.

Moody, Anne. *Coming of Age in Mississippi*. New York: Bantum Doubleday Dell Publishing Group, 1968; reprint, Laurel Books, 1976.

Morris, Aldon D. *The Origins of the Civil Rights Movement: Black Communities Organizing for Change*. New York: Free Press, 1984.

Muraskin, William A. *Middle-Class Blacks in a White Society: Prince Hall Freemasonry in America*. Berkeley: University of California Press, 1975.

Naison, Mark. *Communists in Harlem during the Depression*. Urbana: University of Illinois Press, 1983.

Naples, Nancy A. *Grassroots Warriors: Activist Mothering, Community Work, and the War on Poverty*. New York: Routledge, 1998.

Norrell, Robert J. *Reaping the Whirlwind: The Civil Rights Movement in Tuskegee*. New York: Knopf, 1985.

O'Brien, Gail Williams. *The Color of the Law: Race, Violence, and Justice in the Post–World War II South*. Chapel Hill: University of North Carolina Press, 1999.

Odum, Howard W. *Race and Rumors of Race: Challenge to American Crisis*. Chapel Hill: University of North Carolina Press, 1943.

Oliver, Paul. *Conversation with the Blues*. 2d ed. Cambridge: Cambridge University Press, 1997.

——. *The Story of the Blues*. Rev. ed. Boston: Northeastern University Press, 1998.

Olson, James S., ed. *Historical Dictionary of the New Deal: From Inauguration to Preparation for War*. Westport, Conn.: Greenwood Press, 1985.

Oshinsky, David M. *"Worse Than Slavery": Parchman Farm and the Ordeal of Jim Crow Justice*. New York: Free Press, 1996.

Painter, Nell Irvin. *Exodusters: Black Migration to Kansas after Reconstruction*. New York: Knopf, 1977.

Parker, Frank R. *Black Votes Count: Political Empowerment in Mississippi after 1965*. Chapel Hill: University of North Carolina Press, 1990.

Payne, Charles M. *I've Got the Light of Freedom: The Organizing Tradition and the Mississippi Freedom Struggle*. Berkeley: University of California Press, 1995.

Peery, Nelson. *Black Fire: The Making of an American Revolutionary*. New York: New Press, 1994.

Piven, Frances Fox, and Richard A. Cloward. *Poor People's Movements: Why They Succeed, How They Fail*. Vintage Books ed. New York: Random House, Vintage Books, 1979.

Powell, Lawrence N. *New Masters: Northern Planters during the Civil War and Reconstruction*. New Haven: Yale University Press, 1980.

Putney, Martha S. *When the Nation Was in Need: Blacks in the Women's Army Corps during World War II*. Metuchen, N.J.: Scarecrow Press, 1992.

Raines, Howell. *My Soul Is Rested: Movement Days in the Deep South Remembered*. New York: G. P. Putnam's Sons, 1977.

Ramsey, Ralph J., and Harold Hoffsommer. *Farm Tenancy in Louisiana*. Washington, D.C.: Bureau of Agricultural Economics, 1941.

Record, Wilson. *Race and Radicalism: The NAACP and the Communist Party in Conflict*. Ithaca, N.Y.: Cornell University Press, 1964.

Rosengarten, Theodore. *All God's Dangers: The Life of Nate Shaw*. New York: Knopf, 1974.

Ruchames, Louis. *Race, Jobs, and Politics: The Story of the FEPC*. Westport, Conn.: Negro Universities Press, 1971.

Rudwick, Elliott M. *W. E. B. Du Bois: A Study in Minority Group Leadership*. Philadelphia: University of Pennsylvania Press, 1960.

Russell, Charles W. *Report on Peonage*. Washington, D.C.: GPO, 1908.

Saxon, Lyle, Edward Dreyer, and Robert Tallant, comp. *Gumbo Ya-Ya: A Collection of Louisiana Folk Tales*. Boston: Houghton Mifflin, 1945.

Scherer, James A. B. *The Nation at War*. New York: George H. Doran Co., 1918.

Schipper, Martin, comp. *Guide to the Microfilm Edition of the Peonage Files of the U.S. Department of Justice, 1901–1945*. Bethesda, Md.: University Publications of America, 1989.

Scott, Emmett J. *The American Negro in the World War*. N.p.: Emmett J. Scott, 1919.

Scott, James C. *The Moral Economy of the Peasant: Rebellion and Subsistence in Southeast Asia*. New Haven: Yale University Press, 1976.

——. *Weapons of the Weak: Everyday Forms of Peasant Resistance*. New Haven: Yale University Press, 1985.

——. *Domination and the Arts of Resistance: Hidden Transcripts*. New Haven: Yale University Press, 1990.

Seligmann, Herbert J. *The Negro Faces America*. New York: Harper and Brothers, 1920.

Sepia Socialite. *The Negro in Louisiana: Seventy-Eight Years of Progress*. New Orleans: Sepia Socialite Publishing Co., 1942.

Sernett, Milton C. *Bound for the Promised Land: African American Religion and the Great Migration*. Durham, N.C.: Duke University Press, 1997.

Shannon, Jasper Berry. *Toward a New Politics in the South*. Knoxville: University of Tennessee Press, 1949.

Shaw, Stephanie J. *What a Woman Ought to Be and to Do: Black Professional Women Workers during the Jim Crow Era*. Chicago: University of Chicago Press, 1996.

Shugg, Roger W. *Origins of Class Struggle in Louisiana: A Social History of White Farmers and Laborers during Slavery and After, 1840–1875*. Paperback ed. Baton Rouge: Louisiana State University Press, 1968.

Sindler, Allan P. *Huey Long's Louisiana: State Politics, 1920–1952*. Baltimore: Johns Hopkins Press, 1956.

Sitkoff, Harvard. *A New Deal for Blacks: The Emergence of Civil Rights as a National Issue, Volume I: The Depression Decade*. New York: Oxford University Press, 1978.

——. *The Struggle for Black Equality, 1954–1992*. Rev. ed. New York: Hill and Wang, 1993.

Sitterson, J. Carlyle. *Sugar Country: The Cane Sugar Industry in the South, 1753–1950*. Lexington: University of Kentucky Press, 1953.

Smith, T. Lynn, and Homer L. Hitt. *The People of Louisiana*. Baton Rouge: Louisiana State University Press, 1952.

Stern, Steve J., ed. *Resistance, Rebellion, and Consciousness in the Andean Peasant World, 18th to 20th Centuries*. Madison: University of Wisconsin Press, 1987.

Sullivan, Patricia. *Days of Hope: Race and Democracy in the New Deal Era*. Chapel Hill: University of North Carolina Press, 1996.

Taylor, Joe Gray. *Louisiana Reconstructed, 1863–1877*. Baton Rouge: Louisiana State University Press, 1974.

——. *Louisiana: A Bicentennial History*. New York: Norton, 1976.

Thompson, E. P. *The Making of the English Working Class*. New York: Random House, Vintage Books, 1963.

Tindall, George Brown. *The Emergence of the New South, 1913–1945*. Baton Rouge: Louisiana State University Press, 1967.

Treadwell, Mattie E. *The Women's Army Corps*. Washington, D.C.: Office of the Chief of Military History, 1954.

Tunnell, Ted. *Crucible of Reconstruction: War, Radicalism, and Race in Louisiana, 1862–1877*. Baton Rouge: Louisiana State University Press, 1984.

Tuttle, William M., Jr. *Race Riot: Chicago in the Red Summer of 1919*. New York: Athenum, 1970.

Vandal, Gilles. *Rethinking Southern Violence: Homicides in Post–Civil War Louisiana, 1866–1884*. Columbus: Ohio State University Press, 2000.

Vincent, Charles. *Black Legislators in Louisiana during Reconstruction*. Baton Rouge: Louisiana State University Press, 1976.

Von Eschen, Penny M. *Race against Empire: Black Americans and Anticolonialism, 1937–1957*. Ithaca, N.Y.: Cornell University Press, 1997.

Walton, Hanes, Jr. *African American Power and Politics: The Political Context Variable*. New York: Columbia University Press, 1997.

Warmoth, Henry Clay. *War, Politics, and Reconstruction: Stormy Days in Louisiana*. New York: Macmillan, 1930.

Watters, Pat, and Reese Cleghorn. *Climbing Jacob's Ladder: The Arrival of Negroes in Southern Politics*. New York: Harcourt, Brace and World, 1967.

Weiss, Nancy J. *Farewell to the Party of Lincoln: Black Politics in the Age of FDR*. Princeton, N.J.: Princeton University Press, 1983.

Wells-Barnett, Ida B. *Southern Horrors: Lynch Law in All Its Phases* (1892). In *Selected Works of Ida B. Wells-Barnett*, compiled by Trudier Harris. New York: Oxford University Press, 1991.

Whayne, Jeannie M. *A New Plantation South: Land, Labor, and Federal Favor in Twentieth-Century Arkansas*. Charlottesville: University Press of Virginia, 1996.

Wiener, Jonathan M. *Social Origins of the New South: Alabama, 1860–1885*. Baton Rouge: Louisiana State University Press, 1978.

Wilkerson, Doxey A. *Agricultural Extension Services among Negroes in the South*. Washington, D.C.: Conference of Presidents of Negro Land Grant Colleges, 1942.

Wilkie, Laurie A. *Ethnicity, Community, and Power: An Archaeological Study of the African-American Experience at Oakley Plantation, Louisiana*. Columbia: South Carolina Institute of Archaeology and Anthropology, University of South Carolina, 1994.

Williams, T. Harry. *Huey Long*. New York: Knopf, 1969.

Wilson, Ruth Danenhower. *Jim Crow Joins Up: A Study of Negroes in the*

Armed Forces of the United States. Rev. ed. New York: William J. Clark, 1944.

Woodman, Harold D. *New South—New Law: The Legal Foundations of Credit and Labor Relations in the Postbellum Agricultural South.* Baton Rouge: Louisiana State University, 1995.

Woods, Clyde. *Development Arrested: The Blues and Plantation Power in the Mississippi Delta.* London: Verso, 1998.

Woodward, C. Vann. *Reunion and Reaction: The Compromise of 1877 and the End of Reconstruction.* Boston: Little, Brown, 1951.

——. *Origins of the New South, 1877–1913.* Baton Rouge: Louisiana State University Press, 1951; reprint, with a new preface, 1971.

Wright, Gavin. *Old South, New South: Revolutions in the Southern Economy since the Civil War.* Baton Rouge: Louisiana State University Press, 1986.

Wynn, Neil A. *The Afro-American and the Second World War.* Rev. ed. New York: Holmes and Meier, 1993.

Zangrando, Robert L. *The NAACP Crusade against Lynching, 1909–1950.* Philadelphia: Temple University Press, 1980.

Articles

Alston, Lee J., and Kyle D. Kauffman. "Up, Down, and Off the Agricultural Ladder: New Evidence and Implications of Agricultural Mobility for Blacks in the Postbellum South." *Agricultural History* 72 (Spring 1998): 263–79.

Bates, Beth Tompkins. "A New Crowd Challenges the Agenda of the Old Guard in the NAACP, 1933–1941." *American Historical Review* 102 (April 1997): 340–77.

Beito, David T. "Black Fraternal Hospitals in the Mississippi Delta, 1942–1967." *Journal of Southern History* 65 (February 1999): 109–40.

Bims, Hamilton. "Deacons for Defense." *Ebony,* September 1965, 25–30.

Brown, Elsa Barkley. "Womanist Consciousness: Maggie Lena Walker and the Independent Order of St. Luke." *Signs: Journal of Women in Culture and Society* 14 (Spring 1989): 610–33.

Cecelski, David S., and Timothy B. Tyson. Review of *Trouble in Mind: Black Southerners in the Age of Jim Crow,* by Leon Litwack. *Journal of American History* 86 (September 1999): 735–37.

Cline, Rodney. "Public Education in Louisiana." *Peabody Journal of Education* 35 (March 1958): 259–77.

Cohen, William. "The Great Migration as a Lever for Social Change." In *Black Exodus: The Great Migration from the American South,* edited by Alferdteen Harrison, 72–82. Jackson: University Press of Mississippi, 1991.

Crouch, Barry A. "Black Education in Civil War and Reconstruction Louisiana: George T. Ruby, the Army, and the Freedmen's Bureau." *Louisiana History* 38 (Summer 1997): 287–308.

Daniel, Pete. "The Legal Basis of Agrarian Capitalism: The South since 1933." In *Race and Class in the American South Since 1890*, edited by Melvyn Stokes and Rick Halpern, 79–102. Oxford, U.K.: Berg Publishers, 1994.

Davidson, Chandler. "The Recent Evolution of Voting Rights Law Affecting Racial and Language Minorities." In *Quiet Revolution in the South: The Impact of the Voting Rights Act, 1965–1990*, edited by Chandler Davidson and Bernard Grofman, 21–36. Princeton, N.J.: Princeton University Press, 1994.

Douty, Esther Morris. "FERA and the Rural Negro." *Survey*, July 1934, 215–16.

Engstrom, Richard L., Stanley A. Halpin Jr., Jean A. Hill, and Victoria M. Caridas-Butterworth. "Louisiana." In *Quiet Revolution in the South: The Impact of the Voting Rights Act, 1965–1990*, edited by Chandler Davidson and Bernard Grofman, 103–35. Princeton, N.J.: Princeton University Press, 1994.

Fairclough, Adam. "'Being in the Field of Education and Also Being a Negro . . . Seems . . . Tragic': Black Teachers in the Jim Crow South." *Journal of American History* 87 (June 2000): 65–91.

Ferleger, Louis. "The Problem of 'Labor' in the Post-Reconstruction Louisiana Sugar Industry." *Agricultural History* 72 (Spring 1998): 140–58.

Fields, Barbara J. "Ideology and Race in American History." In *Region, Race, and Reconstruction: Essays in Honor of C. Vann Woodward*, edited by J. Morgan Kousser and James M. McPherson, 143–77. New York: Oxford University Press, 1982.

Flamm, Michael W. "The National Farmers Union and the Evolution of Agrarian Liberalism, 1937–1946." *Agricultural History* 68 (Summer 1994): 54–80.

Grossman, James R. "Black Labor Is the Best Labor: Southern White Reactions to the Great Migration." In *Black Exodus: The Great Migration from the American South*, edited by Alferdteen Harrison, 51–71. Jackson: University Press of Mississippi, 1991.

Hahamovitch, Cindy. "Standing Idly By: 'Organized' Farmworkers in South Florida during the Depression and World War II." In *Southern Labor in Transition, 1940–1995*, edited by Robert H. Zieger, 15–36. Knoxville: University of Tennessee Press, 1997.

Halpern, Rick. "The CIO and the Limits of Labor-Based Civil Rights Activism: The Case of Louisiana's Sugar Workers, 1947–1966." In *Southern Labor in Transition, 1940–1995*, edited by Robert H. Zieger, 86–112. Knoxville: University of Tennessee Press, 1997.

Isaacman, Allen, Michael Stephen, Yussuf Adam, Maria João Homen, Eugenio Macomo, and Augustinho Pililão. "'Cotton Is the Mother of Poverty': Peasant Resistance to Forced Cotton Production in Mozambique, 1938–1961." *International Journal of African Historical Studies* 13 (1980): 581–615.

Jenkins, Alan. "See No Evil." *The Nation*, 28 June 1999, 15–19.

Johnson, Clyde. "A Brief History, Share Croppers' Union, Alabama/Louisiana, 1931–1941." April 1979. (In box 9, Clyde L. Johnson Papers, Southern Historical Collection, University of North Carolina, Chapel Hill.)

Kelley, Robin D. G. "A Lifelong Radical: Clyde L. Johnson, 1908–1994." *Radical History Review* 62 (Spring 1995): 254–58.

Kerkvliet, Benedict J. Tria. "Everyday Resistance to Injustice in a Philippine Village." *Journal of Peasant Studies* 13 (January 1986): 107–23.

Kiffmeyer, Thomas J. "From Self-Help to Sedition: The Appalachian Volunteers in Eastern Kentucky, 1964–1970." *Journal of Southern History* 64 (February 1998): 65–94.

Korstad, Robert, and Nelson Lichtenstein. "Opportunities Found and Lost: Labor, Radicals, and the Early Civil Rights Movement." *Journal of American History* 75 (December 1988): 786–811.

"Labor and the Southern Negro." *The Nation*, 27 September 1952, 261.

Laws, J. Bradford. "The Negroes of Cinclare Central Factory and Calumet Plantation, Louisiana." In Department of Labor Bulletin No. 38, 95–120. Washington, D.C.: GPO, 1902.

Letwin, Daniel. "Interracial Unionism, Gender, and 'Social Equality' in the Alabama Coalfields, 1878–1908." *Journal of Southern History* 61 (August 1995): 519–54.

Lichtenstein, Alex. "Was the Emancipated Slave a Proletarian?" *Reviews in American History* 26 (March 1998): 124–45.

Meier, August. "Toward a Reinterpretation of Booker T. Washington." *Journal of Southern History* 23 (May 1957): 220–27.

Nesom, G. E. "The Louisiana Delta." In *The Call of the Alluvial Empire*, edited by Southern Alluvial Land Association, 21–23. Memphis, Tenn.: Southern Alluvial Land Association, 1919.

Norrell, Robert J. "One Thing We Did Right: Reflections on the Movement." In *New Directions in Civil Rights Studies*, edited by Armstead L. Robinson and Patricia Sullivan, 65–80. Charlottesville: University Press of Virginia, 1991.

Norwood, Stephen H. "Bogalusa Burning: The War against Biracial Unionism in the Deep South, 1919." *Journal of Southern History* 63 (August 1997): 591–628.

O'Hanlon, Rosalind. "Recovering the Subject: *Subaltern Studies* and Histories of Resistance in Colonial South Asia." *Modern Asian Studies* 22 (February 1988): 189–224.

Onkst, David H. " 'First a Negro . . . Incidentally a Veteran': Black World War Two Veterans and the G.I. Bill of Rights in the Deep South, 1944–1948." *Journal of Social History* 31 (Spring 1998): 517–43.

Payne, Elizabeth Anne. "The Lady Was a Sharecropper: Myrtle Lawrence and the Southern Tenant Farmers' Union." *Southern Cultures* 4 (Summer 1998): 5–27.

Prestage, Jewel L., and Carolyn Sue Williams. "Blacks in Louisiana Politics." In *Louisiana Politics: Festival in a Labyrinth*, edited by James Bolner, 285–317. Baton Rouge: Louisiana State University Press, 1982.

Reed, Germaine A. "Race Legislation in Louisiana, 1864–1920," *Louisiana History* 4 (Fall 1965): 379–92.

Reich, Steven A. "Soldiers of Democracy: Black Texans and the Fight for Citizenship, 1917–1921." *Journal of American History* 82 (March 1996): 1478–1504.

Reidy, Joseph P. "Mules and Machines and Men: Field Labor on Louisiana Sugar Plantations, 1887–1915." *Agricultural History* 72 (Spring 1998): 183–96.

Rieder, Jonathan. "The Rise of the 'Silent Majority.'" In *The Rise and Fall of the New Deal Order, 1930–1980*, edited by Steve Fraser and Gary Gerstle, 243–68. Princeton, N.J.: Princeton University Press, 1989.

Rodrigue, John C. "'The Great Law of Demand and Supply': The Contest over Wages in Louisiana's Sugar Region, 1870–1880." *Agricultural History* 72 (Spring 1998): 159–82.

Rogers, Kim Lacy. "'You Came Away with Some Courage': Three Lives in the Civil Rights Movement." *Mid-America* 71 (October 1989): 175–94.

Schultz, Mark R. "The Dream Realized? African American Landownership in Central Georgia between Reconstruction and World War Two." *Agricultural History* 72 (Spring 1998): 298–312.

Scott, Emmett J., comp. "Letters of Negro Migrants of 1916–1918." *Journal of Negro History* 4 (July 1919): 290–340.

——. "Additional Letters of Negro Migrants of 1916–1918." *Journal of Negro History* 4 (October 1919): 412–65.

Scott, James C. "Everyday Forms of Peasant Resistance." *Journal of Peasant Studies* 13 (January 1986): 5–35.

Strain, Christopher B. "'We Walked Like Men': The Deacons for Defense and Justice." *Louisiana History* 38 (Winter 1997): 43–62.

Thompson, E. P. "The Moral Economy of the English Crowd in the Eighteenth Century." *Past and Present* 50 (February 1971): 76–136.

Tolnay, Stewart E., and E. M. Beck. "Rethinking the Role of Racial Violence in the Great Migration." In *Black Exodus: The Great Migration from the American South*, edited by Alferdteen Harrison, 20–35. Jackson: University Press of Mississippi, 1991.

Tyson, Timothy B. "Robert F. Williams, 'Black Power,' and the Roots of the African American Freedom Struggle." *Journal of American History* 85 (September 1998): 540–70.

Vandal, Gilles. "Property Offenses, Social Tension, and Racial Antagonism in Post–Civil War Rural Louisiana." *Journal of Social History* 31 (Fall 1997): 127–53.

White, Christine Pelzer. "Everyday Resistance, Socialist Revolution, and Rural Development: The Vietnamese Case." *Journal of Peasant Studies* 13 (January 1986): 49–63.

White, Walter F. "'Work or Fight' in the South." *New Republic*, 1 March 1919, 144–46.

Woodruff, Nan Elizabeth. "Pick or Fight: The Emergency Farm Labor Program in the Arkansas and Mississippi Deltas during World War II." *Agricultural History* 64 (Spring 1990): 74–85.

——. "African-American Struggles for Citizenship in the Arkansas and Mississippi Deltas in the Age of Jim Crow." *Radical History Review* 55 (Winter 1993): 33–51.

——. "Mississippi Delta Planters and Debates over Mechanization, Labor, and Civil Rights in the 1940s." *Journal of Southern History* 60 (May 1994): 263–284.

Dissertations and Theses

Burran, James Albert, III. "Racial Violence in the South during World War II." Ph.D. diss., University of Tennessee, 1977.

Collins, Gladys Blanson. "Community Activities of Rural Elementary Teachers: A Study of the Community Participation of Negro Rural Elementary Teachers in Louisiana." Ph.D. diss., New York University, 1953.

Crosby, Earl William. "Building the Country Home: The Black County Agent System, 1906–1940." Ph.D. diss., Miami University, 1977.

Dinwiddie, Robert Carlton. "The International Woodworkers of America and Southern Laborers, 1937–1945." Master's thesis, Georgia State University, 1980.

Finnegan, Terence Robert. " 'At the Hands of Parties Unknown': Lynching in Mississippi and South Carolina, 1881–1940." Ph.D. diss., University of Illinois at Urbana-Champaign, 1993.

Hill, Lance E. "The Deacons for Defense and Justice: Armed Self-Defense and the Civil Rights Movement." Ph.D. diss., Tulane University, 1997.

Matthews, Carl S. "American Negro Leadership and World War I." Master's thesis, University of Virginia, 1967.

Neyland, Leedell Wallace. "The Negro in Louisiana since 1900: An Economic and Social Study." Ph.D. diss., New York University, 1958.

Palmer, Leola. "The Evolution of Education for African Americans in Pointe Coupee Parish (New Roads, Louisiana), 1889–1969." Ph.D. diss., Fordham University, 1992.

Rosen, Dale. "The Alabama Share Croppers Union." Honors thesis, Radcliffe College, 1969. (In file 2A, reel 13, Clyde L. Johnson Papers, in *The Green Rising, 1910–1977: A Supplement to the Southern Tenant Farmers Union Papers*. Glen Rock, N.J.: Microfilming Corporation of America, 1977.)

Umoja, Akinyele K. "Eye for an Eye: The Role of Armed Resistance in the Mississippi Freedom Movement." Ph.D. diss., Emory University, 1996.

Wheaton, Donna. "Sheriff D. J. 'Cat' Doucet and the Black Voters of St. Landry Parish." Master's thesis, University of Southwestern Louisiana, 1991.

Williams, Charles E. "A Mighty Fortress: The Black Church as Ancestral Foundation for Black Survival and Civil Rights." Ph.D. diss., The Union Institute, 1997.

Index

Acadiana Neuf, 203

Accommodationism, 51–52, 180–81, 218 (n. 2), 231 (n. 28)

Acheson, Meldon, 189, 265 (n. 7)

Adams, Henry, 13

Adams, Kenneth, 114

Affirmative action, 204

Agricultural Adjustment Administration (AAA), 87, 93, 96–97, 103–5, 110, 111, 112, 152, 199–200

Agricultural Extension Service: origins, 76; discrimination in, 76, 77, 80–81, 108, 113, 199, 237 (n. 50); and African Americans, 76–80, 123, 151–52, 184, 202, 206, 236–37 (n. 45); and plantation owners, 77, 81, 108, 113, 114, 133–35; black agents of, 77–81, 123

Agricultural Soil Conservation Service (ASCS), 152, 199–200. *See also* Agricultural Adjustment Administration

Agricultural workers: conditions for in Jim Crow era, 5, 18, 22–28, 36–37, 42–43, 52–53, 223 (n. 18), 229–30 (nn. 10, 14); as activists, 8–9, 15–16, 17, 42, 45–47, 52–53, 57, 78–80, 152–53, 165–66, 184, 261 (n. 63); violence against, 13, 15, 17, 19, 31, 33–34, 49, 57, 86, 110–11, 165–66, 224 (n. 25); exploitation of, 13, 15, 19–20, 23–24, 26–28, 29–31, 32, 42, 46, 104, 221 (n. 1); and federal agricultural agencies, 76–81, 93, 96–97, 102–5, 106–10, 113, 122–24, 133–35, 151–52, 199–200, 236–37 (n. 45), 239–40 (n. 13), 245 (n. 57), 246–47 (nn. 69, 70, 75); and mechanization, 135, 136–37, 145, 146, 211–12. *See also* Landowners, black; Louisiana Farmers' Union; Plantations

Alabama, 43, 97–98, 100, 106, 143, 155, 172, 173, 174, 190, 192, 248 (n. 80)

Alexander, Tom, 19–20, 221 (n. 1)

Alexandria, La., 58–59, 66, 67, 84, 128, 134, 138, 144, 165, 251 (n. 13)